CONFLICTING WORLDS

New Dimensions of the American Civil War
T. Michael Parrish, Editor

Published with the assistance of the
V. Ray Cardozier Fund
an endowment created to support
publication of scholarly books

JUSTICE OF
SHATTERED DREAMS

Samuel Freeman Miller and the Supreme Court
during the Civil War Era

MICHAEL A. ROSS

LOUISIANA STATE UNIVERSITY PRESS
BATON ROUGE

Published by Louisiana State University Press
Copyright © 2003 by Louisiana State University Press
All rights reserved
Manufactured in the United States of America

DESIGNER: Andrew Shurtz
TYPEFACE: Adobe Caslon
TYPESETTER: Coghill Composition

Library of Congress Cataloging-in-Publication Data:

Ross, Michael A. (Michael Anthony)
  Justice of shattered dreams : Samuel Freeman Miller and the Supreme Court during the Civil
War era / Michael A. Ross
      p. cm.—(Conflicting worlds)
  Includes bibliographical references and index.
      1. Miller, Samuel Freeman, 1816–1890. 2. Judges—United States—Biography. 3. United
States. Supreme Court—Biography. 4. Law—United States—History—19th century. I.
Title. II. Series.
    KF8745.M5R67 2003
    347.73'26—dc21
                                                                                             2003002069
  ISBN 978-0-8071-2924-1 (pbk. : alk. paper)

for my father

SPENCER ROSS

CONTENTS

ILLUSTRATIONS

following page 96

Samuel Freeman Miller in the 1860s
Antebellum Keokuk
Rock Island bridge at Davenport
Estes House in Keokuk during the Civil War
Third and Main in Keokuk
Abraham Lincoln in 1858
Political cartoon, 1860, lampooning the impact of the Dred
    Scott decision
Senate impeachment trial of President Andrew Johnson, 1868
Candlelight meeting of the presidential electoral commission, 1877
Justices of the Supreme Court in 1888
Justice Stephen J. Field
Miller in the 1880s

SAMUEL FREEMAN MILLER'S GENERATION experienced unprecedented change—more change, perhaps, than any other generation of Americans. Born into a small-scale agrarian world of candlelight and horseback, they died in a nation of giant cities and factories, telephones and telegraphs, electric lights and streetcars. In 1816, the year Miller was born, the typical manufacturing concern had fewer than eight workers. By 1890, giant corporations with famous names like McCormick, Armour, Singer, and Swift employed thousands. In one lifetime, the city of Chicago grew from a tiny trading settlement into a skyscraper-filled metropolis with more than a million people—the eighth largest city in the world. In 1816, the open spaces of the West seemed a boundless frontier. By 1890, the year that the U.S. Census Bureau made its famous pronouncement that the frontier had closed, two hundred thousand miles of iron railroad tracks tied the continent together. And slavery, the retrograde institution that had burdened human civilizations for centuries, was gone, destroyed in the United States by a calamitous Civil War that cost more than 620,000 lives. When Americans like Miller, born at the start of the nineteenth century, peered out at their world in 1890, they saw a transformed society that would have left their parents wide-eyed and dumbfounded.[1]

Although many men and women of his generation celebrated the changes they witnessed, Miller was ambivalent about them. Appointed to the United States Supreme Court by President Abraham Lincoln in 1862, Miller served on the bench for twenty-eight tumultuous years. During that time, the Court's justices grappled with the innumerable legal issues that arose from this period of wrenching economic, social, and political change. For Miller, those years were cause for disillusionment. As a young man he had been optimistic about his country's future. Aside from his abhorrence of slavery, he believed that the United States was the most democratic, socially fluid, and economically progressive nation on earth.

After the Civil War, however, his outlook changed. By the start of the Gilded Age, the proponents of corporate industrialism had taken control of his beloved Republican Party, pushing the farmers, small-town merchants, and professionals who had helped found the organization to the periphery. In the nation's cities, a "keensighted well organized class" of capitalists used their unprecedented fortunes to bribe officials, crush unions, and thwart other Americans' economic opportunities. In the courtroom, law-school-trained corporate attorneys filled the Supreme Court's dockets with cases in which they urged the justices to embrace formalistic doctrines that would protect their powerful clients' property from regulatory legislation. In the South, reactionary whites increasingly disenfranchised African American voters, leaving most of the region in the hands of Democrats who refused to abandon their old animosities toward blacks and northerners. In his judicial opinions and private correspondence, Miller revealed that these developments had undermined his faith in the American system. Once sanguine about the prospects for capitalism and democracy, he grew increasingly pessimistic over time. In the process, he became the judicial voice of Americans who were left behind by the postwar economy and felt alienated by the political realignments of the Gilded Age.[2]

Because his bitter critique of capitalists made him distinctive on a Court that became increasingly conservative after the Civil War, historians have long considered Miller one of the Court's most important justices. Even in the sometimes hagiographic field of Supreme Court history, he stands out. One recent survey ranked Miller as one of the hundred individuals in the history of the world who have most influenced the law.[3]

Historians have also been drawn to Miller's inimitable personality. Along with his fellow justice Stephen J. Field, Miller has become emblematic of an era in which many of the Court's justices had larger-than-life personas. Unwilling to couch his opinions about politics, law, or society in temperate language, he was a blunt, passionate man who let attorneys and colleagues know exactly what he thought of them and their ideas. He particularly disliked pretentious lawyers who talked too long or cited too many ancient sources. In one representative incident, Miller, presiding over a hot St. Louis courtroom while a self-important attorney blathered on and on, finally broke in after the attorney ignored his glares. "Damn it, Brown," he snarled, "come to the point." "What point, your Honor?" the startled lawyer replied. "I don't know," Miller fired back, "Any point! Some point!"[4]

Although he was a favorite of the Court's staff—to whom he was always kind—Miller often treated his fellow justices with contempt, and his criticisms of his judicial brethren are the stuff of legend. "I can't make a silk purse out of a sow's ear," he once said of Chief Justice Morrison Waite. "I can't make a great Chief Justice out of a small man." As an in-law of Miller's remarked, "He acts from principle, . . . and is often rather rough and stern with others—I think perhaps he prides himself on his frankness and plain speaking." Although his bluntness understandably irritated some of his judicial peers, it endeared him to others. "I love Miller," Justice Field once remarked, "He has so much backbone!" He was, according to Chief Justice Salmon Chase, "beyond question the dominant personality . . . upon the bench, whose mental force and individuality [were] felt by the Court more than any other."[5]

Although historians agree that Miller was one of the Court's most important justices, there is less consensus about the nature of Miller's legacy. Certainly he was influential, but to what ends—for good or for ill—did he use that influence? In his biography of Miller, former Stanford law professor Charles Fairman portrayed the justice as an agrarian folk hero whose views and positions reflected the keen anger that farmers in Miller's home state of Iowa felt for the new economic order dominated by railroads, financiers, and city dwellers. In this view, Miller was a nascent populist whose Jeffersonian love of the yeoman farmer, agricultural America, and the rich soil of Iowa led him to question the urban, industrial, capitalist system. Writing during the 1930s, Fairman, an ardent supporter of the New Deal, used Miller's judicial legacy as a historical counterpoint to the opinions of the conservative justices who tenaciously fought President Roosevelt's programs and policies.[6]

Fairman's laudatory depiction of Miller has been challenged in recent years by scholars critical of Miller's positions on race. Rather than viewing him as a populist hero, these scholars depict Miller as the key judicial figure in the tragic unraveling of Reconstruction. In particular, historians have focused on his majority opinion in the famous 1873 *Slaughter-House Cases,* the first instance in which the Court interpreted the broad language of the then-new Fourteenth Amendment. In that opinion, Miller gave a constricted construction to the amendment's privileges or immunities clause and, in the process, prevented the Bill of Rights from being applied against state action. After 1877, when southern white Democrats had regained control of all the state governments in the South, they pointed to *Slaughter-House* when defending states' rights to treat African Americans as a separate social and economic caste. As a result, many historians have charged Miller with either intentionally or negligently paving the way for the notorious retreat from Reconstruction.[7]

Because Fairman's 1939 biography has been the only comprehensive study of Miller's life, his work has had a disproportionate influence on current historical interpretations. Many of Miller's critics have relied on Fairman for much of their evidence. Although he cast Miller as a protagonist who fought for economic underdogs, Fairman, like many Dunning-school historians of his era, viewed Radical Reconstruction as a tragic mistake. He concluded—incorrectly, I argue—that Miller shared this assessment. Beginning in the 1960s, as historians' perceptions of Reconstruction changed, Fairman's biography has bolstered the arguments of critics of Miller, the *Slaughter-House* decision, and the late-nineteenth-century Court.[8]

Fairman also based many of his conclusions about Miller on the assumption that Miller's Iowa heritage meant that he shared farmers' agricultural values. Miller's critique of capitalism, however, had little to do with agrarianism. Throughout most of his life, he hoped that a massive urban, industrial metropolis rivaling Chicago would develop in eastern Iowa and that the growth of that city would make him rich. Rather than being an agrarian radical, Miller was instead an important representative of an understudied wing of the Republican Party, a wing that steadily lost influence as financiers and industrialists took control of the party after the Civil War. Miller became a Republican in the 1850s because he opposed slavery and shared the Republicans' optimistic economic beliefs. Their free-labor ideology—an ideology that celebrated Americans' right to rise in life—attracted individuals like Miller and Lincoln because it reflected both their past achievements and their hopes for the future. Born on a crude, preindustrial Kentucky farm, Miller quickly attained a position of social and economic standing. Having elevated his own station in life, he envisioned a world in which all individuals, if freed of constraints, could go as far as their talents and toils could take them.[9]

When Miller helped found the Republican Party in Iowa in the 1850s, the free-labor ideology appeared to be based on an accurate assessment of America's economic system. In the small-scale capitalist world of the old Northwest, social fluidity was the rule rather than the exception. Most Iowans anticipated improving their station and aspired to comfortable prosperity as farmers, shopkeepers, professionals, or small factory owners. The Republican Party's message reflected their aspirations. It was the party of those who succeeded—or expected to succeed—in the new economy.[10]

Miller and Iowa's river-town Republicans also tied free-labor ideology to the western booster ethos. The boosters of the 1850s believed that a person simply had to choose a town with a good location, and with hard work, sound decisions, and promotional zeal, the town would inevitably grow and prosper. And, for a time in the West, the boosters appeared to be right. In the late 1840s and early 1850s, small boomtowns tied to the steamboat trade sprang up all along the Mississippi River, lifting the fortunes of thousands of new settlers with them. For a short period, the views of the Republicans and the boosters intertwined to form a potent ideological affirmation of the dynamic northern economy.[11]

But by the end of the 1850s, the rise of railroads and a new class of eastern financiers brought changes that would undermine the political and economic beliefs of river-town Republicans. By 1860, the outlines of a new world of large corporations, industrialism, concentrated capital, giant cities, and wage laborers were visible. Although some Americans would reap once-unimagined benefits from these changes, the citizens of the Iowa river towns—along with those in countless other communities across the country—fell behind. After the Civil War, the Republican Party would increasingly reflect the values of urban industrialists and financiers rather than the dreams of small-town merchants and professionals.

Miller represented the values of this neglected group of Republicans who lived where growth was expected but never came, who succeeded in the 1850s but who grew embittered when they did not share in the wealth created by the postwar economy. His jurisprudence reflected the evolving ideology of these Republicans, a group that does not fit neatly into the traditional postbellum categories of Radicals, conservatives, Democrats, and labor reformers. Because he served on the Supreme Court at the critical time when the nation's highest tribunal was thrust to the center of the economic and political disputes of the new age, his river-town worldview played an important role in shaping the judicial response to revolutionary change.[12]

Reexamining Miller's life also provides a means to assess the combined effect that the five justices appointed by Abraham Lincoln had on the Supreme Court and American law. Historians generally agree that Lincoln's main concern when choosing his nominees was how prospective justices might rule on his controversial war measures. Lincoln rightly feared that Roger Taney and the other proslavery members of the Court might obstruct his efforts to subdue the rebellion. In response, he appointed five staunch Unionists who he hoped would recognize the need to adapt the Constitution to wartime exigencies. But while scholars have explained why Lincoln appointed the justices he did, less attention has been paid to the collective effect that his appointments had on the Court during and after the war.[13]

I will argue that after Appomattox the rise of a new, large-scale, industrial America and a mighty capitalist class divided Lincoln's appointees into hostile camps. Samuel Miller, on the one hand, and Lincoln appointees Stephen Field and Noah Swayne, on the other, came to lead divergent philosophical wings of the Court. In the process, Lincoln's appointees became, as a group, a metaphor for the postwar unraveling of the antebellum free-labor ideology, an ideology that simultaneously championed both equality and the right to get rich. In the small-scale world of the 1850s, Republicans had yet to face the question of what should happen when some Americans grew so rich and powerful that they threatened other Americans' economic prospects. After the Civil War, the rise of a national market, giant corporations, and a permanent wage-earning class brought this question to the fore. Because the Supreme Court decided many of the disputes that arose from these dramatic postwar changes, Miller and Lincoln's other appointees faced this issue head-on, and the ensuing fierce battles revealed just how different Lincoln's appointees really were. Because Lincoln's sole litmus test for potential Supreme Court justices was their staunch Unionism, he failed to ascertain their positions on other issues. Miller's critique of eastern bondholders and financiers, for example, represented a producerist version of free-labor ideology that Lincoln did not share. As a result, Lincoln lost an opportunity to leave a coherent ideological legacy on the Court.

This book is an effort to reevaluate and recontextualize Miller's positions on the issues for which he is most famous—race, politics, and capitalism. It is not, therefore, a traditional biography. Miller's family life is only briefly touched upon. And because my analysis is as much about politics as it is about law, most of the hundreds of opinions Miller authored on the Court are not discussed.

Instead, I will show that current perceptions of Miller as a lifelong agrarian and an opponent of Reconstruction are wrong. I will argue that Miller was representative of a losing faction of trans-Mississippi Republicanism, a wing of the party that found itself increasingly marginalized as the Republicans turned into the party of big business after the war. I hope to change, complicate, and reshape the current view of Miller's jurisprudence and also to contribute to discussions about the ideological development of the Republican Party and Lincoln's legacy on the Supreme Court.

ACKNOWLEDGMENTS

MY INTEREST IN THIS TOPIC began in 1988 when, as a student at the Duke
University Law School, I took a constitutional history course team-taught by
Walter Dellinger, John Hope Franklin, and William Leuchtenburg. Unlike the
"practical" law school courses on torts, property, and civil procedure, constitutional history captured my imagination. Using the law as a window to the past,
Dellinger, Franklin, and Leuchtenburg revealed the fascinating ways in which
historical context shaped the law. After graduation and a short stint at a law
firm, I returned to graduate school to pursue a Ph.D. in history. I thank Professors Dellinger, Franklin, and Leuchtenburg for their inspiration. To Professor
Leuchtenburg I owe especial thanks, as I had the good fortune to continue my
association with him in the history department of the University of North Carolina at Chapel Hill.

It is also with great satisfaction that I have the opportunity to thank my
graduate school advisers, William Barney and Peter Coclanis. Professor Barney
consistently gave a close and thoughtful reading to even the roughest of drafts
and always welcomed my questions and brainstorming sessions. Professor
Coclanis's legendary breadth of knowledge influenced this study in innumerable
ways. As an adviser, moreover, he is indefatigable. He works tirelessly on his
students' behalf—writing letters, lobbying for them, and providing guidance.
Both men have become close and loyal friends, and this book would not have
been completed without their efforts.

Many other faculty members at the University of North Carolina and the
University of Massachusetts at Amherst also deserve thanks for their guidance
during my graduate career. These include Paula Baker, Milton Cantor, R. Don

Higginbotham, Bruce Laurie, Roger Lotchin, Gerald McFarland, Stephen B. Oates, Leonard Richards, and Harry Watson. In preparing this book, I was also fortunate to receive comments and advice from a number of outstanding scholars to whom I owe a debt of gratitude. These include Richard Aynes, Douglas Atterberg, Gordon Bakken, Michael Les Benedict, Laura Edwards, Mark Fernandez, Paul Finkelman, Christian Fritz, David Moore, John Orth, Lawrence Powell, John Semonche, Ted Tunnell, and all of my colleagues in the Loyola University New Orleans history department. Marvin Bergman, Harold Hyman, Paul Kens, and Timothy Mahoney deserve particular thanks for their thorough and insightful readings of large portions of this manuscript. Gary Frost, Kathleen Roberts, and Robert Tinkler provided their editorial acumen as well. I am also grateful to Michael Parrish, Alisa Plant, Sylvia Rodrigue, and the anonymous manuscript referees at Louisiana State University Press for their highly professional and invaluable assistance. Any mistakes that are found in this book are mine and mine alone.

Two generous grants from the State Historical Society of Iowa, one from the New Jersey Historical Commission, and an American Historical Association Littleton-Griswold Research Grant helped to fund my research. Thanks are also due to the editors of the *Journal of Southern History*, the *Annals of Iowa*, and the *Filson Club History Quarterly* for allowing me to reprint the portions of this book that first appeared in their journals as articles.

Thanks also to Marian and Harold Andersen, Stacy Braukman, Annabel Caner, Eric Carrig, Deborah Coclanis, Missy and Peter Cook, Matt Crocker, Spencer Downing, Michael Flynn, Andrew and Kristi Foster, Lars Golumbic, Mike Haje, Jill and Michael Lloyd, Hans and Jen Mueller, Gregg and Pam Melinson, Allen and Amy Nelson, Steve O'Donnell, Krisi Raymond, Adam and Jen Tuchinsky, Tony Young, Heather Wharton, and my sister Janet Ross for their support and social expertise during my years at UNC.

Finally, this study would not have been possible without the steadfast support of my father, Spencer Ross. During my transition from law to history, and during the many years of graduate school, he was always there with sound advice, a timely check, and an encouraging word. He has done more for his children than any father should be expected to do. This book is dedicated to him.

ABBREVIATIONS

CFDC	Caleb Forbes Davis Collection
FCHS	Filson Club Historical Society
KGC	*Keokuk Gate City*
LC	Library of Congress
SFMP	Samuel Freeman Miller Papers
SHSI	State Historical Society of Iowa
W.P.B.	William Pitt Ballinger

JUSTICE OF SHATTERED DREAMS

CHAPTER I

"The Athens of the Kentucky Highlands"

S AMUEL FREEMAN MILLER never liked farming. Born on a rural
homestead in Richmond, Kentucky, in 1816, Miller grew up on a preindustrial farm. Although Richmond farmers were generally prosperous, agricultural life in the early nineteenth century was arduous for all involved. Unlike
other areas of the national economy, farming had yet to be transformed by tech-
nology, and most agricultural techniques had not changed in two hundred years.
Farmers used fire and ax to clear the land and drew their plows with horses and
oxen. For men, farm life meant rising at dawn, toiling in the fields, and returning, exhausted, to a candlelit house at dusk. For women, rural life consisted of
an endless routine filled with drudgery and childbearing. "Men's hands hard-
ened from gripping plow handles, their legs bowed from tramping over the
clods turned up by the plowshare," one historian has written. "Women's hands
cracked, bled, and developed corns from the hard water of the family wash, their
knees grew knobby from years of kneeling to grit corn or scrub puncheon
floors."[1] For Miller, farming meant a childhood of mind-numbing labor and
agricultural responsibilities that made acquiring an education a continual struggle. For a few months each year he attended school at the Richmond Academy,
but from early spring to late fall his parents kept him at work on the farm. It
was a life of toil for which Miller was not suited.[2]

Six feet tall, over two hundred pounds, with a massive head and square jaw,
as a young adult Miller had the look and build of an ox-driving farmer, but his
physique belied his real inclinations. He was, in fact, never known for a dogged
work ethic. Later in life, he only half jokingly claimed that "it was fortunate [I]
was born poor, as otherwise [I] would never have worked." His dislike for farm

I

life only increased as he took on many of his father, Frederick's, responsibilities. Whether because of Frederick's indolence, alcoholism, or sheer incompetence, Samuel's mother, Patsy, called upon her son—the oldest of her ten children—to help her raise her enormous brood. "Owing to my father's habits," Miller said of his mother, "I was at a very early age taken into her confidence as a substitute, and the care of my younger sisters and brothers were a joint affair." In order to help provide for the family, Samuel quit school at fourteen and went to work in a local drugstore owned by a Dr. Leverill, a friend of his mother.[3]

Liberated from the fields, Miller spent six years working for Leverill, during which he spent long hours poring over the doctor's medical texts. Miller's enthusiasm for medicine impressed Leverill, who convinced his young employee to choose a medical career instead of a life tied to the soil. In the autumn of 1835, at the age of eighteen, Miller entered medical school at Transylvania University in Lexington. Gaining admission to Transylvania was a coup for the son of a rural family. The school—one of the few outposts of medicine in the West—had a national reputation.[4]

At Transylvania, Miller learned the skills he would need to be a general practitioner in the Kentucky countryside. Given the limited number of doctors in the West, Transylvania's medical graduates faced a daunting task. As doctors, they would have to diagnose and treat diseases without the aid of experts or fellow physicians. After only two short years of training, they would be on their own, riding from farm to farm with their medical books in their saddlebags, facing the vast array of maladies from which antebellum Americans suffered. Transylvania's professors accordingly taught students to be medical ombudsmen who could recognize common symptoms of major diseases and turn for guidance to their medical texts.[5]

In addition to learning broad concepts, the school also required each student to prepare a dissertation that focused on one disease. Miller chose the most feared affliction of the antebellum period—cholera. While other diseases might have claimed more lives, cholera's swift, brutal, and deadly effects left those who survived an outbreak permanently shaken. It came on with little or no warning. A person could leave his or her house perfectly healthy in the morning and be dead before nightfall. During an outbreak, it was not uncommon to see someone drop to the street in a fit of spasmodic vomiting and diarrhea and die within hours. Spread by contaminated water, cholera could be devastatingly concentrated in its attacks. Whole families or factory crews could be wiped out in a matter of days.[6]

The first cholera epidemic struck the United States in 1832, three years before Miller enrolled at Transylvania. Initially confined to the dirty and crowded streets of East Coast cities, the epidemic soon spread westward and hit Kentucky with devastating results. Louisville and Lexington were struck first; in the latter city, over five hundred residents died in a three-month period. At its 1833 peak, cholera killed as many as fifty persons per day in a population of a little over six thousand. Lexington became a veritable ghost town as city dwellers trying to escape the pestilence fled into the countryside. Panic and death soon followed cholera to other Kentucky towns.[7]

The cholera epidemic cast a dark shadow over the medical profession during Miller's years at Transylvania as his professors struggled unsuccessfully to find effective treatments for the disease. Rather than giving cholera victims fluids to fight dehydration, doctors at this time favored using calomel and other purgatives to increase the amount of vomiting and diarrhea. Doing so, they believed erroneously, would clear the disease from the victim's system. Transylvania's most noted faculty member, Dr. John Esten Cooke, instructed his students to treat cholera with a combination of calomel and bloodletting, and Cooke became famous during the 1832–33 epidemic because of his tireless efforts in Lexington, where he dashed from patient to patient administering those often deadly remedies.[8]

At Transylvania, Miller and his fellow students zealously scribbled Cooke's theories into their notebooks, and Miller's own dissertation on cholera followed the famous doctor's approach to curing the disease. Cholera victims, Miller wrote, should be given a "full dose of calomel, especially if the attack is violent" for its "proper purgative action." This, in turn, would "establish the secretion from the Liver" and "relieve internal congestion." He also suggested that victims be given doses of turpentine and opium and that blood should be extracted from their temples. In particularly difficult cases, blisters could also be raised on victim's stomach. If the patient's extremities turned cold from dehydration, he advised putting "cayenne pepper in the socks."[9]

Widely accepted by other doctors, the treatments advocated by Cooke and Miller remained the preferred remedies for years. As a result, cholera killed roughly half of those who contracted it during the nineteenth century.[10] Because so many patients died from cholera and other poorly understood diseases, Miller's medical-school professors tried to prepare their students psychologically for the often grim results of a doctor's labors, warning them not to be daunted by a "fatal termination of a case of disease, although all may have been done that the art affords." Students needed to recognize just "how often is the physician doomed to suffer such unkindness."[11]

Miller's professors also advised students to become dependable citizens wherever they chose to begin their careers. Take great care, they cautioned their students, in choosing a community in which to practice. During an age of great migrations, they urged students to pick a locale, establish lasting relationships, and stay put. "When you have made a choice of a place of residence it should not be given up without good cause," Professor Lunsford P. Yandell told Miller's class, as "frequent changes are eminently prejudicial to the character of the young practitioner. They evidence a want of stability and perseverance, one of the most unfortunate of deficiencies. Guard against this. Be judicious in the choice of home, and there plant yourselves."[12]

Miller took this professional advice to heart, and while attending medical school he traveled throughout Kentucky in search of a good town in which launch his career. After canvassing the state, he decided upon Barbourville, a small but vibrant village in the southeastern hill country. For him, the town's appeal lay in its growing economic prosperity and its lack of other doctors. By getting there first, he hoped to hold a "monopoly of the practice for a wide region of country."[13]

Located on the western side of the Cumberland Gap, Barbourville served as a trading point for emigrants traveling on the old Wilderness Road. The road carried traffic from Virginia to the West through the gap in the Cumberland and Pine mountains. Although Barbourville never had more than a few hundred inhabitants, the constant influx of travelers and a thriving merchant community gave the village a cosmopolitan feel.[14] Barbourville's boosters dubbed their town the "Athens of the Kentucky Highlands," and claimed that it would grow into a major city, a "great western gate" to the frontier.[15]

For over a decade, Barbourville prospered. While it had no newspaper or wholesalers and only one bank, busy retail merchants lined its short main street. In the drier seasons, wagons, stagecoaches, horses, and mules clogged the town's roads. Cattlemen drove herds of cows and pigs through Barbourville on their way eastward through the gap to markets in Baltimore and Philadelphia.

Trade continued during the rainy season, although at a reduced pace, with emi-grants' wagons "creaking and rolling through bogs and chuckholes."[16]

In 1836, between his first and second years of medical school, Miller moved to Barbourville. Fast action allowed him to beat other practitioners to the doc-torless town and paid immediate professional and social dividends. Even while returning to Lexington for semesters of school, he developed a solid town and country practice. Upon graduation, he quickly became one of Barbourville's most socially prominent citizens. In 1842, he married Lucy Ballinger, a young woman from a family of lawyers who dominated the local legal community.[17] Lucy's father, James, served as clerk of the county court, over which her uncle, Franklin, presided as judge. Lucy's brother, William Pitt Ballinger, was also an attorney who had an active private practice in writs, warrants, and land titles.[18]

By marrying Lucy, Samuel joined a family not only of lawyers, but of slave-holders. The Ballingers owned over a dozen slaves, and in 1829 James Ballinger gave Lucy five slaves, who, under the property laws of the time, became Sam-uel's upon marriage.[19] By acquiring a small number of slaves, he did not become a great planter rivaling those in Kentucky's tobacco-growing regions. The peo-ple that Miller and the Ballingers enslaved worked as domestic servants rather than fieldhands because slavery had limited economic utility in southeastern Kentucky, a region where the hilly land and thin soil made plantation farming impossible. A lack of access to markets compounded this fact. Even if Barbour-ville's countryside had shared the rich soil and gentle topography of central Kentucky, the lack of suitable transportation inhibited the growth of commer-cial agriculture. The farmers who lived around Barbourville were not slaveown-ers, and most of Knox County's slaves lived in town. By 1850, Barbourville had only thirty male and forty-two female slaves, numbers far smaller than in com-mercial towns in the state's other regions.[20]

Miller also tied himself to slavery by means other than marriage. As part of his medical practice, he accepted mortgages on slave "property" to secure debts owed him for services rendered. If patients could not pay their medical bills immediately, he allowed them to pledge their slaves as collateral until they could do so. In 1842, for example, George McCallister gave Miller a lien-mortgage on three black children to secure a debt of $67.50.[21] Consequently, Miller spent his mid-twenties enmeshed with slavery—a fact he would later regret. Neverthe-less, by the standards of the day, his early career was an unmitigated success. He was a doctor with a prosperous practice, married to the daughter of a prominent family, living in a town he thought would grow into a great city. As he walked the muddy main street of Barbourville in the early 1840s, Miller, fresh from medical school, was already a man of standing.

But his success would soon be undermined by Barbourville's unexpected economic decline. Despite an outward appearance of health, Barbourville's economy had profound structural weaknesses. Although located on the Cumberland River, Barbourville sat well above the "falls line" at a point not suitable for commercial navigation.[22] Lacking a cost-efficient connection to outside markets and cursed with thin soil unsuited for cash crops, the farm families who lived in the countryside around Barbourville wore homespun clothing and eked out a subsistence living. Although some farmers occasionally traded a few surplus crops or furs to Barbourville's merchants in return for cloth, most came to town only to record a deed or pay their taxes. This disconnectedness between town and country did not bode well for Barbourville's future. Economically, Barbourville had no hinterland, and if the emigrant trade dried up, so, too, would the town.[23]

Barbourville's overreliance on the emigrant trade spelled its doom. Beginning in 1835, the old Wilderness Road began facing stiff competition from the newly built National Road along the Ohio River that provided a more direct route east. As steamboats began regularly to ply the Ohio River, emigrants to and from Kentucky increasingly traveled by boat. Louisville, far to the northwest, became Kentucky's commercial center, while the market for Kentucky's cattle and hogs shifted to Pittsburgh and Cincinnati. As a result, travel overland through the Cumberland Gap to eastern markets became prohibitively costly. Towns like Barbourville without river access fell behind. And if the steamboat provided a stiff body blow to Barbourville's economy, railroads landed the knockout punch. Reliable, direct, and fast, railroads made the old plank roads obsolete. At a time when railroads made the hundred-mile trip from Louisville to Cincinnati in a few hours, the eleven-mile journey from Barbourville to neighboring Flat Lick still consumed a full day. While Lexington and Louisville boomed, Barbourville slipped into economic and historical obscurity, plunging into what one historian has called its "dark ages." As it became increasingly remote, Barbourville's development halted, and the Wilderness Road deteriorated into a muddy and largely forgotten byway.[24]

For a short time, however, Barbourville was a flicker of economic light in the shadow of the Cumberland range. Convinced of the town's bright prospects, Samuel's brother, William Miller, followed him to Barbourville and embarked on a career in law.[25] During the 1830s and early 1840s, Samuel, William, and the town's leading citizens had yet to detect the looming economic disaster, believing that Whiggish boosterism would lead to development and growth. As a forum for expressing these views, Samuel and the town's other professional men organized the Barbourville Debating Society.[26]

The debating society met at the courthouse at early candlelight every Saturday night during the summers of 1837, 1838, and 1839. In a town without a newspaper or a theater, the society's meetings provided both information and entertainment to the men and women who filled the gallery. At these meetings, members argued the opposing sides of current issues and then voted, either for or against, a particular position. Miller, a rousing speaker, took center stage in these events. During their debates on political and social topics, Miller positioned himself with a Whiggish coalition that argued for increased government involvement in southeastern Kentucky's economy. Over the course of the three years, he repeatedly spoke and voted in favor of banks, internal improvements, and railroads.

The development-minded members of the society clearly favored government measures that spurred growth. On issues such as the National Bank, Miller joined in resounding 12 to 1 pro-Bank majorities. But on other topics, he often took minority positions. Because of the scarcity of labor, he resisted the anti-Catholic nativist sentiments of the society's majority and opposed a ban on foreign immigration. At this point, Miller had an optimistic view of American capitalism. When asked if the economic system unfairly favored the wealthy, Miller argued that it did not. He believed that talent was more important than wealth in achieving success. He recognized, however, that even talented men sometimes failed through no fault of their own and, accordingly, opposed imprisonment for debt. He also strongly opposed any property restriction on the right to vote.[27]

In many of these debates, Miller revealed a respect for the dignity of human life that many Americans in the Age of Jackson did not share. He opposed, for example, the majority of the debating society who argued that the federal government should "wholly exterminate the Seminole Indians, if they continue their depredations upon the citizens of the United States." And at a time when hangings were a regular occurrence, Miller argued that there was never a "moral justification for capital punishment."[28]

Issues from the growing sectional crisis also made their way into the debating society's forums. During the mid-1830s, abolitionist groups in the North began sending their congressional representatives antislavery petitions to be read on the floors of the Senate and House. Southerners in Congress, led by South Carolina's fearsome John C. Calhoun, argued that these documents were insulting and incendiary and should not be allowed. The infamous "Gag Rules" that followed, banning the reading of antislavery petitions, deeply offended many northerners who believed that the "slave power" had unjustly curtailed their right to free speech.[29] In 1837, the members of the Barbourville Debating Society weighed in on the issue in response to the question, "Should congress refuse the reception of abolition documents as contended by the Southern delegation?" Miller, although a slaveholder, spoke against southern censorship; other members followed his lead and voted 12 to 2 against the rule.[30]

Later in his life, Miller remembered the debating society as one of his most important formative experiences. It was the first time that he truly felt intellectually challenged. He claimed that he heard "as able discussions in the debating society . . . in Barbourville as at any other time or place, not even excepting the Supreme Court of the United States." More importantly, it left him thirsting for something more than the largely anonymous life of a small-town doctor. "It had drawn the mind of a country doctor in a mountain hamlet into the current of national thought," one biographer noted, "and afforded him a means of relating himself to the great public questions of the day."[31] "What gave the turn of [my] mind toward law," Miller later told a reporter, "was developed in [the] debating society."[32]

During the 1840s, Miller's budding antislavery sentiments blossomed into full-blown support of pro-emancipation politician Cassius M. Clay. A slaveholder like Miller, Clay nevertheless criticized slavery's economic grip on the state. He felt that in order to prosper, Kentucky needed a mixed economy with manufacturing and diversified farming. Slavery, Clay came to believe, degraded white labor because it made all labor seem like something that needed to be coerced from a servile class rather than as a redemptive experience. Plantation monoculture, moreover, made Kentucky overly dependent on one or two crops and stifled any hope for the more dynamic growth then occurring in the North.[33]

Clay shaped his views during a tour of New England that left him awestruck over that region's manufacturing and wealth. "I . . . saw a people living *there* luxuriously," he told a Kentucky audience, "on a soil which *here* would have been deemed the high road to famine and the almshouse." By using abundant water to power mills, New Englanders had created wealth out of the seeming adversity of their cold climate and rocky soil. Deeply impressed, Clay's visit sparked his lifelong love affair with industry. When he returned to Kentucky, he promoted manufactures with evangelical zeal. What Kentucky needed, he argued, was a smaller version of his cousin Henry Clay's famed "American System." Under Cassius's "Kentucky System," slavery would end, tobacco plantations would grow foodstuffs, and those crops would be sold to workers in the mills and factories that Clay hoped would develop. And where would these mills and factories be built? They would be built in towns in southeastern Kentucky like Barbourville.[34]

When Clay looked to Kentucky's mountain region, he saw a mineral- and water-rich environment analogous to industrial New England. He thought that with free labor, Kentuckians could turn the region into an "American Switzerland" dotted with factories. For the development-minded boosters of Barbourville, Clay's message must have been intoxicating. As Barbourville's economic weaknesses became increasingly apparent in the 1840s, the idea of worker-filled mills sprouting along the Cumberland River offered the prospect of a cure-all for Barbourville's ills. Not surprisingly Miller joined this crusade, and by middecade, he was an enthusiastic disciple of Clay's.[35]

The most controversial portion of Clay's program was his call for emancipation. He vehemently believed that slavery discouraged industry, and progress. To prove his point, he argued that one need only compare the South and the North. The North, he exclaimed, was "radiant with railroads, the channels of her untold commerce, whilst the South hobbles on at an immeasurable distance behind." In order to change this situation, he believed that the state needed to attract skilled craftsmen, virtuous free laborers, and progressive mill owners, all of whom would never come to Kentucky while slavery existed. Slavery, he charged, "degrades the mechanic, ruins the manufacturer, lays waste and depopulates the country."[36]

Initially, Clay's ideas received enthusiastic support from many Kentuckians. Targeting his message at the state's non-slaveholding majority, Clay vowed to defend the "six hundred thousand free white laborers of Kentucky! . . . against whose every vital interest slavery wages eternal and implacable war!" In 1840, he ran successfully for the Kentucky legislature on a platform that combined support for banks, railroads, and turnpikes with fierce opposition to further importation of slaves into the state.[37]

As national abolitionist fervor grew during the 1840s, however, Kentucky slaveholders were increasingly able to brand emancipationists wild-eyed fanatics. After 1846, Clay's message faced stiff resistance in the slave-dominated hemp and tobacco regions, where his opponents portrayed him as a disguised emissary of radical Boston abolitionist William Lloyd Garrison. In response, Clay focused his attentions on southeastern Kentucky. "I turned my eyes toward the mountains eastward," he remembered, "where few slaves were held." To the mountain towns he made an "increasingly vigorous appeal."[38] Few of Kentucky's 31,000 slaveholders lived in that region, and of those fewer still were unconditionally wedded to the slave system. Slaveholders like Miller, moreover, did not depend solely upon slavery for their livelihood, and Clay believed correctly that the promise of industrial prosperity could convince them to forego the profits from a handful of slaves.[39]

In his speeches and his newspaper, *The True American*, Clay made it clear that his motives were economic rather than humanitarian. "If we are for emancipation, it is that Kentucky may be virtuous and prosperous," he said, "If we seek liberty for blacks, it is . . . that the white laborers of the state may be men and build us all up by their power and energy." Clay, in fact, had an unflattering opinion of African Americans. He feared that his own slaves were poisoning his family's food. Moreover, he felt that free blacks were lazy and unfit for factory work. "I have studied the Negro character," he said, "they lack self-reliance—we can make nothing out of them. God has made them for the sun and the banana!"[40]

Clay's negrophobic sentiments played well in Barbourville, a town with a history of rigid race relations. While the town had few slaves, it was no haven of social equality. Whites were fined "for playing cards with a Negro" or "for playing cards with a free person of color." Lynchings occurred on occasion, and slaves accused of committing crimes received swift and brutal treatment. In 1836, the sheriff ordered Bob George, a slave caught stealing, to be taken "within two miles of Barbourville" and hung "by the neck until he be dead, dead, dead." Town officials then left George's body on display in a tree in front of a school.[41]

Miller's racial views during these years reflected his time and community. While he came to favor emancipation, he opposed Garrisonian abolitionism.

"An abolitionist has been my abhorrence all my life," he wrote. Even after his conversion to antislavery sentiments, he never condemned slaveholders themselves. He later told a crowd that slaveholders were "nearly all the blood relations I have living, and the warmest personal friends and purest men I know on earth. . . . I feel too much compassion for the slaveholder to indulge in any rage against him." Although he lacked the convictions of a true abolitionist, Miller did recognize the humanity of slaves and their right to the fruits of their labor. He also lamented slavery's frequent cruelties, recalling his horror during childhood upon seeing his black nursemaid being whipped. Beginning around 1846, after Clay's writings and speeches convinced him that slavery was an impediment to progress, he freed his slaves at the rate of one per year.[42]

In the mid-1840s, as his views on slavery evolved, Miller also began to question his choice of profession. He was growing tired of the role of small-town doctor. He resented the backward attitude of many of his patients in the countryside and complained that they would not even allow him to perform a simple autopsy. "In consequence of the superstition greatly prevalent among the people with whom I practice," he wrote, "I have never been able to obtain an opportunity of making a post-obituary examination of a subject." He also found Barbourville to be a wretched cauldron of disease. Prone to flooding and bordered by swamps, Miller claimed that Barbourville was "remarkable as being the most unhealthy place in the mountains, or probably in Kentucky, in proportion to its population."[43]

During these years cholera repeatedly struck the town, even though some medical experts believed that rural areas like Barbourville would be spared. Rather than a haven, Barbourville made a likely target. Visited by thousands of emigrants, it was continuously exposed to possible carriers of the disease. Travelers and townspeople alike relied on a common source, the Cumberland River, for their drinking water. The frequent floods that plagued Barbourville—floods that carried contaminated water throughout the village—also aided the spread of cholera. Miller quickly realized that his town was not immune to the epidemic and condemned those who said cholera would not strike "any where else than cities." He pointed out that Barbourville was "certainly as unlike the confined filthiness of a city, as anything can be." Nonetheless, he noted in 1838, the "affliction . . . has for years been very fatal, destroying probably one fourth of the juvenile population."[44]

While some Kentucky doctors attributed cholera to the "free use of vegetables, of an indigestible nature," Miller recognized that it was somehow linked to the river. He noted that around Barbourville cholera was "not confined to the town alone," but was "to be found along the course of the Cumberland, and on every realm which pays its tribute to that river." Unfamiliar with germ theory, Miller and many other doctors blamed the disease on the inhalation of "marsh effluvium." Miller believed that swampy areas near the river produced fumes from decomposing organic matter that created an unhealthy "marsh miasmata." It would be another fifty years before scientists first isolated the bacterium that causes cholera.[45]

After a few years of witnessing medicine's limitations, Miller became dissatisfied with a life of "riding from cabin to cabin on horseback" dispensing questionable (if not deadly) remedies to superstitious, subsistence farmers in Kentucky's sleepy backcountry. He later said that he simply could not bear to see his patients suffer in cases he could not cure and that, as a result, he found the medical profession to be "distasteful."[46] Miller, a man of ambition, must also have recognized the low status of antebellum physicians. "American medicine was provincial," one historian has noted, writing that the "average physician, ill-paid and poorly trained, struggled constantly to retain . . . dignity and prestige." Doctors' lack of success in treating cholera only compounded their low station. Although Miller's marriage into the Ballinger family had solidified his position in Barbourville's social hierarchy, he might well have noted the social advantages held by his in-laws and friends in the legal community.[47]

Spurred by his rhetorical success sparring with the town's lawyers in the debating society, Miller began preparing for a career in law. "After some three or four years' practice I determined to abandon it," he later wrote of his medical career, "and studied law while practicing medicine which was my only means of support." Surrounded in his daily life by lawyers, he had plenty of mentors and role models in his new profession. He and Lucy lived in a room in the large house of his jurist father-in-law James Ballinger, and he shared his doctor's office with lawyer Silas Woodson.[48] Much as he did with the medical texts in Dr. Leverill's pharmacy, Miller pored over Woodson's law books after long days of practicing medicine. Some of his friends tried to discourage him from attempting a risky career change, "being then a married man with two children." But he plowed ahead. "After two years [sic] study," he remembered, "I commenced the practice of law."[49]

Miller's name first appears in legal records as a witness to a will. In 1844, the townspeople elected him justice of the peace. Admitted to the bar in 1846, he became Woodson's law partner, and in 1847 the county court appointed him to the important position of supervisor of the toll roads in Knox County. The job required him to oversee the collection of tolls from Warriors Path, Boone Trace, and the Old Wilderness Road, on which emigrants traveled. As a result of this appointment, he received firsthand knowledge of the way in which the new National Road, steamboats, and the railroad had cut into the emigrant trade through the Cumberland Gap. Barbourville's economic lifeblood was evaporating, and this depressing news pushed him towards another weighty life decision. Within two years of this appointment, he began exploring the possibility of leaving Kentucky and moving west.[50]

In the early autumn of 1849, Miller embarked on a trip to the Mississippi River to investigate possible places to move his family. Although he had not completely given up on Barbourville, he now explored up-and-coming Mississippi river towns in search of locales that might grow as he had originally hoped Barbourville would. On this trip, one river town in Iowa particularly dazzled him. As the first Iowa city encountered by steamboat travelers up the Mississippi, Keokuk served as the entryway to one of the most fertile regions on the globe. The city's location at the base of the Des Moines river valley positioned it to control the trade of an area that contained half of Iowa's agricultural wealth. And, in stark contrast to the sleepy subsistence homesteads that surrounded Barbourville, prolific cash-crop farms filled the fecund countryside around Keokuk.[51]

By the time of Miller's 1849 visit, Keokuk had grown from a rustic trading village with a few rickety cabins into a rising entrepôt with dozens of dry goods stores, harness shops, blacksmiths, coopers, and other businesses. Because all river traffic heading north from New Orleans or St. Louis had to stop at Keokuk to transport goods past an infamous stretch of rapids located there, the city's boosters could rightly claim that their town was an economic necessity. As steamboats had to be unloaded at Keokuk, the town became the natural transshipment point for goods being sent to Iowa's interior towns. On summer days, hundreds of carts and covered wagons full of merchandise bound for Des Moines, Winterset, Ottumwa, and other Iowa towns crowded Keokuk's levee and waterfront streets.[52]

Keokuk also flourished as a processing center for farm products. Mills ground flour, distilleries turned wheat into whiskey, and tanners processed cattle hides into leather goods. In the winter, a time when Barbourville slipped into a deep economic slumber, Keokuk packed meat and lots of it. In 1848, Keokuk slaughterhouses processed 15,000 hogs and stored the meat in Mississippi River ice to be shipped with the first thaw. By 1849, that number had risen to 34,000.[53]

In 1849, Keokuk also served as a jumping off point for emigrants bound for the goldfields of California or the Mormon settlements on the Great Salt Lake. These travelers arrived by steamboat and camped at Keokuk while they outfitted themselves for their westward journey. Mormon encampments could resemble small cities. At one point, "some 3500 souls—besides wagons, cattle, tents and animals numberless" camped outside the town. City boosters took to calling Keokuk the "Gate City" to the West.[54]

The town's economic vibrancy made it a magnet for ambitious young professional men, particularly lawyers. Its bustling commercial life ensured many litigious disputes. Better still were the possibilities that the town might grow into a major city. Lawyers who established a practice early on could position themselves to reap the benefits of unrestrained growth. In 1847, Keokuk had "several" lawyers. By September 1849, it had twenty-two. As he had done while visiting Barbourville thirteen years earlier, Miller realized that if he was going to move his career and family to Keokuk, he needed to act fast.[55]

Miller let his decision of whether or not to move west rest upon the outcome of the 1849 Kentucky Constitutional Convention, called to settle the slavery question in the state once and for all. Delegates to the convention were asked either to leave the constitution's current protections of slavery in place or to provide for gradual emancipation. If the convention added the proposed emancipation amendment to the new constitution, he was inclined to stay put. With slavery abolished and Cassius Clay's Kentucky System implemented, the resulting industrialization might save Barbourville from its precipitous economic decline. But if slavery remained firmly protected under the new constitution, Clay's plan to create an American Switzerland in the Kentucky mountains seemed doomed. Woodson, Miller's law partner, publicly vowed that if the new constitution permanently protected slavery he would leave the state. Because the outcome of the convention depended upon the results of the county elections for delegates, both Miller and Woodson declared themselves candidates for the position of Knox County's delegate to the convention.[56]

No stranger to political activity, Miller had played an "active part in politics as a member of the Whig Party" throughout the late 1840s. But unlike most

Kentucky Whigs who supported Henry Clay, Miller remained a staunch follower of Henry's cousin, Cassius. In the 1848 election, Cassius campaigned for Zachary Taylor, who had beaten out Henry for the Whig presidential nomination. He did so in order to embarrass the "Henry Clay Whigs" who had closed ranks behind slaveholders. Following Cassius's lead, Miller stumped for Taylor as well.[57]

Miller's candidacy for the delegate position would have been his first campaign for public office. But he and Woodson soon recognized that only one of them could fill Knox County's seat at the convention. As a result, Miller pulled out of the race on the condition that Woodson "stand openly in favor of emancipation." He later recalled that "[w]hen the proposition to amend the Constitution of Kentucky was [announced] and delegates were to be elected," he was "ardently in favor of incorporating into the new constitution a provision for the emancipation of slaves and gradual abolition of slavery. . . . I told [Woodson] who was elected from Knox County that unless he would come out in favor of emancipation, I should be a candidate. He did so promise." After withdrawing from the race, Miller actively canvassed for Woodson.[58]

Although most Kentuckians owned no slaves, the campaign quickly turned sour for the emancipationists. Many Kentucky whites continued to associate emancipationists with the despised abolitionists. They feared that immediate abolition of slavery would lead to social chaos. In response, Cassius Clay tried desperately to distance both himself and other gradual emancipationists from abolitionist Garrisonians. He condemned abolitionists as a "horde of fanatical incendiaries rising up in the North." A violent incident on the campaign trail, however, undermined his efforts. Stumping in Madison County, Clay got into a fierce confrontation with Cyrus Turner, a proslavery speaker. Angry words soon led to a physical altercation; in the course of the fight, both men badly wounded each other. Turner later died of his injuries. Although it was not clear who started the brawl, many Kentuckians blamed Clay and made him a symbol of abolitionist violence. The incident turned many voters against the emancipationists.[59]

The emancipationists faced other obstacles as well. The leaders of the two mainstream parties—the Whigs and Democrats—campaigned actively against them and made opposition to emancipation a test of party orthodoxy. "Both parties feared the effect of the mad dog cry of abolitionism throughout the State," the *Louisville Examiner* noted after the campaign, "and the leaders of both for weeks before the election cautioned and besought their friends not to show any respect for emancipation." Many non-slaveholders opposed the emancipationists because they had economic ties to the slave system and defended the institution as if they held slaves themselves. Other white Kentuckians worried that no feasible scheme for emancipation had been offered. Clay's plan was simply to expel freed slaves from the state, except those "we shall absolutely need." Combined, these factors all but destroyed the emancipationists' chances for victory.[60]

In the end, the election did not go well for the antislavery forces. Although they received ten thousand votes statewide, they only commanded a majority of votes in Barbourville's Knox County. Woodson was the only emancipationist delegate elected, and proslavery forces dominated the constitutional convention. The new constitution they drafted kept all the old proslavery clauses intact and added new ones that barred free blacks from entering the state and banned voluntary emancipation unless the freed slaves were immediately exiled from Kentucky. The new constitution also included a clause that stipulated that the "right of property is before and higher than any constitutional sanction; and the right of the owner of a slave and its increase, is the same and is as inviolable as the right of the owner of any property whatever."[61] When the voters of Kentucky subsequently ratified this new, ultra-proslavery document, Miller made up his mind to leave for free-soil Iowa. "The new constitution of Kentucky framed by this convention, and *adopted* by the people," Miller wrote, "fixed slavery more firmly than ever in the state; and left no reason to suppose that any policy eradicating slavery would ever be adopted in my life time." Having determined that slavery "would never be voluntarily abolished in a Slave state," he decided to leave Kentucky.[62]

Miller was not alone in his decision to abandon Barbourville. By 1849, the importance of railroads and steamboats in the new economic order was apparent to all. Barbourville, unfortunately, had access to neither. Furthermore, the possibility of state-promoted industrialization around Barbourville died with Clay's Kentucky System at the constitutional convention. A desperate and fanciful proposal to link southeastern Kentucky to eastern markets by building a canal through the Cumberland Mountains also died quickly, squelched by the railroad forces in the state legislature.[63] As a result, Barbourville's professional men faced a clear choice: stay put and settle for a declining standard of living in an increasingly remote mountain town, or move west. After 1849, both proslavery and antislavery men began to leave Barbourville in droves. One ill-fated group of Barbourville families set out for the goldfields of California. Cholera struck the group around St. Louis, killing seven of the twenty-seven member party. Silas Woodson moved to Missouri, where he later became the Republican governor. Miller's brother-in-law, William Pitt Ballinger, moved his family and slaves to Galveston, Texas. Miller's brother William also migrated to Texas. Even Miller's father-in-law, James Ballinger, a thirty-two-year resident of Barbourville and one of its original settlers, left eventually for the West.[64]

Miller headed for Keokuk. He and Lucy and their two children arrived in the "Gate City" on May 7, 1850, to find their new hometown still dusted by the remnants from a surprise late-spring snowstorm. But the unusually cold weather could not diminish their enthusiasm. For Miller, his family, and Keokuk, the future was full of possibility.[65]

CHAPTER 2
Keokuk Rising

U PON ARRIVING in Keokuk in May 1850, Miller found a small hotel where he and his family could live while he embarked once again on a new career. As a newcomer with no friends or professional acquaintances, he might have struggled initially had it not been for a fortuitous meeting with William Clark, a boyhood friend from Kentucky who had already settled in Keokuk and who had served as the town's first mayor. Clark introduced Miller to Lewis Reeves, a successful lawyer in town who was looking for a partner. Despite being a regular at the gambling tables of Keokuk's saloons, Reeves had built a busy and lucrative practice. He took an immediate liking to the bright and affable Miller, and the two joined forces that summer. Rather than struggling, Samuel found himself almost instantly immersed in a demanding and remunerative legal practice.[1]

Much of Reeves and Miller's practice involved real estate disputes. Frontier boomtowns were notoriously tricky places to secure sound land titles, and Keokuk's situation was worse than most. Part of the town sat on land known as the "Half-Breed Tract," 120,000 acres originally set aside by treaty for the use "of half-breeds belonging to the Sac and Fox nations." Because there were relatively few so-called half-breeds, white families soon overran the sparsely settled tract, established farms, and declared ownership of the land. Despite the best efforts of the frontier judicial system to establish who in fact held legitimate land titles, Keokuk quickly descended into a welter of conflicting claims that would plague the city throughout the 1840s and 1850s. At times, disputes over this land even erupted into mob actions.[2] But for attorneys, the Half-Breed Tract was a boon, because "every parcel of land, every 'corner' lot, and every other lot was good for a law suit." Within a year, Miller had made enough money to move his family out of the Laclede Hotel and into a fine house at the corner of Third and High Streets near the center of town.[3]

Among Keokuk's lawyers, Miller gained a reputation as an attorney who favored reason over precedent. Unlike many antebellum lawyers who relied on long, windy discussions of old cases and Roman law, he favored clarity over profundity. "Miller's method," one Keokuk attorney noted, "was to cite few cases, but to impress the court with the reason of the law."[4] The best lawyers, Miller later wrote, were those with a "capacity to reduce all propositions to the test of sound logic, without regard to the syllogisms of Aristotle or Whately." His distaste for ancient precedents and overly erudite barristers might have stemmed from his insecurities about his own lack of formal legal training, but his practical approach and clear arguments resonated with clients and juries in the West during a can-do age.[5]

Miller's faith in reason also influenced his spiritual life. In Barbourville, he had never been much for church, and as a member of the Barbourville Debating Society he had sided with rationalists who doubted that God intervened in humans' day-to-day lives. Now in Keokuk, Miller gravitated to the Unitarians, a liberal, New England–based denomination that attracted freethinkers. In the 1850s, Unitarian ministers taught that the meaning of the Bible had to be sought in the same manner as in other books. It had to be interpreted using logic rather than faith. This approach appealed to Miller, who employed a similar methodology in his law practice.[6]

The Unitarians were also activists. Like Miller, they opposed capital punishment and slavery, believing that both the death penalty and the peculiar institution violated the tenets of Christian humanism. Although Miller did not endorse the radical abolitionist views of some Unitarian ministers—such as Boston's Theodore Parker—he nevertheless approved of the Unitarian's message of reason and God's infinite goodness. Nineteenth-century Unitarians were, according to one historian, "probably the most convinced believers in progress the world has ever known." In the early 1850s, Miller shared their optimistic outlook. Whether pondering the future of Keokuk or slavery, he believed that progress was inevitable. In 1853, he helped found Keokuk's first Unitarian Church, personally drafting its articles of incorporation.[7]

A double dose of personal tragedy soon tested his optimistic worldview. First, in 1854, a resurgence of Asiatic cholera that had terrorized the nation in

1849 killed Lewis Reeves, leaving Miller to run the large practice the two men had created. Named the executor of Reeves's estate, Samuel also assumed the task of managing Lewis's property for the benefit of his widow, Eliza, and her four-year-old daughter. Then, in November of the same year, Miller's wife, Lucy, died of consumption at the age of twenty-seven. Miller was now a single father with three daughters of his own.[8]

Refusing to be daunted by adversity, Miller continued to pursue a vigorous legal career. For a time after Reeves's death, he worked as a solo practitioner, and business remained brisk. He became the most sought-after attorney in Keokuk and appeared regularly before the state's highest court. In 1855, Miller served as the lead attorney in fifteen of the twenty-four cases Keokuk lawyers argued before the Iowa Supreme Court, and his practice encompassed almost every facet of Keokuk life. He handled divorces, personal injuries, disputes between merchants, bankruptcies, contested wills, and even criminal cases. His all-consuming career took its toll on his ability to care for his children, however, and in 1855 he sent them to live temporarily with their uncle, William Pitt Ballinger, in Galveston, Texas.[9]

In the meantime, Miller rebuilt his life. He formed a new law practice with John Rankin, another prominent attorney in town. And in 1856 he married Eliza Winter Reeves, the twenty-eight-year-old widow of his former law partner. The daughter of one Keokuk's Unitarian ministers, Eliza was a "handsome women with a fine figure" who, it was later said, bore a "feminine resemblance to her husband."[10] With a new stepmother for his children, Samuel traveled to Galveston to retrieve his daughters—Olivia (called Olly), Jane, and Patricia—all of whom were excited to return to their father's care. "Olly's little heart," their uncle noted of Miller's arrival, "almost left her body."[11]

Eliza joined Samuel on the trip to Galveston, where she first met William Pitt Ballinger, the brother of Miller's first wife. From the start, Ballinger had mixed feelings about Eliza. In some ways he admired her, noting in his diary that she had "high animal spirits." She liked to "dance, ride, & take active exercises" and was, he inferred, an "excellent housekeeper & domestic manager." But other aspects of Eliza's personality worried him. "She has too much impulse," he felt, and she was "evidently vain & fond of display—too desirous of admiration." He feared Miller would "be rendered occasionally uncomfortable by her want of discretion & a little oppressed at times by her exacting." Most of all, Ballinger wondered how well Eliza would treat his nieces. He hoped she would "be judicious & get along happily with [Miller's] children," but he suspected she would never have "any warm affection for them."[12]

Ballinger's fears only increased as time passed, particularly after Samuel and Eliza had two children of their own (a daughter named Alida, and a son, Irvine) in 1859 and 1860. "So far as I can see," Ballinger wrote in 1860, "the children are cheerful, but [Eliza] is evidently not a patient person & talks and fusses a great deal & feels that her trouble and responsibility are very great—her manner towards them is not pleasant at all." Many of Ballinger's relatives (including his parents) lived in Keokuk, and they shared his concerns. His Aunt Jane was "not at all satisfied with [Eliza's] treatment towards the children." Ballinger's father, for his part, liked Samuel, but had "no respect for his wife" and thought "as do all the kin that she utterly neglects the children."[13] Miller, of course, did not agree. He adored Eliza. He thought her a "watchful" and "loving" mother and believed, as he told Ballinger pointedly, that she had been "no *step*mother . . . to any of Lucy's children" [emphasis Miller's]. "Miller," Ballinger later acknowledged, "is . . . entirely wrapped up in [Eliza] and thinks her part as a stepmother has been discharged to perfection."[14]

While Miller rebuilt his domestic life and expanded his legal practice, Keokuk boomed. The town's unrestrained growth had only accelerated since his arrival. In the mid-1850s, workers erected scores of buildings each month, and many of Keokuk's streets "were almost completely blocked with great piles of brick, sand, lumber, lime, and mortar beds." "There were about 700 buildings of all kinds put up in the past year," the *Keokuk Post* reported in 1855. "Keokuk will double its population, wealth, and importance in the coming year." "All the dwelling houses are occupied," declared a Keokuk citizen, "and the cry is still for more." During the peak boom year of 1856, the city's twenty-three brickyards produced an estimated 20 million bricks.[15]

As the town thrived, its boosters became increasingly certain that the "Gate City" would soon be one of the great cities of the West. Dubbing Keokuk an "infant Hercules," they predicted that the town would someday "eclipse both Chicago and St. Louis." Immigrants and men of capital, they claimed, would soon bypass other, better-known cities in favor of Keokuk. "The majestic Mississippi will bear the trophies of the advance of Keokuk in every boat that passes St. Louis," one guidebook forecast, "whilst Chicago will strive in vain to recall her truant merchants who have realized the advantages of Keokuk." Promoters added that the only thing the city currently lacked was adequate housing for the expected crowds. "Were it not that our city is not prepared to shelter the people," a Keokuk advocate remarked, "it would be hard to tell how much of Cincinnati and Pittsburgh would be left behind."[16]

By modern standards, a city of fifteen thousand hardly amounts to a major metropolis. But that figure fails to reflect the constant bustle, astonishing growth, and hard-charging attitude in Keokuk and its hinterland. Farmers and merchants alike possessed an aggressive economic outlook. Farmers, responsive to market demands, quickly began corn and hog production on a prodigious scale. The Gate City's Yankee merchants and entrepreneurs had an equally vigorous commercial spirit. When the opportunities arose, they eagerly expanded the size, scale, and scope of their establishments. Intensely individualistic, the merchants and farmers shared an ethos of hard work and economic optimism. As one Keokuk resident wrote in 1853, "No rich man emigrates to the West, and those that are rich have made this money by hard work. 'Every man for himself' is the motto which adorns the armor of each one of us, and no coat of arms ever bore a more truthfully correct or more significant emblem." Keokuk's citizens believed that, unlike eastern cities, theirs was a meritocracy, where talent and effort, rather than birthright, led to success. "Skill and talent are more necessary to success here than in older communities," the *Keokuk Dispatch* avowed, "but with those, the promised success is more certain and abundant here than there."[17]

By 1856, 431 businesses lined Keokuk's streets. Lawyers, doctors, insurers, notaries, and customs collectors occupied another hundred or so offices. Commercial establishments ranged in size from small bookstores to expansive warehouses. Sophisticated, factory-scale slaughterhouses butchered tens of thousands of hogs each winter. Most businesses prospered, with many recording sales increases of 40 to 50 percent per year. Some of the town's dry goods merchants who initially sold only to farmers found themselves wholesaling to the country stores of inland towns. "The merchants coming down from the interior," noted one observer in 1855, "have swept our merchants' shelves faster than they were replenished."[18]

The rapid growth of the wholesale business convinced the citizens of Keokuk that their town would become an entrepôt of the first rank. Once dependent on St. Louis for their goods, many Keokuk merchants now ordered their supplies directly from New York. Instead of viewing their town as an important spoke in St. Louis's economic wheel, Gate City boosters increasingly viewed St. Louis as a competitor. Thanks to growth that "dazzles and bewilders the imagination," Mayor Samuel Curtis claimed in 1856, Keokuk would no longer play second fiddle to anyone. "In the future march of Western cities we claim position in the front rank," he boasted in his 1856 inaugural address, predicting "future wealth and grandeur that may hereafter rival . . . the great cities of ancient and modern times." Having come of age, the Gate City hoped to attract those who previously "would never have forsaken the idea that the sun rises and sets in St. Louis."[19]

Keokuk became a magnet for talented men and women. As was the case in Barbourville, a number of these settlers later found national prominence. Among them was Samuel Clemens (Mark Twain), who came to work at his brother Orion's printing office. A gifted cohort of lawyers also coalesced in the Gate City. Many later became federal cabinet members, influential politicians, judges, and Civil War generals.[20]

Not content to rest on their laurels, Keokuk's builders and elected officials strived to provide the town with expensive amenities normally reserved for larger or more established cities. They built theaters and schools and sold city bonds to pay for the construction of a medical college. They graded the roads, installed gaslit streetlamps, and planned a sophisticated water works. Comfortable homes and regal churches filled the side streets. Determined that Keokuk should have a first-class hotel, developers began work on the grand, multistoried Estes House.[21]

One can imagine how impressive Keokuk must have appeared to steamboat passengers arriving at the city's docks on summer evenings in the 1850s. After the long, two-hundred-mile trip from St. Louis, the Gate City must have seemed a frontier oasis of restaurants, theaters, saloons, shops, hotels, and success stories, a gaslit jewel glimmering on the bluffs overlooking the Mississippi.

Samuel Miller thrived along with the town. The combination of his active practice, his marriage to Eliza, and his own real estate speculations made him an affluent man. Reeves's death had left Eliza independently wealthy; she had inherited real estate holdings worth an estimated $40,000. Miller's own properties in and around Keokuk totaled $50,000. The couple owned several buildings in Keokuk's business district, as well as a number of undeveloped lots on the outskirts of the town and in the surrounding county. Miller also invested in a company that mined coalfields north on the Des Moines River and in the railroad line that would bring the coal to town. If, as he expected, Keokuk swelled into a giant metropolis with hundreds of thousands of citizens, he would become even richer. His landholdings were straight in the path of future development, and he held stock in the coal and railroad companies that would provide energy and transportation for a major city.[22]

Miller's speculations in real estate and coal mining were part of a much broader speculative craze that swept over Keokuk during its boom years, fueled in 1855 when the United States Supreme Court settled the question of land titles in the Half-Breed Tract. Before the Court's decision in *Coy v. Mason,* the uncertainty surrounding the town's land titles had slowed such speculation. Now, Keokukians celebrated the Court's ruling as a sign that their city was ready to enter the next phase of its development. The Court's decision, an 1855 Keokuk city directory proclaimed, had removed the final shackles holding back the town's expansion. "Having burst these fetters," the guide trumpeted, Keokuk was "now coming forward to claim supremacy in the trade of the Upper Mississippi." It soon seemed that anyone with sufficient income was investing in land in and around the city, since growth seemed certain and profits sure. Even ministers and preachers who counseled their parishioners to "lay up ye treasures in heaven" got in on the speculation. The pastor of Keokuk's New School Presbyterian Church owned an entire city block.[23]

While Keokuk's citizens were united in their goal of pecuniary gain, national political events soon divided them. Efforts to organize Nebraska—the flat, fertile land to the west of Iowa—brought the divisive slavery issue to the fore. Initially, many Iowans thought that opening Nebraska for white settlement was a good idea. Few feared the increased competition or agricultural overproduction that might result, holding instead to the nineteenth-century American tenet that unbridled expansion meant progress. Organizing Nebraska would also provide a direct route for a transcontinental railroad that would, Iowans expected, run through their state. The railroad, in turn, would bring new settlers, investment, and wealth to Iowa. And because the Missouri Compromise's time-honored 36° 30′ line had long placed Nebraska north of slavery, the new territory would be free-soil. Nebraska, Iowans predicted, would one day mirror their own state with its prosperous small farms and industrious yeomen.[24]

Southern slaveholders never shared Iowans' enthusiasm for organizing Nebraska as a territory, precisely because it sat above the Missouri Compromise

line. They knew that, inevitably, the citizens of a settled Nebraska would request admission to the Union as a free state and upset the tenuous political and
psychological balance between North and South. Southerners in Congress thus
consistently blocked efforts to organize the territory. As Missouri senator David
Rice Atchison put it, he would see Nebraska "sink in hell" before he would vote
to organize it as a free territory.[25]

Expansion-minded politicians such as Stephen Douglas, the powerful Democratic senator from Illinois, soon grew exasperated over southerners' dogged
opposition to organizing Nebraska. For Douglas, the problem with such sectional squabbling was that it obstructed his cherished dream of a transcontinental railroad linking Chicago to the Pacific coast. Despite hailing from a free
state himself, Douglas did not care whether or not slavery expanded. No railroad could be built until Nebraska was organized; yet it appeared that Nebraska
might never be organized if its status remained intertwined with the slavery
issue. In January 1854, Douglas formulated a plan to solve this dilemma. Then
chairman of the Senate Committee on the Territories, Douglas introduced a bill
that would split the vast lands known as Nebraska into two territories, Kansas
and Nebraska, and that would allow slavery to exist in those territories if the
people who settled there voted for it. In the meantime, Congress could get on
with expanding the American empire.

Douglas cloaked the bill in the democratic language of "popular sovereignty," a phrase he borrowed from Michigan senator Lewis Cass, who had
proposed unsuccessfully a similar concept during the 1848 presidential election.
To guarantee southern support for his plan, Douglas had to convince slaveholders that it was not simply a ploy to add more free states to the Union. Thus, his
bill eventually included an explicit repeal of the Missouri Compromise's revered
36° 30' line. Although Douglas knew his bill would raise a "hell of a storm" in
the North, he felt that some northerners would soon recognize that the benefits
of national expansion outweighed the danger of repealing the 36° 30' line.[26] But
Douglas badly misread the northern mood, and his bill remains one of the great
political miscalculations in American history. Rather than bringing North and
South together, the furious, divisive congressional debates sparked by the bill in
the spring of 1854 convinced many Americans, including Samuel Miller, that
the nation was headed towards civil war.[27]

Miller quickly recognized the threat the Kansas-Nebraska Act posed to the
Union. When Douglas's act passed in the Senate, he predicted that the slavery

issue would split the national parties along sectional lines and that issues that once united northern and southern Whigs and Democrats, such as banks and internal improvements, would be no match for the divisive slavery question. "The passage of the Nebraska Bill as it came from the Senate," he wrote his slaveholding brother-in-law in March 1854, "will arouse a fury in the North which will abolish party ties and create a new organization of parties on sectional bases" that could be "fatal to the Union." There was, he warned Ballinger, "a real danger that you and I shall live in different nations."[28]

Despite his fears, Miller refused to compromise his position on slavery to appease southerners. Like many other antislavery moderates, he had long hoped that slavery, if contained in the South, would eventually exhaust the soil and die out. The Kansas-Nebraska Act dramatically undermined this plan. Miller called the act an "aggressive step in favour of . . . propagating slavery by violating . . . honorable compromises." He warned that the "repeal of the national legislation of the Missouri Compromise Act will be the beginning of the end." Because tens of thousands of other northerners shared his views, visceral reactions to the Kansas-Nebraska Act echoed across the North.[29]

The intensity of the northern reaction to the Kansas-Nebraska Act surprised Douglas. He had hoped that moderate northern Whigs, after some initial protests, would eventually acquiesce to it. When a favorable consensus failed to materialize, however, Douglas refused to back down. Instead he used party discipline and his immense political influence to force the bill through the Democratic-controlled House, gaining just enough support from southern Whigs to carry the day. The Kansas-Nebraska Act passed in the spring of 1854. It was a pyrrhic victory.

The 1854 elections left no doubt as to the scale of the mistake Douglas and the other politicians who supported the measure had made. That fall, northern voters rebuked Douglas and his party, throwing out seventy northern Democratic congressmen. The number of Democrats in the House of Representatives dropped from 93 to 23. The Democrats did not suffer alone; the fallout from the Kansas-Nebraska controversy proved terminal to the Whig Party as well. Hopelessly split along sectional lines, the party collapsed, never again to revive.

Two new political organizations filled the political vacuum that resulted from the Whigs' demise—the nativist, anti-Catholic, American Party (known as the Know-Nothings) and the Republican Party. The Know-Nothings found success for a short time, particularly in the Northeast, but they too soon imploded due to the slavery issue. The Republicans, in contrast, flourished as a result of their antislavery position. In Iowa, former Whigs like Miller flocked to the new party. Initially called the Kansas-Nebraska party, the Republicans formed in opposition to Douglas's act, and its leaders vowed to contain slavery in the South. Drawing their support solely from the North, the Republicans' rapid rise reflected a nation splitting apart. Although Miller feared where this political sectionalization might lead, he joined the party and enthusiastically recruited new members in Iowa.[30]

Events in Kansas and Washington made Miller's recruitment efforts easy. Not only had Douglas misread northern opinion, but he had also underestimated the potential for violence. The new Kansas territory quickly filled with proslavery and antislavery zealots. All settlers recognized the stakes, and Kansas, the southernmost of the two territories, quickly became contested ground. "We will engage in competition for the virgin soil of Kansas," William H. Seward announced in the Senate in May 1854, "and God give the victory to the side which is stronger in numbers as it is in right." For their part, slaveholders believed that the future of slavery in all of the great West rested on the outcome in Kansas. "The game must be played boldly," Missouri's senator David Rice Atchison implored. "If we win we carry slavery to the Pacific Ocean, if we fail we lose Missouri, Arkansas, Texas, and all the territories."[31]

Atchison and other southerners wanted victory by any means, including election fraud and violence. "We will be compelled to shoot, burn & hang," Atchison warned, "but the thing will soon be over." He was as good as his word. When Kansans went to the polls in March 1855 to elect a territorial legislature, he led thousands of armed, proslavery Missourians across the border to vote illegally and to intimidate free-soilers. Of the 6,307 ballots cast that day, 4,908 were illegal. With the aid of Atchison's "border ruffians," proslavery forces easily swept the election, and the resulting proslavery legislature that met in Lecompton, Kansas, proceeded to draft a draconian slave code. Under the new laws, a person could be fined or imprisoned simply for expressing opinions against slavery. Anyone convicted of helping slaves to escape could be put to death. All voters were required to take an oath to uphold these laws. Embattled Kansas free-soilers rightly called the election a farce and established their own legislature in Topeka.[32]

Keokuk's newspapers filled with articles about the controversy, and the town split along proslavery and antislavery lines. While most Iowans favored a free-soil stance, Keokuk's Lee County sat in the southeastern corner of the state, where many southerners with proslavery sympathies had settled. The *Dispatch*, Keokuk's Democratic paper, did its best to portray anti-Nebraska Iowans as extremists who were "polluted by Abolitionism and Niggerism." The antislavery *Gate City*, in contrast, condemned the border ruffians as scoundrels with "whiskey-drinking, filibustering slaveocratic proclivities" and urged northerners to fight the slaveholders and their henchmen. "We are none of your namby pamby, doughfaced, lily livered northerners who stand in constant dread [that] the southern slaveholders will destroy the Union unless they are permitted to have their way on all occasions," the *Gate City* warned. "The North . . . has yielded long enough to the domineering demands of a few southern aristocrats."[33]

The Kansas crisis reached a crescendo in May 1856, when two events galvanized northern opinion. On May 21, an armed group of eight hundred men, deputized as a posse by the proslavery government, descended upon the free-soil center of Lawrence, Kansas, in search of antislavery agitators. The posse proceeded to pillage the town, robbing homes and shops, destroying its two newspaper offices, and torching a hotel and the home of the free-state governor. Reports of the "sack of Lawrence" filled northern newspapers. Under headlines declaring "Kansas War Commenced!" and "Lawrence Destroyed!" the *Keokuk Gate City* provided dramatic accounts of the events and called Republicans to action. "The man that can read [about] it without feeling his blood boil with indignation," the newspaper charged, "is fit only to be a slave and a lick-spittle to aristocrats."[34]

More inflammatory news came from the U.S. Senate, where, on May 19 and 20, Massachusetts senator Charles Sumner delivered his famous speech entitled "The Crime against Kansas." During this lengthy and angry oration, Sumner labeled Atchison's border ruffians as "hirelings picked from the drunken spew and vomit of an uneasy civilization." He excoriated specific southern politicians, such as South Carolina senator Andrew Butler, for lying with the "harlot slavery." Listening to the speech from the Senate gallery was Congressman Preston Brooks of South Carolina, a cousin of Butler's. Brooks believed that Sumner's speech impugned his cousin's honor. Two days later, he took his revenge. Making his way onto the Senate floor, Brooks approached the Massachusetts senator as he sat writing letters at his desk. After informing Sumner that his speech had been a "libel on South Carolina, and Mr. Butler, who is a relative of mine,"

Brooks struck him over the head more than thirty times with a gold-headed cane.[35]

While southerners cheered Brooks's actions, the *Gate City* reflected northern sentiment, calling the caning an act of "unmanly and dastardly baseness never before paralleled in the proceedings of any legislative body in America." The violence in Kansas and the caning of Sumner convinced many northerners that slaveholders would stop at nothing in their campaign to spread slavery to the West. Even sober-minded men began to consider the possibility that a vast slave-power conspiracy was afoot and that the Kansas-Nebraska Act, the "sacking of Lawrence," and the assault upon Sumner represented the acts of a reactionary, antidemocratic cabal determined to further its immoral way of life at all costs. Northern Know-Nothings and free-soil Democrats—now convinced that the slave power represented the most dire threat to northern liberties—left their parties in droves and joined the Republicans. In Iowa, the Republicans became the dominant political force.[36]

Despite his Kentucky roots, Samuel Miller quickly became one of the most influential Republicans in Iowa. Aside from his southern slaveholding background, his profile matched those of other Republican leaders in the state. From the outset, a small elite of merchants and lawyers politically and socially led Iowa's river towns. These men speculated in land, organized efforts to build railroads, and set Iowa's economic and political agenda. In the mid-1850s, when the Republican Party looked for leaders, they turned to members of this river-town elite. As one of the best known antislavery attorneys in southeastern Iowa, Miller was a natural choice to lead the new party in Keokuk.

In May 1856, at the first Republican county convention, it was Miller who expressed Iowans' outrage over recent events by moving resolutions that condemned the sacking of Lawrence and the caning of Sumner. In June, Miller's supporters elected him president of Keokuk's new Republican organization. In his acceptance speech, he portrayed the Republican Party as different from previous political movements. In the past, he argued, politicians had often been driven by self-interest and careerism. But the leaders of this party were spurred to action by something else—their consciences. It was a party, he argued, of "national and patriotic aims, in which good men were combining, without hope of office or pecuniary benefit."[37]

By July 1856, Republicans had assembled a full slate of candidates for the fall elections, and Keokuk's Republicans nominated Miller to run for state senate.

Because of his professional responsibilities, he initially hesitated. "There are on the docket now, for trial at our next term, commencing on the first Monday of September," he wrote, "some three hundred cases in which I am engaged for one side or the other." He also suspected that he had little chance of winning in Lee County. Unlike most Iowa counties, Lee still had a Democratic majority, and the odds of victory for a Republican remained slim. But in the end, Miller concluded that his new party needed to offer a respectable slate of candidates, even in Lee County. "If . . . I were to refuse to accept the nomination it would be equivalent to leaving my political friends without any candidate for Senator," he wrote. "I have therefore concluded to accept the nomination."[38]

Knowing that he faced almost certain defeat, Miller limited his campaign to a public letter to voters, reprinted in local newspapers, in which he summarized his political views. As a lifelong Whig, he wrote, he had shared that party's enthusiasm for banks, tariffs, and internal improvements. But now those issues had been pushed aside by a "new, vastly important, and overshadowing issue, thrust upon us in a manner that admits of no evasion and requiring at our hands a conscientious solution. . . . You will understand at once that I speak of the Slavery question." Because he had once held slaves, he could speak with authority about slavery's horrors. He had lived with slavery for thirty years and had "had ample opportunity of knowing its workings and observing its influences." Slavery, he had concluded, was "to the white man and the black . . . a full evil." He charged that the "institution of African Slavery as it exists in the United States," was in his judgment "the most stupendous wrong, and the most prolific source of human misery, both to the master and slave, that the sun shines upon in his daily circuit around the globe."[39]

While condemning slavery, Miller took pains to note that he and his fellow Republicans were not wild-eyed abolitionists; rather, they pursued a moderate course. The abolitionists, Miller pointed out, had their own candidates in the field in 1856—Gerrit Smith for president and Frederick Douglass for vice president. "The true Abolitionists," he wrote, "hate us worse than they do the Democrats, because we intend to preserve the Union at all hazards." In his view, the real radicals were the proslavery zealots in Kansas and the politicians who had repealed the venerable Missouri Compromise. The Republicans represented the sensible middle ground between the abolitionists and the Democratic Party, "the latter seeking to extend slavery every where, and the former to abolish it every where, and they are equally regardless of the most sacred constitutional and legal compacts and compromises." While moderate, the Republicans would nevertheless be uncompromising in their principles, particularly with regard to Kansas and Nebraska. Miller pledged that the new party was "opposed to the Repeal of the Missouri Compromise; opposed to the extension of Slavery into Free Territory, and will never consent that acts of conquest, achieved by armed invasion, shall impose upon a free people, who are entitled to the protection of the laws of the Union, the institution of Slavery against their will, and with that institution a set of laws more odious than those which govern the serfs of Russia."[40]

Miller found it puzzling that Iowa's Democrats labeled Republicans a band of disunionists. No prominent Republican, after all, had ever called for disunion. On the contrary, it was southern Democrats who, like small children, threatened secession whenever they did not get their way. "We are called disunionists," Miller wrote, but "this charge comes with ill grace from the party which includes within its bosom all the followers of J. C. Calhoun in his nullification doctrine, all the States' rights men of Georgia who openly defied the laws of the Union as decided by the Supreme Court in the case of the Cherokee Indians, . . . and all who at any time have threatened to dissolve the Union, and whose Cabinet officer, possessing more influence than all the others put together, is Jeff. Davis, the notorious Mississippi secessionist." The Republicans, on the other hand, sought change through constitutional processes. If they lost, they would abide by the majority's decision and continue to work for change through lawful means. "We intend to stand by the Union at all hazards," Miller concluded. "If we are defeated we will submit to the rule of the majority."[41]

Although Miller faced an uphill fight in Lee County, Keokuk Republicans fared well when running for statewide office. That fall, Iowans elected Keokuk Republican Ralph Lowe governor, even though he received limited support in his home county. Iowa had turned solidly Republican—presidential candidate John C. Frémont captured the state—but Lee County had not. Southeastern Iowa remained the state's last Democratic stronghold. In the end, Miller's half-hearted campaign failed to sway Lee County's Democratic voters and he lost, as he had expected.[42]

While Miller and Keokuk's Republicans battled the town's proslavery Democrats, new challenges to the local economy forced leaders from both parties to work together. Although at mid-decade Keokuk continued to thrive, there were hints of dangers ahead. The most apparent of these was the threat posed by Burlington, Keokuk's primary economic rival in Iowa. During the 1850s, the two river towns were locked in a fierce competition for control of southern Iowa's farm and steamboat trade. For a time, Keokuk appeared to be slightly ahead in this close race for regional dominance. As part of the contest, the boosters and newspapers of the two towns constantly sparred, attempting promotional one-upsmanship. "The Keokuk papers are making a huge to-do about the immense business of that little hamlet," quipped a typical editorial in the *Burlington Hawkeye*, "but even with all their gas they don't [compare] with the actual state of things in Burlington."[43]

A key turning point in this rivalry came in 1856, when Burlington became the first of the two cities to be reached by a railroad. The arrival of the Chicago, Burlington, & Quincy Railroad gave Burlington a powerful advantage over Keokuk. Swinging south from Chicago, the CB&Q reached the Mississippi at two points, Burlington and Quincy. Farmers near these river cities now had the ability to compare crop prices in two markets, the traditional outlet at St. Louis and newly accessible Chicago. Within a short time, a large portion of Mississippi River traffic was lost to the railroads.[44]

Railroads also gave Burlington's merchants an advantage, since they now had the ability to purchase their goods at the vast Chicago wholesale houses. Inventories could even be acquired during the winter, a season in which the steamboat trade shut down altogether when the river froze. Keokuk almost instantly became a communications backwater. The railroad brought dependable mail service, as well as telegraph lines that soon paralleled the CB&Q tracks. While Keokuk often received no mail for two or three days, Burlington now had the telegraph and two daily mail runs from Chicago.[45]

Initially, the Keokuk papers tried to downplay the importance of Burlington's railroad connection. But such dismissals soon gave way to grave concern that a "very considerable section of trade . . . has been drawn from several of the northern townships . . . to Burlington, on account of her proximity and railroad facilities." Keokuk's leaders recognized that their city needed its own railroad connection. "Railroads wield the power of men and cities," Keokuk mayor Samuel Curtis stated. "They command and commerce obeys. They can create and destroy, restrain and enlarge. . . . Without railroads, Keokuk would sicken and dwindle down to a local village."[46]

Perhaps more than most, Miller understood that Keokuk had to have a railroad. In Barbourville he had seen what could happen to a town that failed to take advantage of transportation innovations. Without steamboats, Barbourville had withered, and Miller hoped to keep his new home from suffering a similar fate. As early as 1852, Miller advocated building railroads for Keokuk, joining others "in favor of an appropriation by Congress of land for the construction of these works."[47]

A direct railroad connection with the East held particular importance for Keokuk's grand aspirations. The great New York to Chicago trunk lines had propelled Chicago's growth. If Keokuk had any hope of matching the success of Chicago or St. Louis, it needed the economic independence provided by its own eastern route. City leaders envisioned an elaborate four-spoked rail system with Keokuk as its hub. One line would head north, paralleling the Mississippi River to Burlington, another would run south to St. Louis, and a third would traverse the fertile Des Moines River Valley to the state capital and then on to Minnesota. The fourth and most important spoke would be the coveted eastern connection.[48]

But who would pay for this grand scheme? Lack of capital presented an obvious hurdle. Eastern and European capitalists had numerous western suitors hoping to lure them to invest in railroad projects. Recognizing the importance of railroads to economic growth, city officials soon came to the fateful conclusion that public monies could and should be used to build private railroads. Like officials in many other towns and counties along the Mississippi, Keokuk's leaders determined that issuing municipal bonds was the best way to finance their railroad projects. Towns typically sold these bonds to investors, guaranteeing a solid rate of interest, and then invested in private railroad companies that promised to build a line to their locale. In return, towns often received company stock. Expecting that the railroad would prosper, town leaders planned to use the profits from the increasing value of their stock to pay the interest owed to the bondholders. Rosy projections helped mask the real possibility that the railroad might not be profitable (or worse, never be completed) and that taxpayers would have to bear the burden of paying the city's debt.[49]

Initially, there were some doubts in Keokuk about the legality of using municipal bonds to finance private corporations. Iowa's state constitution prohibited the state government from becoming a stockholder in any corporation, and it was not clear whether this prohibition applied to counties and cities as well. For their authority to issue railroad bonds, municipalities relied upon section

114 of the Iowa Code, which said that with voter approval towns could provide "aid to construct any road or bridge which may call for an extraordinary expenditure." Did railroads constitute a "road"? Some Iowa jurists doubted that they did. "As a generic term," a leading judge wrote, "the word includes highways, streets, and lanes. The words 'any road' do not to my mind embrace railroads." The Iowa legislature previously had rejected a version of section 114 that would have authorized county aid for "internal improvements," a term that often encompassed canals and railroads.[50]

In 1853, the Iowa Supreme Court, in a brief but sweeping opinion, did its best to squelch any concerns about the legality of municipal railroad bonds. In *Dubuque County v. Dubuque and Pacific Railroad,* the court held that railroads were indeed "roads" for the purposes of section 114, and that the constitution only prohibited the state, not counties or towns, from being corporate stockholders.[51] The court's decision opened the floodgates for the river of Iowa bonds that followed. In 1855, emboldened by the *Dubuque County* decision, Keokuk's leaders proposed to issue $600,000 in bonds to aid three different railroad projects. Assured by town officials that the bonds would pay for themselves, Keokuk voters approved the bonds "with great unanimity."[52]

Although a direct eastern connection was the most coveted of the projected railroads, most city planners believed that the best way to lure the capital needed for its construction was to complete a railroad that would follow the Des Moines River to the west. That line would ensure Keokuk's status as depot for the agricultural products of the fertile river valley. Officials duly earmarked $400,000 of the $600,000 in bonds for the western spoke, the Keokuk, Fort Des Moines, & Minnesota Railroad. Miller was particularly enamored with this railroad. He invested enough of his own money in it to become an important shareholder and served on its board of directors.[53]

As the best-funded railroad project, the Keokuk, Fort Des Moines, & Minnesota Railroad made the most progress. The line received monies from both Keokuk and Keokuk's Lee County. Once again, though, the Gate City faced stiff competition from Burlington. Each city now had a railroad plunging into the interior, and everyone believed that whichever city's railroad went farthest first would claim the agricultural trade of the farmers along the line. The race was on to reach points such as Eddyville and Ottumwa. Unfortunately for Keokuk, Burlington's affiliation with the Chicago, Burlington, & Quincy Railroad, one of the great railroad lines of the West, tipped the balance. Armed with

Chicago's capitalist muscle, Burlington's line expanded west at a rate Keokuk could not match, beating the Keokuk line to Eddyville and then to Ottumwa. Eventually its tentacles fanned out as far as Montana, Wyoming, and Colorado, while Keokuk's line remained relatively small and independent. Because the Keokuk line terminated at the Mississippi River, it continued to depend on the river as an outlet, while goods sent on the Burlington line could be unloaded and shipped on the river or could roll on to Chicago.[54]

Whether Keokuk's boosters recognized it or not, their city's losing struggle with Burlington was really part of the much larger economic competition between St. Louis and Chicago. Despite the grandiose hopes of Keokuk's boosters, St. Louis viewed Keokuk not as a rival, but as a "sister city," an ally in the competition with Chicago. St. Louis merchants cheered the progress of the Keokuk, Fort Des Moines, & Minnesota Railroad, noting that with its completion "most of the produce that might be diverted to Chicago by railroad, will find its way by an easy process to Keokuk and this city . . . and thereby secure to St. Louis a vast amount of business."[55]

Keokuk was thus aligned with the loser in the economic struggle between St. Louis and Chicago. In 1850, St. Louis's trading hinterland had stretched from Wisconsin to the Ohio Valley and out to the western frontier. By 1860, Chicago merchants had claimed much of that territory. St. Louis's loss did not bode well for Keokuk, which continued to serve primarily as a transshipment point for goods coming north from St. Louis or for farm goods headed south to St. Louis markets. While Burlington had a direct rail connection with the triumphant economic metropolis of the West, Keokuk remained wedded to the steamboat and a declining entrepôt.[56]

Recognizing their loss of status to Burlington, the tone of Keokuk's boosters started to sound desperate. Despite its expenditures, Keokuk still did not have an eastern connection, and Burlington's line was outdistancing its western road. Politicians asked the town to go ever deeper into debt. "Although our city has subscribed liberally, she may yet have to do more," Mayor Samuel Curtis warned in 1856. "The county, city and individual effort will have to be strained to the utmost. . . . Such is the vital importance of railroads to our success, that I present their interests as prior and paramount to all others. . . . Upon the success of our roads—upon their progress this year—will depend the future prosperity or adversity of our city. . . . I am convinced that upon this year's success hang such fearful issues that I present it as a crisis in our history." As the *Gate City* concluded, Keokuk needed an eastern connection "or else . . . must remain indefinitely as it is now, especially in the winter, a by-corner of the world."[57]

Unfortunately, Keokuk boosters' obsession with railroads missed one crucial point. The railroad connections they craved were part of an expanding system that would eventually undermine all of Iowa's river towns, including both Burlington and Keokuk. Railroads benefited a river town while it remained a western or eastern terminus of a line or as long as goods had to be unloaded at the river and ferried across. But if railroad bridges ever spanned the Mississippi, goods and passengers could cross the river and speed on to Chicago without ever having to stop at the river towns.[58]

Inevitably, the first railroad bridge was built. In 1856, the Mississippi and Missouri Railroad built the Rock Island bridge, extending the Chicago & Rock Island line to Davenport. The first bridge to cross the Mississippi, it represented a triumph of nineteenth-century engineering. But its potential economic impact made its completion truly momentous. With the bridge finished, goods and passengers no longer had to be unloaded from railroad cars on one side, ferried across the river, and then reloaded on the other side. Cargo could cross the river easily during all the seasons of the year. The potential benefits of the bridge led many commentators to view it as the epitome of western progress. One Chicago newspaper called the bridge the "greatest feat of the nineteenth century."[59]

Not everyone welcomed the bridge so warmly. To St. Louis merchants, it was a threatening example of Chicago's aggressive efforts to seize regional dominance. Steamboat men also cursed the bridge, which had been built on an already treacherous stretch of the Mississippi. Near Rock Island, the river had long been notorious for its powerful crosscurrents and dangerous submerged rocks. Now those problems were magnified as waters eddied and swirled around the bridge's seven immense stone piers. This new hazard jeopardized even slow-moving steamboats with cautious and experienced pilots. Insurance companies understandably raised their rates for boats that had to travel under the bridge. Within a month after the first train chugged across the bridge, twenty steamboats slammed into its unforgiving piers. One of those boats, the *Effie Afton*, exploded, bursting into giant flames that set the bridge itself on fire. Embittered steamboat men mourned the loss of the *Effie Afton* but toasted the flames that scorched the hated bridge. The bridge, of course, was quickly repaired.[60]

For steamboat owners and pilots, the Rock Island bridge represented more than a simple hazard; it was evidence of the railroads' devious attempts to create a transportation monopoly. Lawsuits soon pitted the two great transportation technologies of the nineteenth century, steamboats and railroads, against one another. The outcome of these cases helped shape the destiny of steamboat towns like Keokuk.[61]

Steamboat owners launched their lawsuits against the Rock Island bridge in both Iowa and Illinois. In Illinois, John Hurd, the captain of the *Effie Afton*, sued the bridge company, seeking damages as well as a judicial declaration that the bridge was a nuisance that should be torn down. The case of *Hurd v. Railroad Bridge Company* reached the U.S. Circuit Court in Chicago in September 1857. A young attorney named Abraham Lincoln represented the Railroad Bridge Company. Cities and towns up and down the Mississippi followed the trial intently. Newspapers from St. Louis and New Orleans sent special correspondents to cover it.[62]

In his argument, Lincoln suggested that the steamboat companies were less interested in removing a hazard than they were in ridding themselves of a competitor. The railroad, he argued, was at least as important a mode of transportation as the steamboat; railroads were invaluable when the river froze. He therefore urged the jury not to place the interests of the steamboat owners above those of the equally beneficial railroad industry. "This bridge," he concluded, "must be treated with respect in this court and is not to be kicked about with contempt. . . . The proper mood for all parties in this affair is to 'live and let live.'" While some members of the jury remained sympathetic to the steamboat owners' plight, Lincoln's argument swayed enough jurors for the deliberations to result in a deadlock.[63]

When the Illinois case ended in stalemate, eyes turned to the parallel case taking place in Iowa. There, James Ward, a part-owner of four Mississippi steamboats and captain of one of them, brought suit against the owners of the bridge. The bridge had not actually damaged Ward's boats, but he pointed to the many accidents that had occurred to other boats as evidence that the bridge created an intolerable obstacle to all steamboat traffic. Ward, like Hurd, wanted the bridge destroyed. As his attorney, he hired Keokuk's rising star, Samuel Miller.

Given his ties to the Gate City, Miller really had two clients in the case, Ward and the city of Keokuk. If Miller won, Keokuk would benefit in many ways. First, if the court placed the needs of steamboats over the needs of railroads, the case could protect the vitality of the riverboat trade. Second, if the court ordered the bridge removed, all other plans to build bridges across the Mississippi (and there were many) would be placed in jeopardy, thereby ensuring that river towns like Keokuk would continue to function as indispensable loading and unloading points for goods that needed to cross the river. At the very least, a verdict in Ward's favor could buy Keokuk time. Even if Miller only managed to stop this one particularly dangerous bridge, the case could provide Keokuk the months or years it needed to catch up with Iowa's railroad river towns farther north. Perhaps by the time a new bridge was built somewhere else, Keokuk would have an eastern rail connection or even a bridge of its own. But if the court gave railroads the legal upper hand, Keokuk would certainly suffer. Trade and travel would increasingly take place on an east-west axis, rather than a north-south one. The river would soon be clogged with dozens of similar bridges. Steamboat travel would slow to a crawl, while the unimpeded railroads rolled right along.[64]

Miller brought Ward's case to the federal district court in Iowa. Because the Mississippi & Missouri Railroad (which owned the bridge) was an Iowa corporation and Ward resided in Missouri, the district court could claim diversity jurisdiction. Getting the case into Iowa's federal court was a shrewd strategic decision for Miller. In that venue, he could count on a sympathetic hearing from district court judge James M. Love. Not only was Love a Keokuk citizen, he was the former law partner of Miller's current partner, John Rankin.

In the trial, Judge Love lived up to Miller's expectations. He accepted Miller's assertion that justice demanded that the bridge be removed. Miller charged that the bridge created a serious hazard for steamboats. The steamboats and their owners had been there first. The bridge threatened their livelihood, so, Miller reasoned, it needed to be removed. Love, fearing that if the Rock Island bridge were allowed to stand "we shall probably, in no great period of time, have railroad bridges upon the Mississippi River at every forty or fifty miles of its course," agreed and ordered that the bridge (at least on the Iowa side of the Mississippi) be torn down. In Keokuk, they cheered the decision.[65]

The railroad appealed, and the case reached the United States Supreme Court in 1862. By then, Miller was one of the Supreme Court's justices. Because of his previous role in the litigation, he had to recuse himself. And this time, the outcome did not please Ward or Keokuk. Justice John Catron, speaking for the Court in *Mississippi and Missouri Railroad Company v. Ward,* overturned Judge Love's decision. Catron based his opinion on the grounds that if Love's logic were followed, "no lawful bridge could be built across the Mississippi anywhere; nor could the great facilities to commerce, accomplished by the invention of railroads, be made available where great rivers had to be crossed." Catron spoke for a Court stocked with former railroad attorneys who did not share Love's regional preference for steamboats. The justices allowed the bridge to stand and thus opened the door for other bridges to be built. But by the time the case was decided in 1862, few in Keokuk even noticed. By then, the town had other problems that dwarfed the threat posed by the Rock Island bridge.[66]

CHAPTER 3

The Panic of 1857

IN 1857, AN ECONOMIC CALAMITY struck Keokuk from which Samuel Miller's grand river-town dreams would never recover. As the year began, a sagging market in Europe for produce from the American West raised fears among eastern bankers and investors that they might be sitting on a speculative bubble about to burst. Newly cautious eastern banks stopped extending loans to western enterprises. Some refused to accept western currencies. Financial contraction and conservative decisionmaking became the rule; the wild speculation, growth, and expansion of the early 1850s abruptly halted. By early spring, commercial credit had dried up, forcing already debt-ridden merchants of the West to curtail new purchases of inventory. Dwindling orders threatened New York wholesalers, thousands of retail merchants around the country, and the railroads that linked them. The railroad age had created an interdependent national economy, and now an economic downturn in the West threatened to push the entire nation into economic crisis.[1]

As the financial panic hit with a vengeance in the late summer and fall of 1857, it soon became clear that Keokuk would not be spared. Farm prices crashed. Wheat that had garnered $2.19 a bushel in 1855 fell to 80¢ a bushel by 1858, with other crop prices suffering similar fates. Farmers' buying power evaporated. Merchants who had thrived during the boom years now paid the price for their risk-taking. The Keokuk newspapers filled with advertisements from frantic merchants hoping to sell their inventories at almost any discount. "To raise money," said a typical advertisement, "I am offering my stock regardless of cost for cash . . . at less than the cost of manufacture." In the fall of 1857, one Keokuk observer wrote, "We think we have touched bottom and feel that any change must be for the better." Unfortunately for Keokuk, the next two years were even worse.[2]

While most Gate City residents suffered, lawyers thrived. Business failures, broken contracts, and hard times meant lawsuits. By 1859, two thousand cases crowded the docket of Lee County's district court. Men who heretofore had been land speculators, land agents, and merchants rushed through half-baked legal apprenticeships and opened law offices. Keokuk's bar became so "crowded with attorneys," the *Gate City* complained, that a "stranger might have inferred that our citizens had all turned their attention to the law." Samuel Clemens's brother, Orion, typified this group. In the years preceding the panic, Orion's printing office published a city directory that boosters used to promote the town. After the panic hit, he sold his printing press and became a lawyer specializing in debt collection.[3]

For Samuel Miller and John Rankin, the "hard, selfish times" meant an increase in certain types of cases. Rankin had long held a reputation as the premier collections attorney in town. Now Miller was flush with such cases as well. On any given day in the late 1850s, their firm ran dozens of legal notices in Keokuk newspapers notifying debtors and other creditors of the firm's claims against them. They also served as trustees for defaulted parties and presided over the auctions of debtors' property.[4] But overall, the economic collapse hurt Rankin and Miller. With little money available, few debtors could ever pay. Their firm's thriving land business dried up as land speculation ceased. Miller, with his many personal real estate investments, had as much to lose in the town's demise as anyone in Keokuk. The sheer scale of the catastrophe that hit the town left him dumbfounded and grasping for answers as to how things could have turned sour so quickly. "No one," he lamented in 1858, "anticipated the calamity which has overwhelmed the community."[5]

Many critics believed that the thousands of lawsuits then underway exacerbated Keokuk's economic crisis. The town's businessmen and landowners needed to "quit suing each other, cease mourning over the great collapse and awful shrinkage," and get on with things, complained a typical letter to the editor. Even though he earned his livelihood from such lawsuits, Miller agreed. In 1858 he proposed a special rule requiring that anyone who brought a frivolous lawsuit be fined by the district court. "In short," he explained, "the spirit of the rule is, that when either party commence[s] or protract[s] litigation, evidently for the purpose of evading justice, or to gratify his malice, he shall pay the expenses which he causes the successful party to incur; and it is in my judgment both wise and just." The overburdened judges of the district court welcomed and adopted Miller's rule.[6]

In 1858 and 1859, Keokuk's economic situation further deteriorated. Two years of successive crop failures in the surrounding countryside were compounded by two brutal winters that killed cattle across Iowa.[7] As the depression wore on, Keokuk took on a ghostly aspect. With few customers, the town's gasworks stood "silent and gloomy" at the end of Main Street. Abandoned storefronts lined previously busy streets. In November 1859, the last merchant closed his doors on Keokuk's once-bustling Second Street. "Alas, for Second Street," cried an editor, "Once so grand with its Athenaeum, its Bank, its Auction Stores, Bookstores and crowds of eager speculators! Now so deserted, so quiet!" In the center of town, the Estes House, which was to be the Gate City's "grand hotel," sat unfinished, unfurnished, and unoccupied. A visiting reporter dubbed the roofless hotel a "monument of the folly to which even wise men will be led in a time of general prosperity." In a particularly emblematic move in the frigid December of 1858, the town, unable to pay its gas bill, shut off Keokuk's streetlamps. The lampposts would stand unused for years, looming in the darkness, spectral reminders of better times.[8]

The days when hundreds of wagons from the countryside clogged Keokuk's levee were gone. Railroads had siphoned off some of this business. The economic collapse scared off much of the rest. "This is the deadest, dullest, most quiet place I ever beheld or heard of," wrote a visiting reporter from the *Chicago Tribune*. "When I awoke this morning, I had hard work to persuade myself it was not Sunday—no trade, no money, no life." The reporter may have exaggerated, but he did correctly present a cold truth about Keokuk. The boom was over.[9]

By the end of the decade, only one Keokuk industry remained vital—hog slaughtering. Because the river remained a cost-efficient way to ship meat, in the late 1850s and early 1860s Keokuk's butchers killed over 110,000 hogs each winter. But the slaughtering industry brought with it a host of problems. Keokuk remained a city of only 15,000 inhabitants, and with 110,000 hogs hoofing in from the countryside, the slaughtering industry overwhelmed the town. During slaughtering season, the "shrill and piercing" cries of tens of thousands "kicking, squirming, agonizing" pigs echoed through Keokuk's empty streets. The creeks near the abattoirs filled with bloody slaughtering refuse.[10]

Although the slaughterhouses employed dozens of Keokuk residents, the industry had numerous local critics. Residents soon mounted a successful campaign to regulate it. Fearing disease, city officials passed ordinances to control the driving of hogs through the streets, to keep them from running wild, and to stop the "perfidious traffic" in unwholesome meats. Though town leaders succeeded in passing some public health initiatives, Keokuk remained a town of closed stores, declining population, and squealing pigs headed to death and dismemberment.[11]

Keokuk's boosters knew that their town's reputation for bloody hogs and bankrupt merchants needed refurbishing if they were ever going to lure back capital. To counter reports like the one in the *Chicago Tribune*, city leaders put their own spin on recent events, arguing that their town's problems were no worse than any other Mississippi River community. "It is true," one official wrote, "that we have suffered in common with other towns and cities, from the recent stagnation which has overspread the land. But that we have suffered more than the common average, we have no reason to believe." Despite such efforts to downplay the town's woes, damaging reports about Keokuk's collapse continued to circulate in the East.[12]

One article compared Keokuk to the "doomed city of Jerusalem." Keokuk, it said, had "creditors without and creditors within. . . . Every third man is a lawyer . . . every other man virtually a pauper, and all standing in listless and unprofitable idleness except the police and constables. Three millions of dollars are to be sued for in the courts . . . and 'ruin and degradation' is given as the probable result."[13] Reprinted in newspapers throughout the country, this article was particularly deleterious to Keokuk's reputation. "Every paper from Maine to Texas, and from Minnesota to Florida has given it [a] place," the *Gate City* reported blackly, ". . . and we are waiting anxiously for the next steamer, expecting to see it in the London Times." After the story ran in Baltimore, New York, and Philadelphia papers, Keokuk merchants and their purchasing agents found themselves blacklisted in those cities. Many eastern wholesalers canceled their Keokuk contracts. The town's name became synonymous with the financial revulsion in the West. "Reports more injurious to Keokuk," concluded the *Davenport Gazette*, "have gone out than in relation to any other western city." In an age when eastern perceptions of western cities had a major impact on the flow of capital, a spate of negative publicity could destroy a boomtown in a flash.

After the Panic of 1857, Keokuk's reputation might have been the worst of any town in the West.[14]

A huge municipal debt magnified Keokuk's problems. By 1858, the town owed $900,000, mostly on railroad bonds, while the value of its taxable property dropped by $5.5 million. Lots that brought $1,000 before the crash now could not be sold for $10. Hard-hit property owners were unable to pay their taxes, and thousands of properties slipped into tax delinquency. On June 7 alone, Lee County officials put up for auction more than one thousand lots with unpaid taxes. Keokuk's Union Hotel, bought by an investor in 1856 for $28,000, sold at a tax auction in 1857 for $2,800. Deeply in debt, with tax revenues slowed to a trickle, the town cut back drastically on services. Streets and sidewalks deteriorated into a "condition of decadence." City police went unpaid and morale sank. A crime wave struck. Thieves robbed private homes and merchants' safes. The levee, once the pride of Keokuk, became a haven for violence and thievery. "The wharf," the *Gate City* reported, "is full of teens & urchins . . . and a few adults who raid unloading freights, cut open bags and steal whatever they can dislodge." Pickpockets plagued the packet depot, and unemployed laborers filled the saloons at all hours. Gangs of Irish longshoremen attacked rivals who tried to claim dwindling work.[15]

Boosters and civic leaders desperately searched for solutions to Keokuk's problems. One drastic proposal suggested that in order to lure capital, "it would undoubtedly be good policy for real estate holders to give away every other lot, if necessary." Some suggested that Keokuk build giant grain elevators modeled on those in Chicago. "Where men sell their grain they also buy their goods," went the argument. Others proposed that Keokuk start a hydraulic company to harness the Mississippi's rapids and to use the energy generated to power factories. In June 1858, Miller attended a meeting convened to discuss this plan. The sparsely attended gathering quickly descended into ineffectual bickering after Mayor H. W. Sample shouted that southern Iowa "is not a manufacturing country and never could be a manufacturing country."[16]

Most citizens blamed Keokuk's torpid economic recovery on its debt from railroad bonds. To be sure, Keokuk had received some definite benefits from these bonds. By 1858, the Keokuk, Fort Des Moines, & Minnesota Railroad had thirty-eight miles of track heading west, and the Keokuk, Mt. Pleasant, & Muscatine ran twelve miles north. But construction had progressed slowly, and there was still no eastern connection. The railroads had done little to pull Keokuk's economy back from the brink. Instead, the city's railroad bond debt destroyed its credit. Keokuk still had the "natural advantages" its boosters had long trumpeted, but no capitalist would touch a small city saddled with such a huge debt. Town leaders recognized the problem the bond debt posed. "A crisis has come," Mayor Sample admitted, "the arm of industry is paralyzed, property and business are depressed . . . and we find our city encumbered with a large indebtedness. . . . We cannot carry such a load and prosper."[17]

By 1859, Keokuk's leaders admitted that they could not pay the interest on the city's bonds. The city defaulted, a catastrophic blow to its reputation. Outraged bondholders charged Keokuk with open repudiation and demanded that its citizens be taxed until they honored their debts. When moneyed men pilloried Keokuk's name in the East, Keokuk's leaders offered a simple but painful response: "We can't pay now; we doubt if we can ever pay if the full amount is insisted upon." Civic leaders held out hope that the debt could be renegotiated. With the debt "settled on some honorable basis . . . Keokuk would arouse from her lethargy 'like a giant refreshed with wine.'" Toward that end, in the winter of 1859, Mayor Sample traveled to New York to try to reach a compromise with bondholders. The trip proved spectacularly unsuccessful. Rumors even circulated that angry Wall Street creditors had thrown the mayor in jail for swindling.[18]

Although few Keokuk residents had complained back when their city issued the bonds, many taxpayers now claimed they had never approved of these railroad schemes. With boom turned to bust, angry voices called into question the original constitutional validity of the bonds, even though the Iowa Supreme Court had declared them constitutional in 1853. Local attorneys launched new legal challenges to the bonds, but in an 1857 case, *Clapp v. County of Cedar,* Iowa's supreme court justices again held that it was far too late to turn back. Whatever doubts they may have "tacitly entertained" about the bonds, it was now "impossible to recede." "To change now," Justice William Woodward wrote, "would be the worst form of repudiation, judicial repudiation." The court pointed to the impact such a decision would have on people who innocently bought Iowa's railroad bonds. Besides, Iowa cities had benefited from the bonds. Perhaps all the railroads were not completed, but some had made progress. "Our people," an exasperated Woodward added, "have received the consideration of these bonds."[19]

But by admitting that they "tacitly entertained" doubts about the bonds' original validity, the justices inadvertently encouraged further legal action. Desperate Iowans clung to the thinnest of straws. Encouragement could also be found in Chief Justice George Wright's dissenting opinion, in which he said he believed that the bonds could still be declared void. The citizens of Keokuk and Lee County rallied around the chief justice's dissent. The slightest hope of somehow escaping their debilitating debts provided ample incentive to keep launching challenges to the railroad bonds. Given Keokuk's desperate situation, it is not surprising this litigation continued. More surprising is the name of the lawyer who became the antibond champion: Samuel Freeman Miller.

Miller made an unlikely antibond warrior. He had served on the board of, and held shares in, a Keokuk railroad that had greatly benefited from the bonds. He had made a number of other speculative investments in land and businesses along the routes of the projected railroads. Moreover, a large portion of his legal career in the 1850s had been devoted to cases he described as "suits to collect just debts." One might assume that he would have sided with bond purchasers over those trying to escape their financial obligations. Not so.[20]

Beginning in 1859, Miller handled a number of cases that challenged the validity of the railroad bonds, challenges that relied on the same worn arguments about section 114 and debt limits. In *Robert Moir v. Jefferson County*, Miller defended an Iowa county that had defaulted on its payment to bondholders. He argued that the county officials who had authorized the bonds had no constitutional authority to do so because "any roads" under section 114 did not include railroads. Consequently, the bonds were void, and current county government officials should not be bound by the irresponsible actions of their predecessors. The district court judge in the case was once again Keokuk's James M. Love, someone potentially sympathetic to Miller's claim. In this case, however, local sympathies did not carry the day.

Judge Love rejected Miller's contentions in no uncertain terms. "Our counties have been, it must be admitted, involved in a great misfortune," Love recognized. However, he continued, "it is now proposed that we add to our misfortune the disgrace of repudiation." If the judiciary were to sanction such repudiation, he warned, it "would lead to the distraction of all public credit." He acknowledged that the counties' authority to issue bonds under section 114 had been a stretch. But the benefit of the doubt in such cases should not go to a county that had already profited from the bonds.[21]

With Love siding against Miller and Jefferson County, all further legal efforts appeared futile. Even the *Gate City*, the newspaper that most doggedly urged antibond litigation, wondered whether additional suits were worthwhile. "Considering that the courts of our state have, in numerous cases, decided the same way," the paper asked, "can there be either sense or advantage in agitating the question further?" Despite Love's decision, however, many Keokuk and Lee County citizens vowed to keep up the fight. Thousands attended antirailroad tax meetings, where orators encouraged citizens to resist payment of their taxes. Lee County residents, the protesters complained, were being asked to pay $108,000 in back interest alone. "We are utterly unable to pay the said tax," they contended, "were we ever so willing, and we are not willing." Speakers urged citizens to attend auctions of tax delinquent property and then refuse to bid. One resolution passed by the protestors warned, in a veiled threat of violence against tax collectors, that "while we expect all county officers to do their sworn duty, we have no respect for those persons who may voluntarily undertake to do the dirty work, and we will visit with our indignation all who may do so." Most of all, the protesters beseeched Miller and other attorneys to persist in the antibond fight and to "continue the litigation as long as there is any foothold for us to stand upon."[22]

Normally, one might expect that the tax protesters would also have turned their anger on local politicians who had guided Keokuk and Lee County into debt. Local Republicans seemed particularly vulnerable because their party's ascendancy in Iowa coincided with the panic, and they easily could have been blamed for their state's misfortune. Amidst the economic disaster, however, Iowa's Republican Party found surprising success. Its leaders adroitly shifted much of the blame for the downturn to eastern banks and financiers, whom they accused of hoarding capital in New York. "The great accumulation of specie in the eastern banks is not a very difficult matter to account for," charged the Republican *Gate City*. "Everyone [is] paying off debts." Blaming banks for creating economic problems was a startling turnabout for the Republicans. Traditionally, Democrats specialized in antibank rhetoric. But unlike the Democrats who denounced all banks, Iowa's Republicans ascribed the panic exclusively to those eastern banks that had called in their loans as the panic set in. Iowa suffered, Republicans charged, because capital was "being hoarded up in ever-increasing but useless piles in the hands of distrustful men." Rather than saying all banks were evil, the Republicans argued that had Iowa had its own state bank to provide capital, the region could have been spared the panic's worst effects. Thus, the Republicans managed to turn the issue against Iowa's Democrats, whose uncompromising opposition to a state bank had left Iowa at the mercy of eastern capitalists.[23]

Indeed, in 1857, prior to the onset of the panic, Republicans had called a constitutional convention in Iowa to revise the old constitution that banned state aid to banks. Iowa's farmers and merchants needed a home-grown, western bank, Republicans had argued, so that capital would stay in the state. The antibank policies of the Democrats allowed the profits from Iowa's fertile farms to be siphoned off and forced Iowa's market-oriented farmers and merchants to rely on the dubious notes of out-of-state financial institutions. To solve this problem, the Republican-led convention drafted a new constitution that authorized the legislature to create a state bank. Credit-starved Iowans quickly ratified the new document, and Miller—long a vocal advocate of an Iowa bank—cheered when the legislature voted a state bank into being. He successfully campaigned to get a Keokuk branch of the new bank and was elected its first president. By the time the bank opened, however, the Panic of 1857 had arrived.[24]

By blaming their state's economic woes on eastern banks and financiers, Iowa Republicans began to shape their own western version of free-labor ideology, the value system on which Republicanism was based. While all Republicans championed the benefits of free rather than slave labor, western party members now suggested that northeastern capitalists harmed their region in much the same way that slaveholders poisoned the South. In Iowa and other states along the Mississippi River, they argued, lived the true Americans who created wealth with their own labor. Unlike the corrupt East or the slaveholding South, Iowans came west "with the intention of working—of becoming producers—not of speculation or living off of others." Eastern bankers and railroad bondholders joined southern planters on a list of parasitic villains who obstructed the common man's right to rise. Sitting idly at their desks, overfed bankers sucked the profits from the industrious merchants and laborers of Iowa. The slaveholders, meanwhile, fought to keep western land out of the hands of hardworking family farmers. Eastern bankers and southern slaveholders, the *Keokuk Gate City* complained, wanted a world where "capitalists own the soil and the labor" because they could not "stand it to see territories occupied by 'small fisted farmers' who cultivate their own 'dirty acres.' Not they; they go in for gentlemen owning the soil and the laborers who cultivate it."[25]

As Miller and other Iowa Republicans turned against eastern financiers, events in Washington, Kansas, and elsewhere continued to inflame Iowans' animosity towards slaveholders and the slave power. In March 1857 the United States Supreme Court issued its infamous *Dred Scott* decision. Dred Scott was a slave who had moved with his master, a U.S. army surgeon, to the free state of Illinois and then to the free territory of Wisconsin before returning to the slave state of Missouri in 1838. In 1846, he sued for his freedom on the grounds that his time in a free state and free territory had made him free. After numerous twists and turns, the case eventually reached the Supreme Court.[26]

Chief Justice Roger Taney saw the case as his opportunity to settle the national controversy over slavery once and for all. Rather than concluding that Scott's status was simply a matter of state law to be determined by Missouri courts (as the Court had done in a similar Kentucky case—*Strader v. Graham*—in 1851), Taney offered three sweeping rulings on the slavery question.[27] First, he concluded that Scott, as a black man, was not a citizen of the United States with a right to sue in the federal courts. The framers of the Constitution, Taney argued, viewed black Americans as a "subordinate and inferior class of beings," so far inferior "that they had no rights which the white man was bound to respect." While some states in the 1780s had conferred limited rights on free blacks, he continued, this did not make them United States citizens with all the rights and privileges of citizenship. Southerners, he maintained, would not have entered into the Constitution if they thought that free northern blacks would become full United States citizens. As such, free blacks would have been entitled to travel to the South, flaunting their rights and their freedom in full view of enslaved blacks and thus "producing discontent and insubordination among them, and endangering the peace and safety of the State."[28]

Taney also ruled that Congress acted unconstitutionally when it prohibited slavery in the territories. The Constitution (art. 4, sec. 3), Taney wrote, only gave Congress authority to make needful rules and regulations, rather than laws, for the territories. Thus, the Missouri Compromise was unconstitutional. In addition, because slaves were "property," denying slaveholders the right to bring slaves into the territories deprived them of their property without due process of law, violating the Fifth Amendment.[29]

Taney's decision deliberately targeted the antislavery doctrines of the Republican Party. Up to that point, Republicans had hoped to contain slavery in the southern states, where the peculiar institution might eventually wither and die. Taney's decision, if allowed to stand, made that position obsolete. Slavery could now expand unimpeded into any new territory; it followed the flag. Recognizing *Dred Scott*'s ramifications, the Republican press denounced the Court. The day after the decision, Horace Greeley's *New York Tribune* said that the opinion deserved no more respect than if made by a "majority of those congregated in any Washington bar-room." Republicans in Keokuk agreed. "The decision of the Court," the *Gate City* exclaimed, "goes to the full extent claimed by the ultra slavery-propagandists," and thus warranted condemnation "by every patriot, every friend of human rights, and of constitutional law."[30] Many of *Dred Scott*'s critics saw it as not only flawed, but as further proof of a slave-power conspiracy. Not only were five of the Supreme Court's nine justices from slaveholding southern families, but evidence surfaced that proslavery president James Buchanan had improperly influenced members of the Court. As a result of *Dred Scott,* even sober-minded men began to accept that a slave-power conspiracy existed.[31]

The *Dred Scott* decision intensified Samuel Miller's well-developed dislike for Taney. Miller had detested Taney since the chief justice's days as Andrew Jackson's secretary of the treasury. In that role, Taney had helped to dismantle the Bank of the United States, and Jackson had appointed him to the Supreme Court as a reward for his efforts. Miller later told a friend that Taney "had attempted to throttle the Bank of the United States, and I hated him for it." Taney, he added, took his "seat on the Bench . . . in reward for what he had done in that connection and I hated him for that." Now that Taney became the "chief spokesmen for the Court in the Dred Scott case," Miller "hated him for that" as well.[32]

Eight months after the *Dred Scott* decision, events in Kansas again took center stage when the proslavery Lecompton legislature approved an inflammatory constitution for the territory. Despite the territory's two-to-one free-soil majority, the fraudulently elected legislature remained the territory's official lawmaking body, and it rigged a state constitutional convention guaranteed to create a proslavery document. Not only did the new constitution saddle Kansas with a rigid slave code, it stipulated that "no alteration shall be made to affect the rights of property in the ownership of slaves." When it came to slaveowners' right to own slaves, the constitution was unamendable and would protect slavery in Kansas for all time.[33]

Without giving Kansans a chance to vote against it, the legislature sent the Lecompton constitution to the U.S. Congress and asked that Kansas be admitted to the Union as a slave state. Despite the constitution's fraudulent nature, southerners warned their northern political allies not to reject it. President Buchanan lined up in support of the Lecompton constitution, claiming that if he did not accept it the southern states "would either secede from the Union or take arms against him." But most northerners, including many Democrats, bridled at such a bold-faced attempt to force slavery illegitimately upon Kansans. Senator Stephen Douglas felt that the events in Kansas made a travesty of popular sovereignty, and he urged his Democratic colleagues to reject the Lecompton constitution. Though the Senate eventually approved it, the northern-controlled House rejected it.[34] In Keokuk, Miller and other Republicans closely followed the *Dred Scott* and Lecompton constitution controversies.

During the summer and fall of 1858, those two issues dominated in the famous debates between Abraham Lincoln and Stephen Douglas. Although the Lincoln-Douglas debates involved two Illinois candidates for the U.S. Senate, Republicans in Keokuk followed the proceedings intently and cheered Lincoln's efforts to unseat the "little giant." In October 1858, Miller, then head of the Keokuk Republican Committee, helped organize an excursion to Illinois to watch one of the debates. On October 13, a steamboat filled with Keokuk Republicans chugged thirty-five miles downriver to Quincy, where they saw a rising star in the Republican Party.[35]

During the debate, Lincoln defended positions that mirrored Miller's own views. Although Miller felt that Republicans should respect constitutional protections of slave property in the South, he wanted slavery contained where it existed. And though he did not favor full equality for blacks, he believed black men and women had the same right as whites to be paid for their labor. Now he listened as Lincoln skillfully defended these positions. During the Quincy debate, Lincoln acknowledged that he did not intend to introduce a "social and political equality between the white and black races." Even if his "own feelings would admit of it, . . . the public sentiment of the country would not, and that such a thing was an utter impossibility." Nevertheless, Lincoln declared, this did not mean that blacks should be prevented from rising economically. "There is no reason in the world," he proclaimed, "why the negro is not entitled to all the rights enumerated in the Declaration of Independence—the right of life, liberty and the pursuit of happiness." The negro, he continued, was "as much entitled to these as the white man . . . in the right to eat the bread without leave of anybody else which his own hand earns." Miller liked what he heard and after the Quincy debates became a fervid supporter of Lincoln.[36]

Many Iowa Republicans shared similar racial views. Rather than being radicals, most Iowans were moderates who had once been free-soil Whigs or anti-Nebraska Democrats. Though they opposed slavery, they did not embrace full black equality. Even though African Americans had provided needed labor during the boom years in the river towns, relatively few blacks lived in Iowa, and Iowans did not go out of their way to welcome them. In Iowa's state constitutional convention of 1857, for example, most delegates voted against black suffrage. Yet there were signs that Iowans' racial views were in flux. Although the 1857 convention denied blacks the vote, the new constitution included a personal liberty clause designed to protect free blacks from being falsely seized by slave catchers. That same year, the Iowa General Assembly passed a law allowing blacks to testify in court. After *Dred Scott,* Iowa's Republican press began to portray blacks in Iowa as hardworking and upright individuals. Keokuk's Republican newspaper noted that the city had "half a score or so" black residents who "are seeking to earn an honest living in our midst."[37]

The national obsession with the slavery question caused Miller and Iowa's Republicans to overlook Lincoln's views on other issues. Slavery was the only issue addressed in the Lincoln-Douglas debates, and it was Lincoln's eloquent defense of free soil and free labor that inspired Miller. But on other economic issues, Lincoln held views that, if widely known, might have alienated many Republicans in the indebted Iowa towns along the Mississippi. Although Lincoln was sensitive to the plight of debtors, for example, he abhorred the repudiation of debts. In 1837, as a Whig leader in the Illinois legislature, Lincoln promoted an aggressive campaign of internal improvements that included the issuing of $10 million in state bonds to aid construction of the Illinois Central & Northern Cross railroads. Soon after the legislature approved the bonds in 1837, hard economic times arrived. As the economy soured, the state struggled to make its payments on the bonds; many politicians called for Illinois to stop paying on the debt. Lincoln unequivocally opposed repudiation. He thought it economically counterproductive and immoral.

When it came to individuals' debts, Lincoln proved equally uncompromising. As a legislator, he opposed a stay law that would have suspended the collection of personal debts until the economy improved. He viewed debt repudiation and stay laws, as well as Jacksonian attacks on bank charters, as part of Americans' unfortunate "mobocratic" tendencies. He had read and admired the work of economist Francis Wayland, who saw debt repudiation as little more than an instance of the majority using democracy to do what might otherwise be done by a mob—stealing others' property. "I am opposed to encouraging that lawless and mobocratic spirit," Lincoln wrote, "whether in relation to the bank or anything else, which is already abroad in the land; and is spreading with rapid and fearful impetuosity, to the ultimate overthrow of every institution, or even moral principle, in which persons and property have hitherto found security."[38]

Unlike Iowa's Republicans, Lincoln did not hate or fear rich capitalists. Instead, he saw them as a necessary class. Again, he followed Wayland's imperative that "every man be allowed to gain all he can."[39] Riches were the just reward for one's labor and served as an "encouragement to industry and enterprise." Lincoln believed that there was no need for laws "to prevent a man from getting rich; it would do more harm than good." While he recognized that some capitalists were not ethical—he called them "respectable scoundrels"—he did not criticize capitalists as a class or believe that they had grown too powerful.[40]

Earlier in the decade, Miller and other Iowa Republicans had agreed with Lincoln on this point; but as the 1850s progressed, Republicans soured on the venal ways of eastern railroad promoters who held sway over Iowa's towns and cities. After spending millions of dollars to lure railroad promoters to their locales, Iowa's taxpayers received no corresponding benefits. By the end of the decade, Iowa towns and counties had invested an estimated $7 to 12 million in railroad bonds, yet they had only 731 mostly poorly constructed miles of rail to show for their expenditures. Although the chief villains for the Iowa Republicans remained southern planters, not eastern capitalists, by the end of the decade, Republicans came to view the bondholders and planters as cut from the same cloth. Both were aristocratic economic parasites who lived off the labor of the producing classes.[41]

Iowans also bridled at the practices of the New York bond market, where investors bought western railroad bonds at steep discounts (often 25 to 35 percent below face value). While eastern speculators sitting in leather chairs in their Gramercy Park mansions gambled on discounted bonds, Iowa farmers and merchants broke the soil, stocked the shelves, unloaded the carts, and labored from dawn to dusk. It was the "toiling millions," said a Keokuk Republican, "who conquer all obstacles, provide all the necessaries and luxuries of life, and make all the real wealth of the land." In the midst of hard times, with few railroads completed, Iowans bitterly grudged the indolent bondholders their pound of flesh.[42]

In part because of their prominent roles in bond cases, Miller and Rankin gained fame among Iowa Republicans. As Iowans turned against the railroads and eastern financiers, the party searched for leaders without ties to railroads. Attorneys who fought against the bonds became heroes, and Miller and Rankin adroitly turned their efforts in these cases to their political advantage. "These Republican attorneys," a Keokuk newspaper said of a bond case Miller and Rankin handled in 1859, "have manufactured about all the political capital out of this case that can possibly be made."[43]

By the summer of 1859, the Republican State Central Committee recognized Miller as a man with broad appeal. In August, Miller accepted an invitation from the committee to join other top Republicans on an extensive speaking tour of Iowa. That fall, Miller, then chairman of the Republican Committee of Lee County, barnstormed the state, stumping "with great force and eloquence upon the free and glorious principles of Republicanism" in towns such as Farmington, Montrose, West Point, and Green Bay. Miller privately hoped that his new prominence might lead to his being appointed to the Iowa Supreme Court. Although the appointment failed to materialize, Miller nevertheless became one of the best-known Republicans in Iowa and earned a place on the Republican State Executive Committee.[44]

In October 1859, troubling events in the East captured Iowans' attention. On October 16, 1859, abolitionist John Brown and a small band of followers that included three Iowans raided the federal arsenal at Harpers Ferry, Virginia. Brown hoped the attack would ignite a slave uprising in the South, but the plan was ill-conceived from the start. Brown's men carried few provisions and selected a site from which escape was impossible. Led by Colonel Robert E. Lee, Virginia militia and U.S. Marines soon surrounded Brown's party, killing or capturing most of those involved. Word quickly reached Iowa that three members of Brown's raiding party came from the Hawkeye State.[45]

Initial reports in Iowa of the incident described Brown as insane. Four days after the raid, the Keokuk Gate City labeled him a "monomaniac." But Iowans' views of Brown changed during his trial in Virginia where—contrary to his reputation as a madman—Brown maintained a quiet dignity and faith in the abolitionist cause. His eloquent defense of his actions swayed moderates across the North, who subsequently defended his noble motives while deploring his violent methods. Iowa's Republican governor Samuel Kirkwood called Brown's raid a "great crime" but added that it was "relieved to some extent of its guilt [because] the blow was struck for freedom, and not for slavery." Some northerners likened Brown to a religious martyr. "Brown has become an idea," author William Dean Howells wrote, "a thousand times purer and better and loftier than the Republican idea." On the day of his hanging, church bells rang in Keokuk and across the North. This show of support for Brown confirmed southerners' worst fears. Although Republicans claimed that they simply wanted to prevent slavery from expanding to the territories, they now lionized the perpetrator of a violent attack on slavery in the South. Southerners now saw little difference between the Republicans and abolitionists like John Brown. As a result, the presidential election of 1860 took place in Brown's shadow.[46]

At their party's national convention in Chicago in May 1860, Iowa's delegates supported the nomination of Lincoln, the candidate who shared their moderate antislavery views. For many, Lincoln personified the free-labor western ideal of opportunity and upward mobility. Born in a crude log cabin, Lincoln rose to prominence in the West while retaining his down-to-earth qualities. Although as an attorney he often represented large corporations, such as the Illinois Central Railroad, his folksy demeanor allowed supporters to portray him as a candidate of the common man and the laboring classes. His positions on bondholders, capitalists, and debt repudiation never entered the political debate. Instead, Keokuk supporters lauded him as a man for the "toiling millions who conquer all obstacles, provide all the necessaries and luxuries of life, and make all the real wealth of the land."[47]

With the support of delegates from Iowa and other western states, Lincoln carried the day in Chicago and became the Republicans' nominee. Miller welcomed his victory and served as delegate to the Republican state convention that ratified Lincoln's nomination.[48] During the summer of 1860, Miller campaigned for Lincoln in earnest. In July and August, he crisscrossed Iowa and southwestern Illinois giving pro-Lincoln speeches, and he developed a reputation as one of the top orators in the state. On August 16, he gave the keynote address at a Republican barbecue in Primrose, Iowa, that drew six thousand people. Even his slaveholding brother-in-law William Ballinger gave Miller's oratory high marks. On a visit to Keokuk in July, Ballinger "went over into Illinois to witness a Republican meeting & hear Mr. Miller who was the chief speaker." As he recorded in his diary, "Miller made a sensible and I should think pretty effective speech."[49]

In the fall, Miller stepped up his efforts for Lincoln. At numerous rallies, he addressed hundreds, sometimes thousands, of Iowans in places like Jackson County, Keosauqua, Bloomfield, and Fort Madison. The largest event occurred in October 1860, when 25,000 Republicans from all over Iowa, southwestern Illinois, and northeastern Missouri streamed into Keokuk for a "Grand Mass Meeting." Huge crowds forced ferry operators to turn back scores of Republicans trying to cross the Mississippi from Illinois. For a day, Keokuk streets filled as they had in the boom years. The local newspaper called it a "Grand Outpouring!" and a "Great Day in Keokuk!" Bands marched, and Republican women presented their beaus with campaign flags. Miller served as the meeting's master of ceremonies and introduced luminaries that included Congressman John Kasson, Senator James Grimes, and Lincoln's friend Orville Browning (who stayed at Miller's house). Afterwards, 2,500 Wide-Awakes, a Republican organization of young men, marched wearing hats and capes in a torchlight parade through Keokuk's downtown.[50]

Besides Lincoln, three other candidates joined the field in the 1860 presidential election. Because the Democratic Party had fractured under the weight of sectional tensions, southern Democrats ran John C. Breckinridge of Kentucky, while northern Democrats supported Stephen Douglas. Breckinridge's platform echoed slaveholders' demands that popular sovereignty in the territories be revoked and replaced by a federal slave code protecting slavery. Many of Breckinridge's supporters expected the South to secede if Lincoln won. Douglas ran on the principle of popular sovereignty. Some old-style Whigs from the North and upper South formed the Constitutional Union Party that tried to ignore the slavery issue entirely. Their candidate, John Bell of Tennessee, ran on a platform that pledged "to recognize no political principle other than the Constitution . . . the Union . . . and the enforcement of the Laws."[51]

For all intents and purposes, the contest in the South was between Breckinridge and Bell, as Douglas's equivocations on slavery had long since alienated most southern voters and Lincoln's name did not even appear on the ballot in most southern states. In the North, most voters supported Lincoln or Douglas. In southeastern Iowa, where most of the state's Democrats lived, Lincoln and

Douglas ran neck and neck. With threats of secession in the air, voters in Iowa and across the nation went to the polls in November 1860.[52]

To southerners' horror, Lincoln won the election. With support split among four candidates, Lincoln carried the day with only 40 percent of the popular vote. Nevertheless, it was clear that northerners had rallied behind him; he captured the electoral votes of California, Oregon, and every state in the North (except for a portion of New Jersey). In Iowa, Lincoln received more votes than Douglas, Bell, and Breckinridge combined. While Lincoln lost in Miller's Lee County, in Keokuk he defeated Douglas by 153 votes.[53]

With Lincoln victorious, an elated but cautious Miller tried to reassure his southern brother-in-law about the moderate intentions of the president-elect. Miller urged Ballinger to stay calm and give a Lincoln a chance. "However much we may have differed in our wishes in reference to this event before," he wrote, "I feel sure that we will agree in the desire that he may have a fair trial in the administration of the government." He promised Ballinger that "no cause exists for revolution. My confidence in the real Conservatism of Mr. Lincoln is strong, and my hope is that in this he will be vigorously supported both by the mass of the Republican Party and the better portion of all parties in the South."[54]

Miller recognized that secessionists would use Lincoln's election to advance their cause. "It is . . . undeniable," he wrote, "that a class of men in high confidence of the Southern people, have for many years desired a dissolution of the present Union and a separate Southern Confederacy. That these men will renew and continue the slavery agitation, and that they will seize the occasion of Mr. Lincoln's election to influence to its utmost the discontent of the South is certain." For Miller, this behavior seemed uncivilized. Lincoln had won fairly and deserved a chance. "The Republicans," he noted, "have conscientiously exercised their right and elected a President in a mode pointed out by the Constitution."[55]

Many northerners, including Miller, believed that the southerners who were threatening disunion were bluffing. They had threatened secession many times before. Even Lincoln did not "expect any formidable effort to break up the Union," thinking that the people of the South [had] too much sense to attempt to ruin the government.[56] "All the talk about secession and disunion," Horace Greeley's New York Tribune concurred, "is but the idle gabble of vaporing politicians." In a famous editorial Greeley even challenged secessionists to act on their threats. Suspecting that southerners meant to bully northerners into concessions, and doubting that they really would leave the Union, Greeley dared southerners to go ahead and secede. "If the Cotton States shall become satisfied that they can do better out of the Union than in it, we insist on letting them go," he editorialized three days after the election. "We hope never to live in a republic whereof one section is pinned to the residue by bayonets."[57] Greeley's gambit, one historian has written, operated "like the strategy of parents who tell an obstreperous adolescent son, after his repeated threats to run away from home, 'There's the door—go!'"[58] Many other Republicans, including Miller, followed Greeley's strategy and replicated the famous editor's position in their own arguments. Two days after Greeley's editorial appeared, Miller conveyed the same message to his southern brother-in-law. "It is true we cannot permit a single State to set up for herself in our midst," he wrote Ballinger, "but if enough join the movement to make it creditable let the thing be done decently and in order." Greeley's and Miller's go-in-peace attitude quickly evaporated, however, when it became clear that this time the southern secessionists intended to follow through with their threats.[59]

One month after Lincoln's election, the South Carolina legislature called a convention to consider secession, and on December 20 the Palmetto State voted to secede from the Union. Other Deep South states soon followed South Carolina's lead. In January and early February, conventions in Mississippi, Florida, Alabama, Georgia, Louisiana, and Texas all voted to leave the Union. The states in the upper South did not immediately join the exodus and instead waited while political leaders discussed possible compromises.[60]

In December 1860, Senator John J. Crittenden of Kentucky offered a plan he hoped might resolve the crisis. Crittenden's compromise proposal consisted of appeasing southerners by adding a number of proslavery amendments to the Constitution, including one that guaranteed slavery in the states against future interference by the national government. In addition, the Missouri Compromise line would be restored and extended in all territories "now held, or hereafter acquired." Congress would be denied any power to interfere with the interstate slave trade and would have to compensate slaveholders who were prevented from recovering fugitives in northern states. These constitutional amendments would be valid for all time, and no future amendment could override them (a policy that if implemented would have revolutionized the Constitution, which the founding fathers intended to be an amendable document).

Though proponents labeled the plan the Crittenden compromise, opponents noted that the proposed amendments all made concessions to the South.[61]

Some Republicans seemed tempted to accept the compromise, but Lincoln would have none of it. "Entertain no proposition for a compromise in regard to the extension of slavery," Lincoln instructed key senators and congressmen. In January, Crittenden took his plan to the Senate floor, where it ran into stiff opposition. On January 16, the Senate rejected Crittenden's compromise proposals 25-23, with Republicans casting all 25 votes against it. But supporters continued to push the plan even after its initial defeat.[62]

On three cold nights in January 1861, Miller and other town leaders filled Keokuk's Athenaeum to discuss the Crittenden compromise and other proposed solutions to the crisis. The town's leading Democrats saw Crittenden's proposal as the nation's last hope. Some argued that disunion must be averted at any cost, even if it meant making major concessions to the South. "No concession," lawyer William Worth Belknap asserted, "is too great to save the Union." Democratic judge James Love suggested that rather than threatening the use of force, the North, "like a gentle wife," should quietly and peacefully convince the South to return. What should happen, he asked the audience, "if a man gets drunk and beats his wife? . . . If the wife calls him a drunken brute and beats him with a broom stick, instead of quietly leading him back to temperance and virtue, she is wrong." Love believed that northern support for the Crittenden compromise might serve "quietly" to lead the South back.[63]

Miller disagreed. Tired of placating the South, he dismissed the secessionists as outlaws who should be punished rather than rewarded with compromises. The issue now, he told the audience, was the "necessity of obedience to law." The highest "interests of man and society were involved in the ability of government to assert and maintain its own existence and integrity." He continued, "The government should make no concession to those who have assumed the defiant and treasonable attitude of secessionists," and "Northern men could not yield to the insolent demands of the South on the slavery question, without the deepest humiliation and the most shameful and dastardly cowardice." There would "be time enough for us to talk of conciliation when the people of the South cease from their acts of . . . treason, and put themselves in the right under the Constitution and the laws." Republicans in the audience greeted Miller's remarks with a "perfect storm of applause."[64]

In February, after compromise efforts had failed, war fever swept Keokuk.

Rumors reached the town on February 20 that Iowa militiamen had recaptured Fort Donelson in Tennessee from secessionists who had seized it. Keokukians celebrated as if a war had already begun and a major battle had been fought. Local troops paraded in the street, and Miller delivered patriotic speeches to excited crowds at the Athenaeum and the courthouse.[65]

At 4:30 A.M. on April 12, 1861, the real war began when southern gunners opened fire on Fort Sumter in Charleston Harbor. In response, on April 15 Lincoln called 75,000 militiamen into national service. With hostilities underway, Republicans and northern Democrats temporarily put aside their differences and rallied around the cause of the Union. "There are only two sides to the question," Senator Douglas told a huge Chicago crowd shortly after Fort Sumter. "Every man must be for the United States or against it. There can be no neutrals in this war, only patriots or traitors." In Keokuk, Democrats followed Douglas's example. Recognizing the "momentous fact that the Union is in immediate peril," Democrat William Worth Belknap, who had supported the Crittenden compromise, now vowed to act "without reference to party platforms." He soon enlisted in the Union army, where he later became a decorated general. A united Iowa would eventually provide over eighty thousand soldiers—almost half the state's white male adult population—for the Union cause.[66]

Governor Samuel Kirkwood turned to Miller for help with organizing Keokuk's regiments. At age forty-five, Miller would be more helpful to the cause as a recruiter than by enlisting himself. Kirkwood counted on Miller's rousing speeches to move people to action. "The time for talking is past; the time for action has come," Miller proclaimed at an enlistment rally at Keokuk's Verandah Hall on April 17. "Rebellion is organized, and the very existence of our government is threatened. And now the only question for each one of us is: will we sustain our Government, or will we sustain the rebels." His speech received an "emphatic response" from an audience already eager for war. "The war spirit is rampant here," the *Gate City* noted. Volunteers came quickly, and Keokuk's first regiment was training within the month.[67]

In early May, Governor Kirkwood wrote Miller assuring him that sufficient arms were on the way and asking him to order a second regiment into service. Miller needed these assurances, for early in the war Keokuk's soldiers lacked weapons and equipment, and the strategically located town appeared vulnerable to attack. Initially, Keokuk's militia made do with some 1,500 old muskets, 200 rifles, and six outdated pieces of artillery. Rumors circulated that rebel Missourians planned to rob Keokuk's banks and that the town itself might be captured by invading rebel troops. Until state-supplied arms arrived, Miller used his own money to help pay and arm the local troops.[68]

Miller's anger against the South increased throughout the spring. In May, at an immense picnic for Keokuk's soldiers, he denounced southerners as vile traitors who had defiled America's sacred documents—the Constitution and the Declaration of Independence. The rebels, he charged, failed to appreciate the blessings those documents had conferred upon them. Spoiled rotten, they had seceded even though under the Constitution they had "attained a greatness and prosperity unrivaled." The "glorious Declaration of Independence, which declares that all men are born free and equal," Miller reported, "has been denounced at the South as a tissue of glittering generalities, and the Congress of the Southern Confederacy has abolished the 4th of July." He rhetorically asked the troops, "Shall traitors who thus raise their hands against the Constitution, and declare their enmity to the Declaration of Independence, be permitted to trail our flag in the dust?"[69]

Throughout the difficult first year of the Civil War, Miller's wife Eliza also pitched in to help keep up the morale of Keokuk's citizens and the troops training there. She raised money for the families of volunteers, organized benefit concerts for the Soldier's Aid Society, and presented battle flags—hand-sewn by local women—to the troops. On at least one occasion, she and other women from Keokuk prepared a "luxurious supper" for the soldiers. Because of the Millers' efforts, soldiers came to trust them. In December, Eliza received a thick package in the mail addressed to her husband. He was away attending district court in Fort Madison, so Eliza opened the package. Inside she found $1,250 in small denominations and a letter from Iowa's Third Cavalry Regiment asking Samuel to distribute the money to their families. Eliza delivered the money instead, and the Millers' home thereafter became the place where the wives of Keokuk's soldiers would go to collect remittances from their husbands.[70]

Miller's law partner, Rankin, also did his share for the cause by carrying Governor Kirkwood's war messages to Washington and buying arms for the Iowa militia while he was there. On one of these missions, he met President Lincoln. "This forenoon I called on Mr. Lincoln," Rankin wrote, "He is quite well, though care worn. It is evident that he is conscious of his position and fully determined to discharge all his obligations." Rankin's frequent absences, however, left Miller to handle the law firm's caseload by himself, a problem that only increased when Rankin subsequently enlisted in the army.[71]

While enthusiasm for the war ran high in Keokuk, the conflict exacerbated the town's economic problems. Because the Confederacy's blockade of the Mississippi shut down the steamboat trade, Keokuk's once bustling levee, already suffering before the war, now sat empty. "If our soldiers were not daily exercising on the levee," the *Gate City* lamented, "we would see grass grow there in abundance." With steamboats nowhere in sight and no southern outlets for produce, the economies of Keokuk and other river towns were "prostrated." The Mississippi blockade accelerated the trends that had hurt Keokuk before the war. By necessity, goods now traveled almost solely by trains via Chicago, and the railroads quickly took advantage of their new monopoly by raising rates. "The blockade of the Mississippi, has given railroads a monopoly which they have not been slow to understand," Keokuk residents complained, "and by paying increased tariffs on freights on all we export and all we import, the people of the West, or the farming population, whose prosperity underlies all commercial and other prosperity . . . have been depressed and embarrassed."[72]

The Union troops who camped and trained in the fields outside of town provided a modicum of economic relief for Keokuk's remaining businesses. But the soldiers created new problems. Often poorly supplied, they stole chickens from residents and surreptitiously milked cows in the fields. When they came into town, they often drank, swore, fought, and harassed the local populace. When one saloonkeeper tried to eject offensive soldiers, "they smashed everything in the establishment." "There are a few soldiers in town," the *Gate City* grumbled, "who are, we are sorry to say, making themselves very offensive to our citizens . . . parading through the streets of Keokuk at their leisure, insulting ladies, and committing depredations upon the property of citizens." In July 1861, Miller organized a committee of public safety to help keep order.[73]

The Union army did put the Estes House to use, stretching a tarp over its open roof and using it as a giant hospital. By June 1862, over two thousand wounded soldiers lay in the makeshift floors of the uncompleted hotel. Poorly designed for its new purpose, the hospital had conspicuous sanitation problems. Giant cesspools of filth formed behind it. Some of Keokuk's other abandoned buildings later housed Confederate prisoners and experienced similar problems.

Prisoners were quickly evacuated from one such building before its decrepit walls tumbled in.[74]

Despite the daunting problems of boisterous soldiers, unsanitary hospitals, and crippled trade, Miller refused to give up hope for Keokuk. As the Civil War began, he was back in the courtroom challenging the validity of the railroad bonds in the case of *Beecher v. City of Keokuk*. The case involved one particularly questionable $1,000 bond issue by the city nine years earlier, not to fund a railroad but to pay Mayor Hugh Sample's expenses for a trip to Congress to lobby for railroad appropriations. Even with a broad reading of section 114 of the Iowa Code, this bond's validity seemed dubious. If ever a case existed where the anti-bond forces could carry the day, this seemed to be it. At the trial, Miller convincingly argued that the city never had any authority to issue bonds for such overly broad purposes. In this instance, Judge Love agreed and gave Miller a rare victory in a bond case. Both Love and Miller recognized that the United States Supreme Court would ultimately have to resolve the issue. Miller, in fact, had already secured admission to practice before that Court in hopes that he could argue this and other Iowa railroad bond cases there.[75]

CHAPTER 4
Lincoln Appoints a Justice

W HILE MILLER WAS IN KEOKUK, a climactic struggle was occurring in Washington between the new Republican president and the United States Supreme Court—a struggle that would soon change the course of Miller's life.

Lincoln came to the presidency in 1861 determined to reshape the Supreme Court, which had helped precipitate the crisis that engulfed the nation. Many northerners viewed Chief Justice Roger Taney's opinion in *Dred Scott* as the proximate cause of the Civil War. Lincoln regarded that decision as so inflammatory, so clearly biased, that he—and other Republicans—refused to defer to the judgment of the nation's highest tribunal on the question of slavery in the territories. Instead, he declared that *Dred Scott* was wrong and that it should be overturned. "We think the Dred Scott decision is erroneous," he had argued in 1858, "We know the Court that made it, has often over-ruled its own decisions, and we will do what we can to have it to over-rule this." Campaigning in 1860, Lincoln and other Republicans had pledged to "reconstitute" the Court if their party captured the presidency. As president, Lincoln hoped to reshape the Court in the Republicans' image.[1]

Lincoln had immediate opportunities to leave his imprint on the Court. When he arrived at the White House, the Court already had one vacancy. Justice Peter Daniel of Virginia, a member of the *Dred Scott* majority and a "brooding proslavery fanatic" had died the previous May. President Buchanan, overwhelmed by sectional pressures, had simply left the seat empty. One month into Lincoln's presidency, a second seat on the Court opened when Justice John McLean of Ohio died on April 4, 1861, at the age of seventy-six. A dissenter in

65

Dred Scott, McLean was a hero to many abolitionists, and he would have been a friend of the new administration. Later in April, yet another seat on the Court opened when Justice John A. Campbell of Alabama, a member of the *Dred Scott* majority, resigned to join the Confederacy. As the nation descended into Civil War, many northerners found solace in the fact that the South's viselike grip on the Supreme Court had loosened, and Lincoln would be able to appoint one-third of the Court's personnel.[2]

Even with these vacancies, however, Lincoln still faced a hostile Court, one unlikely to overturn *Dred Scott* or please Republicans. Of the remaining six justices, five—James Wayne, John Catron, Robert Grier, Samuel Nelson, and Taney—had been in the *Dred Scott* majority; the sixth—Nathan Clifford of Maine—was an embittered, proslavery Democrat. Even if Lincoln appointed three zealous Republicans, the Court's majority would still be made up of men unsympathetic to Lincoln and his party. If Lincoln needed any confirmation of this fact, it came very early, with Taney's opinion in *Ex Parte Merryman.*[3]

John Merryman was a wealthy Maryland landowner who, soon after Fort Sumter, joined a secessionist cavalry unit that burned bridges and tore down telegraph wires in his home state. Confederate partisans like Merryman were common in the border states, but their presence in Maryland—a state that enclosed Washington on three sides—was particularly troubling. If Maryland secessionists could not be subdued, the capital could be cut off from the Union. As the fighting began, rumors swirled that a Confederate attack on Washington might come any day and that the invading southerners would be assisted by thousands of secessionist sympathizers.[4]

On April 27, Lincoln responded to these fears by ordering General Winfield Scott to suspend habeas corpus from Washington to Philadelphia, allowing the military to summarily arrest and detain any persons thought to be aiding the Confederacy. Now, suspected secessionists could be rounded up on even the thinnest evidence and imprisoned indefinitely, which is how military authorities came to seize John Merryman on May 25, 1861.

From a constitutional perspective, suspending the writ was a dramatic and drastic decision. The framers of the Constitution considered habeas corpus a fundamental protection that could be suspended only in the direst circumstances. Nevertheless, they recognized that a rebellion or foreign invasion might justify such a course of action, and article 1, section 9 of the Constitution thus stipulated that habeas corpus "shall not be suspended, unless when in cases of rebellion or invasion the public safety may require it." Lincoln reasoned in 1861 that southerners' mass treason constituted a rebellion of that magnitude. Yet it remained uncertain whether the president, rather than Congress, had the authority to suspend habeas corpus. Article 1 of the Constitution described the powers of Congress, not the executive branch, and it seemed clear that the framers did not intend to give the president unilateral authority to suspend such a crucial civil right. But what if Congress was not in session, as was the case in April 1861? Faced with a rebellion that threatened the very existence of the Union, did the president have to sit idly by and wait for Congress to reconvene? Surely, Lincoln argued, this was not the intention of the founding fathers. "Are all the laws, but one to go unexecuted," he asked, "and the government itself go to pieces, lest that one be violated?"[5]

Merryman's lawyer quickly challenged Lincoln on this point. On the day of his client's arrest, he filed a habeas corpus petition at the Baltimore circuit court, where he could count on a sympathetic hearing from Chief Justice Taney, who was then serving as the senior judge of the federal circuit in Maryland and who welcomed an opportunity to rebuke the new president. On May 28, Taney denied Lincoln's authority to suspend habeas corpus unilaterally, and he commanded the military to produce Merryman before the court "with the cause, if any, for his arrest and detention." Lincoln, in turn, ordered the army officer who had arrested Merryman to refuse to accept the writ. Taney responded by ruling that Lincoln was acting unlawfully and claimed that if the president's usurpation of a congressional power did not go unchecked, the people of the United States would be "no longer living under a government of laws." Taney sent Lincoln a copy of his *Merryman* opinion, but Lincoln ignored it, and habeas corpus remained suspended.[6]

Lincoln knew that the Supreme Court would continue to attempt to check presidential war powers. He recognized that a civil war required drastic measures, and he often ignored constitutional niceties. With the list of controversial measures growing rapidly, each new directive that left his desk increased the possibility of a major confrontation with the Supreme Court. During the early months of the war, Lincoln ordered the Union navy to blockade southern ports, and he had several members of the Maryland legislature arrested for advocating secession. In October 1861, he suspended habeas corpus all along the eastern seaboard from Washington to Bangor, Maine, even though the northeastern states were not in rebellion. Although Congress reconvened for an emergency session in the summer of 1861 and promptly passed bills approving Lincoln's extraconstitutional actions, the constitutionality of many of his war measures remained in doubt. At some point, many of Lincoln's policies would inevitably face the judicial scrutiny of the Supreme Court.[7]

The blockade of southern ports made for a particularly sticky question. Much of the problem stemmed from Lincoln's definition of the war and the fact that he refused to recognize the legitimacy of the Confederacy. He viewed the war as an internal "insurrection" of individuals who joined in "combinations too powerful to be suppressed by the ordinary course of judicial proceedings." If he had to refer to the new southern government, he called it the "so-called Confederate States of America." To do otherwise might invite foreign powers to recognize the Confederacy, thereby giving England or France a pretense to intervene on the South's behalf. But if the war was merely a "rebellion" or "insurrection," as Lincoln argued, the blockade's legality became uncertain. Some governments viewed a blockade as an instrument of war to be used only between two sovereign and belligerent powers. If the conflict with the South was only an "insurrection," the United States was blockading itself. A constitutional confrontation with the Court over the blockade loomed, and it seemed that only a change in the Court's personnel could guarantee a favorable decision for Lincoln.[8]

Taney's *Merryman* opinion, combined with lingering anger over *Dred Scott*, fueled new calls by Republicans to pack the Court with Lincoln appointees. The *New York Tribune* proposed increasing the number of seats on the Court to eleven, justifying its position by pointing to the role *Dred Scott* had played in causing the war. "The present rebellion," the *Tribune* noted in its defense of the court-packing plan, "is due quite as much to an unsound and unwise decision of the Supreme Court as to any other single cause."[9]

Other newspapers and politicians rallied behind a proposal to reorganize the nation's judicial circuits in order to decrease the South's disproportionate representation on the Court. In 1861, the nation's federal courts were divided into nine judicial circuits, with each circuit supervised by one of the members of the United States Supreme Court. A justice usually hailed from the region he supervised. Of the nine circuits, five covered slaveholding states.[10] It had been twenty-five years since the last modification of the circuits; during that time, the North's population had exploded while the South's had lagged behind. The resulting imbalance between population and representation on the Supreme Court infuriated northerners. "The twenty millions of the people of the free states are represented by four judges," the *Chicago Tribune* complained, "while the nine millions of whites in the South have five judges." Like the notorious three-fifths clause in the Constitution, which allowed the South to include slaves in the population totals used to determine representation in the House of Representatives, the organization of the judicial circuits seemed designed to give slave states an unfair advantage. The population of the northwestern Seventh Circuit alone equaled that of the five southern circuits combined. Such disparity led Iowa congressman James F. Wilson to call the Supreme Court a "monstrous citadel of slavery." In addition to the longstanding sectional imbalance, reorganization was overdue as a result of the nation's westward expansion. Texas, Florida, Wisconsin, Oregon, Minnesota, Kansas, California, and Iowa had not yet been assigned circuits. Proponents of change could thus cite both practical and political justifications for a major judicial reorganization.[11]

Lincoln joined the chorus of voices calling on Congress to reorganize the circuits and vowed to delay making any appointments to the Supreme Court until this task was accomplished. In his first annual message to Congress, in November 1861, Lincoln announced his support for a plan that would reduce the number of southern circuits and increase those from the North. Pointing to the North's tremendous growth, Lincoln noted that during the late Justice McLean's thirty-two-year tenure, the population of the Seventh Circuit had grown from roughly 1.47 million to 6.15 million, a circuit "altogether too large for any one Judge." A change had to be made. Efficiency, logistics, and simple fairness all pointed to the need for reorganization. Most importantly, reorganization would secure a northern majority on the Court.[12]

Congress heeded Lincoln's call. Six days after the president's speech, Senator John Sherman of Ohio introduced a bill to reorganize the circuits in a manner that would condense the number of southern circuits and add a new circuit in the North. Representative John Bingham of Ohio introduced a similar bill in the House. After a month of deliberations, the Senate Judiciary Committee endorsed Sherman's proposal. Under Sherman's plan, three judicial circuits would be assigned to the Northeast (population 10.6 million), three would cover the South (population 9.9 million), and three would represent the Middle West (population 10 million). If so organized, all three vacancies on the Court would be in western circuits. Lincoln's appointments would thus have a profound effect on the administration of justice in that region.[13]

With a plan on the table, members of the Judiciary Committee urged their fellow senators to approve the bill quickly. The Court had operated for almost a year without a full complement of justices. "The Supreme Court has but six judges on the bench," Senator Trumbull noted. "The other three ought to be appointed . . . [but] they will not be appointed until some bill passes on the subject, and I think it would be best to act upon it as early as we conveniently can." With the constitutionality of Lincoln's war measures hanging in the balance, Trumbull and other senators hoped for quick passage of the judicial reorganization bill so that Republican appointees could begin to reshape the Court's jurisprudence.[14]

Despite the need for expediency, the bill met stiff opposition from an unexpected source—Iowa's staunchly Republican congressional delegation. Even though the nation was at war, Iowa's delegation delayed the circuit reorganization bills in the House and Senate for months. Although Iowa's senators and congressmen welcomed the idea of reorganizing the circuits, the Senate Judiciary Committee's plan placed the Hawkeye State with Illinois in the new Ninth Circuit. Because of the economic and political importance of Chicago and the rest of Illinois, Iowans believed that Lincoln would almost certainly appoint a justice from that state to supervise the circuit. Already rumors were swirling that he would nominate his friend Senator Orville Browning for the position. Indeed, Lincoln had told others that he felt "he must appoint Browning."[15]

Many Iowans knew Browning well and held unfavorable opinions of him. In the campaign of 1860, Browning spoke at Republican rallies in several Iowa cities, and while in Keokuk he had stayed at Miller's house. While most Iowa Republicans shared Browning's moderate views on slavery, other issues made him suspect to them. Before serving in the Senate, he was a fervent booster of railroads who with his friends promoted the Northern Cross, a railroad that had relied heavily upon community subscriptions to railroad stock. In the 1850s, he had encouraged local governments to go into debt to support construction of the line. But after the river-town economies crashed in 1857, Browning steadfastly opposed the repudiation of bonds and other debts, and he later was hostile to the regulation of railroads. Iowa's Republicans had long since turned against politicians who held such views; but in northern Illinois, where the economy had recovered from the Panic of 1857 more quickly, men like Browning succeeded.[16] Because the Supreme Court would soon be hearing numerous cases involving railroad bonds and that pitted steamboat corporations against railroads, Iowans hoped to avoid being saddled with a justice like Browning, who would be unsympathetic to their economic concerns.

At the end of January 1862, as it became clear that the reorganization of the circuits would be delayed, Lincoln was compelled to make a nomination to fill John McLean's vacant seat on the Court (McLean's Seventh Circuit then consisted of Ohio, Indiana, Illinois, and Michigan). The president's hand was forced when two sitting justices, Taney and Catron, became ill; this meant that the already depleted Court could not even maintain a quorum. For the position, Lincoln tapped Noah Swayne, a Republican from Ohio with impressive antislavery credentials. Like Miller, Swayne was born in a slaveholding state, studied medicine, switched to law, acquired slaves through marriage, and then emancipated them. Eventually, he moved to Ohio, where he helped form the state's Republican Party and served as counsel in fugitive slave cases. Lincoln correctly assumed that Swayne would uphold his war measures.[17]

But there was more to Swayne than his antislavery views. As an attorney, Swayne had grown wealthy representing railroads, banks, and other corporations, and he had adopted the economic outlook of America's financial elites. In 1856, for example, he had defended the Mad River & Lake Erie Railroad in a suit by a company brakeman who had been thrown under a train and maimed as a result of defective brake rods. In the well-publicized case, Swayne had successfully argued that by agreeing to be hired, the brakeman had voluntarily assumed the risk of injury and should not be compensated for his injuries.[18]

Swayne also had close ties to New York City wealth. Samuel J. Tilden, a Democrat and leading New York corporate lawyer, actively lobbied for his appointment to the Court. The New York bar also petitioned Lincoln on his behalf. Capitalists who supported Swayne weighed in as well. Chicago railroad magnate William B. Ogden, the first president of the Union Pacific, urged Swayne's nomination. To Lincoln, Ogden touted the fact that Swayne's considerable fortune meant that "he has means to live handsomely independent of his salary."[19] Ogden and other captains of industry got their wish. "The war could not be prosecuted to a successful conclusion without the support of Big Business," one historian has noted. By selecting Swayne, Lincoln "satisfied business interests at the same time that he satisfied Ohio politicians."[20]

With Swayne appointed and Browning rumored as a shoo-in for a reorganized Illinois circuit, Iowans dug in their heels and campaigned for a reorganization bill that would create a new trans-Mississippi circuit that would not include Illinois. In March, the Iowa state legislature passed a resolution urging its congressmen (and requiring its senators) to fight for a circuit made up solely of states west of the Mississippi. They also petitioned Congress for the same.[21]

Unified and determined, Iowa's congressional leaders, led by Senator James Grimes and Congressman James Wilson, stymied the plan that put Iowa in the same circuit as Illinois. Although a promoter of railroads while living in Burlington in the 1850s, Grimes turned, at least publicly, against railroads, bondholders, and capitalists after the Panic of 1857. Wilson had also turned against railroads and financiers after the panic. In 1860 he had supported a controversial plan to regulate railroad rates. Now in Congress, Wilson served as a member of the House Judiciary Committee, a strategic position from which to influence the reorganization process.[22]

Wilson and Grimes proposed creating a new Ninth Circuit out of Iowa, Missouri, Minnesota, and Kansas, on the grounds that the four states shared similar legal codes and that "their commercial relations were closely connected by the Mississippi and Missouri Rivers." Despite all the manic efforts to bring railroads and eastern capital to Iowa in the 1850s, Iowa's leaders still felt more kinship to states built on the steamboat trade, states that now felt the effects of the river trade's decline and the burden of railroad debt.[23]

Wilson reminded his House colleagues of the crucial role Iowa's troops were playing in the war, suggesting that the bravery of their soldiers entitled Iowans to the judicial circuit of their choice. He noted that Iowa had sent "to aid in crushing the atrocious rebellion, almost as many men as she had voters in 1850; men than whom none more true, none more brave, none more gallant ever encountered a foe on this field of battle. The bloody fields of Pittsburgh Landing, Fort Donelson, Belmont, Wilson's Creek, and Blue Mills, all attest how well and nobly the gallant volunteers of Iowa have done." Despite his skillful use of patriotic language, he did not explain why the "gallant volunteers of Iowa" should not share a judicial circuit with the gallant volunteers from Illinois.[24]

As the Iowans successfully delayed the reorganization bills, Republican Senator Jacob Howard of Michigan, a member of the Senate Judiciary Committee, questioned their motives and the idea that "there should be a division of judicial circuits upon the Mississippi River." Under the Iowans' plan, Howard noted, the circuits would once again have wildly disproportionate populations. A circuit made up of Missouri, Iowa, Minnesota, and Kansas would represent a population of only 2.1 million, while Michigan's circuit and the circuit covering Indiana and Ohio would have 3.2 million and 3.7 million residents respectively. Was not one purpose behind reorganization, Howard wondered, to bring circuit court representation in line with population? Under the current system, the South had disproportionate representation. The Iowans' plan would replicate the problem, minus only the disruptive variable of slavery. "All of these inequalities and disproportions," Howard complained, "are introduced . . . for the purpose of carrying out the idea that there must be a separate circuit on the West side of the Mississippi River. . . .Why are these inequalities introduced? What is at the bottom of it?"[25]

Howard perceptively noted that the Iowa plan had broad and disturbing implications—among them, a dangerous sectionalism. By demanding a circuit made up solely of states west of the Mississippi, the Iowans highlighted regional differences and animosities. Against the backdrop of a bloody civil war, such sectional identification made Howard uneasy. "Indeed, I do not like it," Howard worried. "In times like these I am getting a little distrustful of geographical divisions. We do not know what a day or even an hour may bring forth in the midst of the trials and shocks the nation is now undergoing."[26]

Howard's concerns reflected an important development within his party. Although Republicans shared a general view that celebrated free labor, the party also suffered from significant regional tensions. Republicans often divided over economic issues along East-West, North-South, and urban-rural lines. Debates about taxes and tariffs split Republicans residing in New England and the Upper Northwest (i.e., Wisconsin, Minnesota, Michigan, and the northern portions of Illinois and Indiana) from those from the lower portions of Illinois, Indiana, Ohio, and Iowa. Other issues, particularly railroad bonds, widened cleavages between urban and rural Republicans and between easterners and westerners. Many westerners shared a growing resentment of New York and saw a conflict that pitted eastern speculators, brokers, moneychangers, and bondholders against the productive toiling men of the country. The Iowans' battle over judicial reorganization revealed yet another schism, between the steamboat states on the west side of the Mississippi River and the railroad state of Illinois.[27]

From February through May 1862, the Iowa congressional delegation successfully bottled up the judicial reorganization legislation. In early June, the *Chicago Tribune* demanded action. "What has become of the bill reorganizing the Supreme Court?" the paper asked. Pointing to the disparities between the North and the South, and all of the western states that had yet to be assigned a circuit, the *Tribune* urged Congress to not "leave the court in this wretched condition."[28]

Under growing pressure, the House and Senate finally acted. In June, despite the efforts of Grimes, the Senate rejected Iowa's plan and passed a version of the bill that lumped Iowa with Illinois. But in the House, where Wilson sat on the Judiciary Committee, the bill placed Iowa in a judicial circuit with Missouri, Kansas, and Minnesota. When the House and Senate met in a conference committee on the issue, Wilson went to work. Most of the members of the joint committee hailed from eastern states unaffected by the bill, and Wilson reasoned that they would probably accept any version that would allow the drawn-out process to be completed so that new justices could be appointed. Because he stubbornly insisted on his version for the Ninth Circuit, the other members of the conference committee eventually acquiesced, and the bill emerged with Iowa in a new circuit of states exclusively from west of the Mississippi, while Illinois joined Wisconsin and Michigan in the Eighth Circuit.

On July 12, Congress passed the Judicial Reorganization Act of 1862 by a unanimous vote in the House and a vote of 24 to 12 in the Senate. Lincoln approved the measure; on July 15, he signed the bill into law. The Iowans had "delayed and jeopardized circuit reorganization," but they had won. Iowa joined a circuit in which three of its four states were tied to the river trade, and Iowans now urged Lincoln to appoint a justice who knew the hopes, dreams, and bitter disappointments of the river towns all too well: Samuel Freeman Miller.[29]

Miller's supporters had begun lobbying for his appointment from the moment Congress started debating judicial reorganization. In late 1861 and early 1862, Iowa judges and lawyers barraged Lincoln with letters that served a dual purpose. Not only did they tout Miller as the right man for the job; they reminded Lincoln that Iowans desired their own circuit and representation on the Court. "The citizens of the Upper Mississippi Valley believe that this region of the country is entitled to be represented on the federal bench," wrote one Keokuk lawyer. "I hope your excellency will be pleased to compliment Iowa, whose devotion to our Union is so manifest & deserving," former Iowa congressman Daniel F. Miller chimed in, "with the appointment of Mr. Miller."[30] The letters came from both Democrats and Republicans, reflecting Iowans' recognition that Miller represented their best hope for a sympathetic voice on the Court. Almost all spoke of his sharp mind, and many described him as the top lawyer in the state. Some emphasized the steadfast Republicanism of a man who was "an earnest Patriot and conscientious Republican" and "unwavering in his political creed."[31] Iowa federal district court judge James Love wrote on Miller's behalf even though, as a Keokuk Democrat, he had sparred with Miller in the past. "*Personally* I have been a friend of Mr. Miller," Love informed Lincoln, "but *politically* opposed him." As Keokuk neighbors, Love and Miller nonetheless agreed on certain topics. "As Judge of the District Court of Iowa," Love wrote, Miller had "been engaged in constant and extensive practice before me."[32] In the district court, he had heard Miller's argument in the Rock Island Bridge case and had agreed with Miller that the bridge should be destroyed. As a river-town resident and pro-steamboat judge, Love now wanted Miller on the Supreme Court.[33]

Miller was flattered by the fact that so many Iowa Democrats lobbied for his nomination. "It was a time of great political excitement," he later recalled, "and I have always felt peculiarly gratified that members of the bar who were zealous democrats vied with those of the republican party . . . in the sincerity and vigor of their recommendations." The bipartisan support for Miller reflected the fact that Iowa's Democrats and Republicans shared a regional worldview. Outside of Iowa, Democratic Copperheads portrayed the Republicans as the party of eastern bondholders and railroad directors who reaped windfall profits from the war, and they claimed that Lincoln's support for tariffs, the national banking system, and government bonds enriched northeastern capitalists at the expense of farmers and laborers. But in Iowa, Republicans shared the Democrats' views of bondholders and railroad magnates. Thus, men of both parties favored Miller's appointment to the Court.[34]

Some Iowans pressed Miller's case in person. Miller himself asked Lincoln's assistant postmaster general, John Kasson of Des Moines, to meet with the president on his behalf. Lincoln, Kasson soon learned, had not heard of Miller and confused him with the Daniel F. Miller who had once represented Iowa in Congress. Kasson corrected the misunderstanding and touted Samuel Miller's qualifications for the Court.[35] On another occasion, Governor Kirkwood, Senator James Harlan, and several Iowa congressmen went to the White House to urge Lincoln to appoint Miller. At that meeting, the Iowans, assuming that Lincoln knew why they had come, launched into their case without mentioning Miller's name or the position to which they wanted him appointed. Lincoln, who was well aware of their hopes, used the opportunity to humorous advantage. He "picked up his pen, and drawing a paper to him as if to make the appointment in compliance with their wishes, said to them, 'what is the office and whom do you wish to be placed in it?' 'We wish,' an astounded Harlan quickly replied, 'to have Mr. Miller of Iowa chosen by you to . . . the Supreme Bench.' 'Well, well,' Lincoln replied, replacing his pen and pushing back the paper, 'that is a very important position and I will have to give it serious consideration. I had supposed you wanted me to make some one a Brigadier General for you.'" The chagrined Iowans left with no assurances.[36]

As the process moved forward, Iowans back home and in Washington flooded Lincoln's desk with more material in support of Miller. In addition to the numerous letters from the Iowa bar and bench, Lincoln received written entreaties from the Iowa state legislature and "Iowa State Citizens." Wilson and Grimes circulated petitions for Miller's appointment in the U.S. House and Senate and managed to procure the signatures of 120 congressmen and twenty-eight senators.[37]

Lincoln, of course, had other pressing concerns in the spring and summer of 1862 besides judicial reorganization and Supreme Court appointments. In April, the war in the West began to take a gruesome turn. Although the battle of Shiloh was a smashing Union victory, horrific casualties convinced Lincoln that subduing the South would not come quickly or easily. Temporarily demoted from army command (in large measure because of Shiloh's shocking death toll), General Ulysses S. Grant, like Lincoln, concluded that the war could be won only by totally conquering the South. For Lincoln, who did not want the war to become a "remorseless revolutionary struggle," this was a disheartening realization. In the East, matters also looked bleak. In May and June 1862, Stonewall Jackson's Confederate forces scored stunning successes in the Shenandoah Valley, while the carnage at the Seven Days' battle appeared to signal the start of a bloody summer. With the war escalating and the fate of the Union in doubt, it is hardly surprising that Supreme Court appointments did not top Lincoln's agenda.[38]

When Lincoln did consider possible appointees for the Court in July, he sought men who supported both the war effort and even his most constitutionally suspect policies. Miller's supporters let Lincoln know that their man met these criteria. Outspoken in his opposition to the expansion of slavery, Miller had rejected last-minute attempts at sectional compromise that would have required concessions to slaveholders. An active supporter of the war, he had given fiery speeches demanding that the traitorous rebellion be crushed. His supporters emphasized his patriotism and unwavering commitment to Republican principles in their appeals to the president. Preoccupied with the war effort, Lincoln had to rely on the recommendations of others, and Miller's supporters provided him with plenty of material. Lincoln told one Iowan that "he had not known such a unanimous recommendation of any man for any office, and felt he could not err in making the appointment of a Federal Judge so generally approved by an intelligent bar, and, not less important in such a crisis, by a patriotic people."[39]

In the end, Lincoln chose Miller without even meeting him. It is possible that the president thought such a meeting was unnecessary. From Miller's background and qualifications, he must have recognized a familiar tale, for in many ways, Miller's past mirrored Lincoln's own. Born seven years apart in the same state, both men grew up on hardscrabble family farms in slaveholding Kentucky. Both hated the mind-numbing, backbreaking existence on preindustrial farms, and in early adulthood they rejected the life of their parents. As a means to prominence and upward mobility, both eventually chose a career in law and thrived in that profession. Gravitating to the Whig Party, they championed Henry Clay's American System of internal improvements, factories, banks, tariffs, and aggressive economic growth. They embraced the notion of a modern, urbanized America, linked by railroads and teeming with factories. "Lincoln fought his entire political life for industrialization," one historian has written, "and there was not a pastoral bone in his body." Miller shared Lincoln's views. In Barbourville, he had supported industrialization, urbanization, the national bank, and tariffs; he had hoped that Cassius Clay's vision of a Kentucky System would bring factories and economic salvation to his dying town. When he moved to Iowa, it was Keokuk's economic vitality, not the region's fertile soil, that attracted him. In Keokuk, Miller saw an embryonic Chicago, and if it grew into a major metropolis, he wanted to reap the benefits of having been there at the start. When Lincoln grimly described a nonindustrial world where "all is cold and still as death—no smoke rises, no furnace roars, no anvil rings," he could have been describing the Barbourville that Miller fled, or the Keokuk that might be if that city could not escape its disastrous debts.[40]

Lincoln and Miller also both celebrated free labor, the right to rise, and the "self-made man." America was a remarkable land, Lincoln believed, where the "penniless beginner in the world labors for wages awhile, saves a surplus with which to buy tools and land, for himself; then labors on his own account another while, and at length hires another beginner to help him. . . . This is free labor—the just and generous, and prosperous system which opens the way for all—gives hope to all, and energy and progress, and improvement of condition to all."[41] Lincoln had risen in life, and he loved the fact that in America others could too. Miller shared Lincoln's views on this point. As a young man in the Barbourville Debating Society, his boundless optimism about his country had led him to argue that the American economic system did not unfairly favor the wealthy and that talent was more important than wealth in achieving success. Because slavery denied both blacks and non-slaveholding whites the right to rise, both men hated the peculiar institution and moved west to get away from it. When the Kansas-Nebraska Act threatened to bring slavery to what had been free soil, both men vehemently opposed it. And when that act irreparably split the Whigs along sectional lines, they joined the Republican Party and never looked back.

The parallels between Lincoln and Miller are hardly startling, however. Theirs was a common story, played out many times in the antebellum West. America's expansion provided unprecedented opportunities, both for those seeking farmland and for men like Lincoln and Miller who chased urban, bourgeois dreams. Self-made men formed the backbone of the Whig and Republican parties. Much of the support for both parties came from people who had succeeded in the nineteenth-century economy and who believed that others with talent and ambition should follow their example.[42] When Miller's supporters told Lincoln of Miller's rural Kentucky roots, Whig background, career in law, antislavery views, and conversion to Republicanism, the president knew all he needed to know. Based on Lincoln's wartime criteria for Court appointments, Miller was a worthy candidate.

But while they shared similar backgrounds and held many of the same views, wartime priorities masked sharp differences in their economic philosophies. After the Panic of 1857, Miller began to believe that capital had become dangerously concentrated in the hands of parasitical financiers. Lincoln, on the other hand, still believed that capitalists, farmers, laborers, and merchants had a harmony of interests. Because Americans could rise, social mobility assured that today's laborer could be tomorrow's capitalist. Lincoln did not believe the capitalist class had grown unduly large or powerful. Instead, he feared that attacks on capitalists, such as calls for the repudiation of debts, undermined property; and if property was not secure, the incentive to labor diminished. "Let not him who is houseless pull down the house of another," Lincoln admonished, "but let him labor diligently and build one for himself, thus by example assuring that his own shall be safe from violence when built." Although he was willing to tax the rich disproportionately to pay for the war, he almost certainly would have opposed Miller's attempts to manipulate Iowa law so that Iowa river towns could escape their debts to eastern financiers. In different circumstances, Lincoln might have met Miller before nominating him, and discussions of topics such as their mutual participation in the Rock Island Bridge litigation might have revealed Miller as a river-town lawyer who held deep resentment for eastern financiers.[43]

Moreover, in calmer times other factors would have entered the nomination equation. Without wartime distractions, the Iowa river towns' attempts to escape their railroad debts through litigation would almost certainly have caught Lincoln's eye. In the years before slavery took center stage, Lincoln had been obsessed with economic issues, of which the repudiation of railroad bonds in Illinois was one. In a time of peace, Lincoln might have asked Kirkwood, Harlan, Kasson, or the other Iowans pushing Miller's nomination where their man stood on municipal bonds. He would not have liked the answer. But in the maelstrom of civil war, Miller's economic views did not surface. Miller was sound on race, slavery, and the war—and that was all that was required.

On July 16, 1862, the day after the enactment of the Judicial Reorganization Act, Lincoln nominated Samuel Freeman Miller for the seat representing the new Ninth Circuit on the United States Supreme Court. The Senate confirmed the nomination within half an hour.[44] On July 19, Miller received his commission, and on July 21 Chief Justice Taney administered Miller's oath of office. In Washington, "all Iowans . . . most heartily rejoiced." Within the span of a few days, they had scored two dramatic successes with the birth of a trans-Mississippi circuit and Miller's appointment to the Court. Later in life, Miller gave the credit for his appointment to the Iowans' lobbying expertise and the success Wilson and Grimes had in placing Iowa "in a circuit entirely west of the Mississippi River."[45]

In Iowa, Republicans cheered, anticipating that Miller would give their values a voice on the Court. The new justice, Iowa's editors noted, brought with him a western view of the law that favored practicality over precedents. While some historians have charged Miller with having "little systematic approach to the law," his contemporaries saw this quality as a strength. Miller was a judge who sought results first and then found the arguments to justify them. If justice demanded that river towns be freed from their bond debts, for example, Miller would find a way to do so. Unlike men from the tradition-bound East, Miller was not awed "by the dust of antiquated precedents." "He is [the] model," the *Keokuk Gate City* trumpeted, "the beau ideal of a Western lawyer and a Western Judge and his advent to the Bench cannot fail to create a sensation even in that fossilized circle of venerable antiquities which constitutes the Bench of the Supreme Court of the United States. No better appointment has been made in our time." "The appointment is a most excellent one," the *Des Moines Daily State Register* declared, "and grateful to the people of Iowa."[46]

While Iowans cheered, the eastern press met Miller's appointment with confusion. The *New York Tribune* mistook him for Daniel F. Miller (as Lincoln had done earlier). "Mr. Miller's name is printed *Samuel* in the dispatches," the *Tribune* posited, "but we presume it is Daniel F. Miller, the first Whig member of Congress ever chosen from Iowa." Most papers knew so little about Miller that they ran only an abbreviated dispatch stating that the appointment had been made.[47]

One journalist did manage to provide a thumbnail sketch of the new justice. "Many able men, being also modest, remain comparatively unknown," remarked the *Chicago Christian Times*. "In politics, Mr. Miller was originally a Whig, but when that party was destroyed by mint-juleps, his anti-slavery sentiments found early congeniality in the Republican organization." The article also noted that Miller, unlike Swayne, was not wealthy. He is "economical in his way of life, but not parsimonious . . . though not rich."[48]

Shortly after taking his oath of office, Miller returned to Keokuk to accept congratulations and organize his affairs. To celebrate, he and his wife Eliza hosted Iowa's prominent judges and lawyers at their house for a night of dining, toasts, and speeches. "We understand the evening passed very pleasantly," the

Gate City reported, with the "distinguished host and his accomplished lady doing all in their power to render their visitors perfectly at home. The bar of Iowa, as well as the people, feel a just pride in being represented on the Bench of the Supreme Court by Judge Miller." The next day, Miller gave a rousing speech at a war meeting.[49]

Before leaving for Washington, Miller once again proved his commitment to a vigorous prosecution of the war. In August 1862, the Keokuk town council passed an ordinance requiring the city's residents to swear an oath of allegiance to the United States. Although Keokuk never suffered from the internecine warfare between Unionists and southern sympathizers that afflicted neighboring Missouri, plenty of former southerners still lived in town and their loyalty remained in doubt. The town council hoped to root out would-be Confederates with a test oath. Before heading east, Miller helped administer those oaths.[50] If Lincoln wanted a justice who would support his controversial war measures, he had picked the right man.

The fall of 1862 brought the announcement of another sweeping war measure by Lincoln—a preliminary Emancipation Proclamation. On September 22, the president declared that unless the Confederate states returned to the Union by January 1, 1863, he would issue a proclamation that slaves in the rebel states would "be then, thenceforward, and forever free." His emancipation plan reflected the new consensus among moderate Republicans that the cost of the war had escalated to the point where simply restoring the Union would not be enough. Something had to be done to strike at slavery, the institution that had caused the war. "The mere suppression of the rebellion will be an empty mockery of our sufferings and sacrifices," Congressman George Julian of Indiana asserted in January 1862, "if slavery shall be spared to canker the heart of the nation anew, and repeat its diabolical deeds." By midsummer 1862, with no end to the war in sight, all but the most conservative Republicans had reached this same conclusion. To avoid an appearance of desperation, Lincoln waited for a Union military victory to announce his plan. That victory finally came in September with the Union's bloody success at the battle of Antietam.[51]

The high costs of the war led Miller, like other Republicans, to support Lincoln's plan. Everyone recognized, Miller later wrote, that slavery caused the war, dividing the nation between "those who desired its curtailment and ultimate extinction and those who desired additional safeguards for its security and perpetuation." He asserted forcefully, "Whatever auxiliary causes may have contributed to bring about this war, undoubtedly the overshadowing and efficient cause was African slavery." As the war turned into a protracted struggle, limiting northern objectives solely to restoring the Union no longer made sense. Slavery, Miller felt, "perished as a necessity of the bitterness and force of the conflict. When the armies of freedom found themselves upon the soil of slavery they could do nothing less than free the poor victims whose enforced servitude was the foundation of the quarrel." A year and a half of catastrophic warfare had changed him from a moderate free-soiler to a full-blown emancipationist.[52]

The bravery of black soldiers who enlisted in the northern army after the Emancipation Proclamation also influenced him. African American soldiers played a crucial role in winning the war and defining its consequences. By the end of the war some 180,000 blacks served in the Union army—over one-fifth of the nation's adult black males of military age. These troops not only provided needed military manpower, but their courage in combat changed many northern whites' perceptions of African Americans. The valor of the 54th Massachusetts in the assault on Fort Wagner, South Carolina, in July 1863 gained national attention. After that battle, the *Atlantic Monthly* declared, the "manhood of the colored race shines before many eyes that would not see." Black troops from Iowa also served with distinction. Mustered and trained in Keokuk, the 60th U.S. Colored Infantry Regiment fought bravely at Wallace's Ferry in July 1864 and earned the respect of many whites. Miller joined his fellow Iowans in commending African American soldiers who, he thought, "proved themselves men" by fighting bravely for the Union cause.[53]

Yet the constitutionality of the Emancipation Proclamation remained uncertain. Many Republicans feared that the Supreme Court—a Court still dominated by Taney and the other *Dred Scott* justices—would strike it down. "The proclamation of 1863," abolitionist Wendell Phillips later wrote, was "to be filtered through the secessionist heart of a man whose body was in Baltimore and whose soul was in Richmond. It was to pass the ordeal of the bench of Judges who made the *Dred Scott* decision, and announced that a negro had no rights that a white man is bound to respect." Some commentators feared that Lincoln erred in freeing southern slaves by proclamation rather than by military order and that by opting against the latter, he created unnecessary constitutional questions. "It is a matter of utmost importance to the President, to the slaves, and to the country, that [the Emancipation Proclamation] should come in a form to be sustained," the *New York Times* cautioned two days after Lincoln officially issued it. "It must be a legal and constitutional act in form as well as substance." But even if Lincoln had made emancipation a military order, the measure still would have eventually faced an unsympathetic Supreme Court. Although the Court had yet to subject any of the president's war measures to its scrutiny, a showdown with the judiciary appeared unavoidable.[54]

The first case involving a Lincoln war measure reached the Supreme Court in February 1863, when the justices heard arguments in the *Prize Cases*. The plaintiffs challenged the constitutionality of one of Lincoln's earliest and most important orders—the blockade of the southern coastline. Intended to isolate the southern economy, Lincoln's April 1861 order authorized the U.S. Navy to capture any ship suspected of trading with the rebellious states and to claim all such ships and their cargoes as prizes of war. Initially, the blockade existed largely on paper only. With 3,500 miles of coastline to patrol, the small Union navy had little hope of sealing off every river, bay, sound, or inlet. In the conflict's first months, the northern navy managed to capture only one out of every ten ships that ran the blockade. Nevertheless, because of the severe penalties facing owners of seized ships, even a low number of captures led to significant litigation. This was particularly true in the early days of the war, when ship owners could claim that they had not received adequate notice that a blockade had been instituted.[55]

By late 1862, the Supreme Court had a number of blockade cases pending. For efficiency's sake, the most significant cases were grouped together and argued en bloc before the Court. Because the plaintiffs in these cases questioned Lincoln's authority to act without congressional approval, the fate of many of Lincoln's early war measures hung in the balance. Although Congress later officially sanctioned the blockade, it remained unclear whether a congressional resolution could legitimize a presidential measure after the fact.

The Court's decision in these cases—known collectively as the *Prize Cases*— would have a significant impact on the war's outcome. The blockade might prompt foreign intervention, since many of the seized ships belonged to foreign nationals. Moreover, if a blockade signaled a war between two sovereign powers, the Supreme Court would be hard pressed to declare the blockade legal without granting the Confederacy belligerent status. Consequently, the *Prize Cases* provided perilous challenges for the Union war effort and a singular opportunity for Taney and the Court to circumscribe Lincoln's power. Lincoln had to hope that his three new justices could convince at least two of their brethren to join an opinion that would somehow uphold the constitutionality of the blockade while denying the Confederacy sovereign status.[56]

Lincoln's hopes lay in the argumentative skills of Miller, Swayne, and his third appointee, David Davis, his Illinois friend and campaign manager. Lincoln appointed Davis in October 1862, selecting him over the previous frontrunner, Orville Browning, who as a senator lost ground by displaying lukewarm support for Lincoln's policies. As Browning's star faded, Davis's Illinois backers reminded Lincoln of the political debts he owed his former campaign strategist. Davis had provided invaluable advice and support during the 1860 election. Although he came from the conservative wing of the party, as an early Republican and friend of the president, he could be counted on to support Lincoln from the bench. No one viewed Davis as a great intellect or legal scholar, but his presence provided Republicans with added hope for a satisfactory decision in the blockade cases.[57]

Anxiety about the possible verdict spurred Congress to reconsider proposals first floated in 1862 to expand the size of the Court. In February, as the Court heard oral arguments in the *Prize Cases,* the Senate once again considered a plan to add a tenth justice, who would preside over a circuit consisting of California and Oregon. Solid arguments were made that a tenth justice would increase the Court's efficiency, while fears concerning the upcoming decision provided a new incentive for Republicans to approve such a proposal. Despite the fact that Lincoln had already appointed three justices, the Court still had a Democratic majority. Although any new appointee would arrive too late to affect the outcome of the *Prize Cases,* other lawsuits involving Lincoln's war measures were on the way.

Democratic papers warned their readers that the Republicans might try to tamper with the Court. The *New York World* cautioned Democrats "to keep a sleepless eye on the plot that is hatching to destroy the independence of the Supreme Court, by the creation of new abolition judges to outvote the present members." Democrats' concerns were well-founded. On February 25, 1863, the day after oral arguments concluded in the *Prize Cases,* the Senate approved a bill to add a tenth seat to the Court. On March 2, the House followed suit. President Lincoln approved the measure on March 3, one week before the announcement of the decision in the blockade cases. Unremitting in their efforts to create a safe majority on the Court, the Republicans thus scored another major victory. "This judge will be assigned to the Circuits on the Pacific Coast," the *New York Times* noted. "He, of course, adds one to the number which will speedily remove the control of the Supreme Court from the Taney School."[58]

On March 10, 1863, the Court announced its surprising decision in the *Prize Cases*. Miller, Swayne, and Davis joined Justices Grier and Wayne in a majority opinion that both validated the blockade and endorsed Lincoln's view that the Confederacy was not a sovereign nation. The decision was surprising because Grier and Wayne had both been members of the *Dred Scott* majority and were thought to be Taney's allies. Now both men displayed their apparent support for the Union cause. Wayne, a southerner and the senior member of the Court, returned to his ideological roots. No friend of Republicans, he nevertheless was a dyed-in-the-wool Jacksonian nationalist. In 1836, he had supported Jackson's force bill during the nullification crisis. Grier, a Polk appointee, proved to be similarly loyal to the Union. "We must conquer this rebellion or declare our republican government a failure," he wrote privately. The war should continue, he felt, even "if it should cost 100,000 men & 1000 millions of money." Both justices now joined a thin 5-4 majority in upholding the constitutionality of the blockade (and, implicitly, Lincoln's view of the war).[59]

In order to reach a decision, the justices wrestled with two prickly questions. First, they had to determine whether the president had the power to impose a blockade without congressional authorization. Some Democrats feared that granting such power might turn the president into a monarch. But the Court rejected those arguments and instead concluded that the president had the authority to act unilaterally in times of invasion, insurrection, or war if Congress was not in session. In cases of civil war, furthermore, the president did not need to wait for a formal declaration of war. "A Civil War is never solemnly declared," Grier wrote for the majority, "it becomes such by its accidents—the number, power, and organization of the persons who originate it and carry it on. . . . When the party in rebellion occupy and hold in a hostile manner a certain portion of territory; have declared their independence; have cast off their allegiance; have organized armies; have commenced hostilities against their former sovereign, the world acknowledges them as belligerents, and the contest a war." With or without an official declaration, a state of war existed, and Lincoln could act as he saw fit.[60]

This conclusion raised a second and even more difficult question. If the North and South were belligerents, was not the Confederacy by implication an independent state? In answering this question, the majority struck a delicate balance by emphasizing the unique nature of a civil war. Although hostilities might reach the level of a full-fledged war, the majority held that "it is not necessary to constitute war that both parties should be acknowledged as independent nations and sovereign states." The rebellious states could at once be belligerents subject to measures such as blockades and still be considered dependents of the United States. The Court thus provided Lincoln with a plausible legal footing on which to stand as he tried to discourage foreign powers from recognizing the Confederacy.[61]

Even though the outcome of the *Prize Cases* pleased Republicans, the margin of victory was dangerously thin. Had it not been for the recent appointments of Miller, Swayne, and Davis, the Court's decision in the case would have been markedly different. The four dissenters—Taney, Catron, Clifford, and Nelson—did not share the majority's support for the war. Nelson, for example, had privately expressed his hope that a peaceful separation could be achieved between North and South. He and his fellow dissenters sought to constrain Lincoln. The blockade, they concluded in a dissent written by Nelson, was unconstitutional. Only Congress could authorize such war measures.[62] And without a declaration of war, a blockade could not be legally instituted. While the majority contended that a state of war existed even though war had not been formally declared, the dissenters claimed that a blockade could be legally authorized only after a formal declaration of war. Although they acknowledged that hostilities of the "most extensive and threatening dimensions" had occurred, this had "no relevancy or weight when the question is what constitutes war in a legal sense, in the sense of the law of nations, and of the Constitution of the United States." Because Congress had not declared war, Nelson wrote, "I am compelled to the conclusion that no civil war existed between this government and the states in insurrection." Consequently, the government should return all vessels and cargoes seized in the spring of 1861 to their owners.[63]

The dissenters did concede that once Congress authorized the blockade in July 1861, it became constitutional and ships thenceforth could be legally seized. But the act of ordering a blockade, the minority continued, served as a declaration of war upon the Confederate states. "This act of Congress, we think, recognized a state of civil war between the government and the confederate states," Nelson wrote, "and made it a territorial one." The dissenters contended that

Congress had declared war simply by officially instituting the blockade and thus had granted the Confederate states belligerent status.[64]

Had the dissenters carried the day, the Union war effort might have been badly undermined. Assuming that Lincoln did not ignore the decision (as he had in *Merryman*), ships seized in the early months of the war would have been returned to their owners, and as of July 1861, the South would have had all the rights of a belligerent nation under international law. If European powers then formally recognized the Confederacy, they could have pointed to the ruling of the United States' own Supreme Court as providing a justification for their actions. Grier, Miller, and the other members of the majority instead provided Lincoln with a crucial constitutional victory and allowed him "to fight the war as if it were an international war, without actually having to recognize the de jure existence of the Confederate government."[65]

As the war went on and the blockade grew increasingly effective, Miller and the majority of his fellow justices unfailingly sanctioned an aggressive policy of seizures. By the end of the conflict, the Union navy captured one out of every two blockade-running ships. One such vessel was a leaky, worm-eaten ship, the *Cornelius*, that left New York City in June 1862 headed south. The ship's manifest listed its destination as Port Royal, South Carolina, an island that the Union had recaptured and was not subject to the blockade.[66]

In sailing to Port Royal, the *Cornelius* passed suspiciously close to Confederate-controlled Charleston harbor. Because of shortages, Charleston merchants rewarded blockade-running ships handsomely, providing a temptation for unscrupulous northern ship owners to sail towards Port Royal but then make a break for either Charleston or one of the many inlets nearby. On its voyage to Port Royal, the *Cornelius* appeared to be trying to do just that. When the ship veered towards Bull's Bay, a cove neighboring Charleston Harbor, the USS *Restless* fired a warning shot across the *Cornelius*'s bow. Chastened, the *Cornelius* then sailed on to Port Royal, where it partially unloaded its cargo and sat for three months while workmen attempted to repair its old hull. On October 10, 1862, the ship, still leaking badly, left Port Royal to return north. This time it cut sharply towards the shore as it neared Bull's Bay. The *Restless*, still patrolling those waters, again fired a warning shot, but this time the *Cornelius* did not stop. The *Cornelius*'s captain later claimed that his ship was sinking, and he was simply heading to a safe shore. Pursued by the *Restless*, the *Cornelius* eventually ran aground. The crew of the *Restless* seized the *Cornelius* and her cargo as prizes of war.[67]

The owners of the *Cornelius* sued for the return of their ship, but on appeal Miller and the Court had little sympathy for their claims. In his majority opinion in the case, Miller held that the *Cornelius's* suspicious behavior provided enough reason to seize the ship, even though northerners owned the vessel, its paperwork was in order, and its captain had offered a somewhat plausible excuse for his actions. "There are strong reasons to believe the vessel was started from New York on a simulated voyage to Port Royal," Miller wrote for the Court, "with intent to run the blockade before reaching that place." Although the ship might have been sinking, he argued, the captain's "safest course . . . was to approach the *Restless*, explain his condition, and ask for assistance. This duty he avoided, though he had full knowledge of the blockade, and when admonished by the shot from the *Restless*, he made every effort to escape by crowding sail and running toward the blockaded port." The owner of the *Cornelius* deserved to lose his ship and its cargo.[68]

Joining Miller's opinion in the *Cornelius* case was Lincoln's fourth appointee to the Court, Stephen J. Field of California. On the same day the Court announced its decision in the *Prize Cases*, Lincoln had nominated Field for the new Tenth Circuit. Although a Democrat, Field was a strategic choice. During the secession winter, he had publicly declared his allegiance to the Union and had urged his fellow Californians to do the same. Upon completion of the transcontinental telegraph in October 1861, one of the first messages Lincoln received came from Field, who assured Lincoln of California's continued fidelity. In addition, Field came highly recommended by his older brother, David Dudley Field, a barnburner Democrat turned Republican who had strong ties to the antislavery movement and was a key Lincoln supporter at the Republican convention in 1860. According to Field family lore, when Lincoln heard that David Field wanted his brother to get the Supreme Court nomination, he responded, "Does David want his brother to have it? . . . Then he shall have it." As a prowar Democrat of unquestionable loyalty, Field appeared to be a nominee whose appointment could both supplement the thin majority in war powers cases and deflect partisan charges that the president was packing the Court.[69]

Only later would it become evident that Lincoln's court appointments were men with radically divergent economic beliefs. In California, Field had long befriended propertied men and financiers. As chief justice of the California Supreme Court, Field had a knack for using Jacksonian rhetoric about liberty to defend the interests of the moneyed classes. Although his state court decisions helped bring order to chaotic California land titles, he consistently sided with large landholders rather than miners and settlers. Wealthy railroad men and financiers like Collis P. Huntington loved Field, and California governor and railroad magnate Leland Stanford actively urged his appointment. As Field now joined Swayne and the other economically conservative members of the Court, Miller and his Iowa river-town views grew more isolated.[70]

The extent of Miller's isolation soon became apparent. In *Gelpcke v. Dubuque*, a case that revealed the extremes to which the Court's majority was willing to go to side with the bondholders rather than indebted western towns, the justices took the dramatic step of refusing to follow the opinion of Iowa's highest court on a matter of state law. On June 18, 1862, Iowa's anti–railroad bond forces had won their greatest victory in the *Burlington and Missouri Railroad Company v. The County of Wapello* decision by the Iowa Supreme Court. That tribunal reversed its previous decisions and ruled that section 114 of the Iowa state code did not authorize city and county governments to issue bonds to pay for railroads. With one sweeping opinion, the Republican appointees who had gained control of Iowa's highest court denied the validity of the bonds and railroad stock subscriptions of the 1850s. Judge Ralph P. Lowe, a Republican from Keokuk, wrote the opinion for the court—an opinion that cleared Iowa river towns of all of their debilitating debts. Lowe recognized that "by so ruling, at this late date, we are liable to expose our people to the charge of insincerity and bad faith, and perhaps that which is still worse, inflict a great wrong upon innocent creditors and bondholders—consequences which we would most gladly have avoided, if we could have done so, and been true to the obligations of conscience and principle. Yet it is one of those unfortunate misadventures which sometimes will happen in the best governed and best intentioned communities."[71]

Bondholders, Lowe added, were not left totally without recourse. They could still hope that Iowans' "moral sense and public faith" would lead them to pay off the bonds. "These sentiments, we cannot but believe, still reside in the hearts and consciences of our people, and may be invoked to save themselves and their state from seeming bad faith." Given the pent-up animosity Iowans had for the bondholders, however, an appeal to their "moral sense and public faith" was not realistic. Outraged by the court's decision, aggrieved bondholders turned to the federal courts.[72]

The stunning *Wapello* decision set the stage for *Gelpcke v. Dubuque,* the first and best-known of the municipal bond cases decided by the United States Supreme Court during Miller's tenure.[73] *Gelpcke* involved railroad bonds issued by the Iowa river town of Dubuque during the 1850s. Like so many other Iowa towns, Dubuque defaulted on its bond payments and the bondholders sued to collect. When the case reached the U.S. Supreme Court, Dubuque's attorneys came armed with the Iowa Supreme Court's *Wapello* decision. The stakes were high, not just for Dubuque, but for all of Iowa's river towns. If the U.S. Supreme Court allowed the Iowa court's decision to stand, Iowa's river towns could start afresh. Having Miller on the Court provided Iowans with added hope for a favorable decision.

To strengthen his case that the *Wapello* decision freed Dubuque from its railroad debts, Dubuque's attorney pointed to the U.S. Supreme Court's 1862 decision in *Leffingwell v. Warren,* in which the Court unanimously held that federal courts were bound to follow the most recent interpretations given to state statutes and constitutional provisions by the highest court of that state. "The construction given to a statute of a State by the highest judicial tribunal of such State," Justice Swayne wrote in his majority opinion, "is regarded as part of the statute, and is as binding upon the courts of the United States as the text." This was true even if the state court's decision contradicted its previous decisions. In *Leffingwell,* Swayne said that such a reversal was the state court's prerogative. "If the highest judicial tribunal of a State adopt new views as to the proper construction of such a statute, and reverse its former decisions, this court will follow the latest settled adjudications."[74] Under the *Leffingwell* precedent, the Iowa Supreme Court's interpretation of Iowa's constitution had to be respected. Bondholders could only hope that the Court would somehow bypass *Leffingwell.*[75]

The bondholders got their wish. In his majority opinion in *Gelpcke,* Justice Swayne, who had authored *Leffingwell,* distinguished that case from the case at hand. *Leffingwell,* Swayne argued, applied only to "settled opinions" by state courts. Even though the Iowa court's decision in *Wapello* was unanimous, Swayne suggested that the issue could hardly be considered resolved. Instead, he argued that *Wapello* fell so far out of the mainstream that it could be dismissed as a dangerous and temporary anomaly. The U.S. Supreme Court need not follow "every such oscillation" of a state court, particularly when *Wapello* stood "in unenviable solitude and notoriety." For Swayne, justice and morality demanded that Dubuque pay its contractual obligations to innocent bondholders even at the expense of equally innocent taxpayers and state court precedent, his own *Leffingwell* doctrine be damned. "We shall never immolate truth, justice, and the law," he blustered, "because a state tribunal has erected the altar and decreed the sacrifice."[76]

Although Swayne's friends in the New York financial community may have cheered this decision, Miller did not. In a lengthy dissent, he called Swayne's language "unsuited to the dispassionate dignity of this court." State courts, Miller argued, had the exclusive right "to decide as a finality upon the construction of state constitutions and state statutes." By ignoring *Leffingwell,* Swayne and the majority had created a dangerous and confusing situation. Whose ruling, Miller asked, should government officials in Iowa now follow? Because Swayne's opinion applied only to federal courts, Iowa's state courts could still follow the state supreme court's *Wapello* decision that declared the bonds invalid. "Thus we are to have two courts," Miller warned, "sitting within the same jurisdiction, deciding upon the same rights, arising out of the same statute, yet always arriving at opposite results." This confusion would be introduced, he charged, simply to support the claims of rapacious bondholders. Unlike his brethren on the Court, Miller had little sympathy for the potential losses of a "gambling stockbroker of Wall Street [who] buys at twenty-five percent of their par value, the bonds issued to a railroad company, although the court of the state, in several of its most recent decisions have decided that such bonds were issued in violation of the constitution." Miller's was the lone voice of dissent.[77]

Miller soon had another chance to convince his judicial brethren of the error of their *Gelpcke* position. *Meyer v. City of Muscatine* arose from bonds that the Iowa river town of Muscatine had issued in order to buy stock in the Mississippi & Missouri Railroad. Muscatine's town charter authorized the town council to do such things as establish fire companies, build wharves, and grade and pave streets, but nowhere did the charter empower officials to build, fund, or buy stock in railroads. It did, however, authorize the town council to "borrow money for any object in its discretion." Even though the charter did not expressly authorize the funding of railroads, during the boom year of 1855 town officials invoked this clause in order to issue bonds, using the proceeds to subscribe to railroad stock. A small group of voters subsequently approved the decision. As was often the case with western bonds, the railroad sold the bonds to New York investors at steep discounts. After the Panic of 1857, Muscatine—like Keokuk—fell on hard times and could not pay interest due on the bonds. The bondholders sued to collect. In their defense, the taxpayers of Muscatine now claimed that the town's charter did not authorize the town council to issue the bonds, and even if it had, the bonds had been sold so far below value as to make the bargain unfair and invalid.[78]

When the case reached the U.S. Supreme Court, Muscatine's hard-pressed taxpayers received little sympathy from Swayne, Field, and the other members of the Court's pro-bondholder majority. In an 8 to 1 decision, Swayne delivered an opinion that rejected all of Muscatine's arguments. Swayne asserted that when the town's charter authorized officials "to borrow money for any object in its discretion," it did not refer only to those objects expressly delineated in the charter such as the "grading of streets." According to him, town officials could borrow money for any object whatsoever. Swayne also rejected Muscatine's argument that the railroad company had sold the bonds at a price so undervalued that the town should not be held to its obligation. "It does not appear anyone objected then, and no one can object now," he concluded. "After the bonds passed into the hands of the railroad company, the company was at liberty to sell them on such terms as it might deem proper."[79]

In his dissent, Miller reiterated his position in *Gelpcke* and said that it was fully applicable to this case as well. The Iowa Supreme Court had declared that municipal railroad bonds were invalid, and the *Leffingwell* doctrine required the United States Supreme Court to follow the decisions of state courts in matters of state law. Miller also took issue with Swayne's conclusion that the town's charter gave Muscatine officials unlimited discretion to borrow money. He pointed to the first fourteen paragraphs of the charter that gave officials authority to accomplish very specific tasks, such as building wharves or establishing firehouses. The fifteenth paragraph, he noted, then authorized them "to borrow money for any object in their discretion." "Nothing can be more reasonable," he continued, "than to suppose that the discretion so conferred was limited to the objects enumerated in the fourteen preceding paragraphs." Buying stock in railroads had not been included in those paragraphs, Miller added, "nor does any of them include anything from which railroad enterprises can possibly be implied." If Swayne was correct and town officials could borrow for any purpose whatsoever, those officials could now "borrow money to enter into the banking business, to speculate in gold, or flour, or grain, or to establish mercantile houses, or to build steamboats, and enter into the trade that flows past the city on the waters of the Mississippi River, or to organize mining companies in Colorado." The intent of the town's charter, Miller wrote, could not possibly be so far-reaching. "It makes every man's entire property, within the limits of the city, the common property of the community, and converts the citizen, against his will, into a member of one of those Shaker or French communities in which the individual merges his rights into those of the association." Swayne's reasoning, he concluded, was a "stretch of fancy, only to be indulged in railroad bond cases."[80]

The Court, Miller believed, had effectively declared war on the river towns. His fellow justices seemed not to care about the impact their decisions had on the lives of ordinary citizens. The Court's "latitudinary construction" in *Meyer* was an attempt to burden Iowans with a "debt of twenty millions of dollars, involving a ruin only equaled in this country by that visited upon the guilty participants in the current rebellion." And this destruction was carried out not by armies fighting in the name of freedom, but by judges defending the rights of New York bondholders and financiers.[81]

On October 12, 1864, Chief Justice Roger Taney died at the age of eighty-eight, having served on the Court for almost three decades. The very embodiment of the values of the antebellum Court, no justice evoked stronger emotions. Although Miller had come to respect Taney, other Republicans cheered the chief justice's death. "Providence has given us a victory," Charles Sumner wrote Lincoln. "Thus far the Constitution has been interpreted for slavery. . . . It may now be interpreted wholly for liberty." Many Republicans hoped that Taney's demise meant that the Court could finally move out from under the long shadow cast by *Dred Scott.* "Nobody doubts that Taney died," the *Philadelphia Press* concluded, "with his heart beating for the Rebellion."[82]

The chief justice's death gave Lincoln the opportunity to make a fifth appointment to the Court. He selected his secretary of the treasury, Salmon P. Chase, even though he believed Chase was an overly ambitious man who tirelessly connived for the presidency and who would continue to do so as chief justice. Chase, Miller later agreed, had "discipline, a warm heart and vigorous intellect, but all these usurped, perverted, shriveled by the selfishness generated by ambition." Chase's first thought upon meeting "any man of force," Miller believed, was "invariably how can I utilize him for my Presidential aspirations." Nonetheless, Lincoln knew he could count on Chase to support Republican measures vigorously. As secretary of the treasury, Chase had overseen the implementation of the controversial Legal Tender Act that created the country's first national currency. Chase also had the strongest antislavery views of any member of Lincoln's cabinet, and during the war Lincoln's racial views had evolved closer and closer to Chase's positions. Chase would thus be a positive force when the Court faced controversial issues regarding freed slaves. "We wish for a Chief Justice," Lincoln reportedly told Massachusetts congressman George Boutwell when he appointed Chase, "who will sustain what has been done in regard to emancipation and the legal tenders."[83]

Even with the appointment of Chase, Congress still did not trust the Court to uphold emancipation. In February 1865, with Lincoln's enthusiastic endorsement, Congress sent the proposed Thirteenth Amendment to the states for ratification. Designed to resolve any lingering doubts about the constitutionality of emancipation, the amendment also raised questions as to what black freedom would mean. It banned slavery or involuntary servitude anywhere within the United States except as a punishment for a crime, and it gave Congress power to enforce its provisions with appropriate legislation. But what kind of legislation would be deemed appropriate? Did the Thirteenth Amendment simply end slavery, or did it empower Congress to make sure that freedmen and women would not be treated as a separate caste? Many Republicans insisted that it did more than just abolish slavery: it provided blacks with full legal equality by barring states from passing laws that treated them differently than whites. Radicals like Charles Sumner went even further and argued that the amendment incorporated the Bill of Rights. Previously, the protections of the Bill of Rights had restrained only the federal government. Radicals now claimed that the Thirteenth Amendment empowered Congress and the federal courts to protect all the civil rights of African Americans from state action as well. Other Republicans disagreed, as they did not believe the amendment substantially altered federalism. The great debates that would continue throughout the era of Reconstruction had begun.[84]

In March 1865, Congress took a tentative step toward defining the parameters of black freedom when it passed the Freedmen's Bureau Act. This legislation created the Freedmen's Bureau, a civil-military hybrid that would help freed slaves and white refugees protect their legal rights and gain an economic foothold after the war. One of the bureau's major tasks would be to provide freedmen and -women with legal protection from racist customs and discriminatory enforcement of state criminal and civil laws. The new agency would create "bureau courts" as an alternative to biased local tribunals. These courts would handle both civil and criminal matters, punishing violence against blacks, handling disputes between black workers and white employers, and protecting the freedmen's new rights to marry, sign contracts, and testify in legal proceedings. Hobbled from the start by lack of funding, the bureau ultimately lacked the necessary means to address the needs of millions of freedmen. Nevertheless, the Freedmen's Bureau Act revealed that Congress did not want simply to end slavery and then turn African Americans' fate over to their former masters.[85]

On April 11, 1865, with the war winding down, Lincoln weighed in on the question of black freedom in a speech at the White House. Blacks, Lincoln felt, deserved full civil rights. By civil rights he meant that blacks deserved legal rights such as the ability to contract, sue, and acquire wealth. African Americans, in other words, should have full equality in their ability to rise economically. Lincoln also suggested that at least some African Americans should have the right to vote. "I myself prefer," he said of black suffrage, "that it were now conferred on the very intelligent, and on those who serve our cause as soldiers." Whether he would have insisted that black voting rights be a part of Reconstruction is a question that has long intrigued historians and that will never be fully answered. Three days after this speech, Lincoln was assassinated.[86]

A significant part of Lincoln's legacy was his five appointees to the Supreme Court, men he chose because of their shared commitment to the Union and the war effort. When the war ended in April 1865, war issues would be replaced by those of Reconstruction and of a society grappling with the jarring changes produced by industrialization and urbanization. As a result, the five men who in a national emergency had agreed on the need for Lincoln's war measures would find out how different their peacetime visions for the country were. At Appomattox, Miller and his fellow justices stood at a crossroads. All born in a small-scale agrarian America, they now would serve in an age of iron and steel, giant cities and factories, Newport mansions and urban squalor. Justices who came of age in a world of competitive capitalism would adjudicate the disputes spawned by a world of large-scale industry, concentrated capital, and labor unrest. For his part, Miller still held faith in the Republican free-labor ideology that he and Lincoln had embraced in the 1850s. Although this ideology had already been rendered obsolete by the industrial revolution, Miller believed it remained viable. If the former slaveholders and eastern capitalists could be constrained, the heady days of social fluidity that he once knew in Keokuk and Barbourville might return.[87]

Samuel Freeman Miller in the 1860s   *Library of Congress*

Antebellum Keokuk *State Historical Society of Iowa*

The Rock Island bridge at Davenport was the first bridge across the Mississippi River and the focal point of one of Miller's major cases as an Iowa attorney. *State Historical Society of Iowa*

Intended to be a grand hotel, the Estes House in Keokuk foundered on the rocks of
the Panic of 1857. At the time of this Civil War drawing, it was a military hospital for
the Union army.   *State Historical Society of Iowa*

Above and top of facing page: A panoramic photograph taken in 1907 at the corner of
Third and Main in Keokuk showed a town that had changed little since the 1850s.
Library of Congress

Abraham Lincoln in 1858, two weeks before the final
Lincoln-Douglas debate. *Library of Congress*

An 1860 political cartoon lampooned the impact of the Dred Scott decision on the presidential race. *Library of Congress*

The 1868 Senate impeachment trial of President Andrew Johnson as depicted in *Harper's Weekly* magazine. *Library of Congress*

The March 10, 1877, issue of *Frank Leslie's Illustrated Newspaper* purported to show a secret candlelight meeting of the presidential electoral commission. Miller is shown seated, second from right, near the far end of the table. *Library of Congress*

The justices of the U.S. Supreme Court in 1888   *Library of Congress*

Miller's respected colleague and politico-philosophical enemy Justice Stephen J. Field in 1890. *Library of Congress*

Miller in the 1880s   *State Historical Society of Iowa*

CHAPTER 5

The Consequences Attendant upon Treason

W ITH THE CONFEDERACY DEFEATED, southerners expected the
worst. Northern troops occupied southern soil and the once-proud,
now demoralized, southerners waited to see what social, political, and economic
changes the nation's new president, Andrew Johnson, would force upon their
region. With Congress adjourned for eight months, Johnson would set the tone
for the course of Reconstruction. If he immediately demanded significant
changes in the South, the beaten rebels might see no choice but to acquiesce.
The president had a unique opportunity to reshape the supine South that, if not
seized, could easily be lost.

At the outset, both Radical and moderate Republicans had high hopes for
the new administration. While Johnson favored leniency toward common
southern soldiers, whom he saw as misguided victims of planters' propaganda,
his legendary hatred for aristocratic southern planters led Republicans to believe
that he would propose tough policies for reconstructing southern society. Born
into poverty, poorly educated, and socially unrefined, Johnson detested the
wealthy planters who had snubbed him throughout his life. He called the
planter class a "pampered, bloated, corrupted aristocracy." In Tennessee politics,
Johnson envisioned himself as the champion of small, non-slaveholding farmers. In 1861 he gained national prominence as the only southern senator who
opposed secession and remained loyal to the Union.[1]

Johnson blamed the planters for the war and branded them as traitors. During the conflict, he insisted that the planters' betrayal of the Union warranted
harsh punishments, including the confiscation and redistribution of their lands.
"Treason must be made odious," he declared in 1864, "and traitors must be pun-

ished and impoverished." He also left open the possibility of wholesale treason trials and death sentences for rebel leaders. "I would arrest them," Johnson said of Confederate leaders. "I would try them, I would convict them, and I would hang them."[2]

Given his tough talk, Radical Republicans spent the first month of Johnson's administration believing that he shared their goals. In previous statements, Johnson had revealed compassion for the plight of the freed slaves; upon assuming the presidency, he had assured Radicals of his commitment to providing justice for freedmen and women. But few seemed to notice how vague he remained about specifics. He had not, for example, embraced black male suffrage—Radicals' sine qua non for Reconstruction. Nevertheless, Radical senator Charles Sumner convinced himself that Johnson supported full equality for black men. In the spring of 1865, Sumner described the new president as the "sincere friend of the negro and ready to act for him decisively."[3]

Justice Miller also had high expectations for Johnson's presidency. Although often immersed in his responsibilities on the Court, he closely followed the unfolding political drama of Reconstruction. He particularly liked Johnson's punitive plans for the leaders of the former Confederacy. Ever since the outbreak of war, Miller had insisted on the need to punish treasonous rebel officers and politicians, and his anger towards secessionists only increased as the war grew in intensity and bitterness. Now that victory belonged to the Union, Miller wanted swift and effective retribution. He rejected the views of conservative Republicans who called for a speedy reconciliation between the sections and instead hoped that Johnson would disenfranchise, bankrupt, and, in some cases, try and hang prominent southerners.

Miller's views on race and Reconstruction continued to evolve after Appomattox, as revealed by an extraordinary series of letters with his former brother-in-law, William Pitt Ballinger. Ballinger, a lawyer, judge, and antebellum slaveholder, had supported the Confederacy, and the two men's relationship had been nearly severed by the war. Although they subsequently reconciled, Miller—always candid—did not sugarcoat his anger toward the South. In his letters to Ballinger, Miller laid out his views on Reconstruction and postwar politics in blunt and powerful language. When Ballinger suggested that the country would benefit from a quick and lenient Reconstruction, Miller balked. Ballinger naturally favored a sweeping amnesty and pardons for Confederate leaders (himself included). Pardons and amnesty, he told Miller, would create the goodwill necessary for a smooth restoration of the Union. But Miller summarily rejected this view and let Ballinger know that when it came to Confederate leaders, he was not particularly interested in goodwill or reconciliation. He wanted at least some traitors executed. "I cannot regard the men who participated in this rebellion, as having incurred no personal guilt," he wrote. "They violated a well known existing law whose penalty is death. This heavy penalty is imposed because of the awful consequences usually attendant upon treason." If anyone needed evidence of treason's dreadful outcome, it had "been furnished by the misery and horror incapable of description which have attended this rebellion!"[4]

In calling for trials and executions of top Confederates, Miller fell outside of the Republican Party mainstream. Few Republican leaders, Radical or otherwise, wanted Jefferson Davis and his followers to die for their crimes. Only the most extreme supported Ohio senator Benjamin Wade when he said he wanted to "force into exile or hang about ten or twelve of the worst of the fellows."[5] Miller shared Wade's view and advocated the "penalty of death" for a "half dozen of the most *prominent* and most *wicked*" Confederates. He believed those men had "been governed alone by a selfish and wicked personal ambition" and now should pay the ultimate price. Miller even asserted that if Ballinger himself had been a key leader of the rebellion, he would advocate the same fate. Despite "my affection for you," he told his Texas ex-brother-in-law, "I cannot less deny . . . that you should suffer the highest punishment that the law provides for all."[6]

While Miller limited his desire for capital punishment to the highest ranking Confederates, he favored stiff measures to ensure that lower-ranking rebel leaders would never return to political power. Although subordinate Confederate officials and officers had also committed treason, Miller recognized that widespread and prolonged trials would be unwieldy and counterproductive. Executing a handful of top leaders would send a clear enough message to future would-be secessionists. Yet since lower-ranking rebels had aided what he called the "great crime of the age," they too needed to be punished and barred from power. Ballinger naturally disagreed and tried to persuade Miller that allowing ex-Confederates to regain power would promote reconciliation and stability. Miller, in turn, suspected that the reverse would be true—that forgiven secessionists would soon return to their old mischief. "It is my profound conviction," he wrote, that allowing the leaders of the Old South to return to political power would "prolong indefinitely the struggle which led to the war, and . . . would occasion its early renewal." He doubted whether the rebel leaders had lost their "ambition to become leaders of a southern aristocracy" and feared that if restored to power, they would once again foment animosity between North and South. That is what they had always done, he reasoned, and that is what they would do again if given another chance. Like the slave-power conspirators of old, the "forgiven" rebels would seize upon "any occasion of weakness in [the] government, as a foreign war, [or] an imbecile or treacherous President" to promote secession again. "Their constant effort," he predicted, "would be as it has been for many years, to stir up strife between northern and southern interests."[7]

Miller wanted ex-Confederate leaders ostracized, barred from power, and closely watched. They should be kept "in a condition where they can exercise no *legitimate* influence on popular opinion, where they can hold no office, and by depriving them of all of their property by confiscation in cases when they show a sullen or an evil tendency, I would cripple their influence in all possible ways." He wanted rebel leaders to be "steadily branded as objects of suspicion," not pardoned. As he wrote, by "holding their lives and property at the mercy of the government, they would soon either leave it, or become engaged in active efforts to prove their devotion to it. . . . In short, I believe in the policy of committing the political power of the rebellious states to other hands than those which have caused the rebellion."[8]

If Confederate leaders chafed under these policies, Miller hoped they would do the country a great favor and leave. Like the Radical Thaddeus Stevens, Miller suggested that an added benefit of punitive reconstruction policies might be that disgruntled ex-Confederates would exit the country in disgust. "If they go, all the better," Stevens remarked in September 1865, adding that it would be "easier and more beneficial to exile seventy thousand proud, bloated and defiant rebels" than to try to placate them at the expense of other goals. Miller shared this view. "The duty these men owe to the people whom they have misled is obvious," he remarked. "It is either to leave the country, . . . or otherwise to come forward actively as the advocates of any policy which the government . . . may deem necessary for the pacification of the country." But he resigned himself to the fact that "very few of them will be found equal to either of these courses" and that a voluntary exodus of unrepentant rebels was unlikely.[9]

The only group to whom Miller would extend clemency were the poor white foot soldiers who had constituted the Confederate army. He believed that the common soldier had been misled by secessionist politicians and therefore deserved less blame for the war (a rationale that also would spare Republicans the practical problems associated with disenfranchising hundreds of thousands of southern whites). But he conditioned amnesty and pardons for common soldiers upon evidence of genuine repentance and a willingness to embrace a new political, social, and economic order in the South. "I think that towards them," he wrote of rank-and-file Confederates, the government should provide "clemency, liberality, forgiveness, and a restoration to their civil rights as soon as they *abandon their former leaders* and evince a sincere intention to yield slavery, and give a true and loyal support to the federal government" (emphasis Miller's). If they did not do so, and Reconstruction dragged on and on, so be it. "I do not believe in the necessity or policy of a *speedy* reconstruction," Miller warned. "And such I believe is the *growing* sentiment of the north."[10]

To Miller's dismay, portions of President Johnson's first major statement of postwar policy seemed unduly lenient. Under the president's May 1865 "Proclamation of Amnesty and Pardon," rank-and-file Confederates would be immediately pardoned if they swore an oath of future allegiance and promised to obey the Emancipation Proclamation. Miller would have delayed such a sweeping amnesty until southerners displayed true repentance. But other aspects of Johnson's policy were more punitive. People who held positions of authority in the Confederacy, those who left federal government positions to join the rebellion, and former rebels who owned property worth $20,000 or more were barred from public life and prevented from practicing licensed professions. Their property might be confiscated, and they could be tried for treason and executed. If rigorously pursued, Johnson's policies promised to decrease significantly the influence of the South's old elites. And while members of that elite, including former Confederate officials, could apply to the president for pardons on an individual basis, Johnson's history of animosity toward wealthy southerners suggested that large numbers of clemency proclamations would not be forthcoming.[11]

Initially, Johnson's Reconstruction policies met with overwhelming northern support. Many believed that the president's measures, stringently applied, would bring meaningful change to the South. At least initially, wealthy southerners did think that a day of judgment was at hand. Many planters genuinely feared that Johnson might demand treason trials, plantation confiscations, and land redistribution. Republicans, hoping that he would do just that, praised his early pronouncements.

Not everyone applauded Johnson, however. Republican Radicals like Sumner and Stevens, who had hoped Johnson would endorse suffrage for freedmen, now recognized that the new president did not fully share their political vision. Although Stevens, Sumner, and other Radicals often argued among themselves about the details of particular Reconstruction policies (for example, the extent of land to be confiscated and redistributed), they all agreed that authentic change could not come without giving black men the right to vote. When Johnson's early Reconstruction proclamation failed even to mention black suffrage, some Radicals turned against him.

The Radicals who opposed Johnson after May 1865 remained a minority within the party. Most Republicans, including Miller, had yet to commit to the idea of black suffrage and feared splitting the party over the issue. Moderate Republicans wanted the old order in the South destroyed, but they had not concluded that universal suffrage was essential to the process. Instead, they wanted to wait and see how effective Johnson's policies would be. If his policies failed, they could always be modified later. Johnson himself assured moderates that his program was only temporary. As a result, a broad coalition embraced his goals, and he went about the task of appointing provisional governors in the occupied states to oversee his version of Reconstruction.[12]

By the early fall of 1865, however, Johnson's actions had led even moderate Republicans to question his commitment to genuine change in the South. Despite the president's tough rhetoric about punishing rebel leaders, the army arrested only a few high-ranking Confederates, and only one, Henry Wirz (commandant of the infamous prison camp at Andersonville), was put on trial and executed. In most cases, planters had their property returned rather than confiscated. And much to everyone's surprise, Johnson readily granted thousands of pardons—sometimes hundreds in a single day—to wealthy ex-Confederates. Despite his previous criticisms of aristocratic slaveholders, Johnson quickly pardoned over seven thousand southerners who would otherwise have been denied amnesty under the $20,000 clause.[13]

Johnson seemed determined to complete the process of Reconstruction before Congress returned in December. He ordered his provisional governors in the southern states immediately to initiate special elections to elect delegates for constitutional conventions. The conventions would be required to repudiate secession and renounce slavery, but that was all. Provisional governors could then hold elections to select a full slate of officials, from county legislators to congressmen. At that point, Reconstruction would be finished, after only a few short months. It was, as historians have noted, the most spectacular exhibition of unilateral national executive authority in American history. Johnson, it appeared, was trying to circumnavigate Congress completely.[14]

White southerners breathed a collective sigh of relief in the summer and fall of 1865. Most had expected much harsher terms from the North. "In the immediate aftermath of defeat," one historian has written, "a considerable number of southerners had been prepared to acquiesce in whatever directives emerged from Washington." The mildness of Johnson's terms restored southerners' old confidence. As Miller had predicted, impertinent talk of states' rights re-emerged. Ballinger's claim that leniency would lead to an atmosphere of goodwill and cooperation proved badly off the mark.[15]

When the southern state conventions met in the summer of 1865 to draft new constitutions, the delegates adopted an air of defiance. Rather than graciously accepting Johnson's lenient terms and at least feigning contrition, they seemed determined to prove that they had not been subjugated. The simple requirement of renouncing secession seemed too much for many delegates to swallow, even though northerners considered this a non-negotiable requirement. Northerners insisted that the southern states had to declare their secession ordinances illegitimate, thereby repudiating the whole doctrine of secession and displaying at least a modicum of repentance. But many members of the southern conventions instead suggested repealing rather than renouncing the secession ordinances. More than a semantic difference was at stake in these proposals. Repealing rather than renouncing secession implied that the ordinances were legitimate at the time of their enactment—a position that could be useful to future secession movements.

As he read reports of the debates in the southern conventions, Miller grew livid. Reflecting the anger of most northerners, he told Ballinger that the doctrine of secession was illegal and must be explicitly forsworn. Allowing southerners to cling to the myth of secession's legality, Miller feared, would bear "pernicious fruits." Left unrepudiated, the secession doctrine meant that "whenever in our history it shall happen again that on some point of practical value, the governing majority shall differ in considerable view with the minority, north or south, that minority may resort to arms to maintain their views. . . . This doctrine contains a standing invitation to revolution, and can be tolerated by no government which expects to be . . . more than a temporary arrangement of convenience." The constitutional system provided Americans with stability, prosperity, democracy, and the rule of law. The doctrine of secession threatened to make the United States as unstable as "Mexico and the South American Republics."[16]

Despite admonitions from Republicans like Miller, many members of the southern conventions refused to back down. Their intransigence did not bode well for the future of Johnson's Reconstruction policies, for they were as moderate a group as the old order in the South had to offer. Because the conventions met before Johnson had pardoned most high Confederate officials and men of wealth, most of the delegates were former Whigs who had supported the Confederacy only after their home states had left the Union. If these men were unrepentant, what could be expected from the South as one avid secessionist after another regained his citizenship? After much debate, only North Carolina, Florida, and Mississippi heeded northern opinion and agreed to nullify their secession ordinances. Other conventions tried to obfuscate the issue by declaring the secession ordinances null and void as of 1865. And South Carolina and Georgia, defiant as ever, merely repealed their secession ordinances without renouncing them. This defense of the "dead issue of secession," one historian has commented, "revealed a postwar southern leadership at its most inept: prideful, arrogant, and blinded by the constitutional dogma of the past." Although for many northerners the actions of the southern conventions provided the first warnings that Johnson's lenient polices might backfire, the president, for his part, was satisfied. All the state conventions had, in some way, forsaken secession and abolished slavery. To Johnson these seemed major concessions, and he encouraged his provisional governments to take the next step and elect state legislators, governors, and members of Congress.[17]

The ensuing elections confirmed northerners' worst fears about the intractability of white southerners. Many northerners had once believed that a large group of unconditional Unionists—men whom the Confederates had suppressed and persecuted during the war—existed in the South, and that they would now step forward to take control of the reconstructed governments. But southerners instead filled their state legislatures with unrepentant former Confederates, exposing the fact that a critical mass of white Unionists in the South had never existed.[18] The new southern congressional delegations included ten

Confederate generals, nine Confederate congressmen, and the one-time vice president of the Confederacy, Alexander Stephens.[19]

In southern statehouses, moreover, legislators reaffirmed their lack of contrition by immediately attempting to legitimize their states' war debts. During the war, individual Confederate states had amassed a total of $54 million in debt. Wealthy southerners who had loaned much of this money now wanted to be paid back. While the states' combined debt paled in comparison to the $700 million in notes, bonds, and securities issued by the Confederate government in Richmond, everyone recognized that with the death of the Confederate States of America those larger investments had been irretrievably lost. But because the individual state governments continued to exist, those who held state notes "tenaciously fought to salvage a portion" of their investments. In doing so, the newly elected legislators displayed a complete lack of understanding of the consequences of the war. They failed to recognize that northerners considered these debts immoral and "irrevocably tainted with the odor of rebellion." Southerners' attempts to collect on them revealed yet again a total lack of repentance.[20]

Southern legislators also griped about the clause of the Thirteenth Amendment that gave Congress power to enforce the amendment by passing "appropriate legislation." They feared the enforcement clause would bring endless federal interference in state affairs. As a result, even though Johnson's Reconstruction policy required the southern states to ratify the amendment, the ratification process proceeded slowly, if at all. This recalcitrance deepened northern ire. The South had lost a war that it had started and should, northerners felt, immediately accept the winner's terms. It was only through the intervention of Secretary of State William Seward, who pressured provisional governors to ratify the amendment or face indefinite military rule, that all southern states except Florida and Texas capitulated.[21]

But even as southern legislators ratified the Thirteenth Amendment, they passed the quickly infamous Black Codes, laws designed to make African Americans a legally subjugated class. When white southerners peered out at their world at the end of the Civil War, they saw a terrifying landscape of depleted plantations, empty slave quarters, and roads choked with recently freed men and women whom southerners believed were angry, lawless, and shiftless. Accordingly, they sought a legal means to restore some semblance of the old order and to ensure a productive, pliant, and deferential workforce. The central assumption underlying the Black Codes was that former slaves were lazy and had to be forced to work. White southerners remained skeptical of the northern system of free labor that emphasized incentives over compulsion. With slavery destroyed, southern legislators sought new ways to coerce labor out of freedmen and women. While the Black Codes did include some concessions to African Americans' freedom (blacks could now acquire property, make contracts, get married, and sue and be sued), they also included an elaborate body of laws meant to force blacks into agricultural labor and place them in a separate social caste. The new laws required blacks to sign agricultural contracts at the start of each year and honor those contracts or face severe criminal penalties. Each January in Mississippi, for example, blacks had to have written proof of employment for the coming year. If they did not, they could be charged with vagrancy and punished by fines or involuntary plantation labor. In Louisiana, a freedman who signed a labor contract could be fined or jailed for "bad work," "leaving home without permission," or "impudence, swearing, or indecent language to or in the presence of the employer, his family, or agent." Apprentice clauses placed black minors from poor families under white employers' control. Other statutes forbade blacks from owning firearms, serving on juries, or pursuing certain occupations and professions. Disgusted northerners regarded the Black Codes as a return to slavery.[22]

Southern courts also proved racist, biased, obstructionist, and oblivious to northern opinion. Southern judges and law enforcement officials zealously enforced the Black Codes but looked the other way when ex-rebels committed violent crimes against blacks and white Unionists. State courts forbade testimony by blacks, making crimes against African Americans nearly impossible to prove. Black veterans of the Union army were particular targets of unpunished violence. When the Freedmen's Bureau and the Union army responded to these inequities by creating special courts and military commissions where blacks could receive justice, state officials charged bureau and army personnel with civil and criminal sanctions for interfering with the Black Codes.[23]

The actions of white southerners in the summer and fall of 1865 left most Republicans horrified. What had the war been fought for, they wondered? As a northern editor remarked, in the state legislatures and U.S. Congress the rebels were "all to be let back . . . and made a power in the government again, just as though there had been no rebellion."[24] Southerners seemed blind to the consequences of the war and were, in the words of historian John Hope Franklin, "pursuing most of their prewar policies as though there had been no war." Even one of Johnson's cabinet members lamented in 1865 that the "entire South seems to be stupid and vindictive."[25]

Miller hated the Black Codes. "The laws proposed by Mississippi, Alabama, South Carolina, &c.," he wrote Ballinger, "do but change the form of slavery. As it *was*, the individual slave belonged to, and laboured for the individual white man. As it is *proposed to be*, the whole body of the negro race in each state, must belong to and labour for the whole body of the white people of that state, under compulsion of law." He had little patience for southerners' argument that blacks were naturally indolent and would only work under compulsion. "The pretence," Miller acerbically noted, "is that the negro won't work without being compelled to do so, and this pretence is made in a country and by the white people, where the negro has done all the work for four generations, and where the white man makes a boast of the fact that *he* will *not* labour."[26]

Radical Republicans responded to the white South's intransigence by trying to convince Republican moderates like Miller that the only way truly to reconstruct the rebel states was through black suffrage. Southerners' behavior, Radicals argued in the fall of 1865, plainly established that suffrage was the necessary next step. Although increasingly receptive to this argument, moderates still feared forcing a decisive break with Johnson. Most moderates came from border states or the southern parts of Illinois, Indiana, Ohio, and Iowa, places where success often hinged on compromise and restraint. Fearful of splitting the party on the suffrage issue, moderates trusted their political instincts, which told them to seek some sort of compromise with the president. To do otherwise, men such as Senators James G. Blaine, John Bingham, and John Sherman feared, would divide the Republicans and offer the Democrats an opportunity to regain power. If that happened, all hope for change in the South would be lost. For this reason, even some Radicals recommended against breaking with Johnson. "We ought to do all in our power," Radical senator Jacob Howard advised in November, "to keep him with us."[27]

Moderate Republicans also recognized that most northerners had not yet embraced the principle of black suffrage. Advocating universal suffrage would move their party perilously ahead of public opinion in the North, where blacks still could not vote in most states. Moreover, many moderates still hoped to create a stable Republican Party in the South by attracting forward-looking white southerners to their cause. Black suffrage would kill those plans. They therefore searched for solutions that would provide more protections for black civil rights without giving African Americans the right to vote.[28]

While Miller feared that black suffrage might be politically impracticable, he was not opposed to the idea in principle. In his private correspondence, he proposed a unique plan that would allow men, and possibly women, to vote. "If I had it in my power to make any modification on this subject . . . ," Miller wrote in February 1866, "I would allow every person (perhaps women about which I am not clear) to vote for members of the state legislatures and for members of the House of Rep in Congress." At the same time, he would "have no person whose duty it is to enforce or administer the law dependent for his office on the popular voice." Thus he would "remove Presidents, Governors, Judges, Sheriffs . . . from the class of persons elected by the general voice." Miller knew that such a plan was merely a stretch of fancy. "I have no time to elaborate this abstraction," he concluded, "which is never likely to become a practical question in my time." Instead, he let pragmatic political considerations shape his views.[29]

Miller and other moderates hoped that upon the return of Congress in December, Republican congressional leaders could convince President Johnson that his Reconstruction policies needed substantial modification. After all, Johnson had claimed that his program could be reformed if need be. The moderates failed to recognize, however, that Johnson believed that he had already reconstructed the South. Men who had accepted the end of slavery and had sworn future loyalty to the Union controlled his provisional governments; only a year earlier, this would have been virtually unthinkable. Moderates nonetheless hoped that once Johnson got beyond self-congratulation, even he would recognize that more had to be done to protect blacks' fundamental rights. Miller reflected moderate opinion when he predicted that Johnson would embrace the emerging Republican consensus. "As far as I can form an opinion the President will not break with the majority . . . if he can avoid it," he conjectured, adding that Johnson "will make every concession consistent with any due regard to his personal dignity, and his own convictions of his duty. I believe that he will assent to almost any means of securing the civil rights of the negro, short of imposing negro suffrage on the states in rebellion against their will."[30]

One issue upon which Republicans uniformly agreed was that the ex-rebels should not be allowed to return to Congress. When the Thirty-Ninth Congress opened in December 1865, Republicans, citing the constitutional right of that body to determine the qualifications of its own members, refused to seat the

Confederate-filled delegations elected by the southern states. Congress insisted that its "ironclad test oath" of past as well as future loyalty remained in effect. As a result, the secretaries of the House and Senate purposefully omitted southerners' names at the opening roll call. Miller cheered this decision and agreed that Congress had the right to bar the ex-rebels. To admit them would mean that, for all intents and purposes, Reconstruction had come to a close. In Miller's view, it was far too early to declare Reconstruction over. At the very least, he wanted to deny congressional admission to southerners as long as the Black Codes remained in place. "One thing . . . I think is clear," he told Ballinger in January 1866, "there is no hope for southern members being admitted into this Congress, unless some security is given against the manifest intent thus far shown by every southern state, to refuse to place the negro on an equality with the white man in all his civil rights. The power to make laws which are to operate on the black man and not on the white, will be taken from those states, before the present Congress will admit their delegations. This may be relied on."[31]

With southerners excluded from the Congress, Republicans outnumbered Democrats three to one, dominating both houses. If they remained united, they could dictate their own Reconstruction policy even over Johnson's vetoes. Moderates hoped that Congress would devise a compromise civil rights measure that could earn the president's support. But given the volatile environment, many feared the debate might turn ugly and hopelessly divide the Republican forces. "The discussion on reconstruction is just opened in both houses," Miller fretted in early January 1866, "and promises to be . . . somewhat bitter."[32]

Miller worried that Congress would split into four factions, three "whose powers of mischief" were "very great." "The most potent of these," he thought, were those Radicals who had "no faith in the President giving aid to their policy, and who desire to precipitate a rupture." These "impracticables" included men like Sumner, Stevens, and others who refused all compromises. Unlike the moderates, the Radicals hailed from New England and regions in the path of the New England migration, such as upstate New York, Ohio's Western Reserve, and northern Illinois. In these districts, which had few settlers from southern backgrounds, political success could often come without compromise. Hence the Radicals did not face the political constraints encountered by moderate Republicans and could insist on uncompromising and potentially divisive measures. "If Sumner and Stevens, and a few other such men do not embroil us with the President," moderate senator William Pitt Fessenden believed, "matters can be satisfactorily arranged—satisfactorily, I mean, to the great bulk of Union men throughout the states."[33]

Miller also worried that some conservative Republicans might urge Johnson not to compromise. "The next most mischievous class is composed of certain men who are Republicans," he noted, "but are anxious to signalise themselves as special friends of the President and his policy, in order that they may monopolize the executive patronage." This group, led by Johnson's staunchest defenders—James Dixon, Edgar Corwin, and James Doolittle—often claimed they knew the president's mind, although Miller suspected otherwise. "These [men] while claiming to speak for the president and thus making him . . . responsible for their utterances, really know little more of his views than I do." If these "Johnson conservatives" claimed the president was not willing to budge on black civil rights, they, too, could quickly polarize the debate. The conservatives were most likely to ally with the third faction Miller feared, the Democrats, who would do all they could to foster and exploit differences among the Republicans. The "only hope of a return of their party to power," Miller allowed, was "in the breakup of the great party which has suppressed . . . the rebellion against their wishes and efforts."[34]

As the Reconstruction debate opened, Miller placed his faith in the Republican moderates who hoped to bring President Johnson back into the fold while providing new protections for the civil rights of freedmen and women. "There is . . . a large body of influential republicans," Miller wrote, "who are determined that the civil rights of the negro must be rendered safe, before the members from those states are permitted to take part in the legislation of Congress; but who are quite anxious to prevent a rupture with the President. I hope much for them and [Johnson]."[35]

The key moderate leader in the Reconstruction debates was Senator Lyman Trumbull of Illinois. Trumbull, like Miller, had initially supported Johnson's policies, but his views had slowly turned against them. He did not support black suffrage, yet by January 1866 the excesses of white southerners had convinced him of the need for further federal measures to ensure southern unionism and to protect blacks' civil rights. His support for such measures reflected a larger trend among Republicans. White southern intransigence and Johnson's lack of concern for blacks' rights had pushed the party's center of gravity to the left.[36]

On January 5, 1866, Trumbull introduced two major Reconstruction bills.

The first indefinitely extended the life of the Freedmen's Bureau and gave the agency its first direct funding. Initially envisioned as a one-year operation, the bureau would now become a fixture in southern life for the foreseeable future. The bill made a gesture toward providing freedmen with land by authorizing three million acres of public land in the South for homesteading by blacks. But the bill's most important feature assigned an official law enforcement role to the bureau. To combat the numerous state and local laws, police regulations, customs, and other practices in the South that denied blacks the same civil rights or immunities as whites, jurisdiction would now be officially given to Freedmen's Bureau courts to handle such cases. If local laws denied blacks the right to contract, sue, give evidence in court, or bear arms, African Americans could turn to the bureau's courts for justice. In addition, the bureau would claim jurisdiction if state or local criminal codes subjected blacks to different punishments than whites for committing the same illegal acts. The bureau, furthermore, would provide military protection to African Americans and loyal whites threatened by political and racial violence.[37]

Trumbull supplemented the Freedmen's Bureau bill with a Civil Rights Bill that would extinguish the Black Codes and provide blacks with equal rights under the law. It stipulated that any citizen born in any state, regardless of that person's color, would get full and equal benefit of its laws. The act prohibited criminal laws that stipulated different penalties for blacks and whites or laws that limited blacks' access to the courts. In addition, the bill gave U.S. circuit and district courts jurisdiction over these matters, and all federal law officers, including those of the Freedmen's Bureau, could initiate proceedings against violators.[38]

Trumbull's Civil Rights Bill embodied the moderates' conception of civil rights. Where Radicals believed that fundamental rights included every phase of public life, moderates sought to protect only those rights blacks needed to be free laborers. All citizens, moderates believed, needed to be secure in their persons and property so that they could acquire and hold the fruits of their labor and have an incentive to improve their individual economic status. Voting rights were not considered essential. Women, immigrants, and other groups had long been denied the right to vote. Though Trumbull's bill did not provide for black suffrage, it empowered the federal government to guarantee the right of African Americans to make and enforce contracts, to bring lawsuits and give evidence in court, to own property, and to enjoy the "full and equal benefit of all laws and proceedings . . . as is enjoyed by white citizens."[39]

The Civil Rights Bill had the potential drastically to expand national power. For the first time, the federal government would accept ongoing responsibility for protecting the rights of its citizens.[40] At the same time, the moderates did not intend for the bill to undermine federalism in any significant way. Trumbull did not envision continual federal intervention in local affairs; states would still be responsible for protecting most rights of their citizens. Once the Black Codes were extinguished, his act would create a latent federal power to be triggered only when state laws specified unequal treatment. If state laws treated blacks and whites differently or provided different criminal or civil penalties for the two races, federal courts could step in. Otherwise state authority remained unimpeded. Nevertheless, the bill would create unprecedented federal powers. Moderates' support of the measure once again reflected the Republican Party's leftward shift.

Some Republicans worried that the Civil Rights Act would do nothing to thwart private violence against blacks or to stop discriminatory treatment by white sheriffs, judges, and juries. Moderates countered that the Freedmen's Bureau—as a result of Trumbull's Freedmen's Bureau Bill—would, for a time, prevent such injustices by protecting blacks from physical violence and by providing alternative tribunals for African Americans' legal claims. Soon, moderates hoped, the bureau would not be needed, because equal laws would ultimately result in equal treatment. As to the possibility of black suffrage, Trumbull felt that his bills were "as far as the country will go at the present time." At once radical (in comparison to what came before) and conservative (in comparison to the desires of the freedmen and Radical Republicans), Trumbull's proposals reflected the mood of the Republican majority, and both the House and the Senate passed his bills by large majorities.[41]

Virtually all Republicans, including Miller, assumed that Johnson would sign the Freedmen's Bureau and Civil Rights Bills, which provided him with a chance to stand with his party without seeming to capitulate to the wholesale demands of the Radicals. But in early 1866, Johnson shocked everyone by vetoing both bills. In his veto message, Johnson questioned Congress's power to pass the Freedmen's Bureau Bill during peacetime and suggested that the bureau's assistance to blacks would lead them to a "life of indolence." He called the Civil Rights Bill an "unconstitutional invasion of states' rights," proclaiming, "In all our history, in all our experience as people living under the Federal and State law, . . . no such system as that contemplated by the details of this bill have ever been proposed or adopted."[42] He charged that the two bills constituted a "stride towards centralization and concentration of all legislative powers in national government." In speeches defending his vetoes, he said the legislation operated "in favor of the colored and against the white race" and would eventually lead to interracial marriage and miscegenation.[43] He vowed to approve no further Reconstruction measures until Congress admitted what he described as its loyal members from southern states. While Radical Republicans expected nothing less from Johnson, moderate Republicans could only shake their heads in disbelief.

Early in April, for the first time in American history, Congress enacted substantive legislation over a president's veto, and the Civil Rights Act and the Freedmen's Bureau Bill became law. On April 2, 1866, Andrew Johnson, in turn, proclaimed that the rebellion was entirely suppressed and the southern states fully restored to the Union.[44]

In March 1866, the Supreme Court entered the Reconstruction debate, hearing three landmark cases that the justices, politicians, and the press knew could have a significant impact on Republican Reconstruction policies. The first of these cases, *Ex Parte Milligan*, arose from the military arrest in October 1864 of an Indiana civilian and militant Copperhead, Lambdin P. Milligan, whom officials accused of conspiring to aid the Confederacy, a charge he did not deny. Milligan, a successful railroad attorney before the war, became a "grimly fanatical" proslavery partisan as a result of the Kansas controversy in the 1850s. During the war, he helped organize the Indiana chapter of a pro-Confederate secret society, the Order of American Knights (also called the Sons of Liberty). The Lincoln administration considered rebel sympathizers like Milligan particularly dangerous in border regions such as southern Indiana that were "constantly threatened to be invaded by the enemy." Milligan's activities therefore soon drew the attention of federal agents. If an invasion came, officials feared that Milligan and the Sons of Liberty might aid the invaders by sabotaging Union forces.[45]

In May 1864, Milligan began plotting an ambitious pro-Confederate uprising. With a scheme vaguely reminiscent of John Brown's ill-fated Harpers Ferry raid, Milligan and his co-conspirators planned to seize the weapons in federal and state arsenals throughout Indiana and the old northwest and use them to overpower the guards at prisoner-of-war camps in Chicago, Indianapolis, Rock Island, and Columbus. After arming the prisoners, the freed Confederates and the Sons of Liberty would embark upon a guerrilla campaign behind the Union lines, presumably picking up reinforcements from disgruntled draft resisters and antiwar Copperheads along the way. When Union forces turned to fight this fire in their rear, the Confederate army would launch a swift and decisive offensive from the South. Confederate officials took Milligan's plan seriously, and rebel commissioners in Canada smuggled funds for the operation to the Sons of Liberty. In the fall of 1864, however, federal agents got wind of the plot, and soldiers arrested Milligan at his home on October 5. A military court in Indiana quickly tried Milligan and sentenced him to hang.[46]

Milligan never denied his guilt, but his attorneys nevertheless argued that he should go free. As a civilian, they claimed, Milligan should never have been tried by a military tribunal. The civilian courts were open in Indiana, and Milligan was part of neither the military nor the Confederacy. Furthermore, under the Habeas Corpus Act that Congress had passed in 1863, Milligan had procedural rights that had not been granted. Although the law authorized Lincoln's suspension of habeas corpus throughout the United States, it also provided safeguards to ensure that arrested civilians would receive justice. It stipulated that whenever the military arrested civilian political offenders in states where the federal courts remained open, the secretary of state or secretary of war had to notify that region's circuit or district courts of the arrests and to provide a list of detained civilians within twenty days. The federal court then was supposed to convene a civilian grand jury, which would decide whether the arrests were necessary. If the grand jury did not indict a prisoner, he or she went free. Congress had effectively declared that where the civilian courts operated unimpaired, the military could not hold political prisoners indefinitely and eventually had to submit to civilian authority.[47]

In Milligan's case, military officials did not follow the procedures outlined in the Habeas Corpus Act. Instead, in a thirty-day period, they arrested, tried, and condemned Milligan and never gave his name to the circuit court. As a result, no grand jury ever indicted him. On May 10, 1865, nine days before his scheduled execution, his lawyers petitioned Justice David Davis, who sat on the circuit court in Indiana, demanding their clients' release. Davis had long been opposed to military courts operating where civilian courts remained open, and he granted the request. His fellow judge on circuit, David McDonald, disagreed and voted to reject Milligan's petition. With the circuit judges deadlocked, the case went to the Supreme Court based on a certification of division.[48]

James Speed and former Civil War general Benjamin Butler served as the government's attorneys in the case. Butler, commander of the Union forces that had occupied New Orleans during the war, had plenty of experience with disloyal civilian provocateurs and brought a veteran's credibility to the argument that Milligan's arrest and swift conviction were just and necessary. He might have undermined this credibility, however, by taking the extreme position that the president could exercise sweeping war powers even without congressional authorization. The decision to suspend habeas corpus, Butler and Speed argued, belonged solely to the president, who should be the sole judge of when, where, and for how long it would be invoked. In addition, they contended that the protections of the Fourth, Fifth, and Sixth Amendments, such as due process and the prohibition against illegal searches and seizures, were "all peace provisions of the Constitution, and . . . like all other conventional and legislative laws and enactments, are silent amidst arms . . . when the safety of the people becomes the supreme law." Calling Indiana a theater of military operations, Butler and Speed claimed that the president had unchecked power to arrest and punish men like Milligan, particularly "in a state which had been and was threatened with invasion, having arsenals which the petitioner plotted to seize, and prisoners of war whom he plotted to liberate." In short, during wartime the president had unlimited power over civilians.[49]

In the event the Court did not accept this broad assertion of executive war powers, Speed and Butler also maintained that the Habeas Corpus Act did not apply to Milligan's case. That law, they argued, applied only to civilians who were held as "state or political offenders." Milligan was no political prisoner, they asserted; he was a prisoner of war. He had received Confederate funding for his plot to attack Union forces. "The petitioner," Speed asserted, "was as much a prisoner of war as if he had been taken in action with arms in his hands." The Habeas Corpus Act applied only to prisoners held indefinitely without being charged. "The law was framed to prevent imprisonment for an indefinite time without trial," Speed and Butler averred, "not to interfere with the case of prisoners undergoing trial. Its purpose was to make sure that such persons should be tried." Milligan certainly could not claim that he had not been promptly tried. Within a month of his arrest, he had been tried and sentenced to die.[50]

Milligan's attorneys were also famous men. In addition to James Garfield and Jeremiah Black, his defense team included Stephen J. Field's brother, David Dudley Field. A Democrat who had joined the Republicans on the eve of the Civil War, David Field had become a staunch opponent of his new party's Reconstruction policies and had soon returned to the Democratic fold. During Reconstruction, Field was one of a cohort of Democratic lawyers who regularly argued cases before the Court, hoping to win decisions that would undermine the Republicans' southern agenda. These attorneys, who included prominent politicians such as Reverdy Johnson and Montgomery Blair, willingly accepted greatly reduced fees (and in some cases no fees at all) in order to participate in cases that might help preserve white Democratic rule in the South. Compensation, David Field wrote, was "of no consequence to them." As he noted later while defending the perpetrators of the Colfax massacre, "I had rather receive nothing but the thanks of my clients and the consciousness of doing what I could do to avert a great public calamity and wrong."[51]

Field challenged the government's claim that during wartime Lincoln could suspend important constitutional rights wherever and whenever he wanted. "Has the President," he asked, "in time of war, upon his own mere will and judgment, the power to bring before his military officers any person in the land, and subject him to trial and punishment, even to death?" Alleging that such authority would give the president "kingly" powers, Field reminded the Court that "our executive is in no sense a king, even for four years." When the civilian courts operated unimpaired, as they had in loyal and peaceful Indiana at the time of his client's arrest, civilians deserved a jury trial and the full protections of their constitutional rights. Building on Field's argument, Jeremiah Black added that Congress had clearly curtailed Lincoln's authority when it passed the Habeas Corpus Act.[52]

In his rebuttal, Butler questioned Field's bucolic portrayal of wartime Indiana. Rather than a haven from the war, Butler argued, the state was a critical theater of military operations, and Milligan's nefarious actions reflected this fact. Butler noted that Milligan "and his felonious associates" plotted an insurrection designed to facilitate invasion. While it was true that Indiana's civilian courts remained open, they would not have been able to do so without the presence of federal troops. Had the military, Butler asserted, "not kept the ten thousand rebel prisoners of war confined in the neighborhood from being released by these Knights and men of the Order of the Sons of Liberty; there would have been no courts in Indiana."[53]

Oral arguments in the *Milligan* case concluded on March 13, 1866, and the Court announced its decision on April 3. In what has been hailed by some as a great victory for civil liberties, the nine justices of the Supreme Court unanimously agreed that Milligan should go free.[54] In his majority opinion, Justice Davis stated that the case's importance "cannot be overstated; for it involves the very framework of the government and the fundamental principles of American liberty." Although a wartime case, Davis noted that it was fortunate that *Milligan* was decided after the conflict was over. "The late wicked Rebellion," he wrote, "did not allow that calmness in deliberation . . . so necessary" in a case of this magnitude. "*Then,* considerations of safety were mingled with the exercise of power. . . . *Now,* that the public safety is assured, this question . . . can be discussed and decided without passion." The Court, in other words, could decide a wartime case using peacetime sensibilities.[55]

Davis and the other members of the majority rejected the government's contention that the Fourth, Fifth, and Sixth Amendments applied only in peacetime. Instead, they held that fundamental constitutional rights could never be undermined "where the courts are open and their process unobstructed." Milligan deserved a trial by jury, and the fact that Congress had made Indiana part of a "military department" did not change that requirement. Otherwise, Davis wrote, whenever "war exists, foreign or domestic, and the country is subdivided into military departments for mere convenience, the commander of one of them can . . . with the approval of the executive, substitute military force for and to the exclusion of the laws, and punish all persons, as he thinks proper, without fixed and certain rules." This power, if established, could be abused by a president with evil motives. "Wicked men, ambitious of power, with hatred of liberty and contempt of law, may fill the place once occupied by Washington and Lincoln; and if this right is conceded, and the calamities of war again befall us the dangers to human liberty are frightful to contemplate."[56]

Davis did acknowledge that martial law could be declared in communities where actual fighting was taking place. But for him, the mere threat of invasion did not warrant military arrests and trials of civilians. "Martial law cannot arise from a *threatened* invasion," he concluded. "The necessity must be actual and present; the invasion real, such as effectually closes the courts and deposes the civil administration." In this instance, it was "difficult to see how the *safety* of the country required martial law in Indiana."[57]

Davis's sweeping conclusions appeared to allow no exceptions. Whereas Butler and Speed had overstated their case in regard to the president's war powers, the majority opinion went to the opposite extreme. Using Davis's rationale, even if enemy armies had been marching towards Indiana or a foreign armada had already set sail to attack the coast, the military could not arrest and try treasonous civilians plotting to aid an imminent invasion. Moreover, neither the president nor Congress could approve such arrests. "Not one of these safeguards can the President, or Congress, or the Judiciary disturb," Davis determined. Otherwise, "it could be well said that a country preserved at the sacrifice of all the cardinal principles of liberty, is not worth the cost of preservation."[58]

Davis's ringing rhetoric has led some historians to portray *Milligan* as a bulwark for American civil liberties. Historian Allen Nevins called the decision a "great triumph for the civil liberties of Americans," asserting that the "heart of the decision is the heart of the difference between the United States of America and Nazi Germany or the Soviet Union."[59] But many accounts discuss only Davis's majority opinion in *Milligan,* giving the inaccurate impression that all the other justices uniformly agreed with his reasoning. In fact, four justices, including Miller, filed a separate opinion that provided a very different rationale for freeing Milligan. This separate opinion reveals that *Milligan* was as much about Reconstruction politics as it was about timeless principles.

Although the "crimes with which Milligan was charged were of the gravest character," Chief Justice Chase noted in the minority opinion that Miller joined, it was "important to the country and every citizen that he should not be punished under an illegal sentence." But the minority's reasoning was far less expansive than Davis's capacious language about fundamental rights, relying instead on one simple procedural point. The military court had not followed the guidelines established by Congress in the Habeas Corpus Act, which had stipulated that civilians arrested by the military had to be indicted by a civilian grand jury before they could be tried. The military court had tried Milligan without an indictment. As a result, his conviction was not valid.[60]

Chase, Miller, Swayne, and Wayne sharply disagreed with the majority's conclusion that, short of an actual invasion, Congress could never authorize military trials of civilians. In *Milligan* Congress explicitly chose not to do so, but that need not always be the case. "As we understand it," the four justices said, the majority opinion "asserts not only that the military commission held in Indiana was not authorized by Congress, but that it was not in the power of Congress to authorize it." While the four justices could "assent fully, to all that is said in the opinion, of the inestimable value of the trial by jury, and of the other constitutional safeguards of civil liberty," they could also envision situations where Congress could and should be able to circumvent the civilian courts. In Milligan's case, Congress determined that the civilian courts remained competent. But in other situations, "those courts might be open and undisturbed in execution of their functions, and yet wholly incompetent to avert threatened danger, or to punish, with adequate promptitude and certainty the guilty conspirators. . . . In Indiana, the judges and officers of the Courts were loyal to the government. . . . But it might have been otherwise. In times of rebellion and civil war it may often happen, indeed, that judges and marshals will be in active sympathy with the rebels, and courts their most efficient allies. . . . We are unwilling to give our assent by silence to expressions of opinion which seem to us calculated . . . to cripple the constitutional powers of the government, and to augment the public dangers in times of invasion and rebellion."[61]

The difference between the two opinions reflected the contemporary issues surrounding Reconstruction. Although they never explicitly stated their sentiments, Miller and the other justices in the minority knew that the majority's opinion could adversely affect the course of Reconstruction in the South, where state courts had shown themselves to be "in active sympathy with the rebels." Because southern courts were unwilling to protect African Americans and loyal white Unionists, the Freedmen's Bureau had established alternative tribunals that operated even though the civilian courts were up and running. Republicans justified these special courts on the grounds that the southern states remained in the "grasp of war," and were thus subject to military authority and military courts. When the four justices in the minority said they could envision a situation where civilian "judges and marshals will be in active sympathy with the rebels, and courts their most efficient allies," they did not need to imagine future scenarios. They needed only to point to the civilian courts in the South.

Although the Court rendered its decision to free Milligan on April 3, the justices postponed the release of the opinions by Davis and Chase until the following term. Both justices recognized the landmark nature of the case and wanted more time to polish their prose. This postponement also temporarily muted the fury that would have accompanied a decision that not only released

Milligan but placed the Freedmen's Bureau tribunals in jeopardy. Nevertheless, some Democrats claimed the opinionless decision as a great victory. "We express our thanks to the Supreme Court," said one Democratic paper on April 5. "It stands by Johnson in attempting to bring back Union and a Government of laws."[62]

In March 1866, the Supreme Court also heard arguments in the "test-oath cases," *Cummings v. the State of Missouri* and *Ex Parte Garland*.[63] These cases involved plaintiffs who questioned the legitimacy of the oaths of past loyalty that had been—and continued to be—required by cities, states, and the federal government. Although test oaths in America dated back to the anti-Tory laws of the Revolution, they proliferated during the Civil War. Faced with the nearly impossible task of distinguishing friend from foe in a population with a common culture and language, the loyal state governments in Missouri, Maryland, Tennessee, and Louisiana passed rigorous test-oath statutes. Congress did the same, requiring anyone who wanted to hold a federal office or argue cases in front of the federal courts to take an ironclad test oath of both past and future loyalty. The military also administered oaths throughout the South during the war as it tried to find a critical mass of loyal whites with which to assemble Reconstruction governments. Even small cities like Keokuk passed test-oath statutes. The *Cummings* case arose from Missouri's test-oath law, perhaps the strictest of its kind in the country.[64]

In the spring of 1865, Missourians ratified a new state constitution that required anyone who wanted to vote, hold elective office, work as a professor, teacher, or clergyman, or serve as an officer of a public or private corporation to take a loyalty oath. To prove that they had "always been truly and loyally on the side of the United States," individuals had to swear they had committed none of eighty-six different acts that the law delineated as evidence of disloyalty. Those who had fought with the Confederacy naturally could not take the oath. But the law also barred anyone who had given "aid, comfort, countenance, or support" to a Confederate, or who by "act or word manifested his adherence to the cause of such enemies, or his desire for their triumphs over the arms of the United States, or his sympathy with those engaged in exciting or carrying on the rebellion against the United States," or who in any way indicated "his disaffection to the Government of the United States in its contest with rebellion." Depending on how broadly one interpreted these provisions, Missouri's oath could penalize a significant portion—perhaps a majority—of the state's population.[65]

The punitive nature of Missouri's test-oath provisions reflected the bitterness of the internecine warfare that had occurred there. While all the border states suffered from internal struggles during the war, the viciousness of the guerrilla fighting in Missouri exceeded anything experienced elsewhere. Evenly split between secessionists and Unionists, Missouri quickly descended into a deadly "bushwhacking" war, in which paramilitary bands brutally killed civilians suspected of sympathizing with one side or the other. The pro-Confederate guerrillas in Missouri included the infamous William Clarke Quantrill, who, a historian has noted, assembled a "gang of some of the most psychopathic killers in American history," including Frank and Jesse James and "Bloody Bill" Anderson. Quantrill's raid on Lawrence, Kansas, which left 182 civilian men and boys dead, was just the most notorious example of countless atrocities committed by both sides in Missouri. Since Missourians frequently sheltered guerrillas in their homes, Union commanders grew frustrated in trying to determine the difference between civilians and pro-Confederate guerrillas and resorted to brutal search-and-destroy tactics of their own. Few civilians remained neutral. Guerrillas' demands for sanctuary and the Union army's tough tactics forced Missourians to choose sides. Because of this tangled struggle, test oaths became an important cornerstone of the loyal Missouri government.[66]

The expansive test-oath provisions in Missouri's new constitution quickly led to legal challenges. The *Cummings* case resulted from the indictment and conviction of John Cummings, a Roman Catholic priest from a small town north of St. Louis, for preaching without first taking the loyalty oath. The Catholic archbishop of St. Louis had instructed Cummings and other clerics against taking the oath, which he believed was an unjustifiable infringement of religious freedom. The government did not present evidence that Cummings had ever been disloyal, although the links between urban Roman Catholics and Copperhead Democrats often made priests in the North objects of suspicion. Officials arrested, tried, and convicted Cummings, fining him $500 for continuing to preach after refusing to swear an oath. Cummings, who refused to pay the fine, was thrown in jail and appears to have embraced his role as martyr in the test case on the test oaths. After the Missouri Supreme Court subsequently upheld his conviction, Cummings became a *cause célèbre* when he appealed his case to the United States Supreme Court.[67]

Oral arguments in the *Cummings* case began on March 15, 1865, on the heels of the arguments in *Milligan*. While the Court had temporarily dodged criticism by postponing the release of the written *Milligan* opinions, the justices now faced another incendiary case. Both the federal and state governments had made test oaths central to their Reconstruction policies, and Republicans feared the Court might declare them to be unconstitutional. Democrats recognized the importance of the case as well. Thus, Cummings's cause, like Milligan's, attracted the best legal talent available. Cummings's attorneys included Maryland senator Reverdy Johnson, Missouri powerbroker Montgomery Blair, and David Dudley Field. Each of these men had well-deserved reputations as opponents of Republican Reconstruction policies. Reverdy Johnson had even publicly recommended that ex-Confederates in Maryland deliberately commit perjury and sign the state's required loyalty oath so that they could vote.[68]

In his argument for Cummings before the Court, Field asserted that Missouri's test oath amounted to an unconstitutional ex post facto law, because it made punishable acts that had not been crimes when they were committed. The test-oath law, for example, made it illegal for a person to have expressed sympathy for those in rebellion. If Cummings expressed his sympathies for those fighting the war, Field argued, he was merely fulfilling his priestly duties, an act that was legal at the time of commission. "It would be strange, indeed," Field asserted, "if a minister of the Gospel, whose sympathies are with all the children of men—the good and the sinful, the happy and sorrowing—might not manifest such sympathy by an act of charity or a word of consolation." Cummings had been forced from the pulpit simply for performing his role as a priest.

By focusing on the allegedly ex post facto nature of the Missouri law, Field was able to downplay the fact that he was asking the Court to take the extraordinary step of declaring that the provisions of a state constitution violated the federal Constitution. Only once before had the Supreme Court even accepted such a case. If the Court sided with Cummings, it would signal an unprecedented enlargement of the scope of federal judicial review.[69]

Missouri's counsel, J. B. Henderson, argued in response that his state's test oath was well within a state's right to qualify its own voters, teachers, lawyers, and other licensed groups. It was not within the Supreme Court's purview, he emphasized, to question the content of state laws of this type. The federal government's judicial power only extended to the federal Constitution, not to that of a state. In this instance—as would often be the case while the Republicans held the upper hand in Reconstruction—the counsel for a Republican state government took a firm states'-rights position. Whatever the justices thought about the soundness of Missouri's loyalty oath did not matter, Henderson insisted. The war had not destroyed federalism. States, rather than the federal government, still decided which civil rights to protect.[70]

Henderson nevertheless attempted to convince the justices of the necessity of the Missouri law. He asked the Court to view the issue in the context of the debilitating struggle that had taken place in the state. While the test-oath provisions might now "fall harshly on the public ear," he remarked, the "provisions themselves are no more extraordinary than the circumstances which called them into existence." During the war, Missourians' loyalties had split on a house-to-house basis. "Neighbors and friends of long standing," he recounted, "separated and joined hostile forces." Each town had its opposing military and paramilitary organizations. Rebels and spies infiltrated from Arkansas and Texas "and found shelter and food in the houses of the disloyal." Some rebel sympathizers, too old to join the conflict, instead "urged others to go and furnished the means and money to equip them." Traitors were everywhere. "The merchant in his store-room talked treason to his customers; the school teacher instilled its poison into the minds of his pupils," Henderson explained, "and even the minister of heaven . . . went forth to perform the part allotted to him in this great work of iniquity." When rebel armies marched into Missouri in 1864, disloyal Missourians, seeking retribution against their Unionist neighbors, "joined the advancing hosts, to assist in the work of devastation and death." In Missouri the war became a "hand-to-hand contest." Everyone took a stand: "They were for, or they were against."[71]

Given this context, Henderson argued that test oaths were both necessary and reasonable. He reminded the justices that on the very day Missouri's Unionist voters elected delegates to their constitutional convention, Confederate armies swept through parts of the state, leaving behind "smouldering ruins and human suffering," while thousands of disloyal Missourians greeted the invaders "with shouts of joy and approbation." He concluded that although Missouri's oaths might seem harsh for another state, in Missouri they were needed. Without them it would be impossible to determine who had been loyal and who had not, or to create a society led by loyal citizens.[72]

Henderson's argument seemed likely to resonate with Justice Miller. Keokuk, only a few miles from the Missouri border, harbored numerous southern sympathizers, and Miller knew the difficulties faced by loyal town and state governments in distinguishing friend from foe. When the Keokuk town council demanded loyalty oaths from everyone in the city in 1862, he had volunteered to administer them.[73]

During the same week that the Court heard arguments in *Cummings,* it also heard a second case involving a test-oath law, *Ex Parte Garland.* This case involved a lawyer, Augustus H. Garland, who was prevented from arguing before the Supreme Court by the ironclad loyalty test oath that Congress had required since 1862. The oath, originally proposed in Congress by Keokuk's representative, James Wilson, required all government officials to swear an oath that they had not borne arms against the United States and that they had "given no aid, countenance, counsel, or encouragement to persons engaged in armed hostility thereto." In January 1865, Congress extended the ironclad oath requirement to include lawyers who practiced before federal courts. Not nearly as stringent as the Missouri oath, the oath nevertheless contained enough broad language to disqualify many northerners as well as southerners from federal positions.[74]

In December 1860, Garland had been admitted to practice before the Supreme Court bar. When the Civil War began, however, he accepted a commission as a general in the rebel army and later served in the Confederate House and Senate. After the war, President Johnson pardoned Garland as part of his pardoning spree in the summer of 1865. Garland now hoped to reclaim his position as a member of the Court's bar. His attorneys claimed in their oral arguments that the ironclad test oath constituted both an ex post facto law and an illegal bill of attainder. In addition, they argued that Johnson's pardon made Garland oath-proof, as it absolved him of any acts performed in the service of the rebellion.[75]

In his closing argument, Garland's lawyer, Reverdy Johnson, appealed to the justices' patriotism and the spirit of forgiveness. "I think every man who has within his bosom a heart capable of sympathy," Johnson said, "who is not the slave to a narrow political feeling . . . must make it the subject of his daily thoughts and of his prayers to God, that the hour may come and come soon, when all the States shall be again within the protecting shelter of the Union." This result, he added, "will be hastened by bringing within these courts of the United States, a class of men, now excluded, who, by education, character, and profession are especially qualified by their example to influence the public sentiment of their respective states." This argument made Miller wary, as he had heard it before. Like Ballinger had done the previous summer, Johnson implied that a speedy restoration to power of the South's antebellum elites would lead to a smooth reconciliation. But in the past year Miller had seen the devilish results of lenient policies. Moreover, the argument now came not from his friend Ballinger, but from a man Miller described as an "old political prostitute" who was "hated by all loyal men worse than a thousand times than they hate many honest rebels."[76]

When the oral arguments in *Cummings* and *Garland* concluded, it soon became apparent that the justices were "nearly equally divided," as Miller noted. It became clear that Stephen Field's would be the key swing vote, and that Field was leaning toward declaring Congress's test oath constitutional but invalidating Missouri's. Miller found Field's position problematic. It seemed illogical to vote to "sustain the congressional oath, but . . . hold the Missouri oath which is almost identical void as in conflict with the federal Constitution!!" Miller feared that the two decisions would send contradictory messages to lawmakers and make the Court look indecisive and hopelessly fragmented. Given the highly charged nature of these cases, the justices had hoped for unanimous agreement; decisions by a divided Court on contentious topics often fueled rather than settled controversies. In the Court's history there had been only a few 5-4 decisions, the most notorious of which had been *Dred Scott.* The memory of the violent northern reaction to that infamous opinion haunted the Court. As a result, Miller urged the other justices to postpone the vote on both *Cummings* and *Garland* until the next term so that Field might clarify his muddled thinking during the summer.[77]

Over Field's objections, the other justices followed Miller's advice and postponed the final vote in both cases until December. Combined with the delay in publishing the opinions in *Milligan,* this action risked giving the appearance of a Court incapacitated by the issues of Reconstruction, but Miller hoped it would allow Field time to reach a logically consistent position. To Miller, consistency meant deciding that both the federal and state test oaths passed constitutional muster. Given Field's awkward reasoning thus far, Miller admitted that he had no idea how his colleague would vote in December even with nine months to ruminate. "What a Judge will do next winter who could come to such conclusions," he lamented, "no man can tell now from any thing he . . . said."[78]

After the Court announced the postponement, an angry Reverdy Johnson publicly told Democratic politicians in Missouri that he had learned from one of the justices that the Court would declare the Missouri oath unconstitutional during the next term. In Missouri, election campaigns were underway for state and federal offices, and even with most secessionists barred from voting by the test oaths, the contests promised to be close. Democratic candidates pledged that if elected they would amend the state's constitution to repeal the test-oath provisions and restore ex-rebels to full citizenship. The fate of Reconstruction in Missouri hung in the balance, and Democratic orators took full advantage of Reverdy Johnson's inside information to argue that the Supreme Court was on their side. For Miller, the rumor confirmed his worst suspicions about Johnson's motives. When Johnson spoke at the end of the oral arguments in *Garland* about the need for national reconciliation, what he really wanted was a reconciliation premised on the return of rebels and Democrats to power and an end to Republican Reconstruction. Outraged at Johnson's actions, Miller wrote Chief Justice Chase requesting that the Court make a formal announcement stating that no decision had been made in the case. "Now shall this falsehood be permitted to work successfully its injurious effects," Miller asked, "or shall it be contradicted?" He saw a "manifest propriety in contradicting the assertion that the Court has decided an important case, or an important principle when it has done no such thing." Johnson's announcement, he warned Chase, was being used to manipulate political events in Missouri. "A very animated political contest is now going on in the state of Missouri," Miller wrote, "between the radicals and their opponents; the latter including every returned rebel in the state. This contest is looked upon by both parties as settling the future of the state for years to come." He warned Chase that in that political contest Johnson's "assertion that the Supreme Court of the United States has decided [the test oath] to be in conflict with the Constitution of the United States is telling with fatal effect on the radicals."[79]

Stephen Field, then riding circuit in California, also criticized Reverdy Johnson's machinations. "The conduct of Johnson is indefensible—more it merits some rebuke," Field wrote Chase on June 30. "How foolish he would appear if the decision of the Court should be different from what he supposes it will be." Field's letter, if Miller learned of it, might have given him some hope that Field had rethought his position in favor of both the federal ironclad oath and the Missouri loyalty oath. It might have seemed to Miller that his strategy of postponing the cases had paid off. The constitutionality of both state and federal test oaths would be established, and Reconstruction could proceed in the way he favored—with ex-rebel leaders barred from office and loyal Union men firmly in control.[80]

CHAPTER 6
Men Incapable of Forgiving or Learning

TWO TRAGIC EVENTS in the South in May and July reinforced Samuel
Miller's conviction that white southerners remained unreconstructed
and that measures such as test oaths remained necessary. The first took place in
Memphis, where on May 1, 1866, two horse-drawn cabs—one driven by a black
man, the other by a white—collided. When police arrested only the black
driver, a group of recently discharged African American soldiers intervened. A
white mob, incensed by black soldiers challenging white policemen, attacked
the veterans; three days of racial violence followed. White mobs poured into
Memphis's black neighborhoods, beating men, raping women, and burning
hundreds of homes, churches, and schools. Forty-eight people died in the riots,
all but two of whom were black. "If anything could reveal, in light as clear as
day, the demoniac spirit of southern whites toward the freedmen," remarked
one northern paper, "it is such an event as this."[1]

A second riot in New Orleans arose directly from Reconstruction politics.
In July 1866, Governor J. Madison Wells, concerned with the growing power of
ex-Confederates in the state legislature, endorsed a radical plan to reconvene
Louisiana's constitutional convention of 1864 in order to enfranchise blacks,
prohibit "rebels" from voting, and establish a new state government. When the
convention met in New Orleans, an armed white mob that included New Orleans police officers surrounded the hall, broke down the doors, and killed the
delegates inside. In what General Philip H. Sheridan labeled an "absolute massacre," white terrorists murdered thirty-four blacks and three whites. Miller's
reaction to the violence in Memphis and New Orleans mirrored that of many
other northerners. The riots, he later noted, had confirmed for him that south-

ern whites, with "their peculiar hatred . . . for the negro," were men who were "incapable of forgiving or learning." It was clear that Johnson's Reconstruction policies had utterly failed.[2]

After his vetoes of the Civil Rights and Freedmen's Bureau Bills, Johnson had hoped to form a new coalition of conservative Republicans and Democrats. He even gave his proposed coalition a name—the National Union movement—and called for a National Union convention to meet in Philadelphia in August 1866 to organize the new party. But the New Orleans riot, occurring two weeks before the National Union convention, doomed his plans. Plagued by dissension in their ranks, the convention's delegates failed to establish the new party John-son wanted. Instead, they simply called for voters to elect pro-Johnson candi-dates in the congressional contests that coming fall. Despite the convention's failure, the president began removing thousands of federal patronage appointees who refused to pledge loyalty to the National Union movement. Most of those removed were Republicans, whom Johnson replaced with Democrats. By the fall of 1866, any Republicans with lingering sympathies for Johnson had aban-doned him.[3]

Another issue that occupied Republicans' minds in the summer of 1866 was the struggle over the proposed Fourteenth Amendment. In June, Republicans in Congress finally agreed upon the wording for an amendment that would em-body the central tenets of their party's agenda for Reconstruction. Section 1 of the amendment declared that all persons born or naturalized in the United States were citizens of the United States. This language invalidated Taney's in-famous ruling in *Dred Scott* that African Americans could never be U.S. citi-zens. Section 1 also included language that invalidated state and local laws like the Black Codes by barring states from making or enforcing any law that denied any citizen the "privileges and immunities of citizens of the United States, . . . equal protection of life, liberty, and property," or "due process of law." Section 2 addressed the question of black suffrage. Rather than affirmatively guarantee-ing black voting rights, the proposed amendment reduced the representation in the House of Representatives of states that denied any male citizens suffrage (thereby ridding the Constitution of the three-fifths clause). Section 3 excluded anyone who had voluntarily aided the Confederacy from holding public office until 1870 unless Congress granted them a pardon. The final two sections pro-hibited repayment of the Confederate debt and empowered Congress to enforce all the foregoing provisions with appropriate legislation.[4]

The men who drafted the Fourteenth Amendment had the upcoming elections of 1866 very much in mind during their deliberations, and most of its provisions reflected the moderates' influence. The amendment sidestepped the
divisive issue of black suffrage, and the five-year ban on rebels holding office
applied only to those who voluntarily aided the Confederacy, not to the hundreds of thousands who had been drafted. Much of the language of section 1
remained deliberately vague. What were the "privileges and immunities" of national citizenship? The amendment's framers never reached a consensus on this
point, and the resulting ambiguity allowed various factions to see in the amendment's broad language whatever it was they wanted to see. Some of the amendment's framers thought the privileges and immunities clause dramatically
altered federalism. Whereas the protections of the Bill of Rights had previously
applied only to the actions of the federal government, Radicals believed that
those protections would now extend to state action as well. Other Republicans
had a more conservative view of the amendment's effect and thought that it
simply wrote the Civil Rights Act of 1866 into the Constitution. The amendment, they believed, permanently protected African Americans against state
and local laws and customs that discriminated on the basis of race, while leaving
the states in control of most other civil rights. In other words, a state law could
still limit rights (such as free speech) as long as it treated blacks and whites
equally.

The Fourteenth Amendment's framers also left the exact meaning of the
equal protection and due process clauses unsettled. The broadest interpretations
of those clauses came from President Johnson and the amendment's other opponents, who hoped to discredit the measure by claiming it would destroy the
power of the states, establish complete equality between whites and blacks, and
empower Congress to legislate on any local matter it chose. Throughout the
1866 campaign, Republicans repeatedly denied those charges.[5]

The midterm elections become a dual referendum on the Fourteenth
Amendment and Johnson's Reconstruction policies. On election day, voters
flocked to the polls and delivered a powerful message to the president. In the
upcoming Congress, Republicans would outnumber Democrats by well over the
two-thirds majority required to override Johnson's veto. So stern was the voters'
rebuke of Johnson that some die-hard optimists hoped that he might finally
recognize his mistakes and shift course. But Johnson remained unwilling to
compromise and flatly opposed the Fourteenth Amendment. Congress, now

armed with a powerful popular mandate, made its position clear. The southern states would have to ratify and comply with the Fourteenth Amendment before normal relations could resume.[6]

Given the election results and his party's new unity of purpose, Miller hoped the southern states would quickly comply with the Republicans' conditions. White southerners could no longer cling to the belief that President Johnson might save them from a rigorous Reconstruction. "The recent elections seemed to have extinguished the Johnson Philadelphia Convention Party, . . ." Miller wrote David Davis in October. "I ardently wish, I can hard[ly] say I hope that enough of the Southern States may adopt the constitutional amendment to make it the law of the land."[7] But Miller had once again underestimated the obstinacy of Johnson and the white South. After the elections, Johnson actively encouraged the southern governments to reject the Fourteenth Amendment. Emboldened by the president, the provisional legislatures in the South did just that. One by one, through the late fall and early winter of 1866, all ten southern legislatures that considered the amendment repudiated it by overwhelming majorities.[8]

In December 1866, the second session of the Thirty-Ninth Congress opened with Republicans in an angry mood. Determined to force Reconstruction upon the South, Republicans planned to override and ignore the president with whom they had once hoped to compromise. "The President has no power to control or influence anybody," Iowa senator James Grimes pronounced, "and legislation will be carried on entirely regardless of his opinions and wishes." Increasingly, Republican politicians and editors used the language of revolution to define their objectives. The president, the *New York Herald* noted, "forgets that we have passed through the fiery ordeal of a mighty revolution, and that the pre-existing order is gone and can return no more—that a great work of reconstruction is before us, and that we cannot escape it." This language of revolution would also soon be invoked in a new round of attacks upon the Supreme Court.[9]

In December, rumors began circulating in Washington about the contents of the impending *Cummings, Garland,* and *Milligan* decisions. Papers in New York and Washington reported that the Court had decided 5-4 against both the Missouri and the federal loyalty oaths. While the public already knew that Milligan had been freed, they had not yet seen the opinion, and rumors about the scope of the decision began leaking out. Although the chief justice denied these rumors, angry Radicals warned that if they proved true, the Supreme Court would feel the Republicans' wrath. Republican editors once again demanded that the Court either be packed with friendly justices or destroyed. Reconstruction policy, the *New York Herald* demanded, should include reconstructing the Court. "By increasing or diminishing the number of judges," the *Herald* advised, "the court may be reconstructed in conformity with the supreme decisions of the war."[10]

Much to most Republicans' displeasure, the rumors about the *Milligan* decision were accurate. Revealed officially to the public on January 1, 1867, Davis's majority opinion unleashed a storm of protest. By freeing Milligan and denying Congress's power to authorize military tribunals where the civilian courts were open, the Court, it seemed, had joined with Johnson to thwart the popular will. "The Supreme Court, we regret to find," lamented the *New York Times*, "throws the great weight of its influence into the scale of those who assailed the Union and step after step impugned the constitutionality of nearly everything that was done to uphold it." But the decision, its critics knew, was not just about the past; it had dangerous implications for current Reconstruction policies. The *Indianapolis Journal* predicted that *Milligan* was "clearly a forerunner of other decisions looking to a defeat of Republican ascendancy and a restoration of Southern domination." The Court, John Jay complained, seemed ready to team up with an "obstinate President" in "defying the will of the people . . . and checkmating Congress at a most eventful moment by denying its powers and annulling its legislation." Some critics even questioned the justices' courage, charging that true patriots had fought the war rather than sitting safely in Washington holding court and "poring over dusty, musty tomes."[11]

While some attacks implicated the Court as a whole, other commentators recognized that the concurring opinion in *Milligan* by Chase, Miller, Swayne, and Wayne supported the Republicans' view of Congress's Reconstruction powers. These commentators reserved their criticism for the justices in the *Milligan* majority, calling the majority opinion a "sorry attempt of five not very distinguished persons to exhibit themselves as profound jurists." Justice Davis suffered particular condemnation. "The constitutional twaddle of Mr. Justice Davis," one paper claimed, "will no more stand the fire of public opinion than the *Dred Scott* decision."[12]

Newspapers North and South quickly realized the possible implications of *Milligan* for current Reconstruction policies. If Congress could not authorize military tribunals in any location where civilian courts were open, then the Freedmen's Bureau courts were unconstitutional. "The Indiana decision," *Harper's Weekly* warned, "operates to deprive the freedmen, in the late rebel states whose laws grievously outrage them, of the protection of the freedmen's Courts." Southern papers happily concurred. With Milligan "vindicated," the *Richmond Enquirer* trumpeted, "the South is safe and the end of her troubles approaches."[13]

Although Davis's opinion in *Milligan* said nothing about the South, President Johnson also concluded that the decision made the military tribunals in the South unconstitutional, and he immediately issued orders dismissing all military trials of civilians in southern states. Irate Republicans warned that Johnson's orders exposed freedmen and white Unionists in the South to grave danger. "The President holds that this decision applies to every rebellious state as well as to the loyal," a Republican paper counseled, "and the bloodhounds are loose all over the South, and the freedmen must take their chances." As Representative Thaddeus Stevens exhorted on the House floor on January 3, "If the doctrine enunciated in that decision be true, never were the people of any country, anywhere, or at any time, in such terrible peril as our loyal brethren in the South."[14]

With the release of the *Milligan* opinion, calls for packing or reorganizing the Court grew louder. "Let the Supreme Court be swamped," demanded *Harper's Weekly*, "by a thorough reorganization and increased number of justices." Although reorganizing the Court was an "extreme measure," it would be essential "if the five Judges should deliberately undertake to nullify the will of the majority of the people of the United States in reorganizing the Union." Politicians matched the editors' wild threats. Ohio's John Bingham warned that he would propose a "constitutional amendment and ratifying the same, which will defy judicial usurpation, by annihilating the usurpers in the abolition of the tribunal itself." Even in Miller's hometown, Republicans called for punishing the Court. "A Supreme Court that tries after the events of these six years to preserve a scintilla of the spirit of [the *Dred Scott*] decision . . . ," the *Keokuk Gate City* argued on January 8, "should have no agency in moulding the new Union to grow out of the late war, a Union founded in justice and the rights of man."[15]

On January 14, 1867, as this rhetoric reached a fevered pitch, the Court issued its decisions in both *Cummings* and *Ex Parte Garland*, the test-oath cases. The timing could not have been worse. Miller had hoped that Field, given a summer to cogitate, might recognize that he could not deem Congress's ironclad oath constitutional without doing likewise for Missouri's oath. He also hoped that these two cases, if decided correctly, would bring the Court back in line with the Republicans' Reconstruction policies.

When the Court finally voted in these two cases, Field had indeed resolved the logical incongruities in his position from the previous spring. Much to Miller's displeasure, however, Field now held both test oaths unconstitutional, tipping the Court's balance 5-4 in both cases. Joined by Wayne, Nelson, Grier, and Clifford, the four justices appointed by antebellum presidents, Field wrote the majority opinion for the two cases.

In his *Cummings* opinion, Field acknowledged the bitter context in which the drafting of Missouri's constitution with its loyalty oath provisions took place. Given the situation, he agreed that it would be strange had the document "not exhibited in its provisions some traces of the excitement amidst which the convention held its deliberations." But now that the war had ended, he insisted, more reasoned judgments needed to prevail; the Missouri oath was simply too harsh in its effects. "The oath . . . is, for its severity," he wrote, "without any precedent we can discover." Under the oath, even a tenuous relationship with the Confederacy disqualified a person from many aspects of public and private life. "If one has ever expressed sympathy with any who were drawn into the Rebellion," Field noted, "even if the recipients of that sympathy were connected by the closest of ties of blood, he is as unable to subscribe to the oath as the most active and the most cruel of the rebels."[16]

To declare the Missouri oath unconstitutional, Field had to pin his decision on more than the oath's broad language and effects. The Court was, after all, taking the unprecedented step of declaring a provision of a state constitution to be unconstitutional. In the past, conservatives like Field might have viewed the *Cummings* decision as a dangerous usurpation of state authority. Now he marshaled arguments that greatly increased the power of federal courts. He agreed with Cummings's lawyers that Missouri's oath violated the federal Constitution's prohibition of ex post facto laws, defining such a law as "one which imposes a punishment for an act which was not punishable at the time it was committed." How was Cummings to know, Field wondered, that simply expressing sympathy for the sufferings of the Confederates would later cost him his career? He could not have known. The Missouri law thus unconstitutionally punished Cummings and denied the priest his "inalienable" right to pursue his vocation.[17]

In the second test-oath case, *Ex Parte Garland*, Field built on his arguments in *Cummings* and declared Congress's ironclad test oath unconstitutional as well. Again, Field argued that a test oath of past loyalty amounted to an ex post facto law that punished Garland by denying him his right to practice before the Supreme Court. Like Missouri's provision, the ironclad oath punished behavior that had not been illegal at the time of commission, such as the "giving of assistance of any kind to person engaged in armed hostility to the United States." Field ignored the fact that Garland had done far more than give "assistance" to the rebels. As a general in the Confederate army, Garland had taken arms against the United States.[18] Field also asserted that the oath amounted to an unconstitutional bill of attainder. "A bill of attainder is a legislative act," he argued, "which inflicts punishment without a judicial trial." Garland, he claimed, had certainly been punished, and no trial had ever taken place. Lastly, Field noted that President Johnson had pardoned Garland. This pardon, he argued, made the former Confederate officer as innocent as if he had never committed any offense, since a pardon removed all penalties and disabilities and restored to him "all his civil rights." Field concluded, "It makes him, as it were, a new man, so far as that offence is concerned, he is thus placed beyond the reach of punishment of any kind."[19]

Justice Miller, along with all of Lincoln's appointees except Field, strongly disagreed with Field's reasoning, and Miller wrote a stinging dissenting opinion that applied to both *Cummings* and *Garland*. In it, he charged that amidst his professed concern for the careers of Cummings and Garland, Field had lost sight of the big picture. The cases were not about Garland's law practice or Cummings's freedom of religion; rather, they concerned the right of the nation's legislatures to exclude from government offices and places of high public trust "those among its own citizens who have been engaged in a recent effort to destroy that government by force."[20]

Miller contended that in *Ex Parte Garland*, Field wrongly concluded that Garland had an inalienable right to practice law. Practicing law, Miller argued, was a privilege granted by the state. Most states required lawyers to be of good moral character. "Attorneys are often deprived of this right," he pointed out, "upon evidence of bad moral character, or specific acts of immorality or dishonesty." For him, an armed effort to destroy the U.S. government clearly revealed "evidence of bad moral character." "That fidelity to the government under which he lives, a true and loyal attachment to it, and a sincere desire for its preservation, are among the most essential qualifications which should be required of a lawyer," Miller bitingly added, "seems to me to be too clear for argument."[21]

Miller rejected Field's conclusion that the ironclad oath amounted to a bill of attainder. A bill of attainder, Miller explained, occurred when the legislative branch convicted and sentenced someone without a trial. In these cases, no one was convicted of anything. Congress and Missouri only required oaths from individuals who wanted to fill one of four or five jobs covered by the statutes. If someone did not want to take the oath, they could instead pursue countless other careers. The test oaths actually allowed Garland "to determine his own guilt or innocence, and pronounce his own sentence." The oaths, Miller continued, also were not ex post facto laws. Field had conveniently ignored the fact that the Court had long since determined that that constitutional prohibition only applied to criminal cases and not to civil proceedings. "As far as I am informed," Miller observed, "this is the first time in the history of jurisprudence that taking an oath of office has been called a criminal proceeding."[22]

As he expounded on Field's inclination to place the rights of traitors over the right of the government to keep ex-rebels out of positions of influence, Miller grew angry and sarcastic. People like Garland had committed offenses that made them "liable to be punished with death and confiscation of all their property." Yet Field complained because Garland was "made liable to the enormous additional punishment of being deprived the right to practice law!" Miller resented the fact that President Johnson had never tried any rebel leaders for treason or confiscated traitors' lands. At the very least, he believed, the government should be allowed to strike Garland's name from the roll of attorneys.[23]

Miller also rejected Field's claim that Johnson's pardon completely absolved Garland of prior deeds. While conceding that the former rebel general could no longer be tried for treason, Miller insisted that the pardon relieved him from that and nothing more. He could still be kept out of elected office and licensed professions. Garland, Miller concluded, "may be saved by the executive pardon from the penitentiary or the gallows, but is not thereby restored to the qualifications which are essential to admission to the bar."[24]

Miller applied many of his arguments in *Ex Parte Garland* to the *Cummings* case. His positions concerning ex post facto laws or bills of attainder applied to

Missouri's loyalty oath as well. The *Cummings* case was complicated by the charge that the Missouri oath unconstitutionally interfered with Cummings's freedom of religion. But this complication left Miller unperturbed. The First Amendment, he succinctly concluded, only applied to the federal laws. If Missouri wanted to allow only loyal priests and ministers to preach, it could do so.

Miller found the Court's positions in all of the war powers cases disturbing. In his dissent, he accused his fellow justices of contorting logic in order to aid former rebels. "No more striking example of this could be given than the cases before us," he concluded, "in one of which the Constitution of the United States is held to confer no power on Congress to prevent traitors practicing in her courts, while in the other it is held to confer power on this court to nullify a provision of the constitution of the State of Missouri, relating to a qualification of ministers of religion." Field's language of inalienable rights, Miller implied, masked his true desire to undermine attempts by state and federal officials to create loyal governments. Although Field was a Lincoln appointee, as a Democrat he almost certainly recognized that in many states loyal governments meant Republican governments.[25]

In the end, Miller's strategy of postponing *Cummings* and *Garland* had backfired spectacularly. Not only did Field change his mind in the wrong case, but these inflammatory opinions were announced on the heels of *Milligan*. The Republican press howled. *Harper's Weekly* claimed that the new cases provided additional "proof of the disposition of the Court to withstand the National will and reverse the results of the war." The *Washington Chronicle* warned that *Cummings* and *Garland* would be the "fortification behind which impertinent rebels may renew or continue their war upon the Government." But, the paper noted, the Court had also "produced a reaction, which will not stop until the exact relation of that tribunal to other departments of government is absolutely and irrevocably fixed."[26]

The Court's critics demanded change. The *New York Herald* accused the justices of being the voice "of the intractable, ruling classes of the South" and endorsed a measure recently introduced in Congress that required unanimous decisions in any case involving a constitutional question (a bill that implicitly acknowledged that Miller and Swayne could be counted on to vote on the side of Republican Reconstruction). Such measures, editors insisted, were a necessary part of a righteous crusade that would now push Johnson, the Court, and unrepentant southerners to the side. "They are demands of a great revolution," the *New York Herald* claimed, "which cannot be resisted but which must run its course."[27]

Talk of impeaching President Johnson grew stronger. By January 1867, many Radical Republicans concluded that for Reconstruction to succeed, Johnson would have to go. In Congress, George Boutwell, Thaddeus Stevens, and James Ashley spearheaded the campaign to impeach the president. Although many moderates appeared reluctant to take the unprecedented step of impeachment, they did not rule out the possibility. In February 1867, the *New York Times* reported that some moderates felt that if the president continued to urge the South to resist, he would soon "come to be regarded as an 'obstacle' which must be 'deposed.'"[28]

Miller found the assaults upon and threats against the Court and the presidency deeply disturbing, despite the fact that many critics specifically exempted him and Swayne from their attacks. He viewed the plans to pack, reorganize, or even abolish the Court as a dangerous assault upon the Constitution. With all the revolutionary rhetoric coming from Congress and Republican editors, he feared that many of the best principles of the constitutional system might be lost. He steadfastly supported Republican Reconstruction, but he did not want to see the Constitution's separation of powers undermined in the process.

Miller found it particularly disheartening that men he respected, such as his former law partner John Rankin and Massachusetts representative George Boutwell, supported the effort to impeach Johnson and reconstruct the Court. "If I understand it," he wrote to Rankin on February 4, 1867, "you would, if you had the power, impeach and remove the President, would abolish or reconstitute the Supreme Court, begging pardon of the Constitution for any infraction of the instrument this action would require." Miller reminded Rankin of Alexander Hamilton's view that "there can be no liberty where the power of judging, is not kept separate from the executive and legislative powers." "If the Supreme Court is to be reconstructed for what reason is it to be done?" he asked. "Not for any crimes or misdemeanors of the judges . . . it is simply because a majority of the Court have the misfortune to be compelled to construe the Constitution, and in doing this their judgment differs from that of the majority in Congress, and from yours." As for the president, Miller added, "he will be impeached, if at all, because like the Supreme Court he stands in the way of certain political purposes of the majority." Although Miller shared Rankin's goal of creating a new South, he could hardly believe that men like Rankin and Boutwell would take the Constitution's separation of powers so lightly. "Mr. Boutwell who is perhaps the ablest member of the Judiciary Committee, declared last summer, that the President must be removed, because what the radical majority wants to do cannot be accomplished while he remains," Miller lamented. To his surprise, Rankin had joined that chorus. "I confess that when I see a man of your constitutional training, a sound lawyer, a moderate reasonable man in ordinary affairs, favoring these things, my confidence in the people has received a sensible shock."[29]

But while the assaults on the separation of powers concerned Miller, he still blamed white southerners for the nation's troubles. Three days after he chided Rankin for favoring impeachment and court packing, he lashed out at Ballinger for supporting the president and obstructionist ex-Confederates. Calling Ballinger and other former rebels "you southern people," Miller made clear his view that, whatever excesses took place among Republicans, southern whites were at the root of the problem. "For with all its faults, and all the dangers I see driving it," he wrote, "the Republican Party is the only one from which I can have any hope for the country." As he continued, "The democratic party . . . could not be in full power two years, before Mr. Davis . . . Mr. Vallandigham . . . J. C. Breckinridge, and that class of men, would again become its leaders." The president had already gone beyond the pale. "Mr. Johnson," Miller noted, "is now more odious than the democratic party." And although he feared that Republican attacks on the judiciary and executive were "risking . . . the eventual destruction of some of the best principles of our existing constitutions," this fear did not move him from his support for Reconstruction. "I am," he told Ballinger, "still unwilling to trust you, I mean the Southern people, with full power over the negro, and the Union man of the South."[30]

Miller did not stop there. As he discussed white southerners' refusal to ratify the Fourteenth Amendment, his tone grew angrier and more cutting. "We cannot in the face of events that have occurred since the war," he continued, "trust the South with the power of governing the negro and Union White man without such guarantees in the federal Constitution as secure their protection. . . . Of course, I do not believe that all the stories I see in the papers about killing, beating, shooting these men are true. If you are fair minded you must admit that many of them are true. You will say that they are done by low degraded men who are found in all communities, and that your leading men disapprove of it. That is always the reply."[31]

Then, in language as tough as any Miller used during his life, he challenged Ballinger to offer even a shred of evidence that leading southerners opposed the violence against blacks and white Unionists. "Show me how you disapprove of it," he demanded angrily. "Show me a single white man that has been punished in a State court for murdering a negro or a Union man. Show me that any public meeting has been had to express indignation at such conduct. Show me that you or any of the best men of the South have gone ten steps to prevent the recurrence of such things. Show me the first public address or meeting of Southern men in which the massacres of New Orleans or Memphis have been condemned." Miller knew no such evidence existed. "You may say there are two sides to the stories of Memphis and New Orleans," he concluded. "There may be two sides to the stories, but there was but one side in the party that suffered at both places, and the single truth is undenied that not a rebel or secessionist was hurt in either case, while from thirty to fifty negroes and Union white men were shot down precludes all doubt as to who did it and why it was done."[32]

Miller's letters to Rankin and Ballinger reveal his anguish over events in the North and the South. Caught between northern Radicals who threatened the separation of powers and intransigent white southerners wedded to violence, he longed for a solution that might bring this seemingly endless struggle to a close. He hoped to find a way to save the existing structure of the Constitution while protecting blacks and white Union men in the South. Despite lingering doubts about its political consequences, he acknowledged he was moving towards the idea of black suffrage. In early February, Miller briefly flirted with a compromise plan offered by John Bingham and some southern governors for a revised Fourteenth Amendment that would replace the ban on ex-rebel leaders holding office with a provision for "universal suffrage and universal amnesty." The plan would allow all males, including former rebels and blacks, to vote, provided that they either owned $250 in taxable property or could read the Declaration of Independence and the Constitution. Miller recognized the plan was far from perfect—he certainly feared allowing ex-rebels to have any say in the government—but it was a compromise to which the South might agree, and one that might thus end the struggle that was "demoralizing us worse than the war did." Within the month, however, Miller abandoned this compromise measure and instead endorsed the Military Reconstruction Act that Congress was about to pass.[33]

After southern legislatures rejected the Fourteenth Amendment, Radicals found moderate Republicans increasingly receptive to two key points: existing southern governments needed to be superseded, and black men needed to vote. Moderates began to recognize that black suffrage might be a sound solution in that it allowed federalism to survive by providing freedmen with a means to defend their own rights. Black suffrage, together with the Fourteenth Amendment, would make a powerful combination. Blacks could protect their rights by voting for sympathetic officials, and in the event that African Americans were outvoted by racist whites, section 1 of the amendment could be used to strike down laws that discriminated on the basis of race. Eventually, white politicians would have to start appealing to black voters, which was the first step in bringing a new order to the South.[34]

To achieve these goals, in March 1867 Congress passed the Military Reconstruction Act over Johnson's veto. The act divided the former Confederate states (except for Tennessee) into five military districts. Johnson's provisional governments would not be immediately replaced, but conventions would be called to rewrite each state's constitution. African American males would be allowed to vote for delegates to these conventions, and, if the convention so decided, black male suffrage would be written into the new constitutions. States would also be required to ratify the Fourteenth Amendment. Because Republicans recognized that Johnson and his provisional governments might try to obstruct this process, a supplemental measure gave the Union army responsibility for registering black and white voters and holding elections. During military Reconstruction, Union military forces would also protect the lives and property of the freedmen and loyal whites. In addition, Congress passed the Habeas Corpus Act of 1867, which, by increasing citizens' ability to remove cases to federal courts, protected federal officials and loyal southerners from harassment by obstructionist state tribunals. Overall, the plan was designed to prolong Reconstruction long enough for loyal public opinion to grow and for the Republican vision of commerce, internal improvements, education, and enterprise to attract southern voters to the party. This idea appealed to former Whigs like Miller, who had favored economic development in the South since his early days in Kentucky. He looked forward to the day when the South would "forget the past" and instead the "great interests of finance, currency, [and] internal improvements . . . shall absorb us all."[35]

Later in April, Miller expressed his support for the Military Reconstruction Act in a letter to Ballinger. "How is reconstruction going in Texas?" he asked.

"Will the State adopt the programme laid down by Congress? It is in my opinion as necessary for the north as for the south, that this should be generally adopted by the southern states." Miller believed the act provided a sound basis for completing Reconstruction, and he hoped the South would acquiesce in the plan so as to prevent further Radical attacks on the Court, federalism, or the Constitution's separation of powers. "The strain upon the constitutional government," Miller warned, "from the pace at which the majority is now going, is one which cannot be much longer continued without destroying the machine." But, he admonished Ballinger, if the South remained uncooperative, ever more drastic measures were inevitable. "As long as there is southern resistance," Miller cautioned, "there is no power in the north capable of arresting the onward course of public affairs."[36]

Despite Miller's support for military Reconstruction, however, the act's ability to survive judicial scrutiny was unclear. Legal challenges to the Military Reconstruction Act were inevitable, and, given the Supreme Court's decisions in *Milligan* and the *Test-Oath Cases*, they stood a good chance of succeeding. *Milligan* implied that military authorities had no rightful role in the states in the absence of war or invasion. *Cummings* and *Garland* struck down test oaths identical to those still being used by the military in the southern states. Together, these precedents left the ultimate fate of the Military Reconstruction Act in doubt.[37]

Within three weeks of its passage, the first cases challenging the act reached the Supreme Court. In *Mississippi v. Johnson,* Mississippi's provisional government requested an injunction against the enforcement of the Military Reconstruction Act. As counsel for Mississippi, former senator Robert J. Walker and provisional governor William Sharkey asked the Court to prevent the president from enforcing what they believed to be an unconstitutional act. But because the injunction was directed against the president—who under the act was given the duty of assigning military commanders for each of the five military districts—rather than against Congress, the case took an unexpected turn. Even though Johnson opposed the act, he viewed Mississippi's request as a threat to presidential authority. Not wanting to concede the Supreme Court's right to issue injunctions against the executive branch on political questions, he ordered Attorney General Henry Stanberry to oppose Mississippi's request.

Radical and moderate Republicans worried about the outcome of the case as well. They feared the Court might use this opportunity both to declare military

Reconstruction unconstitutional and to expand its own powers vis-à-vis the executive and legislative branches. As usual, nervous Republicans threatened anti-Court legislation. If the Court struck down the Military Reconstruction Act, they warned, Congress would respond with severe measures. "This tribunal, already suspecting that as now constituted, it is regarded as a diseased member of the body politic," a Republican newspaper predicted, "will not run the risk of amputation by touching the edged tools of Sharkey and Walker."[38]

On April 12, 1867, the Court heard Sharkey, Walker, and Stanberry present their arguments in a courtroom packed with leading senators and congressmen, including Trumbull and Reverdy Johnson. Three days later, a unanimous Court, through Chief Justice Chase, ruled that it had no authority to enjoin the president from enforcing the act. "Can the President," Chase asked, "be restrained by injunction from carrying into effect an act of Congress alleged to be unconstitutional?" Not, he answered, without undermining the separation of powers. "The Congress is the legislative department of the government; the President is the executive department. Neither can be restrained in its action by the judicial department; though the acts of both, when performed, are . . . subject to its cognizance." In other words, only after Johnson acted, not before, were his actions subject to challenge in the courts.[39]

In May, the Court heard a second injunction request. In *Georgia v. Stanton*, the states of Georgia and Mississippi hoped to enjoin Secretary of War Edwin M. Stanton and General John Pope from enforcing the Military Reconstruction Act in their states on the grounds that it unconstitutionally annulled the existing state governments and subjected the people to military rule. But once again a unanimous Court dismissed the suit, saying that it called for an adjudication of political rights, not those of person or property, and was therefore not within the Court's purview. Republicans hailed the decisions in *Mississippi v. Johnson* and *Georgia v. Stanton* as great victories. Many now believed the Court would no longer obstruct congressional Reconstruction. "No State in the Union . . . can rely upon the Supreme Court for protection against . . . Congress," the *Nation* crowed. "The speedy reorganization of the South is now made all but certain." The Court, it appeared to many Republicans, had backed down.[40]

With the Court checked, Congress sought a means to constrain President Johnson during the upcoming summer when Congress would be out of session. Republicans feared that with Congress away, Johnson would harass or fire the federal officials responsible for enforcing military Reconstruction. To prevent this, on March 2 a worried Congress passed the Tenure of Office Act, which required Senate approval for removal of any officeholder whose confirmation had required Senate consent. To assuage Republican concerns that Johnson might order military officials to stop enforcing the Military Reconstruction Act, Congress also passed a regulation requiring that all military orders be directed to the head of the army, General Ulysses S. Grant, whom Republicans trusted.[41]

Despite these measures, Johnson did obstruct Reconstruction's progress in the summer of 1867, removing those military commanders in the South who used their authority to remove uncooperative southern officials. When, for example, Phil Sheridan, military commander in Louisiana, fired state officials implicated for their role in the New Orleans riot, Johnson fired him, against the advice of Grant and all the members of his cabinet besides Gideon Welles. In August, Johnson dismissed Daniel Sickles in the Carolinas for similar acts. In defense of his actions, Johnson argued that the military commanders had authority under the Military Reconstruction Act only to keep peace and punish crimes, not to remove officials. That summer, Johnson also demanded the resignation of Secretary of War Stanton and suspended him until Congress returned. Because Stanton supported military Reconstruction, Johnson considered him a traitor in his midst.

In response, Republican editors once again called for the president's head. Even the most cautious Republicans questioned Johnson's judgment. "Is the President crazy, or only drunk?" asked the conservative editor of the *Boston Daily Advertiser*. "I am afraid his doings will make us all favor impeachment." For his part, Johnson believed that black suffrage in the South had alienated so many northerners that angry voters would rally to his cause in the off-year elections that fall.[42]

The 1867 elections did buoy Johnson's confidence. Although the Republicans triumphed in the South, they took heavy losses in key northern states, where many voters felt the Republican Congress had grown too radical. Republicans retained control of Congress, but the party suffered a significant setback nevertheless. The results frightened many moderates and slowed the leftward shift of the party. Many, including Miller, began to express concern that the Republicans had moved beyond public sentiment. Proponents of impeaching Johnson had also been dealt a blow. When Congress returned in December, an impeachment vote pushed by Radicals failed as moderates retrenched. With a presidential election coming the next year, many Republicans favored nominating a conservative candidate who could help reverse the losses of 1867. Miller, following politics closely as usual, predicted that they would turn to the previously apolitical, probably conservative, and very popular Ulysses S. Grant. "There seems to be no doubt that Grant will be the nominee of the convention called to meet at Chicago next May," Miller wrote in December 1867. But with the tide apparently turning against the Republicans, he worried if even Grant's prestige could change the party's fortunes. "Many thinking men among the Republicans," he moaned, "doubt whether even his name can secure victory."[43]

Adding to his concerns, December 1867 brought further controversy to the Supreme Court. In *Ex Parte McCardle*, the justices faced another lawsuit challenging the constitutionality of the Military Reconstruction Act. The case arose from the arrest of William McCardle, an unreconstructed and fiercely racist newspaper editor in Vicksburg, Mississippi. Military authorities arrested McCardle for printing "incendiary and libelous" articles that allegedly threatened public order. To get McCardle's case to the Supreme Court, his lawyers had ingeniously turned to the Habeas Corpus Act of 1867, which gave federal courts expanded power to grant writs of habeas corpus in all cases where any person might be restrained of his or her liberty in violation of the Constitution. It also allowed appeals of these cases from lower federal courts to the Supreme Court. Ironically, Congress had designed the law to save federal officials and other Unionists from the clutches of biased southern courts, not to aid rebellious newspaper editors. But McCardle used the measure as a means to challenge both his arrest and military Reconstruction in its entirety.[44]

Upon his arrest, McCardle petitioned a lower federal court for a writ of habeas corpus. When the lower court issued the writ, the military commander in Vicksburg duly responded, produced McCardle, and provided the reasons for his arrest—disturbing the peace, libel, impeding Reconstruction, and inciting insurrection, disorder, and violence. The military commander argued that the Military Reconstruction Act authorized the arrest, while McCardle's lawyers claimed that *Ex Parte Milligan* made his arrest and imminent trial by military courts unconstitutional. The lower court decided against McCardle and remanded him to military custody. McCardle's lawyers appealed the case to the Supreme Court. The justices accepted the appeal and again found themselves in the center of the storm.[45]

By January 1868, rumors circulated in Washington that the Court planned to use McCardle's case to declare the Military Reconstruction Act invalid. Of the eight justices on the bench (Justice Wayne had died the previous July), it was predicted that five—Grier, Clifford, Nelson, Davis, and Field—would decide that both McCardle's arrest and military Reconstruction were unconstitutional. Only Chase, Swayne, and Miller could be counted on to support the constitutionality of Congress's Reconstruction legislation. As a result, worried Republicans renewed efforts to thwart the Court's majority. In early January, the House passed a bill that required two-thirds of the Supreme Court to concur before any law passed by Congress could be declared unconstitutional.

Although Congress's constitutional power to pass such a law was questionable, Radical newspapers supported the measure. "The Reconstruction Acts are full of rights and liberties of millions of men," one editor wrote, "and to have these stricken down, by the decision of some old fossil on the Supreme Bench whose political opinion belongs to a past era, would be an outrage to humanity." Radicals believed requiring a two-thirds majority would "lift judicial decisions into universal respect, while the present close divisions exposed the Court to imputations of partisanship." But not all Republicans agreed. The *Chicago Republican* claimed that nine-tenths of the Republicans in the Northwest opposed the measure, that Congress needed to respect the separation of powers, and that most Republicans would never "sit by quietly and see a hand lifted against the Court or the Constitution, whether by the National Congress or by Southern traitors." The next step, another paper feared, would be "to suspend the action of the Court on constitutional questions, during the existence of the present Congress." While the two-thirds bill passed in the House, moderates in the Senate managed to kill the measure. Still, the message to the Court was clear.[46]

As the Court prepared to hear arguments in *McCardle*, efforts to impeach Johnson revived. The 1867 election results and the failure of the impeachment drive in December had emboldened the president, who concluded that voters had tired of Reconstruction and were swinging in his direction. On December 28, he relieved General Pope of his command in Alabama, Mississippi, and Arkansas. Hoping to produce a dramatic confrontation with Congress, he also contemplated firing Secretary of War Stanton in a purposeful violation of the Tenure of Office Act. Johnson believed that if a showdown took place, the country would rally around him, moderate Republicans would split from the Radicals, and congressional Reconstruction would falter.[47]

Miller's mood grew darker as he found himself surrounded on all sides by bitter partisanship. Johnson's boorishness, the new legislative assaults on the

Court, the revived impeachment issue, and the growing factionalism of his fellow justices made him apprehensive. He feared the confrontation that both Johnson and the Radicals seemed to want might irreparably damage the Constitution by undermining permanently the system of checks and balances. After a wrenching civil war that had severely tested the nation's governing institutions, Miller worried that politicians and jurists had lost the proper respect for the Constitution and the principle of separation of powers. "The political situation looks to me more gloomy than it has ever looked," Miller wrote Ballinger on January 19, because "in the threatened collision between the Legislative branch of the government and the executive and judicial branches I see consequences from which the cause of free government may never recover in my day." Miller blamed everyone—the president, the Congress, and the Court—for the disaster he saw coming. "The worst feature I now see is the passion which governs the hour in all parties and all persons who have controlling influence," he bemoaned. "In this the Supreme Court is as fully involved as the President or House of Representatives."[48]

The confrontation Miller dreaded began on February 21, 1868, when Johnson fired Stanton. For House Republicans this was the last straw, and they drafted eleven articles of impeachment. Most of the articles focused on the removal of Stanton as a violation of the Tenure of Office Act. Two others charged the president with denying the authority of Congress and attempting to bring it "into disgrace." These came closest to expressing the real reason for impeachment: Johnson's aggressive obstruction of congressional Reconstruction. Republicans' pent-up anger at the totality of Johnson's behavior, not his sacking of Stanton, drove the impeachment effort. On February 24, the House, voting along party lines, successfully impeached Johnson and the proceedings moved to the Senate, where the president would be tried.[49]

Miller, fed up with the behavior of both the president and Congress, deplored the carnivalesque atmosphere that surrounded the impending trial. "You can no doubt imagine," he wrote disgustedly to Ballinger on March 1, "that we are in the midst of a great excitement on the subject of the impeachment of the President." Indeed, "you would not be likely to overestimate it." If there was any silver lining to be found, he jokingly told his brother-in-law, it was the fact that the Supreme Court's annual dinner with the president at the White House—held on February 28 in the midst of the swirling events—was more exciting than usual. "The evening," he blithely noted, "was not so dull as one I attended last winter at the same place." At the dinner, Johnson's demeanor surprised him; he seemed unaffected by the crisis. "The President," Miller wrote, did not "seem more silent or nervous than usual. He conversed freely . . . about the impeachment."[50]

In the Senate trial, the effort to remove Johnson ran into early trouble. Because the articles of impeachment focused primarily on the technical issues surrounding Stanton's removal, rather than on Johnson's obstruction of congressional policies, the trial quickly bogged down in legal particulars. Johnson's attorneys argued that only a clear violation of law warranted removal, and on that point the House managers had a weak case. The Tenure of Office Act stipulated only that the president could not fire any cabinet members he appointed during his term. But Stanton was a Lincoln appointee, and it was not clear that the act pertained to him. Some Senate moderates, moreover, shared Miller's concern that convicting the president would undermine the separation of powers, while others disapproved of the economic policies of Johnson's heir-apparent, Benjamin Wade. As the trial wore on and it became clear there would not be a speedy conviction, the Republicans' "confidence in ultimate success wilted." In the end, doubts about the validity of the charges against Johnson, concerns about the separation of powers, and fear of Wade's economic policies convinced enough senators to vote against removing the president. In mid-May, thirty-five senators voted for conviction, one short of the required two-thirds.[51]

Johnson's impeachment and trial served as the backdrop for the oral arguments in *McCardle*, the case many thought would determine the fate of the Military Reconstruction Act. On March 2, Senator Matthew Hale Carpenter spoke for two and half hours on the side of the government, delivering a flowery and sentimental speech about the Court's high purpose and the need for judicial restraint. At the end of this oration, Secretary of War Stanton, sure that Carpenter had convinced the Court to uphold the validity of the act, exclaimed with tears in his eyes, "Carpenter, you have saved us." Carpenter, though, was not so sure. Based on the justices' questions and facial expressions, he feared the Court would instead vote to free McCardle and declare the Military Reconstruction Act unconstitutional. He worried that Nelson, Clifford, and Grier had appeared "dead set against" him, and that Davis and Field looked "troubled." Only Miller, Carpenter remarked, seemed convinced. "Miller's face," he said, "was as the face of an angel, radiant with light and joy."[52]

Many Republican congressmen shared Carpenter's apprehension. Three days after the conclusion of oral arguments, Congress resorted to a drastic measure. On March 12, 1868, the House and Senate passed a bill designed to remove the Court's jurisdiction in the case. Since McCardle's ability to appeal his case to the Supreme Court was based on the Habeas Corpus Act, Congress rescinded the portion of that act that allowed habeas corpus appeals. In addition, the bill prohibited the Court from exercising jurisdiction in appeals already taken. It appeared that Congress's act required the Court to dismiss McCardle's case immediately for want of jurisdiction.

Republican editors considered the bill a brilliant tactical maneuver. The Constitution, they noted, gave Congress the power to determine the Court's appellate jurisdiction, and although the decision to pull the rug out from under it with the *McCardle* case already underway was unprecedented, it was not expressly prohibited. "The passage of that little bill which put a knife to the throat of the *McCardle* Case," one editor wrote, "was a splendid performance." Another declared, "Congress does not intend to permit the Supreme Court to overthrow it or revive the rebellion, if it can help it." On March 25 Johnson vetoed the measure, but the Senate and House overrode his veto that same week.[53]

Some of the president's supporters hoped that the Court might outmaneuver Congress by quickly deciding the case during the eighteen days between the close of arguments in *McCardle* and the final passage of the bill that removed its jurisdiction. The *Boston Post*'s correspondent insisted that the justices should immediately decide the case "in defense of its own dignity, and to show that the Court cannot be trifled with by reckless partisans who flippantly speak of 'clipping the wings of the Court.' It is well ascertained that Justices Chase, Nelson, Grier, Clifford, Davis, and Field believe the Reconstruction Acts to be unconstitutional. . . . The decision is made up, and they have the power and the right to deliver it. Whether they have the nerve to be an independent Judiciary remains to be seen."[54]

Only Justices Field and Grier favored reaching a decision immediately. The rest preferred to avoid a direct confrontation with Congress and voted to postpone the decision until the next term, by which time it would no longer have jurisdiction in the case. While Democrats sharply criticized the justices for their alleged cowardice, Republican editors applauded this prudent act. "The Supreme Court, acting with more discretion and better taste than the President," the *Springfield Republican* remarked, "bows down to the will of Congress, and has postponed the *McCardle* case till Congress has more definitely settled the Reconstruction question."[55]

Despite their delaying tactics, the Court could not avoid the new question raised by Congress's action—did the legislature have the ability to abolish its right to adjudicate pending cases? Some Democrats argued that with regard to *McCardle,* the law was in essence "*ex post facto* and cannot apply." Cases already underway had to continue unimpeded, Democrats warned; otherwise, in the future anytime an unpopular decision appeared to be forthcoming, Congress might try to remove the Court's jurisdiction.[56]

During its next term, the Court heard arguments on this question. McCardle's lawyer, William Sharkey, asserted that the Court took its authority from the Constitution, not from Congress, and that Congress could not remove the Court's jurisdiction mid-trial simply because "they anticipate that it will soon deliver [an opinion] contrary to the views of the majority of Congress, of what it ought to decide." To do so, Sharkey warned, amounted to "an exercise by Congress of judicial power." In response, Matthew Carpenter and Lyman Trumbull contended that the Court's appellate jurisdiction under the Constitution was subject to such exceptions as Congress might make. Congress gave the Court jurisdiction in *McCardle* with the Habeas Corpus Act, and it was perfectly acceptable for Congress to take that jurisdiction away. It did not matter that deliberations were already underway when jurisdiction ceased. Instead, Trumbull and Carpenter claimed, that when jurisdiction ceases "no judicial act can be performed." In the end, in an opinion written by Chief Justice Chase that Miller joined, the justices agreed that they no longer had jurisdiction. Chase acknowledged Sharkey's argument that "appellate jurisdiction of this Court is not derived from acts of Congress. It is strictly speaking, conferred by the Constitution. . . . But it is conferred with such exceptions and under such regulations as Congress shall make." Once again the justices had deferred to Congress. It seemed that the Court might no longer interfere with congressional Reconstruction.[57]

With the Court subdued, congressional Reconstruction proceeded apace. In the spring of 1868, biracial electorates in six southern states approved new state constitutions, and all but three of the southern states resumed normal relations with the Union. Although northern troops remained in the South to protect the new governments, only Virginia, Mississippi, and Texas remained politically unreconstructed. This return to normal relations marked a critical juncture in the history of Reconstruction. To be sure, the new forward-looking state constitutions reflected a major victory for blacks and Republicans; but with their passage, Congress's justification for using extraordinary war powers in the restored states ended. Congressional legislation once again needed to be based on the peacetime Constitution and the principles of federalism. As a result, historian Michael Les Benedict noted, "those Republicans who wished to preserve the old . . . conception of national power began to draw apart from those who were willing to see the national government assume broad, new responsibilities for the protection of citizens' rights."[58]

Miller, exasperated by what he perceived as repeated assaults upon the Constitution, was among those reluctant to expand national power further. He convinced himself that the new constitutions and biracial electorates in the South could adequately protect individual rights. The federal government and courts should intervene only if state laws discriminated on the basis of race. In those instances, the Fourteenth Amendment allowed Congress and the federal judiciary to act. In the three remaining unreconstructed states, he still supported Congress's use of extraordinary powers.

On April 12, 1869, the same day the Court rendered its *McCardle* opinion, the justices decided *Texas v. White*, another case with important implications for Congress's Reconstruction program. The case arose from a dispute involving bonds that the federal government had issued in 1851 to Texas as a part of the Compromise of 1850. In order to settle Texas's boundary claims, the federal government gave $10 million in bonds to the new state. They were transferable, so the state could hold on to them or sell them to third parties. During the 1850s, Texas did sell most of the bonds. When the Civil War began, however, some of the bonds remained unsold in the state treasury. Desperate for money to fund the war effort, the Confederate state legislature decided to try to sell the remaining bonds. Before the war the Texas legislature had required that the state's governor endorse with his signature all of the bonds that were sold. But during the war, this requirement created an obstacle to the bonds' successful sale. The legislators recognized that the bonds' value might be diminished by fears that the U.S. Treasury would refuse to honor bonds peddled by a Confederate state. If, as the law required, Texas's Confederate governor endorsed the remaining bonds, it would clearly tie them to the rebellion, further reducing the chance that they could be redeemed. To mask their bonds' origin, the legislature dropped the requirement for the governor's endorsement. "It was supposed . . . that negotiation of them would be less difficult," Chief Justice Chase wrote, "if they bore upon their face no direct evidence of having come from the possession of an insurgent state government." Before the bonds were sold, however, a Unionist Texan tipped off the U.S. secretary of the treasury about the scheme. The Treasury Department then ran advertisements in the *New York Tribune* warning investors that Texas bonds not endorsed by a prewar governor would not be honored. Undeterred by these warnings, two Texas businessmen, George White and Jon Chiles, bought 135 of the bonds and then resold many of them to secondary investors in the United States and England.[59] When the war ended, the provisional governor of Texas attempted to reclaim the bonds. Certain that the illegitimate Confederate government in Texas had no right to sell them, the governor sued in federal court asking for an injunction to keep the Treasury from paying any of the bondholders and asking the Court to instead order that the bonds be returned to the state.[60]

At first glance, the issues in *Texas v. White* seemed very straightforward. Most northerners agreed that the wartime rebel legislature in Texas was illegitimate and had no authority to sell the bonds, particularly for the noxious purpose of funding a rebellion against the United States. Credible evidence existed that all of the bond purchasers either knew or should have known that the bonds had a dubious origin. The provisional Texas government appeared entirely justified in its efforts to reclaim them. As often happened with issues involving Reconstruction politics, however, the case turned out to be far more complex than it first appeared.

The issues in *Texas v. White* were complicated by the fact that in order for the Texas suit to continue, the Court had to determine that the Johnson-appointed provisional government in Texas constituted the legitimate government of the state and could therefore sue in federal court. Many Radical Republicans opposed this, as they had long since turned against Johnson's Reconstruction policies and the provisional governments he appointed. Many moderate Republicans had grown weary of the barrage of lawsuits initiated by the provisional southern governments designed to obstruct congressional Reconstruction; they, too, wanted the provisional state governments disqualified. By 1868, most Republicans had rejected Lincoln's wartime idea that the Confederate states had never the left the Union. They wanted to treat the southern states as conquered territory that could be subjected to any measure Congress deemed necessary. If the justices concluded that the provisional government was not legitimate and that the Court therefore did not have jurisdiction, the remaining provisional governments would be discredited and their obstructionist lawsuits would end.[61]

Democrats, on the other hand, hoped that the Court would declare that Texas could sue in federal court and that the provisional government appointed by Johnson was the official government of Texas. That would mean Texas had already been readmitted as a state and that Congress had no power to withhold any rights the state possessed before the war. The Military Reconstruction Act, it followed, might then be considered an unconstitutional infringement of the state's rights. Adding complexity to the matter were the concerns of Wall Street investors and bondholders. In an era of bond repudiation, investors feared any court decision that denied bondholders their right to collect, as they felt that anyone holding negotiable bonds that were valid on their face should be paid.[62]

In his majority opinion, Chief Justice Chase reached a decision that had something in it to displease everyone. First, he decided that Texas could sue in federal court. Chase shared Lincoln's position that the "Constitution in all its provisions, looks to an indestructible Union, composed of indestructible states" and that Texas's ordinance of secession was "utterly without operation in law." But while Texas remained a state, Chase continued, secession had suspended the rights of its government and citizens. It therefore became the federal government's responsibility to provide the state with a new, republican form of government.[63]

The president, Chase continued, had the authority as commander-in-chief to establish provisional governments in the rebellious states. Thus, Johnson's provisional governments were legitimate. But, he added, it was Congress, under the guarantee clause of article 4 of the Constitution, that had the final say about what constituted a republican government. "The action of the President must," Chase reasoned, "therefore, be considered as provisional." Using this rationale, he declared that Congress did have the authority to pass the Military Reconstruction Act of 1867, even if certain provisions of that act might still be held unconstitutional. With that, the Democrats' last hope that the Court might find the Military Reconstruction Act wholly unconstitutional disappeared. But Chase's opinion also discomfited many Republicans. By concluding that the provisional governments and the military governments were both legitimate, it allowed officials of either government to sue in federal court. Federal courts could continue to accept suits from provisional governors that challenged portions of Congress's Reconstruction policy (including those that challenged the ongoing role played by federal troops in all of the southern states).[64]

Having determined that the Court had jurisdiction, Chase then decided the question of whether Texas still had title to the bonds. On this point, he made a concession to practicality. Although its acts were unlawful, Chase recognized that the rebellious Texas state legislature did amount to the de facto government of Texas, as it was the one that the people of Texas agreed to have regulate their actions during the war. Accordingly, measures passed by the legislature that were necessary to peace and good order among citizens—such as marriage or property laws—would be recognized as valid. This conclusion avoided the legal maelstrom that would have followed if it was determined that every governmental act of the Confederate legislatures was inoperative. In various circuit court opinions, Chase had upheld previously the validity of marriage licenses, market transactions, and other day-to-day acts legally sanctioned by the Confederate state governments. Acts that furthered the rebellion against the United States—such as the wartime Texas legislature's decision to sell U.S. bonds in order to fund the war effort—were the exceptions to this rule. The state's contract with White and Chiles was therefore treasonable and void. The secondary bondholders, despite their claims to the contrary, were hardly innocent purchasers. They had more than sufficient notice that something was awry, namely that the bonds sold at prices well below what they would have been had their title been unquestioned. Consequently, the bondholders accepted the risk. Texas, Chase concluded, could reclaim the bonds.[65]

Miller, Swayne, and Grier dissented from the majority opinion, instead agreeing with the Radicals' position that Texas was not yet readmitted as a state and could not sue in federal court. Texas's status did not differ, Justice Grier wrote, from the "Indian tribes, who are governed by military force" and who "cannot claim to be States of the Union." "Is Texas a state, now represented by members chosen by the people of that State and received on the floor of Congress?" Grier asked rhetorically. "Has she two senators to represent her as a state in the Senate of the United States? . . . Is she not held and governed as a conquered province by military force?" No, Grier resolved, Texas was not a state. Texas officials could bring their suit only if and when Congress readmitted their state to the Union.[66]

In a separate dissent, Miller and Swayne concurred with Grier "as to the incapacity of the state of Texas, in her present condition, to maintain an original suit in this Court." They did not believe that the Court had any authority to determine when Texas regained its status as a state for matters of jurisdiction or for any other purpose. The status of Texas was a legislative matter beyond the purview of the Court. "The question," they argued, was "one in relation to which this Court is bound by the action of the legislative department of the government." They deferred to the legislative branch and to the Radicals' position that Texas would be readmitted when Congress, not Chief Justice Chase, determined.[67]

But while the three dissenters agreed that Texas could not sue in federal court, Miller's and Swayne's reasons for dissenting differed from Grier's. Grier's primary concern was the bondholders. Seventy-four years old, Grier, a dough-face from Pennsylvania who opposed Radical Reconstruction, worried that innocent bondholders would be denied payment. The U.S. bonds that the bondholders bought, Grier argued, were negotiable paper and freely transferable. From the moment the federal government issued those bonds to Texas in 1851, he felt, it lost any control over them, and the U.S. Treasury had to honor them no matter who presented them for payment. To do otherwise, he concluded, would be morally wrong.[68]

Miller and Swayne's dissent had a different goal. Although Swayne normally carried bondholders' interests close to his heart, in war powers cases he staunchly supported the Republicans' position. Miller and Swayne concurred with the majority that the bonds had been sold illegitimately and should not be honored. The status of Texas, however, was a different matter. Here, Miller and Swayne came down on the side of those who favored a rigorous Reconstruction. But because Chase's views on this point carried the majority, Miller once again dissented in a decision that caused a furor among congressional Republicans.[69]

The Court's opinion in *Texas v. White* led Lyman Trumbull to team with the Radicals in support of a bill designed to overcome Chase's decision. In December, Trumbull reported a bill designed "to define the jurisdiction of the Supreme Court in certain cases." The bill's language mirrored Miller and Swayne's dissenting opinion, providing that "under the Constitution, the judicial power of the United States does not embrace political power, or give to judicial tribunals any authority to question the political departments of the Government on political questions." The bill directly challenged Chase's opinion by stipulating that "it rests with Congress to decide what Government is the established one in a State, and that it is hereby, in accordance with former legislation, declared that no civil State Government exists in Virginia, Mississippi, or Texas." Although Miller's reaction to Trumbull's bill is not known, he had previously reacted to similar measures with mixed feelings. He supported Republican Reconstruction, but he did not approve of legislative attempts to control the Court; he probably did not mourn when conservative opposition defeated Trumbull's bill.[70]

In May 1868, the Republicans, as Miller had predicted, chose Ulysses S. Grant as their nominee for president. Back in December, Miller had feared that even Grant's popularity might not be enough to restore voters' enthusiasm for the Republicans. Fortunately for Grant and his party, the Democratic candidate, New York's wartime governor Horatio Seymour, drove many disaffected northerners back into the Republican camp. During the war, Seymour had called Lincoln a despot and the New York draft rioters "my friends." Campaigning against Grant, he declared that military Reconstruction was entirely unconstitutional; he promised that, if elected, he would destroy the new southern governments. Most northerners regarded Seymour's views as anathema. In November, despite widespread Ku Klux Klan violence against Republicans in the South, Grant swept to victory in a contest in which an estimated half-million black votes were almost certainly the deciding factor.[71]

Violence against black voters in that election confirmed Republicans' growing conviction that a constitutional amendment was needed to guarantee black suffrage. If African Americans were going to be able to protect themselves after northern troops left the South, they needed to be able to vote. Miller and other moderates recognized that blacks' votes represented the "only chance for a Republican Party in the South." As a result, in January 1868 Republicans drafted an amendment intended to provide for and protect black suffrage. The proposed amendment stipulated that no citizen's right to vote could be denied or abridged on account of "race, color, or previous condition of servitude." This language was, in many respects, quite conservative. The amendment's framers rejected proposals to include "education" along with race, leaving open the possibility of literacy tests (and poll taxes and other arbitrary and unfairly administered barriers to black voting). They also did not include women's suffrage. Nevertheless, the ratification of the Fifteenth Amendment in February 1870 represented a dramatic culmination of the liberalizing trends in American life in the late 1850s and 1860s. The amendment authorized black votes in the North, where in many states whites had also long resisted black suffrage.[72]

To be sure, there were limits to most Republicans' liberality. Many, including Miller, accepted charges made by white southerners concerning the supposed ignorance and corruption of black and white politicians in the reconstructed governments. "It is not to be denied," Miller wrote in August 1869, that some of "the leaders of the radical party in the gulf states since the rebellion have . . . been men of bad character, and without principle, and that still more of them are ignorant, and unused to the exercise of political power." But for this, he told Ballinger, southern whites had only themselves to blame. What did they expect after vilifying respectable "scalawags" like James Longstreet who had aided the Republican governments? The social ostracism and violence that southern elites had visited upon anyone who cooperated with the Reconstruction regimes, Miller wrote, drove out "all good men who had anything to lose and created the necessity which placed the leadership in the hands of the class of men of who you complain." If Ballinger wanted changes, he should aid the Republican Party in its "attempt to organize a more conservative republicanism in the South." In the meantime, Miller let Ballinger know that he fully supported the Fifteenth Amendment. Blacks had to be able to protect their rights because southern whites had proven themselves unable to control their "fiendish hatred . . . for the negro."[73]

Whatever the faults of the new southern governments, Miller remained firmly committed to Republican Reconstruction policies. In July 1869, he flatly rejected a suggestion from Ballinger that it was perhaps time to appoint a southerner to the Supreme Court. "All the lawyers now of sufficient years, educated in the South," Miller reasoned, "whether whig or democratic in politics, are more or less imbued with the strict construction principles as regards the Constitution." He knew this would lead them to challenge Reconstruction. "The more honest they are as men, therefore, the greater danger that when in the future, great questions shall arise before them, affecting the validity of the various legislative steps involved in the reconstruction policy, intended to give peace and stability to the government and country, they may feel bound to hold those acts unconstitutional." He feared that result. "I think the mere possibility of this to any general extent, would be a calamity hardly second to the rebellion itself."[74]

Miller's positions had dramatically liberalized during the 1860s. At the start of the decade, he was resigned to an indefinite continuation of slavery in the South. By 1870, he supported constitutional amendments giving blacks freedom, civil rights, and the right to vote. Miller's transformation was, of course, not unique. As Robert Dykstra has shown, most Iowa Republicans experienced a similar shift. Before the war, Iowans had overwhelmingly rejected an amendment to the state constitution that would have provided for black suffrage. By 1868, they rewrote their state's constitution in order to give African Americans voting rights. Unlike southerners, Iowans had no economic investment in the theory of black inferiority; the events of the 1860s could and did change their views. The performance of black troops during the war deeply impressed Miller and other Iowans, and during Reconstruction they recognized that it was hypocritical to demand black suffrage in the South while denying it in their own state. Although most still did not embrace social equality between the races, by 1869 a remarkable transformation among Iowans had already occurred. Rather than being deeply and immovably racist, they proved susceptible to pressure and persuasion. "The circumstances, processes, and strategies that won frontier Iowans to the civil equality of blacks," Dykstra concludes, "remind us that there are egalitarian precedents as well as a racist tradition in America's past."[75]

Miller's metamorphosis on issues of race reinforces Dykstra's claim. Miller certainly was never in the vanguard on racial questions. But he did, when pushed by events and the intransigence of others, reveal a remarkable ability to change his views. Once a slaveholder, by the 1850s he favored gradual emancipation and the containment of slavery where it existed. By the end of the Civil War, he embraced immediate abolition and black civil rights, and a few years later he advocated suffrage for African Americans. All black men, Miller believed, should be treated as citizens with full political and legal rights. By 1870, his positions on race made him indistinguishable from many of the antebellum abolitionists he once claimed to abhor.

CHAPTER 7

A New Class That Produces Nothing

B ECAUSE OF HIS DUTIES on the Supreme Court, Miller was able to return to Keokuk for only a few months each summer. He regretted this absence because many of his best friends were in Keokuk, the place he considered home. "I am so little at Keokuk now," he wrote from Washington in March 1868, "and the position of Judge of the Supreme Court is so much one of isolation, that my social feeling is now very much to two classes outside of my own family. There are the friends whom I have made in this city and the old friends and family of years ago. Some of the former class are pleasant friends and agreeable companions, but the feelings they call into life want the fervor and completeness of those made in former days."[1]

Throughout the 1860s, Miller's family remained in Keokuk and he lived in hotels while in Washington. After fulfilling his circuit duties at the end of each term, he returned to Iowa and there passed the summer, spending evenings with old friends and playing cards with Eliza and his children on their porch. "Miller is enjoying his vacation—and takes his life philosophically," William Ballinger wrote in his diary after visiting Samuel and Eliza in July 1867. "I don't [know] any one who seems to have a truer contentment. His health is fine—They have a good pair of horses & drive out every evening."[2]

Despite his air of contentment, Miller had reason to worry during those summers. He was living beyond his means, and, like his hometown, he owed money to creditors. "I have never been out of debt since the first year after I came to Iowa," he wrote in July 1866. In the 1850s, he had borrowed freely in order to pay for his real estate investments in and around Keokuk. Certain that the bustling river town would grow into a major metropolis, he believed that his investments would make him rich. The Panic of 1857 and the decline of the river trade destroyed that dream, and he now held worthless lands and burdensome debts. Year after year he waited for Keokuk's economy to revive. "I have been making a vigorous effort to sell our lands here," he wrote in July 1866, "but find it is a very poor business. . . . I may be able to sell some . . . this summer but the prospect seems dull. It is not so much a matter of price, as finding purchasers at any price." Although Miller enjoyed returning home each summer, the trips always reminded him of financial troubles, both his own and the town's. "I have not," he lamented in July 1867, "been able to make my income meet my accrued expenses."[3]

By the late 1860s, Keokuk's economy had not improved. The unbridled growth and crowded streets of the 1850s were distant memories. By 1868, the town's population had dropped below 15,000. Railroads finally connected Keokuk to the rest of the world, but only long after rival towns had secured the best routes. The grand plans from the boom years for a direct trunk line to New York had been abandoned. Miller and other town residents placed their hopes in building a canal at Keokuk that would allow boats on the Mississippi to circumnavigate the nearby rapids that slowed river traffic. "There is a strong probability that the appropriations . . . to be made for improving the rapids of the Mississippi River," Miller wrote Ballinger in 1866, "will be used for building a canal on the Iowa side. In that event I hope to sell the property." Upon some reflection, however, Miller recognized that a canal might not improve the city's fortunes. Although it would speed river travel, it would also provide boats with the means to bypass the Gate City entirely. "The canal is in progress," he wrote in 1868 as construction began on the project, "but its blessings to Keokuk are not as certain."[4]

Hog slaughtering remained the backbone of Keokuk's economy although that industry, too, was in decline. Health problems, particularly cholera, continued to plague the town. "We have cholera in Keokuk now and have had for several weeks," Miller wrote in September 1866, doubtless recalling that the disease had killed his first law partner, Lewis Reeves, as it would take his second partner, John Rankin, in an 1869 outbreak. Miller had grown accustomed to pigs, befouled rivers, cholera, and unexpected deaths, but this was not the future he had envisioned for Keokuk when he first had arrived there in 1850.[5]

In the late 1860s, when Keokuk's citizens looked for someone to blame for their town's troubles, they still were able to point to the railroad bondholders.

Local Republicans and Democrats, though deeply divided on national issues, shared a hatred for bondholders who continued to insist that the ailing city pay its debts from the 1850s. Miller and Keokuk's Republicans portrayed bondholders as parasites who, like antebellum slaveholders, lived off the labor of others; Keokuk's Democrats lumped bondholders and African Americans together with other groups who, they believed, received special favors from the federal government (a list that included "railroad companies, New England manufacturers, officeholders, the Southern Negro, and the bondholder"). "You freed the negro . . . ," a Democratic stump speaker told an audience, "and fastened eternal white slavery upon yourselves and [your] children by lowering and knuckling to . . . the monied monopolies of the country." With the advent of African American suffrage in Iowa, the speaker warned, cheap labor would flood into the state and benefit only the "wealthy bondholder who is to be their employer."[6]

In 1868, Iowans' anger at the bondholders and the federal courts boiled over. Throughout July and August, during what Miller described as the "hottest summer here ever known," thousands attended antibondholder rallies in Keokuk and Lee County. At these mass meetings, angry taxpayers, enraged by the *Gelpcke* decision and the federal circuit court rulings that followed, complained of "being persistently pursued in the federal courts by certain holders of . . . railroad bonds." Lee County alone, taxpayers bitterly noted, owed nearly $1 million plus interest to bondholders, "a sum, if collected, sufficient to reduce [taxpayers] to bankruptcy." Taxpayers' meetings passed resolutions protesting the payment of the "so-called . . . bonds." Iowans continued to embrace the decisions of their state courts that held that the bonds were invalid. Rather than accepting the *Gelpcke* decision as final, protesters demanded "vigorous and untiring legal opposition to the bonds in question."[7]

In his dissent in *Gelpcke,* Miller had predicted that the decision would create a legal crisis in Iowa, pitting state and federal judges against one another and sandwiching county and town officials between the two. With the U.S. Supreme Court upholding the validity of the bonds and the Iowa Supreme Court declaring them invalid, municipal officials did find themselves in a legally precarious position. Mayors and aldermen regularly faced competing injunctions from state and federal judges. Federal courts ordered local officials to raise taxes in order to pay bondholders, while state courts issued injunctions barring the collection of such taxes. Either way, officials faced fines or imprisonment for violating the courts' orders. In Keokuk and Lee County, irate taxpayers joined the fray and demanded that county supervisors follow the state court decisions and refuse to collect taxes to pay the bonds. Taxpayers thanked the judges of the Iowa Supreme Court for "their manly, dignified and unswerving position in regard to those so-called bonds" and pledged to indemnify city and county officials for any fines imposed on them by the federal courts. But the officials risked more than just fines; they could be jailed. In one instance, Justice Davis, following two suits by Chicago bondholders in his northern Illinois circuit court, ordered U.S. marshals both to arrest Lee County officials and to collect the tax.[8]

These disputes resulted in a second generation of Iowa bond cases that revolved around the question of whether municipal officials could refuse to collect taxes to pay railroad bondholders because state courts had enjoined them from doing so. Not surprisingly, the Supreme Court in two 1868 decisions, *Riggs v. Johnson County* and *Weber v. Lee County*, ruled that the tax collectors had to follow the federal courts' orders. For Justice Clifford, who wrote the majority opinion in *Riggs*, the issue was simple. A state court, he wrote, could not enjoin the process or proceedings of a federal circuit court. Miller, "being a tax-payer in Lee County," took no part in the *Weber* decision.[9] But in *Riggs*, he dissented once again, reiterating his arguments from the previous bond cases. In particular, he believed the Court's decision in *Knox County v. Aspinwall* had led to "evil consequences." After that decision, he charged, "no matter how illegal, fraudulent, or unauthorized were corporation bonds, no defence could be made to them in Federal courts, and, of course, they were all sued upon in those courts." Now state officials were "commanded to disobey an injunction of a state court, . . . in a matter of which that court had undoubted jurisdiction, concerning the levy of a tax under state laws." To reach their conclusions, Miller added, the Court's majority had once again resorted to "judicial subtleties of which the corporation bond litigation seems to be the prolific parent."[10]

The justices faced an even more complex question a year later in *Butz v. Muscatine*, a case that arose when a Pennsylvania bondholder sued in federal court in order to collect on delinquent railroad bonds that the Iowa river town of Muscatine had issued back in 1854, at the height of the railroad hysteria. Had the suit been brought in Iowa's state courts, Muscatine might have successfully claimed that city officials had violated their municipal charter by issuing railroads bonds and that the bonds were therefore invalid. But in federal courts, that battle had already been lost in *Gelpcke, Knox County*, and subsequent cases.

Out of necessity, Muscatine officials devised an ingenious new rationale for refusing to pay Butz.[11]

Two laws, one state and one municipal, applied to the case. Given that federal courts had ruled that the railroad bond debts must be paid, Iowa's state code, which required Iowa cities to pay their debts in a timely manner, actually seemed to favor Butz. The state code obligated indebted Iowa municipalities to pay judgments with a tax "levied as early as practicable to pay off the judgment, with interest and costs." If city officials failed to assess such a tax, they would be held personally responsible for the debt, a provision that prompted Keokuk's antibond protesters to promise to indemnify city officials against such penalties. In addition to the state statute, Muscatine officials had to consider a provision in their city's charter that limited the amount that property taxes could be raised in a single year. Adopted in 1852, and mirroring provisions in the charters of many Iowa cities, the statute stipulated this limit to be only 1 percent of the town's estimated property value per year. During the boom years, as rivertown property values soared, a 1 percent increase appeared to be a sensible cap. But in 1867, with prices moribund, a 1 percent restriction choked off needed municipal revenues. Many property owners, moreover, could not afford to pay even modest taxes. As a result, when ordered by a federal judge to pay Butz, Muscatine officials protested that they needed every penny of the 1 percent tax increase just to keep their city government afloat. Although the state code said city officials had to pay creditors "as soon as practicable," the 1 percent limit allowed city officials to argue that payment was not practicable at that time.[12]

Bondholders quickly recognized that the 1 percent defense might allow some Iowa towns to avoid paying their debts indefinitely. Creditors therefore argued that the state statutes requiring prompt payment of judgments preempted the tax provisions in municipal charters. But the Iowa Supreme Court sided with the debt-ridden municipalities on this issue. City officials, Iowa's highest court held, were bound to follow the tax provisions in their city charter. In order to circumnavigate these unfavorable state court precedents, Butz sued in federal court, where he asked that a writ of mandamus be issued against Muscatine's officers, requiring them to ignore the 1 percent provision and to raise whatever taxes were necessary. Butz won his case, and in May 1867 the federal circuit court issued the requested judgment and writ. Nevertheless, Muscatine officials, citing the rulings of the Iowa Supreme Court, steadfastly refused to collect the new taxes. When the case reached the United States Supreme Court, Muscatine's municipal government protested the federal courts' interference in state affairs by refusing to file a brief or to present arguments. Given the Supreme Court's position in previous bond cases, Iowa officials might well have believed that the outcome was preordained.[13]

In *Butz*, the Supreme Court faced two important questions. The justices needed to determine whether or not the construction given to the provisions of the state code by the Iowa Supreme Court was sound. If it was not, was the U.S. Supreme Court then obligated to follow the decisions of Iowa's highest court on a matter of state law? In his majority opinion, Justice Swayne once again sided with bondholders, maintaining that the Iowa Supreme Court had misinterpreted state statutes and that the U.S. Supreme Court need not follow its decisions. Because the state court decisions deprived creditors of their ability to collect against some cities, he concluded, the U.S. Supreme Court would not "adhere to its rule, confessedly obligatory in most cases, that it would follow, irrespectively of what it might itself think of the correctness of such decisions, the decision given by the State courts in construction of their own State statutes." Although Swayne claimed he entertained the "highest respect" for the state courts of Iowa, he argued that the U.S. Supreme Court's duty "cannot be performed . . . by blindly following in the footsteps of others and substituting their judgment for our own." Instead, he offered his own interpretation of Iowa state law. The provision in the state code requiring towns to pay their debts promptly, he asserted, applied to every town in Iowa, and Muscatine could not carve out its own private exemption. Otherwise, Muscatine's creditors might never get paid, since the city could always claim that municipal expenses used up the 1 percent tax increase. "Until the debtor chooses to pay," Swayne said in horror, "the creditor can get nothing. The usual relations of creditor and debtor are reversed. . . . Nothing could bring us to the conclusion that it was the intention of the law-making power of so enlightened a State to produce, by its action, such a condition of things in its jurisprudence."[14]

Although Miller disagreed with the majority opinion, he expected nothing less from Swayne, whom he had grown to hate even though the two men were staunch allies in the Reconstruction cases. "He is an extremist in upholding all negotiable bonds and especially Rail Road securities," Miller wrote in June 1869. "He is not a man much affected by the justice of the case as distinguished from the principles of law which ought to govern it." Swayne, he believed, often relied on long discussions of ancient precedents in order to mask his biased reasoning. "He is much governed by authorities and is fond of the older decisions especially of the English Courts," Miller wrote. "He is very fond of the literature of the profession in which he believes himself to be remarkably well read."[15] Swayne, he would later say, was a "selfish unlikeable man" and "never of much value to the Court. . . . I have always liked him less than any man on the bench."[16]

In his dissent in *Butz,* Miller sarcastically referred to Swayne as "my learned brother," while noting the painful lengths to which Swayne had to go in order always to side with the bondholders. It was Swayne, Miller reminded the Court, who had argued in 1862 in *Leffingwell v. Warren* that the "construction given to a state statute by the highest tribunal of such state, is regarded as part of the statute and is as binding upon the Courts of the United States as the text." But Swayne felt free to abandon this time-honored position when the interests of wealthy capitalists were at stake. He had first done so in 1863 in *Gelpcke v. Dubuque,* when he concluded "that in cases of contracts [the Supreme Court] would not follow . . . decisions of State courts construing their own constitution where the consequence would be to declare such contracts void." In *Butz,* Swayne stretched this reasoning to the point of absurdity. "The opinion of the court in the present case, delivered by the same learned judge," Miller continued, ". . . now holds, in a matter that does not involve the validity of contracts, but a construction of State statutes on the amount of tax which may be levied under them, that the repeated decisions of the State courts on that subject . . . will be disregarded entirely, and that this court will give to such statutes a construction directly opposed to that by which the State courts are governed." To save the bondholders, Swayne brazenly threw important precedents away. "It is an entire and unqualified overthrow of the rule imposed by Congress and uniformly acted on by this court up to the year 1863," Miller concluded, "that the decisions of the State courts must govern this court in the construction of State statutes."[17]

Although he did not enjoy his repeated role as angry dissenter in bond cases, Miller resented even more having to send Iowa officials to jail for actions he thought were just. "These frequent dissents in this class of subjects are as distasteful to me as they can be to anyone else," he said in closing his *Butz* dissent. "But when I am compelled, as I was last spring, by the decisions of this court, to enter an order to commit to jail at one time over a hundred of the best citizens of Iowa, for obeying as they thought their oath of office required them to do, an injunction issued by a competent court of their own State, . . . an injunction which, in my own private judgment, they were legally bound to obey, I must be excused if, when sitting here, I give expression to convictions which my duty compels me to disregard in the Circuit Court." Unwilling to sit idly by as bondholders' rights trumped his own conceptions of justice, Miller dissented more frequently in municipal bond cases than in any other type.[18]

Based on his positions in these cases, some scholars have portrayed Miller as an advocate of judicial restraint, an "exemplar of the wisdom of judicial forbearance." At first glance, Miller's dissents in the bond cases appear to support this thesis. His belief in deference to state courts and his respect for *stare decisis* (with regard to *Leffingwell*) seem to illustrate an essential conservatism in his judicial philosophy. But this view of Miller fails to square his calls for judicial restraint with his opinions in other cases, such as *Loan Association v. Topeka*. That case involved bonds that the city of Topeka issued in order to aid and encourage the opening of an ironworks. The Topeka city government claimed authority to issue the bonds under an act of the Kansas legislature that arguably allowed it to do so. Miller nevertheless argued that the bonds were void on the grounds that they funded a private enterprise and thus did not serve a public purpose. By issuing the bonds, Topeka's elected officers violated the spirit of the Constitution and the "limitations on such power which grow out of the essential nature of all free governments."[19]

In the end, Miller cared less about espousing a consistent judicial philosophy than he did about practical results. Unable to make a specific constitutional objection, he relied on an expansive reading of the Constitution. Rather than using judicial restraint, his majority opinion nullified a legislative act on the grounds that it was "opposed to a general latent spirit supposed to pervade or underlie the Constitution." The common thread between his *Topeka* opinion and his dissents in *Gelpcke, Butz,* and many other bond cases was that the needs of an indebted community took precedence over those of bondholders—hardly the philosophy of judicial restraint.[20]

After the Civil War, Miller came to believe that the Supreme Court had become a tool of the relatively small but powerful class of investment capitalists. Even if a state's highest tribunal ruled against the efficacy of a bond issue, when a case involving those bonds reached the Supreme Court their validity was a "foregone conclusion." "Our Court or a majority of it," Miller complained, "are, if not monomaniacs, as much bigots and fanatics on that subject as is the most unhesitating Mahemodan in regard to his religion."[21] In the late 1860s and 1870s, he grew even more disgusted with both the Court and the capitalists themselves. "I have met with but few things of a character affecting the public good of the whole country," he wrote, "that has shaken my faith in human nature as much as the united, vigorous, and selfish effort of the capitalists,—the class of men who are as a distinct class are but recently known in this country—I mean those who live solely by interest and dividends."[22]

Miller saw the financiers as a new and menacing force that undermined free labor. "Prior to the late war they were not numerous," he explained in a letter to Ballinger. But the war had vastly increased the amount of commercial paper, thereby increasing the opportunities for individuals to grow rich simply by speculating on bonds, stocks, and notes. When the government turned to national bank notes and greenbacks, it benefited speculators by increasing the quantity of the "circulating medium" and by creating a "national funded debt, exempt from taxation." The amount of commercial paper, Miller added, "was quadrupled by the bonds issued by the States, by municipal corporations, and by Rail Road companies." Suddenly the nation was awash in negotiable instruments. "The result has been the gradual formation of a new kind of wealth in this country, the income of which is the coupons of interest and stock dividends, and of a class whose only interest or stake in the country is the ownership of these bonds and stocks. They engage in no commerce, no trade, no manufactures, no agriculture. They *produce nothing*" (Miller's emphasis).[23]

Miller's one-dimensional explanation for the rise of the capitalists was partially correct. The railroad bonds of the 1850s did multiply capitalists' investment opportunities, and the federal government's wartime financial policies did increase the bonds and notes available for speculation. The National Banking Act of 1863, furthermore, had helped to concentrate capital in the hands of established New York bankers. But Miller ignored the fact that even without the war or the municipal bonds, the capitalist class would have grown larger and more powerful. With the rise of an integrated national market, national railroads, and sophisticated corporate structures, capital would have inevitably concentrated in established commercial centers. Miller's producerist ideology unfairly singled out these new capitalists for keeping towns like Keokuk down. To be sure, the bondholders' unwillingness to forgive Keokuk's debt played a central role in that city's continued malaise, but even without its bond debt, Keokuk would have been an unlikely place for new capital to gravitate. With the rise of railroads, it no longer provided an economic function that could attract the massive capital necessary to make the town prosperous again.[24]

By the summer of 1868, Keokukians felt the economic noose tightening. Although many citizens attended antibond rallies and vowed to fight the bondholders to the last, a smaller, more conciliatory group of merchants and businessmen determined that the city could not win this war of resistance and that the time had come to negotiate with its creditors. Hoping that the bondholders might recognize that Keokuk no longer had the means to repay the bonds at their original terms, they proposed issuing new bonds with a longer repayment period and a lower interest rate. Keokuk's creditors could then trade in their old bonds for the new ones and repayment would begin promptly. Other capitalists could buy the new city bonds as well, providing the city with desperately needed funds. "With our financial honor untarnished," the *Gate City* argued, "such bonds will be sought after by capitalists everywhere." Former mayor Hugh Sample, former congressmen Daniel F. Miller, and other men of standing called for the "City Council to compromise the debt, and issue new bonds which shall be valid."[25]

In July 1868, the city council persuaded Miller, Keokuk's most prominent citizen, to lend his support to this effort and to join a special commission established to renegotiate the city's debt. Unable to sell his property and discouraged by the town's continuing decline, Miller recognized that Keokuk had reached a fork in the road. The city's leaders could either compromise with the hated bondholders and reestablish Keokuk's credit or resign themselves to the fact that Keokuk would never achieve greatness. "I have been devoting myself this summer . . . ," Miller wrote to Ballinger in August 1868, "to an effort to compromise our city debt. I am in the midst of the labor now, with some hope of success, but not sanguine. It is indispensable to any progress in our town. If I succeed I shall feel that I have conferred an immense benefit to my neighbors and fellow citizens, and have added largely to the value of my own property."[26]

By November, Miller was not optimistic about matters in Keokuk. The bondholders stubbornly resisted compromises, and his efforts to sell his land in order to pay off his own debts had met with little success. "I have found it impossible to sell any of my real estate . . . at any price," he wrote. "I have had no offers of any kind for a year. The truth is Keokuk is in a crisis. We are trying hard to compromise our city debt. I think the next year will settle our destiny.

Either we shall take a new start in the race of prosperity or we shall be compelled to content ourselves with a second rate position in our own state."[27]

Bondholders were in no mood to negotiate in 1868. The United States Supreme Court had sided with them, making their hard-line position virtually unassailable. Armed with the leverage to have Iowa municipal officials jailed and fined, bondholders would eventually get their pound of flesh. Since Keokuk was just one of many towns faced with a bond crisis, any compromise settlement might lead indebted towns across the Old Northwest to expect similar concessions. Bondholders also took an adamant position with regard to the national debt, as Democratic presidential hopeful George Pendleton learned firsthand in 1868. When he proposed a plan to compromise the federal government's massive war debt by paying interest on government bonds with greenbacks instead of gold, horrified businessmen, bankers, and bondholders destroyed his candidacy.[28]

By 1870, Keokuk's effort to compromise its debt had failed, and Miller's enmity for bondholders solidified. For the rest of his life he would maintain a deep hatred for "money men." Blinded by greed, they destroyed towns like Keokuk, the very towns that had made them wealthy. Miller expressed utter contempt "for the selfish, cunning, organization of bond holders whose only object in life" seemed to be to "have their golden egg, shell, meat and all, though they destroy the goose from which they know it must come if it come at all." Before the war, the Republicans had targeted slavery and slaveholders as the greatest threat to free labor. Now, Miller and other Iowans viewed bondholders as an equally insidious and intractable foe.[29]

In 1870, Miller once again found himself embroiled in a tense and emotional struggle with his fellow justices over an issue involving debtors. Although the *Legal Tender Cases* did not involve bonds per se, they raised many of the same issues as the bond cases and served as one more battleground in the contest between debtors and creditors. Designed to ameliorate the nation's financial crisis during the war, the Legal Tender Act of 1862 authorized the U.S. Treasury to issue over $400 million in non-interest-bearing treasury notes. These paper notes, commonly known as greenbacks, were not backed by gold or silver and were made legal tender for all public and private debts (except customs duties and interest payments on federal debt). Because of wartime financial exigencies, most Republicans, including fiscal conservatives like Noah Swayne, had supported the greenbacks as a war measure. After the war, many conservatives saw the continued use of greenbacks as irresponsible, even immoral, and worried that the government's printing presses would manufacture paper money day and night until inflation crippled the nation. Greenbacks particularly alarmed creditors who had loaned money in gold and other specie, only to be paid back in devalued paper money. With the war over, creditors and fiscal conservatives hoped that Swayne and the other justices of the Supreme Court would deem greenbacks unconstitutional. Five years after Appomattox, the Supreme Court heard arguments in *Hepburn v. Griswold,* the first of the *Legal Tender Cases.*[30]

In June 1860, "a certain Mrs. Hepburn," of Kentucky borrowed money from Henry Griswold and signed a promissory note obligating her to repay him in February 1862. At the time Hepburn and Griswold negotiated their contract, gold and silver coins were the understood medium of exchange. On February 25, 1862, five days after the note came due, the federal government passed the Legal Tender Act. Hepburn then offered Griswold payment in greenbacks. Griswold refused her offer because he had originally lent her gold coin. In the litigation that followed, Hepburn argued that Congress made the greenbacks legal tender for all debts, including those incurred before the passage of the Legal Tender Act. The Louisville chancery court sided with Hepburn, but on appeal the Court of Errors of Kentucky sided with Griswold. At that point, Hepburn brought the case to the United States Supreme Court.[31]

In one sense, *Hepburn* was little different from the other war powers cases the Court had already decided. Like the suspension of habeas corpus or test oaths, the federal government had passed the Legal Tender Act as a war measure. Had the extent of the government's war powers been the only issue involved, the votes of many of the justices would have been easy to predict. Miller, Swayne, and Chase would hold that the act was constitutional; Field, Nelson, Grier, and Clifford would most likely declare it unconstitutional; and the unpredictable Justice Davis would determine the fate of the measure. But in *Hepburn,* much more than the extent of the government's war powers was at stake.

Hepburn presented the Court with a divisive and volatile mix of issues. In 1870, greenbacks remained in wide circulation and had become an important part of the economy. If the justices now declared the Legal Tender Act to be unconstitutional, the nation could expect a jarring deflationary effect; yet creditors hated greenbacks. This mix of issues—war powers, economics, and creditors' rights—placed several of the justices in uncomfortable positions. Swayne, for example, had resolutely upheld all of the Republicans' war and Reconstruction measures but had been similarly consistent in defending creditors' interests. *Hepburn* pitted one of his values against another.[32]

Personnel matters on the Court further complicated the situation. The Court was already one justice short as the term began, and it had become increasingly clear that Grier's mental faculties had badly deteriorated (at the request of his fellow justices he resigned later that year). The Court was in the unhappy position of deciding controversial issues with a depleted bench, a fact that would make its decisions vulnerable to criticism. Such criticism would be inevitable if, as some commentators feared, the justices used *Hepburn* to declare the Legal Tender Act wholly unconstitutional.[33]

The central question the Court faced in *Hepburn* was whether the federal government could compel creditors to accept its paper money as payment for debts in instances where a contract was negotiated before the Legal Tender Act was passed. Specifically, could the federal government force Griswold to accept payment different in nature and value from that which had been contemplated in his contract with Hepburn? In his majority opinion, Chief Justice Chase—who was joined by Justices Nelson, Clifford, Grier, and Field—opened by saying that the Court recognized the "delicacy and importance of this question." The Court, Chase went on, "approaches the consideration of questions of this nature reluctantly; and its constant rule of decision has been, and is, that acts of Congress must be regarded as constitutional, unless clearly shown to be otherwise." But, he added, acts of Congress had to be consistent with the Constitution, as the "Constitution is the fundamental law of the land."[34]

When Congress made greenbacks legal tender for the payment of debts, Chase continued, it overstepped its constitutionally enumerated powers. No one, "however slightly conversant with constitutional law," would "think of maintaining that there is in the Constitution any express grant of legislative power to make any . . . currency a legal tender in payment of debts." If Congress had such authority, it would have to be an implied power—one that combined Congress's expressed powers to regulate commerce, to coin and borrow money, and to raise and support armies according to the necessary and proper clause in article 1, section 8 of the Constitution (a clause that had been interpreted broadly ever since John Marshall's famous *McCulloch v. Maryland* decision upholding the constitutionality of the Bank of the United States).

In *Hepburn*, Chase gave the necessary and proper clause a fairly narrow construction and concluded that Congress's expressed or implied powers did not justify making greenbacks legal tender for past debts. Chase, who had been secretary of the treasury under Lincoln, now claimed that by making greenbacks legal tender for all debts, Congress violated perhaps the "most valuable provision of the Constitution of the United States, ever recognized as an efficient safeguard against injustice," that "no State shall pass any law impairing the obligation of contracts." To make this argument, he had to overcome the fact that the contracts clause applied only to state, and not federal, laws. To do so, he went out on a limb, claiming that the contracts clause represented the "spirit" of the Constitution. It was clear, he wrote, that "those who framed and those who adopted the Constitution, intended the spirit of this prohibition should pervade the entire body of legislation," and that any federal law "not made in pursuance of an express power" which "impairs the obligation of contracts, is inconsistent with the spirit of the Constitution." This was a new and expansive interpretation that had the potential to circumscribe congressional authority for years to come.[35]

Chase also argued that making greenbacks legal tender for past debts violated the Fifth Amendment's due process clause. Any legislative act, he claimed, that forced persons who held contracts for the payment of gold or silver to accept payment in a currency of inferior value deprived such persons of their property without due process of law. At a time when voices calling for repudiation of debts echoed across the country, Chase's language must have warmed the hearts of nervous creditors. "A very large proportion of the property of civilized men exists in the form of contracts," he wrote, and it was thus essential that contracts be protected. The Legal Tender Act was passed during a national emergency when the "time was not favorable to considerate reflection upon the Constitutional limits of legislative or executive authority." In a veiled reference to his own wartime support of the act, he acknowledged, "Not a few who then insisted upon its necessity, or acquiesced in that view, have since the return of peace, and under the influence of the calmer time, reconsidered their conclusions and now concur" that the legal tender portion of the act violated the "letter and spirit of the Constitution." For Chase and the majority, creditors' interests and the "spirit" of the Constitution were the same. Debts needed to be paid in full, and the Constitution could and should be used to bring about that result.[36]

Miller disagreed in a dissent joined by Davis and, remarkably, Swayne as well. After their bitter struggles in the bond cases, it was perhaps surprising that

Swayne would join in a dissent that sided with a debtor rather than a creditor. For him, however, the case was not about debtors and creditors but Congress's war powers. He agreed with Miller's impassioned argument that the Legal Tender Act had grown out of military necessity. "We were in the midst of a war," Miller wrote, "which . . . if we take into account the increased capacity for destruction introduced by modern science, and the corresponding increase in its cost, brought into operation powers of belligerency more potent and more expensive than any that the world has ever known." Paying for this kind of war caused a financial crisis. In February 1862, he continued, "with the spirit of the rebellion unbroken, with large armies in the field unpaid, with a current expenditure of over a million dollars per day, the credit of the government nearly exhausted, and the resources of taxation inadequate to pay even the interest on the public debt, Congress was called on to devise some new means of borrowing money on the credit of the nation." The nation's banks were out of specie. Even if all the coins in the United States had been placed in hands of the secretary of the treasury, Miller argued, it "would not have made a circulation sufficient" to meet the war effort. Thus the Legal Tender Act had not only been necessary and proper; it had been a turning point in the war. It gave the capitalists means to buy war bonds, it stimulated trade, and it "revived the drooping energies of the country and restored confidence in the public mind."[37]

Without the act, Miller concluded, an economic collapse would have occurred, the people's "faith in the ability of the government would have been destroyed, the rebellion would have triumphed, the States would have been left divided, and the people impoverished." He added caustically, "The national government would have perished, and with it the Constitution which we are now called upon to construe with such nice and critical accuracy."[38]

But why did these notes have to be legal tender for all debts? Why didn't the U.S. Treasury simply issue notes—notes bearing a pledge on their face for eventual payment in coin—that people could use voluntarily? Would not those notes also have expanded the circulating medium? Miller argued that such currency would have quickly lost its value. "All experience shows that a currency not redeemable promptly in coin, but dependent on the credit of a promissor whose resources are rapidly diminishing, while his liabilities are increasing, soon sinks to the dead level of worthless paper." But when, by law, greenbacks could be used to discharge debts, "they had a perpetual credit or value." As Miller charged, "To say, then, that this quality of legal tender was not necessary to their usefulness, seems to be unsupported by any sound view of the situation."[39]

Satisfied that the Legal Tender Act could be fully justified as a war power, Miller then expressed his discomfort with Chase's insinuation that the Constitution was a creditors' document. He took issue with Chase's argument that the act, as it applied to past debts, was "in conflict with the spirit if not the letter, of several provisions of the Constitution." While he agreed that the Legal Tender Act impaired contracts like Griswold's, he was certain that Congress had the constitutional authority to pass such a law. "While the Constitution forbids the States to pass such laws," Miller wrote, "it does not forbid Congress." Congress, he believed, could do so in times of war and peace alike. The Constitution expressly authorized Congress "to establish a uniform system of bankruptcy, the essence of which is to discharge debtors from the obligation of their contracts." If Congress could set up bankruptcy laws to wipe away individuals' debts during peacetime, how could Chase conclude that a creditors' contract could not be impaired to save the nation? "How it can be in accordance with the spirit of the Constitution," Miller continued, "to destroy directly the creditor's contract for the sake of the individual debtor, but contrary to its spirit to affect remotely its value for the safety of the nation, it is difficult to perceive." Rather than being a document to protect creditors, Miller's Constitution allowed Congress to side with the have-nots rather than the haves.[40]

Miller also passionately challenged Chase's assertion that the Legal Tender Act deprived creditors of their property without due process of law. "The argument is too vague for my perception," he said, "by which the indirect effect of a great public measure, in depreciating the value of lands, stocks, bonds, and other contracts," constituted taking that property without due process. If that were true, any major law that depreciated the value of private property would violate due process. "The abolition of the tariff on iron and sugar would in like manner," Miller analogized, "sink the capital employed in the manufacture of these articles." Chase's rationale would jeopardize every successive issue of government bonds "because by increasing the public debt it made those already in private hands less valuable."[41]

With the massive debts of Keokuk and the Old Northwest heavy on his mind, Miller attacked Chase's conclusions about the "spirit of the Constitution." The whole idea of a law violating the "spirit of the Constitution," Miller fumed, "is too abstract and intangible for application to courts of justice." He did not trust the Court, stocked with bondholders' advocates and railroad attorneys, to determine fairly what the "spirit of the Constitution" was. "It would authorize this court to enforce theoretical views of the genius of the government," he wrote. "It substitutes our ideas of policy for judicial construction, an undefined code of ethics for the Constitution, and a court of justice for the national legislature." In the *Topeka* case, Miller had used his own version of the "spirit of the Constitution" argument to declare that bonds issued to fund private enterprises were invalid. But, as always, Miller adjusted his legal arguments to meet practical political and economic ends, rather than adhering to a consistent judicial ideology.[42]

When the *Hepburn* decision was announced in February 1870, some Republican newspapers denounced it as simply another unjust attack on a Republican war measure. The decision, the *Washington Chronicle* concluded, was "an insidious assault upon the great measure which saved the country during rebellion." Other commentators soon realized the broader economic ramifications of Chase's opinion. If Chase refused to acknowledge the right of Congress to make greenbacks legal tender for past debts, it seemed possible that the Court might apply this reasoning to all contracts, including those made after the act. The Republican press accordingly began warning that the constitutionality of the Legal Tender Act as a whole had been placed in jeopardy. "Upon a careful examination of the reasoning of the case . . . ," one editorial warned, "we see nothing in it which is not just as applicable to contracts made since the passage of the act, and we think that its supporters look upon the decision as but one step towards the repeal of the legal-tender act in all its bearings." Financiers and bondholders had long advocated a return to gold and silver coins, and the Court now seemed to support their views.[43]

On the same day that the Court announced its decision in *Hepburn,* however, President Grant's appointment of two new Republicans to fill the empty seats on the Court allayed fears that the Legal Tender Act would be declared wholly invalid. There was good reason to believe that both appointees—Joseph Bradley and William Strong—supported the act. Strong, a member of the Pennsylvania Supreme Court, had already upheld it, and Bradley had long served as counsel for debt-ridden New Jersey railroads that were sure to suffer if the law were overturned. If the Court were to consider another case involving greenbacks, debtors, and creditors, the votes of Bradley and Strong could carry Miller and the other dissenters in *Hepburn* into the majority.[44]

Many Republicans thus called for the Court to reconsider quickly the issues in *Hepburn* and overturn the decision before it became settled policy. Miller favored this idea and proposed that the Court reopen the issue by hearing reargument in two Legal Tender Act cases that had been argued but not decided in November 1869—*Knox v. Lee* and *Parker v. Davis*. He hoped the Court would revisit the central questions from *Hepburn,* only this time in front of a realigned Court. Word soon leaked of his plan, and an outraged conservative press charged Grant, Miller, and the Republicans with undermining the independence of the judicial branch. "Reopening of the Legal Tender Cases," the *American Law Review* warned, "would be a terrible blow at the independence and dignity of the profession."[45]

In April 1870, the normally calm relations among the justices deteriorated into bitter partisanship over Miller's proposal. "It is evident that there is a state of feeling in the Court by no means pleasant," one newspaper noted. "We have had a desperate struggle in the secret conference of the court for three weeks over two cases involving the legal tender question," Miller wrote on April 21. "The Chief Justice has resorted to all the stratagems of the lowest political trickery to prevent their being heard, and the fight has been bitter in the conference room." Miller led the campaign to reopen the question and did his best to shore up his temporary alliance with Swayne, who might at any moment switch to the position favored by creditors. "The excitement has nearly used me up. It has been fearful," Miller reported to Ballinger, "and my own position as leader in marshaling my forces, and keeping up their courage, against a domineering Chief, and a party in court who [have] been accustomed to carry everything their own way, has been such a strain on my brain and nervous system as I never wish to encounter again." Much to the dismay of the chief justice and the Democratic justices on the Court, Miller's proposal carried the day. All of the controversial questions surrounding the Legal Tender Act, including those just decided in *Hepburn,* would be reconsidered and reargued.[46]

In its next term, the Court heard arguments in *Knox v. Lee* and *Parker v. Davis,* issuing a decision in those cases on May 1, 1871. As expected, the tables had turned; the two new justices voted with the dissenters from *Hepburn.* Miller's strategy had paid off. The Court reached a 5-4 decision upholding the constitutionality of all aspects of the Legal Tender Act. Justice Strong's majority opinion declared that the government could require creditors to accept greenbacks for past debts without violating the "spirit of the Constitution." "We hold the acts of Congress constitutional as applied to contracts made either before or after their passage," Strong wrote. "In so holding, we overrule . . . much of what was decided in *Hepburn v. Griswold*." After reiterating the arguments Miller made in his dissenting opinion in *Hepburn*, Strong also offered a justification for overturning *Hepburn* so quickly. "That case was decided by a divided court, and by a court having a less number of judges than the law then in existence provided this court should have," he argued. "These cases have been heard before a full court, and they have received our most careful consideration."[47]

Justice Bradley added a concurring opinion in *Knox* that again revealed the role of the struggle between debtors and creditors in the case. For Bradley, the main objection to the Legal Tender Act seemed to be that the "creditor interest will lose some of its gold!" "Is gold the one thing needful?" he asked. "Is it worse for the creditor to lose a little by depreciation than everything by the bankruptcy of his debtor? Nay, is it worse than to lose everything by the subversion of the government? What is it that protects him in the accumulation and possession of his wealth? Is it not the government and its laws?" It appeared to Bradley that the creditors, blinded by greed, had lost sight of the common good and were selfishly placing their own needs ahead of the nation's.[48]

In their dissents in *Knox*, Field and Chase acknowledged that the case was as much about creditors' rights as Congress's war powers. In his opinion, Chase, who was recovering from a mild stroke, turned to a theme that would be used throughout Reconstruction and the Gilded Age to protect corporations, private property, and creditors from regulatory or redistributive legislation. The majority opinion, Chase asserted, "violates that fundamental principle of all just legislation that the legislature shall not take from A. and give it to B." Justice Field built on this theme, asking the majority to consider what would happen if Congress now reversed its position and demanded that contracts loaned in greenbacks be paid back in gold. "The debtor could only satisfy his contract in such case by paying ten times the value originally stipulated," Field charged. "The natural sense of right which is implanted in every mind would revolt from such supreme injustice. Yet there cannot be one law for debtors and another law for creditors." What if the U.S. government borrowed in gold and repaid in dollars? Field asked. It would be repudiation, and "repudiation in any form, or to any extent, would be dishonor." For Field and Chase, the Constitution remained a creditors' document that would not allow repudiation of debts. "For commission of this public crime," Field concluded, "no warrant in my judgment can ever be found in that instrument."[49]

Field's great fear of debt repudiation reflected the widespread sense of uneasiness felt by men of property during the late 1860s and 1870s. Industrialists and financiers amassing great fortunes were terrified that the laboring majority might attack their property both through violence and the ballot box. Some conservatives worried that black freedom and suffrage were only the beginning, and that Republicans would pander next to the uneducated, poor, and immigrant masses in the Northeast. The efforts by municipalities and courts in the Old Northwest to repudiate their railroad bonds served as further evidence of a democratic spirit gone awry.

Descriptions of the Paris Commune, the brief period when workers and anarchists seized control of the French capital in the spring of 1871, had a similarly disquieting effect on propertied men. "Let some such opportunity occur as was presented in Paris . . . ," the *New York Times* warned solemnly in June 1871, "let this mighty throng hear that there was a chance to grasp the luxuries of wealth . . . and we should see a sudden communistic revolution, even in New York such as would astonish all who do not know these classes." For conservatives, the Court's dramatic reversal in the *Legal Tender Cases* seemed to be one more example of a disconcerting trend. Now even the Supreme Court had capitulated to the indebted masses.[50]

With respect to the Court, conservatives had little reason for concern. In most instances, the majority of the justices remained firmly in the creditors' camp, and Miller's success in shaping a new majority in the *Legal Tender Cases* constituted a victory in a losing cause. While Strong and Bradley shared his view of the Legal Tender Act, they opposed him in the railroad bond cases, guaranteeing that Miller's dissents in those cases would be exercises in futility. Throughout the 1870s, in one case after another, the Court upheld the validity of municipal railroad bonds. Increasingly disheartened and tired of writing the same dissenting opinions over and over again, Miller adopted the practice of dissenting without writing an opinion. His fellow justices knew his position even before he put pen to paper. "I have grown more adverse to dissents," he wrote in 1871. As a result, in important cases such as *Railroad Company v. County of Otoe* and *Olcott v. The Supervisors,* in which the Court again held bonds to be valid that a state court had held invalid, Miller silently dissented. The battle, he knew, had been lost. "It is the most painful matter concerned with my judicial life," Miller wrote of the bond cases, "that I am compelled to take part in a farce whose result is invariably the same, namely to give more to those who have already, and to take away from those who have little, the little that they have."[51]

Miller also had to face distressing realities in his personal life. Throughout the 1860s he still considered Keokuk his home and kept his house and family there. But in 1872, his debts, Keokuk's decline, and the inability to sell his undeveloped land outside of town forced him to make a painful decision. In June, he sold his house in Keokuk, purchased a residence on Capitol Hill, moved his family to Washington, and left Keokuk behind for good. "As I should never probably live in it again," Miller wrote of his Keokuk home, "and as in the event of my death my family could not *afford* to live in such a house, to sell it was . . . prudence, however it tortures the heart to give it up. And it does almost break . . . I think for a man whose local attachment was so strong." In a letter to Ballinger, he ruminated, "I have been peculiarly the native of necessity. Richmond, Barbourville, Keokuk, Washington have in turn become home to me and that home broken until I feel almost as homeless in fact and in feeling as a nomadic Tartar."[52]

In September of 1872, Miller also returned for the last time to his birthplace in Richmond, Kentucky, and visited his widowed mother, Patsy, for the last time. "In a busy life of many years passed far away from her," he wrote, "I have only on one occasion (during the war) permitted more than two years to lapse without visiting her." But in 1872 she was failing, and Miller knew this visit would probably be his last. "I think she knows how much I value her, . . . and how much of the success that has attended my life I attribute to her example, her instruction, and the qualities I have inherited from her," he wrote Ballinger. "I will never see her again and the parting was for me inexpressibly painful. She was with a few faults a great and noble women."[53]

Miller led a transient life, a "migratory tale of necessity" that reflected many of the revolutionary changes that took place during his lifetime. He left his family's home in Richmond, Kentucky, in order to escape the backbreaking, mind-numbing labor of preindustrial farming. In Barbourville, his town fell victim to the steamboat; in Keokuk, to the railroad. For most of this period, Miller nevertheless maintained his faith that America was a land where people could improve their station in life. Having risen from a hardscrabble farm to the Supreme Court of the United States, Miller need only have looked at his own success to confirm this vision. But by the 1870s, he recognized that many people in places like Barbourville and Keokuk were being left behind and that selfish capitalists in the North, as well as unrepentant rebels in the South, were destroying the ability to rise for many millions more.

CHAPTER 8

The *Slaughter-House Cases*

IN 1873, THE SUPREME COURT heard oral arguments in a case brought by white butchers from New Orleans who challenged a slaughterhouse law passed by Louisiana's biracial Reconstruction legislature. The butchers claimed that the law, passed as a health regulation, violated their Fourteenth Amendment rights. Because the case presented the justices with their first opportunity to interpret the broad language of that amendment, all involved recognized what was at stake. It was in *Slaughter-House* that the Court would begin to determine what effect the Fourteenth Amendment would have on the South and the rest of the nation.

Of the 616 majority opinions written by Samuel Miller, none is more important than his opinion in the *Slaughter-House Cases*. It is the opinion for which he is most remembered, as it influenced the course of American race relations for almost a century and continues to shape constitutional law today. It is also one of the most criticized opinions in the history of the Supreme Court. Other than *Dred Scott v. Sandford*, *Plessy v. Ferguson*, and *Roe v. Wade*, few opinions have received more withering attacks from historians and legal scholars.

To fully understand Miller's opinion in the *Slaughter-House Cases*, one must begin in the noisome slaughterhouses of New Orleans. Though the case is infamous for its deleterious effects on American race relations, it arose from a seemingly benign attempt by Louisiana's biracial Reconstruction legislature to limit the filth, stench, and sanitary shortcomings of New Orleans's slaughterhouses. In March 1869, the Louisiana state legislature passed a law entitled, "An act to protect the health of the City of New Orleans," which required all of the city's butchers to relocate across the Mississippi River in a new state-of-the-art "grand slaughterhouse." The act also required that all livestock arriving from the countryside and the West be landed and penned at this new site, and that the meat produced there pass inspection by a public health official before being shipped to market. Angered by this law, hundreds of New Orleans butchers sued to enjoin the Crescent City Slaughter-House—the "grand slaughter-house"—from asserting any of its rights under the 1869 act. The butchers claimed that their "right to pursue an occupation"—a right they argued was protected by the privileges or immunities clause of the new Fourteenth Amendment—had been violated.[1]

Stringent sanitary regulations were long overdue in a city infamous for its squalor. The streets of New Orleans—most of them unpaved—were filthy. The city had no public sewer system; toilets of homes and hotels emptied into open gutters, and residents tossed garbage into streets and vacant lots. When the sultry heat of midsummer descended on the city, the smell of rot and decay was overpowering. Travelers compared the streets of New Orleans unfavorably with those of Cairo and Constantinople. Naturalist John James Audubon called the Crescent City's French Market the "dirtiest place in all the cities of the United States."[2]

Of all the noxious nuisances in a city infamous for its filth, the slaughter-houses and bone-boiling establishments were by far the worst. Scattered throughout the city's neighborhoods (with a heavy concentration in an area known as Slaughterhouse Point, located a few miles upstream from the city), slaughterhouses operated side by side with hospitals, schools, businesses, and crowded tenements. In a raucous daily event, stock dealers landed hundreds of cattle, pigs, and sheep at the river and drove them to various slaughterhouses. The terrified animals rushed "wildly and madly through the streets endangering the limbs and the lives of men, women and children." Butchers slaughtered over 300,000 animals in New Orleans each year, and the conditions surrounding these operations were ghastly.[3]

The abattoirs were bloody, filthy, and unregulated. Burly butchers killed the animals with hammers or knives, then skinned, gutted, and hung their fly-covered carcasses on hooks to dangle unrefrigerated for hours, even days. The mass of gory waste generated by these squalid businesses was thrown directly into either the streets or the Mississippi River. "Barrels filled with entrails, blood, urine, dung, and other refuse, portions in an advanced stage of decomposition are constantly being thrown into the river," a New Orleans doctor testified to a legislative committee, "poisoning the air with offensive smells and necessarily contaminating the water near the bank for miles."[4] Much of the rotting refuse from the slaughterhouses collected in the river around the giant intake pipes from which New Orleans drew its water supply. Pilings designed to stop the bulk waste matter from entering the pipes proved inefficient, and the pumping system repeatedly clogged.[5]

New Orleans slaughterhouses had undermined the public's health for many years. Attempts to regulate them had begun as early as 1804, when the new U.S. territorial government ordered all butchers to move their slaughtering operations out of the city and over to the west bank of the Mississippi River. As the city grew, however, the butchers' political and economic clout increased; after persistent complaints about the inconvenience of shuttling back and forth across the river, they forced their way back to the opposite bank upstream from the city. As New Orleans' growth continued, housing and businesses quickly sprouted up alongside these new slaughterhouses. In 1866, one thousand outraged New Orleans citizens petitioned the Louisiana legislature to force the slaughterhouses and stock landings across the river once again.[6]

Extending their concerns beyond foul odors and unhealthful meat, many officials in New Orleans (and other locations around the country as well) blamed slaughterhouses for deadly diseases such as yellow fever and cholera. This pertained particularly to New Orleans, which had been repeatedly and ferociously plagued by these two nineteenth-century scourges. Nearly every summer of the antebellum period, yellow fever or cholera closed businesses, forced quarantines of New Orleans shipping at other ports, and sent the rich into the countryside and the poor to their deaths. In 1853 alone, yellow fever and cholera afflicted forty thousand Crescent City residents.[7]

When the Louisiana legislature passed the 1869 slaughterhouse act, it did not act in a vacuum, but as part of a national sanitary reform movement that had begun before the Civil War. By the time Louisiana lawmakers acted, San Francisco, Boston, Milwaukee, and Philadelphia had already passed slaughterhouse ordinances. New York City was in the vanguard for these measures; its dynamic Board of Health regulated slaughterhouses and other unhealthful nuisances, thereby contributing to the eradication of cholera. Among the New York board's most effective laws was an 1866 regulation that required all butchers located below 40th Street to use a centralized slaughterhouse. The new facility operated away from the crowded downtown neighborhoods and allowed for efficient inspection of the city's meat supply. Although New York's butchers bitterly opposed the law, it was widely popular with most of the city's middle- and upper-class inhabitants.[8]

The Louisiana slaughterhouse law closely imitated its celebrated New York predecessor. However, despite the obvious benefits of the law, white residents of New Orleans vehemently opposed slaughterhouse regulation. The butchers' self-interest explains their strong opposition to the slaughterhouse law; for New Orleans tradesmen used to a completely unregulated business environment, the statute was a bitter pill. But why did the rest of white New Orleans rally around them? Before 1869, the butchers had never been well-liked as a group. They had conspired for years to keep prices high and had assaulted the senses and health of the residents of New Orleans. At the urging of the citizenry, the city government had tried many times in the past (albeit unsuccessfully) to force the butchers to clean up their operations.[9] Most historians and legal scholars have argued that many residents resented the fact that the "grand slaughterhouse" was built by a private corporation that was allowed to collect fees from butchers, who were required to use it. The popular opposition, some historians suggest, was a traditional Jacksonian response to a monopoly. Furthermore, the timing of the slaughterhouse investors was unfortunate; one historian has argued that "they had obtained their franchise at a time when the public was beginning to have serious second thoughts about the subsidies and franchises they had lavished on corporations in the past as a means of stimulating growth."[10] The fact that many of the slaughterhouse's investors were from the North only intensified public opposition. Locals accused carpetbaggers of bribing the legislature in return for the monopoly. White newspaper editors repeatedly raised unproved charges of corruption, alleging that the legislature passed the slaughterhouse law for the benefit of a few bribe-wielding Yankee businessmen.[11]

Yet these explanations overlook the context of contemporary Louisiana politics and society. No hard evidence has ever surfaced that bribery factored in the law's enactment. Those charges originated with white editors of New Orleans newspapers searching for arguments against it.[12] Even if there had been bribery, legislative corruption was common in Louisiana and usually stimulated little public outrage, leaving open the question as to why the slaughterhouse bill—a bill that achieved longstanding objectives of Democrats and Republicans—would cause such a furor.[13]

To be sure, ever since the Civil War, the idea of enforced health codes had taken on the appearance of a Yankee-directed enterprise. General Benjamin F. "Beast" Butler, who commanded the Union occupation of New Orleans, had forced the city to undergo a rigorous wartime sanitation effort. In order to protect the health of his troops, the much-despised Butler had organized an extensive cleanup of the city and the riverbank. Locals had expected Butler's soldiers to drop dead during their first summer in the Crescent City. Instead, the epidemics of cholera and yellow fever had ceased, largely because Butler put "thousands of unemployed Louisianians to work removing garbage, patrolling the river, and closing the slaughterhouses north of the city."[14] New Orleanians refused to grant Butler any credit for the improvements in public health. They characterized the break from yellow fever and cholera as purely coincidental, even though the epidemics ceased during the occupation and resumed after Butler and his troops left the city and the sanitation program ended. In 1867, yellow fever killed three thousand New Orleans citizens.[15]

It was true that the slaughterhouse bill had been pushed, in part, by transplanted northerners. The law was part of a broader effort by carpetbaggers in the Louisiana legislature to reshape and modernize the state's economic and social life. Many Yankee legislators were shocked and disgusted by the backwardness of New Orleans and Louisiana as a whole. While conceding that New Orleans had enjoyed economic success in the antebellum period, they attributed the city's fortune to its position on the Mississippi River rather than to the acumen or enterprise of its citizens. Northerners saw a decaying, primitive, reactionary city that had succeeded in spite of itself. Sporting little Yankee-style prosperity, it was served by few railroads and a single, six-mile canal. There were only four paved streets and a small number of covered warehouses and wharves; on most sides marshy, unnavigable swamps and bayous still surrounded the city. To many northerners, New Orleans seemed a rotting Gomorrah run by corrupt and ignorant officials and filled with gamblers, prostitutes, drunkards, duelists, and thugs. Henry Clay Warmoth, Louisiana's Illinois-born Reconstruction governor, called New Orleans a "dirty, impoverished, and hopeless place." As if to support the impression of general backwardness and disregard for public health, the malodorous, polluting, pathogenic slaughterhouses sat squarely within New Orleans' most populous areas; each summer business ground to a halt as citizens fled the "necropolis" of America for the countryside in order to avoid yellow fever and cholera.[16]

As part of the plan to reshape New Orleans and Louisiana in the northern image, the Republican legislature authorized an aggressive plan of internal improvements. They chartered railroad and canal companies and other corporations charged with repairing the dilapidated levees along the Mississippi. The legislature gave a private company, much like the one authorized in the slaughterhouse bill, the task of building a modern facility for the Crescent City Water Works. Another company acquired the monopoly on cleaning the city's privies. The legislature created steamboat companies and other enterprises to build warehouses and docks. They drew up plans to make nearby bayous navigable. "There was a conscious purpose," wrote one Dunning-school historian, "to introduce in the South the energy and methods of the North and West in the hope of similar economic results." Carpetbaggers in the Louisiana legislature envisioned a new South, with railroads, canals, schools, and free labor, all modeled on those of the North. Eventually, they hoped, white southerners would see the benefits of these changes and join the Republican crusade. But when Republican legislators turned to bonds and exclusive private charters to fund their improvement plans, they armed their opponents with ammunition for potent charges of corruption and monopoly.[17]

Because of the lack of capital in Louisiana after the war and the dire financial circumstances of the Reconstruction government, legislators had little choice but to turn to creative methods of funding their Whiggish development program. At the end of the war, Louisiana's economy lay in shambles. The plantations had been decimated by war. Trade dropped to a fraction of prewar levels, as did sugar production. Fleeing Confederate troops had torched wharves, steamboats, and warehouses full of cotton. Severe crop failures and cotton blights in 1866 and 1867 compounded these problems. Most ominously, the river trade, the lifeblood of the New Orleans economy, steadily continued to lose business to northern railroads. Midwestern crops that had previously come south on the river began to move east on iron rails.[18]

With the economy prostrate and many whites simply refusing to pay taxes to the Reconstruction government, tax revenues slowed to a trickle, and legislators opted for issuing bonds to pay for their ambitious modernization plans. But as Louisiana's credit plummeted, state bonds became hard to sell; in order to achieve its public goals, the legislature granted exclusive privileges to private corporations like the Crescent City Livestock Landing and Slaughtering Company. The plan worked. Sensing a sound venture, investors—who included former officers of both the Union and Confederate armies, brokers, shippers, and merchants—bought the company's publicly traded stock, and construction of the new slaughterhouse progressed quickly. The founding of the Crescent City Slaughter-House appears to have been a rational response to the city's sanitation needs and the state's shortage of capital. It hardly amounted to the monopoly decried by New Orleans's white press.[19]

In the end, the real reason for resistance by the white residents of New Orleans to the slaughterhouse bill was their opposition not to monopoly and corruption, but to the biracial Reconstruction legislature. The charges of monopoly and corruption served as useful rhetorical devices for white editors and lawyers intent on thwarting every effort, beneficial or otherwise, of a legislature that contained black elected officials. This context, and the circumstances leading to the passage of the law, must be examined to understand white opposition to the slaughterhouse bill and how the controversy reached Justice Miller and the United States Supreme Court.

White New Orleans never acquiesced in the idea of a biracial state government. In July 1866, Governor J. Madison Wells, a Republican, called for the election of additional delegates to a reconvened state convention authorized to draft a new constitution that would enfranchise blacks and prohibit many former rebels from voting. This effort led to the notorious New Orleans riot that helped to galvanize the North against Andrew Johnson's presidential Reconstruction and brought about the military Reconstruction directed by Congress. The riot had confirmed for Miller that southern whites' hatred for blacks meant that they could not be trusted.[20]

It seemed that change in Louisiana could be brought about only by force. Under the aegis of federal troops, state constitutional conventions charged with reshaping the South's legal, political, social, and economic order met throughout the South in 1867 and 1868. Before the election of convention delegates in Louisiana, General Sheridan enforced Reconstruction laws that disenfranchised many former rebels and allowed 83,000 black men to register to vote. The "Louisiana convention was the first major elective body in Southern history dominated by a black majority," and it produced a constitution that seemed to promise a new day in the state.[21] The new document desegregated education, prohibited racial discrimination in public places, and denied former Confederates the right to vote. It also included a bill of rights—the first in Louisiana's history—that voided the Black Codes, outlawed slavery, and guaranteed trial by jury, the right to assemble peacefully, and freedom of religion and the press.

Most white Louisianians reacted with hostility. Editors of the *New Orleans Bee*, for example, called the new constitution the "work of a few white men who were elected to the convention by the votes of ignorant negroes, and by means of disenfranchising those who by their ownership of the soil, their birthright as free men, and their education as citizens ought to be [Louisiana's] masters and its law givers."[22]

The new Louisiana legislature, charged with enacting measures that would support the goals of the new constitution, included African Americans. Although not a majority by any means (35 out of 101 members in the house and 7 out of 30 in the senate), blacks joined with white Republicans to form pluralities in both branches. The election of blacks to the legislature, combined with the presence of carpetbaggers, enraged many New Orleans whites. Opponents labeled the new legislature a horde "of ignorant negroes cooperating with a gang of white adventurers."[23]

Louisiana newspapers issued a racial call to arms, urging citizens to fight any and all acts passed by the legislature, and New Orleans papers branded its laws as merely a "parody of legislation." In January 1869, the *New Orleans Bee* loudly charged, "We are now laboring under the evils brought upon us by ignorance, the incapacity, and the notorious corruption of our so-called representatives in the General Assembly." Using the rallying cry "that the 'white man's flag' shall be upheld," editors claimed that the laws being passed "by the Legislature are of no more binding force than if they bore the stamp and seal of a Haytian Congress of human apes instead of the once honored seal of the state." In February 1869, the *Bee* called one African American state senator a "coal black negro with kinky hair, thick lips, and the feet the size of a sauce pan," and in July asserted that "no true citizen of Louisiana can ever coalesce with such men."[24]

Louisiana whites were most opposed to laws that attacked racial segregation. In February 1869, the biracial legislature passed what its opponents derisively called the "Social Equality Bill." This act made it a criminal offense to deny African Americans entry to hotels, steamboats, railroad cars, barrooms, and other public places. The *New Orleans Daily Picayune* called the act the work of "misguided black men and very worthless and wicked whites, the object of all being strife and subsequent bloodshed." The *Bee* chimed in, "It will be defied and condemned by every white man who has any sense of dignity and superiority of his race over that of the negro."[25] In the following month the legislature passed a law to enforce the article in the 1868 constitution that required public schools in Louisiana to be open to all races. This further enraged whites, who labeled the enactment the "School Integration Bill." "The white people of the city and the state," warned the *Bee,* "will not consent to the commingling of their children with the children of negroes in any school whatever." The newspaper urged that whites resist the law, asserting that the legislature wants to "drive us as equals into association with a servile race. Let us show them that laws are helpless to enforce such a commixture." White men reacted to such editorial calls for resistance by joining terrorist organizations—the Knights of the White Camelia and the Ku Klux Klan—and, in so doing, indicated their intent to destroy the biracial Republican government. By the early 1870s, nearly half the white males in New Orleans were members of such groups.[26]

In March 1869, less than a month after the passage of the Social Equality Bill, and within weeks of the adoption of the School Integration Bill, the Louisiana legislature approved the slaughterhouse law. Given this context, white New Orleanians opposed the legislation even though it finally ameliorated the terrible conditions in and around the slaughterhouses. The *Bee* called the bill a "monstrous perversion of law." It was "no law, although a law," a "wicked imposition which deserves the respect of nobody." Saying that the act was the work of "ignorant and corrupt, not enlightened and virtuous lawmakers," a white editor asked "Why is it that legislation since the adoption of the Constitution of 1868 has been uninterruptedly for plunder and oppression?"[27]

Louisiana Republicans did not hesitate to point out the disingenuous nature of conservatives' charges against the legislature and the slaughterhouse law. "In an effort to keep up the old prejudice against the new order of things," the editor of the *New Orleans Republican* wrote in March 1870, "the opposition have failed to see any good in the work of those who have been called upon to take part in the state government under the new constitution." Because the Republican Party had had the temerity to pass laws protecting blacks' civil rights, conservatives felt obligated to attack all things Republican. "Everybody had been proclaimed infamous, vile, ignorant and corrupt, that had had anything to do with a state government that recognized the civil and political equality of the colored man."[28]

In different times the community would not have rallied around the butchers, who were unsympathetic protagonists at best. In addition to operating businesses that produced filth and stench, they had also conspired for many years to inflate meat prices. New Orleans papers conceded as much. "But admitting the butchers may have practiced a monopoly," the *Bee* argued on June 22, "you do not destroy a monopoly by setting up another as bad or worse." In the racially charged atmosphere of 1869, white New Orleans residents formed an alliance of convenience with the butchers and stock dealers. "We make common cause with the butchers and stock dealers," said the *Bee*, "because their interests just now happen to be our interests." In another article, the paper argued, "The butchers are not only fighting their own battle, they are fighting the battle of the community." Perceptions of the once-troublesome butchers had changed, "and public opinion is unmistakably with them." The butchers' legal challenges to the slaughterhouse law became a New Orleans *cause célèbre*, which the newspapers and populace closely followed.[29]

Because the butchers' grievances became intertwined with Louisiana whites' opposition to the Reconstruction government, they acquired the best legal representation that the old order could offer. The lead attorney in most of the hundreds of cases individual butchers brought against the state was John A. Campbell, the former United States Supreme Court justice who had resigned from the Court at the start of the Civil War to join the Confederacy. While on the Court, Campbell had concurred with the majority in the *Dred Scott* decision. During the war, he served as the Confederacy's assistant secretary of war and was a leading theorist for the secessionist slaveholders. After being imprisoned for four months by northern troops at the end of the war, Campbell moved to New Orleans and developed a successful legal practice, much of which was devoted to fighting the Reconstruction government and returning the old elites to power.[30]

Campbell ardently believed that Reconstruction governments in the South had to be destroyed at all costs. He detested the new order that permitted blacks to serve in public life. "We have the African in place all about us," he wrote his daughter. "They are jurors, post office clerks, custom house officers & day by day they barter away their obligations and duties."[31] He felt that whites should resist the biracial government by any means necessary. "The Southern communities will be a desolation until there is a thorough change of affairs in all the departments of government," he wrote in 1871. "Discontent, dissatisfaction, murmurings, complaints, even insurrection would be better than the insensibility that seems to prevail." Defenders of the old political, economic, and racial order placed so much faith in his legal maneuverings that a saying developed in New Orleans: "Leave it to God and Mr. Campbell." Campbell was a true believer in the Old South. He would not rest until the social equality law, the school integration law, and the slaughterhouse statute were overturned. He became the white South's champion—the lawyer who would take the *Slaughter-House Cases* to the highest court in the land.[32]

In February 1873, after four years of pleading for New Orleans butchers in state and federal courts, Campbell finally challenged the slaughterhouse law before the United States Supreme Court. In his written brief and oral argument, he ladled out a thick soup of rhetorical excess. Quoting from Turgot, Tocqueville, Dalloz, and Leiber, he portrayed the butchers as patriotic citizens and lovers of liberty oppressed by a heavy-handed legislature. He likened the slaughterhouse legislation to the onerous regulations of seventeenth-century European monarchies, imposed at a time when the "peasant could not cross a river without paying to some nobleman a toll, nor take the produce which he raised to market until he had bought leave to do so; nor consume what remained of his grain till he had sent it to the lord's mill to be ground." Escape from such petty tyrannies, Campbell added, was "exactly what the colonists sought and obtained by their settlement here, their long contest with physical evils that attended the colonial condition, their struggle for independence, and their efforts, exertions, and sacrifices since." The "right to exercise their trade" unfettered by government intrusion was one of the fundamental rights for which the founding fathers had fought and died. Now, he asserted, the Fourteenth Amendment's privileges or immunities clause definitively protected this fundamental right from autocratic state legislation like the slaughterhouse law.[33]

Amidst all his lofty rhetoric, posturing, and bluster about liberty, Campbell inadvertently revealed his true fears and base motivations. He dreaded not the rise of a new monarchy, but the development of a democratic system in which blacks and immigrants could participate. The Fourteenth Amendment, he claimed, was framed at a moment when "more than three millions of a population lately servile, were liberated without preparation for any political or civil [life]. Besides this population of emancipated slaves, there was a large and growing population who came to this country without education in the laws and constitution of this country and who had begun to exert a perceptible influence over our government." He argued that the amendment's purpose was to keep a democracy composed partly of blacks and immigrants from running amok. Hence, he asserted, the duty of the Supreme Court was to declare unconstitutional laws like the slaughterhouse statute, which were rooted in black ignorance and Yankee greed.[34]

Miller did not like Campbell's attempts to stand the Fourteenth Amendment on its head. And he loathed Campbell personally for resigning from the Court to join the Confederacy and for refusing to give up the fight after the war. "I have neither seen nor heard of any action of Judge Campbell's since the rebellion which was aimed at healing the breach he contributed so much to make," Miller wrote privately. "He has made himself an active leader of the worst branch of the New Orleans democracy. Writing their pronunciamentos, arguing their cases in our Court, and showing all the evidences of a discontented and embittered old man, filled with the disappointments of an unsuccessful partisan politician." He felt that Campbell's lack of repentance should be punished. "I think no man that has survived the rebellion is more saturated today with its spirit. . . . [H]e deserves all the punishment he . . . can receive, not so much for joining the rebellion as for the persistency with which he continues the fight when all men ought to seek to forget it as much as possible." It is not surprising that Miller listened to Campbell's arguments in *Slaughter-House* with skepticism.[35]

In his majority opinion—joined by Justices Clifford, Davis, Hunt, and Strong—Miller concluded that the Fourteenth Amendment's privileges or immunities clause did not make the federal government the protector of all civil rights, such as the right to exercise one's trade. While the federal government could and did protect a more narrow list of rights—those traditionally associated with national citizenship, such as habeas corpus or the right to assemble peaceably to petition for redress of grievances—citizens still had to seek protection for most of their civil rights from state governments and state courts.[36]

Many historians have long criticized Miller's narrow interpretation of the privileges or immunities clause. Defined broadly, that clause might have given the federal government greater powers to protect the civil and natural rights of African Americans from discriminatory and violent acts. The Court could have ruled that the Fourteenth Amendment's privileges or immunities clause meant that the federal government had the power to protect citizens' basic rights—both those enumerated in the Bill of Rights and others, such as the right to pursue an occupation—from infringement by state governments. In declining to do so, the Court left to southern state governments the responsibility of protecting the rights of African Americans. "By strangling the privileges or immunities clause in its crib," one scholar has remarked, Miller either purposefully or negligently left the freedmen and women at the mercy of their former masters.[37]

Historians, jurists, and law professors have repeatedly raised two key questions in their discussions of *Slaughter-House*. First, they have debated whether or not Miller's interpretation of the Fourteenth Amendment's privileges or immunities clause was correct. In recent years, as scholars have sought a scapegoat for the unraveling of Reconstruction, most have concluded that Miller ignored the intention of some of the Fourteenth Amendment's framers that the privileges or immunities clause should extend the protection of the Bill of Rights to state laws and actions.[38] Although the evidence of the framers' intent is by no means conclusive, it is clear that at least two of the amendment's proponents (Jacob Howard and John Bingham) did want the Fourteenth Amendment to incorporate the Bill of Rights, and that Miller could have found support for that argument had he so desired. Fatefully, he chose otherwise, which has led many historians to ask: why? What compelled a Court dominated by Republicans to reach a decision seemingly so at odds with the Republicans' Reconstruction agenda?[39]

Historians have often suggested that *Slaughter-House* reflected a growing disgust among northerners with Radical Reconstruction. These scholars view the 1873 decision as the first step in conferring second-class status on blacks while restoring control of the South to white conservatives.[40] If the Civil War and postwar amendments were revolutionary, Miller's opinion marks the point where the "forces of contraction and counterrevolution" regained control. Some have even suggested that the Court deliberately selected a case that involved white plaintiffs (i.e., the white butchers) so that they could constrict the Fourteenth Amendment and the rights of black people without causing widespread outrage in the North.[41]

In hindsight, the *Slaughter-House* decision does seem to be a portent of the tragedy that befell African Americans after Reconstruction; yet those effects were far from certain at the time of the decision. When viewed within the political, economic, and social context of the early 1870s, the *Slaughter-House Cases* may be read as a progressive—though ultimately failed—attempt to affirm the authority of the biracial government of Louisiana, to grapple with the horrible sanitary conditions in New Orleans, and to thwart conservatives such as Justice Field, who hoped to defeat state regulation of private property.

When placed within the context of Louisiana politics, Miller's majority opinion in *Slaughter-House* seems hardly a racist attempt to retreat from Reconstruction. On the contrary, it was a vote of confidence for a biracial Reconstruction government then struggling to overcome the forces of reaction. Miller found it scandalous that the Fourteenth Amendment, which he considered a means for protecting African Americans in the South, might be used to strike down a sanitation law with such obvious social benefits. Even with the "most casual examination," he argued, "no one can fail to be impressed with the one pervading purpose" of the Fourteenth and Fifteenth Amendments. "[W]e mean the freedom of the slave race, the security and firm establishment of that freedom, and the protection of the newly-made freeman and citizen from the oppressions of those who had formerly exercised unlimited dominion over him." The Fourteenth Amendment was not designed, Miller felt, to thwart a valuable health measure that removed slaughterhouses from a crowded city.[42]

Miller's support for the slaughterhouse law also reflected his deep interest in the sanitation movement, an interest rooted in his personal experience and medical expertise. In Kentucky, he had spent years as a physician studying the causes and treatment of cholera. Ahead of his time in recognizing the connection between cholera and fouled water, Miller's long residence in Keokuk had given him firsthand knowledge of pigs and slaughtering.[43] In the 1850s and early 1860s, despite a population of only 15,000 inhabitants, Keokuk butchers killed over 110,000 hogs a year. Given the high pig-to-human ratio, the swine-killing industry dominated the town. Despite the money that slaughtering pumped into Keokuk's economy, the industry had numerous critics among the local populace. During Miller's years in the "porkopolis" of Iowa, residents mounted a successful campaign to regulate the industry.[44]

These experiences had a lasting impact on Miller's views. By the time the *Slaughter-House Cases* reached the Supreme Court, he had long since recognized the need for regulating the slaughtering industry. He was uniquely knowledgeable among the Court's justices about cholera, medicine, hogs, and slaughterhouses. He was sympathetic to the efforts of the Louisiana legislature to regulate New Orleans' abattoirs and resistant to interpretations of the Fourteenth Amendment that would undermine those efforts. It must have pleased him to see a southern city adopt modern health measures, as he always believed that southern doctors remained a backwards group. "I do not believe that the southern medicine men . . . ," Miller wrote in 1871, "have kept pace with the march of science."[45] He now welcomed New Orleans' cutting-edge public health legislation. "It cannot be denied," he said of the slaughterhouse law, "that the statute . . . is aptly framed to remove from the more densely populated part of the city, the noxious slaughter-houses, and large offensive collections of animals necessarily incident to the slaughtering business of a large city. . . . And it must be conceded that the means adopted by the act for this purpose are appropriate, are stringent, and are effectual."[46] He continued, "The regulation of the place and manner of conducting the slaughtering and butchering of animals, and business of butchering within a city, and the inspection of animals to be killed for meat, and of the meat afterwards are among the most necessary and frequent exercises of [a state's police] power."[47]

Just as he recognized the need to regulate slaughterhouses in order to thwart deadly epidemics, Miller shared the Republican legislators' dynamic economic vision for the postwar South. Throughout his life he had championed such efforts. In trying to reshape the South in the image of the North, the Louisiana legislators were doing exactly what Miller had attempted to do in Kentucky years earlier. There, he had been an ardent supporter of Cassius Clay's plan to replace Kentucky's plantations with food-producing farms and, with the aid of government-funded internal improvements, to turn that state's water-rich mountain region into a manufacturing paradise modeled on bustling New England mill towns. When Miller left for the free soil of Iowa, he took with him Clay's message that the South would always lag behind unless Yankee-style enterprise was imposed upon it. This was also the outlook of Louisiana's Republican legislators in the 1860s, a viewpoint many white southerners continued to resent deeply.[48]

In addition to trying to validate and protect the legislation of Louisiana's Republican legislature, Miller also sought in *Slaughter-House* to prevent his more conservative colleagues from turning the Fourteenth Amendment into a weapon with which they could defend propertied elites. He did not want the amendment to give the notoriously conservative federal judiciary the power to strike down state regulatory laws. To confirm his fears, he needed only to look to his left, at the stark visage of archconservative Stephen J. Field, who was anxious to have the authority strike down state regulations. By 1873, Miller had grown distrustful of the judgment of Field, Swayne, and his other brethren on the Court and feared the mischief they might cause in national affairs if the Court accepted Campbell's arguments.

In his famous dissent in *Slaughter-House*, Field took up Campbell's cause and criticized Miller for his limited interpretation of the privileges or immunities clause. If Miller were correct, Field charged, then the Fourteenth Amendment "was a vain and idle enactment, which accomplished nothing, and most unnecessarily excited Congress and the people on its passage." Instead, he believed, the privileges or immunities clause carried a "profound significance and consequence." He asserted that the clause had revolutionized the constitutional system by giving the federal government and—most importantly—the federal courts the authority to protect all fundamental rights from state interference. The privileges and immunities of national citizenship, Field claimed, included all the protections contained in the Bill of Rights as well as the "natural and inalienable rights which belong to all citizens." He continued, "The privileges or immunities of citizens of the United States, of every one of them, is secured against the abridgment in any form by any state. The Fourteenth Amendment places them under the guardianship of national authority."[49]

Conveniently ignoring the fact that all butchers could still pursue their vocation in the new slaughterhouse, Field charged that the slaughterhouse law was an "odious" violation of the butchers' constitutional right to pursue an occupation. "The Act of Louisiana presents the naked case . . . ," he argued, "where a right to pursue a lawful and necessary calling . . . is taken away and vested exclusively . . . in a single corporation." Because the Constitution does not contain an expressed right to pursue a vocation, Field found that right in natural law and the rights which "belong to citizens of all free governments." The right to pursue freely one's vocation, he asserted, grew out of the spirit of the Declaration of Independence, Adam Smith's economic theories, the rights of Englishmen, and the gifts of the Creator.[50]

Although Miller's twentieth-century critics charge him with unnecessarily constricting the meaning of the privileges or immunities clause, Field hoped to expand its meaning well beyond what most of the amendment's framers ever contemplated. If the right to pursue an occupation became a fundamental right protected by that clause, it would open the door for any number of rights derived from natural law to receive Fourteenth Amendment protection. From such an unlimited conception of privileges or immunities, the Court could create innumerable new rights not expressed in the Constitution and then strike down state legislation that interfered with those rights.

Field's argument that the Fourteenth Amendment gave the federal government extraordinary new powers vis-à-vis the states did not stem from a desire to protect the rights of African Americans. As a Democrat and presidential hopeful who often curried favor with southern whites, he opposed Reconstruction and the biracial Republican governments in the South. He wrote a friend that he longed for the day when "by the mercy of God, the Congress of the United States can be induced to think of anything but our 'colored brethren.'" His dissent instead reflected a growing fear of the democratic process. Ever since his days in gold rush California, Field had been suspicious of the masses. In the 1870s, the Paris Commune, the rise of organized labor, and other class movements convinced him that property rights were under siege. He believed that it was the Supreme Court's duty to ensure that the grasping majority could not use the democratic process to achieve what otherwise might be done by a mob—taking property from the haves and giving it to the have-nots. He viewed the Louisiana's slaughterhouse law not as a health regulation, but rather as redistributive legislation that took the property of white butchers and gave it to corrupt carpetbaggers and their black lackeys. If the Court allowed the slaughterhouse "monopoly" to survive, Field warned, similar regulations might soon be imposed on "ovens, machines, grindstones, wine presses, and for all the numerous trades and pursuits for the prosecution of which buildings are required." He feared that a flood of redistributive legislation would follow *Slaughter-House,* and he looked to the broad language of the Fourteenth Amendment to hold back the deluge.[51]

In a separate dissent, Justice Bradley agreed with Field that the privileges or immunities clause incorporated all of the Bill of Rights and those fundamental rights granted to Englishmen under the Magna Carta. In addition, Bradley argued that the slaughterhouse law violated the Fourteenth Amendment's due process clause. By prohibiting a large class of citizens from pursuing lawful employment, he believed, the state legislature deprived them "of their liberty and property without due process of law."[52] In so arguing, he advocated a dramatic new interpretation of the meaning of constitutional due process. The Fifth Amendment had long protected citizens' due process rights, but courts had always interpreted due process to involve procedural matters, such as whether persons had had a fair trial. Now, Bradley asserted that due process included more than procedural protections; it also allowed the Court to scrutinize the substance of state and federal legislation (a doctrine subsequently known as "substantive due process") and to strike down laws that unnecessarily infringed on property rights. Miller summarily dismissed this contention. He saw no reason why the Fourteenth Amendment's due process clause should receive a different reading than the comparable clause in the Fifth Amendment had received in the past. "And it is sufficient to say," Miller wrote, "that under no construction of that provision that we have ever seen . . . can the restraint imposed by the State of Louisiana . . . be held to be a deprivation of property within the meaning of that provision."[53]

Noah Swayne, the justice whom Miller liked least of all his judicial colleagues in his twenty-eight-year tenure on the Court, wrote the third dissent. Adding little to what had already been said by Bradley and Field, Swayne instead chastised Miller and the majority for allegedly supporting one of the worst laws ever passed. "A more flagrant and indefensible invasion of the rights of the many for the benefit of the few," Swayne blustered, "has not occurred in the legislative history of the country." In order to uphold this law, he charged, the majority had purposefully misinterpreted the Fourteenth Amendment. For Swayne, the language of the Fourteenth Amendment was pellucid. "No searching analysis is necessary," he said. The amendment's "language is intelligible and direct. . . . Nothing can be more transparent. Every word has an established signification. There is no room for construction. There is nothing to construe." In other words, the broad language of the Fourteenth Amendment—the meaning of which is still be debated by jurists and scholars well over a century later—could be intelligently interpreted only in the manner in which Swayne interpreted it. Miller had heard arrogant arguments like this before from Swayne in the bond decisions, but now he had the satisfaction of writing the majority opinion.[54]

In the end, Miller and the majority rejected the dissenters' view that the Fourteenth Amendment "radically changes the whole theory of the relations of the State and Federal governments to the people." The founding fathers, Miller argued, added the Bill of Rights to the Constitution in order to prevent the federal government from becoming too powerful. Under the guise of protecting individual rights, the minority wanted to increase dramatically the power of the federal government and Supreme Court. If the Court had adopted the positions of Field and Bradley, state legislatures that attempted to address the problems associated with industrialization, urbanization, and the concentration of capital would have to adjust their legislation to the views of conservative justices. Every piece of state regulatory legislation would be scrutinized by a Supreme Court that jealously guarded the interests of the propertied classes. The dissenters' construction of the Fourteenth Amendment, Miller warned, "would constitute this Court a perpetual censor upon all legislation of the states, on the civil rights of their citizens, with authority to nullify such as it did not approve as consistent with those rights." Increasingly mindful of the influence that bondholders and financiers had over his judicial brethren, he refused to accept an argument that would give the Court this power. "We are convinced," he wrote, "that no such results were intended by the Congress which proposed these amendments, nor by the legislatures which ratified them." The Thirteenth, Fourteenth, and Fifteenth Amendments were designed to protect the freedmen, not completely revolutionize the system.[55]

Some critics have suggested Miller and the rest of the majority could have upheld the slaughterhouse law and still allowed the federal judiciary to accept a new role as the defender of personal rights. The Court could have ruled that the Fourteenth Amendment allowed the Supreme Court to scrutinize and strike down state laws that interfered with the fundamental rights enumerated in the Bill of Rights (i.e., free speech or freedom of religion), but that "natural rights," such as the right to operate a slaughterhouse in the midst of a crowded city, were not fundamental rights. "But Justice Miller," one historian has written, "went far beyond the needs of the case before him in an obvious attempt to destroy, as far as possible, any affirmative reading of the Fourteenth Amendment."[56] Other historians, such as Michael Les Benedict, have persuasively countered this argument by suggesting that Miller and the majority were unable to accept the idea that the Fourteenth Amendment's unadorned language had completely altered the traditional system of federalism that they had always known. They welcomed the end of the era of Taney and *Dred Scott* and recognized that the system had fundamentally changed. They sought a middle ground where the Fourteenth Amendment could be used to protect African Americans' rights, but without making the national government the primary defender of all the rights of all citizens.[57]

Miller believed that African Americans should still look first to their state constitutions for protection of their civil rights. Most state constitutions contained provisions that, if vigorously enforced, would adequately protect blacks' rights. Louisiana's constitution, for instance, contained strong provisions barring discrimination in public accommodations, businesses, and schools. In early 1873 it was still not clear that congressional Reconstruction would fail or that the old economic and racial order of the South would return. Although ex-

Confederates had regained power in some southern states, biracial Reconstruction governments remained firmly in control in others. Congressional Republicans, moreover, had not given up the fight. To shore up Republican governments in the South, Congress had just passed the powerful Ku Klux Act. Up until the final blow dealt by the Compromise of 1877, Louisiana Republicans believed that their Reconstruction government would endure, as evidenced by their reaction of utter disbelief when President Rutherford Hayes agreed to remove federal troops from the South. In 1873, Miller's opinion in *Slaughter-House* affirmed the validity of a biracial legislature that many expected would survive. Had the Court ruled against the slaughterhouse law, it would have supported the Reconstruction legislature's critics who alleged that blacks and Yankees were either too ignorant or too corrupt to adopt legislation that could pass constitutional muster.[58]

Miller did not pin all his hopes on the survival of the Reconstruction governments. He had faith in the power of the Fourteenth Amendment's equal protection clause to achieve its objective of protecting black rights. Rather than a radical transformation in the federal system that would have resulted from a broad reading of the privileges or immunities clause, the equal protection clause held out the promise of a powerful enforcement mechanism requiring minimal federal interference in most state activities. The equal protection clause, Miller argued, allowed the Supreme Court to strike down any state law "which discriminated with gross injustice and hardship against [blacks] as a class." If "[s]tates did not conform their laws to its requirements," Congress could pass suitable legislation to bring the offending states into line. For Miller, this was the perfect balance, offering strong federal assurances that even if the Reconstruction governments faltered, the onerous Black Codes would not be restored because the federal government would intervene on behalf of southern blacks. Most important, by relying on the equal protection clause, the federal judiciary could protect the rights of African Americans without assuming the power to overturn valuable state health and economic regulatory measures. "We doubt very much," Miller wrote of the equal protection clause, "whether any action of a State not directed by way of discrimination against the negroes as a class, or on account of their race, will ever be held to come within purview of this provision. It is so clearly a provision for that race and that emergency, that a strong case would be necessary for its application to any other."[59]

Though a number of Republicans eventually criticized Miller's *Slaughter-*

House opinion for not incorporating the Bill of Rights into the Fourteenth Amendment, others embraced the decision as a powerful affirmation that the overriding purpose of the Fourteenth Amendment was to protect the rights of African Americans. Republican supporters of *Slaughter-House* used it to defend the constitutionality of the Civil Rights Act of 1875. Miller's opinion, Congressman Oliver Morton of Indiana argued, "shows that the very history and purpose that called the Fourteenth Amendment into existence was to protect the colored race from all unjust discriminations in the law, of whatsoever kind," which included even discrimination by owners of those private businesses and public accommodations licensed by the State. "Rights are of no avail unless they are enforced," Morton declared, adding that *Slaughter-House* confirmed that "Congress has the power to protect rights if states won't." He concluded, "The States have the same right they always had to make police regulations, with this single difference, that whatever regulations they make must operate equally upon men of all colors coming within the same conditions." Senator Timothy O. Howe of Wisconsin concurred, proclaiming during the Civil Rights Act debates that "Judge Miller, then, is of the opinion that under the [equal protection] clause no state can oppress a colored citizen by virtue of its laws," and adding that "the very object of the bill now before us is therefore sanctioned by the opinion of that one judge."[60]

Despite much evidence to the contrary, many historians continue to charge that Miller's *Slaughter-House* opinion reveals a Court tired of the "excesses" of Radical Reconstruction and motivated by a reactionary desire to restore stability in the South by returning the old racial and economic order to power. Miller's critics can accurately claim that his views on race consistently trailed behind those of Radicals such as Charles Sumner and Thaddeus Stevens. But they ignore how much Miller's racial views, like those of many thousands of other white Iowans and Americans, changed as a result of the sweeping events of the Civil War and Reconstruction.

In his *Slaughter-House* opinion Miller attributed the transformation of his views both to the courage of black troops during the war and to the rise of the infamous Black Codes afterwards. After the war, he lamented, the southern states quickly "imposed upon the colored race onerous disabilities and burdens, and curtailed their rights in the pursuit of life, liberty, and property to such an extent that their freedom was of little value." Northerners soon recognized, that "without the further protection of the federal government," the freed slaves' plight would "be almost as bad as it was before."[61] The southern states should, and would, be forced "to place the negro on an equality with the white man in all his civil rights." As Miller had warned recalcitrant southerners in 1866, "The power to make laws, which are to operate on the black man and not on the white, will be taken from these states. . . . This may be relied on." The privileges or immunities and equal protection clauses of the Fourteenth Amendment, Miller accurately noted, were the logical remedies to the Black Codes. Never again could a state pass laws specifically designed to degrade a particular race. Those clauses thus served an important and virtuous purpose, but they did not prevent states from passing health regulations that had nothing to do with race.[62]

In the end, Miller's critics are placed in the paradoxical position of arguing that the *Slaughter-House Cases*—an opinion full of rich language emphasizing the need to protect black civil rights—was actually an attempt to undermine those rights. This charge simply does not ring true. While admitting that the Reconstruction governments in the South had made some mistakes, Miller did not want to see them destroyed. He did not trust southern whites, when left to their own devices, to protect the rights of blacks.[63]

With one opinion Miller hoped to preserve the federal system while at the same time providing protection for black civil rights. He wanted to support the biracial Reconstruction government in Louisiana and uphold the ability of states to pass economic and health regulations that affected private property. He also wanted to prevent the Supreme Court, with its archconservatives like Stephen J. Field and Noah Swayne, from becoming the perpetual censor of state regulations. Tragically and ironically, the opinion would fail on all counts. But the ultimate victory of virulent racism and laissez-faire jurisprudence was not what Miller and the Court's majority in the *Slaughter-House Cases* intended.

In 1879, two years after reactionary Democratic regimes replaced the Reconstruction governments, Miller noted that northern businessmen avoided New Orleans, thereby eluding the yellow fever epidemics that continued to plague that city. In the past, businessmen often emerged from New Orleans having contracted tropical diseases. But by the end of the 1870s, he wrote, the "ostracism or fanaticism which has grown out of the war and politics has put a stop to the Northern man going down to New Orleans to do business and there is then no more disease and no more trade." The Republicans' efforts at modernization had failed, and northerners washed their hands of the Crescent City. New Orleans, Miller said, is "delivered over to yellow fever . . . and folly."[64]

CHAPTER 9
Shattered Dreams

AFTER SELLING HIS KEOKUK HOME, Miller bought a large brick Capitol Hill house in a genteel neighborhood on Massachusetts Avenue. The house had a book-lined study outfitted with soft leather chairs and plush sofas where he could be found on many mornings before court, drafting opinions at his cluttered desk. He worked in furious spurts, often sitting for four or five hours without breaking. "When he gets at it," a visitor wrote, "he works like a well-fed, well-contented steam engine." But when he finished, he knew how to take his mind off his work. He relaxed by reading fiction on his couch, and he often said that he hoped to retire one day and write his own novel. In the evenings, he played card games with his family while enjoying a glass of whiskey with a plate of soda crackers. He had, in short, a sense of perspective not shared by some of the other members of the Court. Justice Field, for example, was famous for his relentless work ethic. Whereas Miller quipped that his motto in life was "Never walk when you can ride, never sit when you can lie down," a plaque in Field's study offered a very different aphorism. "My ideal recreation," Field's plaque read, "is to keep on working."[1]

Although Miller enjoyed having his family with him in Washington, their arrival also brought emotional tumult. By the 1870s, the relationship between his daughter Pattie and his wife Eliza had deteriorated. Pattie was "on the point of having to leave home," and she accused her stepmother of excessive drinking and "soliciting presents." The two women bickered frequently, and this consistent antagonism pained Miller. "She and Mrs. Miller are implacables," he later said of Pattie. "She will not yield an inch to Mrs. Miller's peculiarities and argues and sets her down all the time—keeping up perpetual discord and warfare."[2]

Despite these uneven moments, Miller was glad that his family had joined him. In the 1860s, he had led something of a bachelor's existence, renting rooms in hotels and dining with male friends and the other justices. He found it a lonely life, brightened on occasion by surprise visits from his wife. With Eliza in Washington, Miller not only "relieved the lonesomeness"; he could also fully participate in Washington's social life.[3] Wives played an important role in the elaborate rituals that defined the capital city's elite society. When the social season opened each fall, wives of top officials were expected to receive callers, host luncheons, throw parties, keep impeccably clean houses, wear fashionable gowns, and follow the intricate protocols and manners outlined in Washington etiquette books. On each Monday, for example, wives of Supreme Court justices were instructed to be at home in "street costume" so that "persons in social relations with the Court circle, or others in polite society, may call."[4]

Eliza Miller welcomed these duties. Even during her Keokuk years, she had prided herself on her social sophistication, and she enthusiastically embraced the role of Washington socialite. She soon became a leading expert on how the rules of protocol applied to the justices' wives. "Mrs. Miller . . . ," a social commentator wrote, "is held in high esteem among the ladies of the Court circle as the authority on the social etiquette which attaches to their position in fashionable life." With Samuel standing proudly at her side, Eliza threw stylish dinner parties that attracted influential guests. In addition to the other justices and their wives, the Millers regularly entertained cabinet officers, senators, and famous men such as Civil War general William Tecumseh Sherman.[5] "Mrs. Justice Miller," a society reporter wrote, "gives elegant dinners, not only to the Supreme Court, but other distinguished people at the Capital. She is a charming hostess. Her residence is in the best of taste, and in all her surroundings, there are many marks of luxurious refinement." Samuel also enjoyed these events. At parties and gatherings, he was known as a witty and genial raconteur. "Justice Miller," the same observer noted, "has abstracted hours, but is full of life and fun when wakened up in society."[6]

Eliza particularly loved the prestige that came with her husband's job. In the early 1870s, Supreme Court justices and their wives stood near the top of the Capital's social pyramid. In Washington, official position dictated social standing, and, after the president, U.S. senators and the Court's justices held the highest rank. "There can be no doubt as to the precedence of a Justice . . . over a member of the Cabinet," a society expert wrote, "as the Constitution provides that there shall be 'One Supreme Court,' but it does not provide there shall be any Cabinet." Later in his career, when Samuel considered retiring, Eliza insisted that he could not, for she feared their social status would be diminished.[7]

At times, Miller shared his wife's passion for social advancement. In the early 1870s, he set his sights on the Court's most prestigious title—chief justice. Even though the position would mean more work and only a $500 pay increase, he coveted it because of the increased status that came with the job. When Chief Justice Chase died in May 1873, Miller engaged in elaborate machinations in an effort to succeed him. While he thought his chances of being appointed were "good," his brother-in-law Ballinger feared that somehow Eliza might undermine his efforts. Despite Eliza's attempts at refinement, Ballinger thought she was still a liability. Her aggressive social climbing, he believed, worked against her husband's chances for advancement. "I am afraid his wife will hurt him," he wrote, "She is ambitious, imprudent & unscrupulous."[8]

Miller's best hope for securing the nomination lay with two influential members of Grant's cabinet—Secretary of War William Worth Belknap and Attorney General George Williams. Both men were former Keokuk residents whom Miller had befriended during the boom years of the 1850s. It was a testament to Keokuk's former dynamism that three men from a town of only 15,000 played such an important role in national events. Even though Belknap and Williams had long since left the Gate City behind, Miller hoped they still felt emotional ties to their Keokuk acquaintances. And Belknap, whom Miller called "my earnest active friend," did indeed try to influence Grant on Miller's behalf. Rumors spread that Miller, Williams, and Belknap envisioned a scenario in which Miller would be appointed chief justice and Williams would then himself be appointed to the Court. Even the Court's other justices speculated that such a plan was afoot. "I had thought, perhaps, if Miller was made chief," Justice Bradley observed, "Williams would be put in his place. I think that is the Keokuk Programme."[9]

The three Keokuk men undertook these efforts despite the fact that Miller had some small misgivings about the job. He worried that becoming chief justice might expose "original defects" in his "education as regards the languages, and some of the sciences." Although he prided himself on his practical approach to the law, he feared that the role of chief justice might require a more sophisticated education than the one he had acquired in frontier Kentucky. "I might also feel embarrassed," he fretted, "by a want of familiarity with other systems of jurisprudence besides our own." Miller also suspected that the job might be a thankless task. The chief justice, he knew, often found himself caught in the middle of the other justices' petty squabbles. "I doubt if my effective influence in the court would be increased by being made its chief," he wrote, "while I know I should be subjected to much criticism from my associates which I now escape." The Court's figurehead, moreover, often bore the brunt of any public displeasure with the tribunal and was often "held responsible by the public for all its acts." Despite these doubts, Miller continued his quest.[10]

In addition to the efforts of the Keokuk members of Grant's cabinet, editors of Iowa's newspapers did their best to drum up support for Miller's appointment. On their editorial pages, they portrayed Miller as the lone uncorrupted voice of Republican values then serving on the Court. "We hope and expect to see the position accorded to Judge Miller," the *Des Moines Daily Republican* announced. Of all the justices, Iowans believed, Miller was the only one in "full accord and sympathy with the people on the leading constitutional questions of the day." "He is the man," the *Gate City* chimed in, "to put the best results of the war and equally important questions of . . . Corporation franchises and rights, soundly interpreted, into our settled jurisprudence."[11]

Unfortunately for Miller's aspirations, it soon became clear that the Keokuk contingent in Grant's cabinet was not as unified as Bradley thought or Miller hoped. While Belknap supported Miller's cause, Attorney General Williams harbored his own ambition to become chief justice. In order to thwart Miller's nomination, he helped convince Grant that elevating one of the Court's current justices was a bad idea. On Williams's advice, Grant concluded that to "raise any Associate Justice over his brothers would be to deepen jealousies not wholly invisible there."[12] Williams then pushed for his own appointment. After offering the position to Senator Roscoe Conkling and Secretary of State Hamilton Fish—both of whom turned it down—the president did indeed nominate Williams. Miller felt betrayed, even as he tried to remain stoic. "Williams was an old friend of mine," he lamented. "He has been the rock on which my own fortunes were wrecked as regards to this office. . . . But he had a right to get it if he could, and I do not know that he did or said any thing personally against me. He had the shuffling of cards and stacked them for his own benefit. Most other men would have done the same, and I have no quarrel with him about it."

Miller might well have taken some pleasure from the fact that the Senate rejected Williams's nomination. During the confirmation hearings, credible accusations surfaced that Williams had, among other improprieties, misused Justice Department funds to pay for an elaborate carriage for his wife.[13]

With Williams disgraced, Grant next nominated seventy-four-year-old Caleb Cushing, then serving as minister to Spain. But Cushing's nomination ran into trouble as well when the Washington press reminded the public of his doughfaced, proslavery past. In the 1850s, Cushing had served as attorney general in Franklin Pierce's cabinet and had publicly defended the *Dred Scott* decision. The *Washington Chronicle,* edited by Miller's son-in-law George Corkhill, led the attack and lambasted Cushing for being "steadily on the side of the slave-master." Miller approved of Corkhill's efforts. Cushing's nomination, he wrote, "was considered an insult to the Bench by every man on it except [Justice] Clifford, who is himself over 70 and a life long bitter Democrat."[14]

After Cushing's defeat, Grant finally found a passable nominee—Morrison Waite, a little-known Republican lawyer from Ohio. Waite had neither judicial experience nor a national reputation, but he was free of scandal, and the Senate promptly confirmed his appointment—much to the disgust of several of the Court's justices. "He is a new man that would never have been thought of for the position by any person except President Grant," Field complained. "My objection to the appointment is that it is an experiment whether a man of fair but not great abilities may . . . be a fit Chief Justice of the United States—an experiment which no President has a right to make with our Court." Miller, disappointed at not having been nominated himself, also regarded Waite as "mediocre." Although he would grow to like Waite's gentle nature, Miller complained that the new chief justice had limited legal acumen.[15]

Miller grew particularly unhappy with Waite's inability to rein in the long, rambling, and sloppy opinions of Justices Swayne and Clifford. A stronger chief justice, Miller believed, would set strict limits on the discursive efforts of his aging brethren. "The truth is," he wrote, "that the one man of our court who ought to take the lead and without whose courage and firmness nothing can be done is sadly wanting in both those qualities. He is much more anxious to be popular as an amiable, kind hearted man (which he is) than as the dignified and capable head of the greatest court the world ever knew. Of what is due to that court, and what is becoming its character, he has no conception."[16]

Having been thwarted in his efforts to become chief justice, Miller saw his status in Washington society not only fail to grow but positively diminish, due to an influx of rich newcomers into the capital during the 1870s. These arrivistes who came to Washington only after the capital became fashionable did not hold official positions and cared little for the city's traditional hierarchy. Western mine owners, rich industrialists, and other new millionaires built ostentatious mansions and entertained lavishly during the three- to six-month social season. Before the 1870s, Washington had a reputation as a slovenly, dirty, southern town—a fact exacerbated during the Civil War, when soldiers and hospitals filled every open lot. But in the early 1870s, Congress spent over $5 million on roads, sewers, parks, and other improvements in an effort to build a more sanitary, efficient, and handsome city. Washington gained a reputation as a place where nouveaux riches could buy their way into society. Unlike Boston, Philadelphia, or New York, Gilded Age Washington did not have a viable, closed upper class. In the past, government officials had dominated Washington society, but they were an ever-changing group with limited financial resources. As rich industrialists amassed great fortunes in the integrated postwar economy, they gravitated to a city where their wealth could instantly catapult them to the top of fashionable society. Status could be achieved simply by building a mansion and hosting extravagant soirées.[17]

Miller hated the influx of the newly rich, criticizing those who came "to Washington with nothing but money to commend them, showering expensive gifts on their friends and taking place only by virtue of wealth." This disdain was understandable, as the arrival of wealth diminished the importance of rank. "The seat of government has become the winter residence of men of . . . means, with their families, from all parts of the country," a reporter noted. "The prestige of rank has therefore very materially diminished as a passport to polite recognition."[18]

While parvenus built mansions all over town, Miller was living beyond his means. Already indebted from their Keokuk days, in Washington Eliza and Samuel had splurged on home furnishings, dinner parties, and fine wines, and they regularly traveled to Newport, Block Island, and Saratoga. A justice's salary of $10,000 per year hardly covered their expenditures. Although Miller supplemented his income by teaching courses at Georgetown Law School, it was not enough, and he constantly worried about his finances. Compounding the Millers' financial difficulties, Washington's nouveau-riche millionaires threw parties that made Eliza's dinner parties seem pedestrian. Having long hated bondholders and greedy capitalists, Miller had even more incentive to detest the idle rich. His distaste for the excesses of the wealthy only grew as the nation's economic situation deteriorated in the years following the great financial panic of 1873.[19]

Precipitated by the collapse of Jay Cooke and Company, one of the nation's largest and most respected banking firms, the Panic of 1873 struck Wall Street in September. Cooke, whose ingenious marketing of Union war bonds had once made him a national hero, overextended his bank in the early 1870s to fund the construction of the Northern Pacific Railroad. When his firm went under, Wall Street depositors feverishly pulled their money out of banks. The banks promptly called in their loans, and financiers attempted to unload watered-down stocks and depreciating bonds. As capital dried up, the economy foundered. Within two years, 18,000 banks and businesses failed, and unemployment rose to 14 percent. The panic, combined with a glut of manufactured goods, plunged the nation into the longest depression in American history.[20]

Although the worst of the panic was over within a month, the resulting depression lingered for years. Across the political spectrum, Americans looked for people and policies to shoulder the blame. Conservatives believed that the continued use of paper money caused the wild speculation that precipitated the crash. Other people took the opposite view, attributing the slow recovery to a lack of circulating currency. Still others felt that the demands of blacks in the South and militant workers in the North had weighed the economy down. For Miller, the explanation was simple: bondholders and capitalists were responsible. As long as they hoarded their money and sucked the lifeblood out of the West, he predicted hard times would remain. He was incredulous that despite the depression, bondholders continued to demand full repayment of the debts owed by western states, counties, and municipalities, and he was certain that their inflexibility would continue to hold the economy back. "There is no mode of creating wealth but by manufactures, or by the productions of the soil," he wrote. "If they are to be forever crippled both by the diversion of capital to these public securities, and by having all the taxes which support government and pay the interest on the capital invested adversely, it is hard to see when prosperity will return."[21]

Miller believed the only solution was to find a way to let western communities compromise or escape their bonded indebtedness, and he hoped that hard times might soften the Supreme Court's hard-line position on this issue. Although many of the legal questions surrounding municipal bonds had already been resolved in favor of the bondholders, new cases kept arriving on the Court's docket, and Miller hoped the Court might use these opportunities to overturn its previous bond decisions. Many of the new cases involved municipal officials who had ignored strict limitations that state and local laws placed on their power to issue bonds. Some laws required that bond issues receive voter approval or the written assent of two-thirds of a city's voters. Other laws limited the amount of interest a bond could pay. In a number of instances, municipal officials issued bonds without meeting these preconditions. Sometimes these oversights were due to negligence, but town officers often deliberately disregarded the restrictions. In these cases, the Supreme Court had to determine whether to protect municipal taxpayers from the abuses of elected officials or to protect the investments of the bondholders who ultimately bought the bonds.

For a moment, Miller thought his judicial brethren had seen the error of their ways. In 1874, he rejoiced at the outcome of *The Mayor of Nashville v. Ray,* a case that arose from an elaborate scheme used by the elected officials of Nashville, Tennessee, to borrow money despite statutory restrictions on their ability to do so. Unlike most municipalities, Nashville's city charter did not authorize officials to borrow money for public purposes; they could not, therefore, issue bonds in order to meet their city's expenses. To get around this prohibition, town officials wrote special checks for large amounts that they then sold to private individuals for a lesser value. The purchasers could use these checks as coupons with which to pay their taxes, or they could resell them to third parties, who paid their taxes with them. The checks thus became a form of commercial paper, closely akin to a non-interest-bearing bond, and with them Nashville officials raised funds and circumnavigated their city's charter. Lawsuits followed only when a new administration refused to accept these checks at tax time.[22]

In *The Mayor v. Ray,* the United States Supreme Court finally drew a line that government officials could not cross. In the past, the justices' sympathies had been with the innocent secondary purchasers of negotiable instruments, and they had upheld the validity of almost any form of commercial paper issued by a state, county, or town, no matter how fraudulent its issuance had been. But in this case, a 5-3 majority (including Miller, Bradley, and Field) focused on the fact that Nashville's officials had possessed absolutely no authority to borrow money. It would be one thing, Justice Bradley suggested, had they enjoyed some authority to borrow funds, but had done so in an improper manner. "But where the power has not been given," he concluded, "parties must take municipal orders, drafts, certificates, and other documents of the sort at their peril." Any other conclusion would inevitably lead to "fraudulent issues, peculations, and embezzlements, and the accumulation of vast amounts of indebtedness, without any corresponding public benefit."[23]

Justice Miller cheered the decision and thought it represented an important turning point. The case, he wrote hopefully, reflected "a disposition on the part of the court to return to the old principle" of holding city officials "within the just limits of their granted powers and protecting the citizen against contracts made without authority."[24] Justice Swayne, the Court's most adamant defender of bondholders' rights, disagreed with the majority's opinion; he and Justices Clifford and Strong dissented. For over a decade, the Court had upheld the validity and enforceability of negotiable instruments like those issued by the city of Nashville, and the dissenters correctly recognized that the majority's opinion ran counter to those precedents. "The doctrines of the opinion," the dissenters concluded, were "repugnant to the well-settled rules of law established by repeated decisions of this court."[25]

Miller's hopes proved premature. In the years that followed, it became clear just how limited a victory *The Mayor v. Ray* was for the indebted West. The *Mayor* decision represented an unusual case in which city government had no authority to borrow money whatsoever. It did not involve the interests of large bondholders in distant markets and adversely affected only a handful of small investors in and around Nashville. In the years following the *Mayor* decision, the Court faced a whole series of less clear-cut cases where cities, counties, and towns did have authority to issue bonds or borrow money but ignored strict limitations on that authority. In each case, municipal officials violated statutes that required them to meet certain conditions before issuing bonds. In each instance, when these municipalities subsequently defaulted on their bond payments, aggrieved bondholders sued.[26]

One such case, *Town of Coloma v. Eaves*, arose after the town of Coloma, Illinois, defaulted on bonds it had issued in 1872 to help fund the construction of the Chicago & Rock River Railroad. Although Coloma's officials had authority under Illinois law to issue the bonds, the statute also required that the bond issuance be approved by a popular vote of the town's citizens. That vote never took place. When the bondholders sued to recover, a newly elected group of Coloma officials argued that their predecessors had acted without authority "because the legal voters of the town had not been notified to vote upon the question of the town's making the subscription in question."[27]

Miller saw this case as a perfect opportunity for the Court to build on its decision in *The Mayor v. Ray* by holding that all municipal bonds issued without proper authority were invalid. But instead of picking up where they had left off in the Nashville case, Miller's fellow justices returned to their old ways and sided with the bondholders. How, Justice Strong asked for the majority, could bondholders in "distant markets" have known that no vote had taken place? Surely, he argued, the Illinois legislature did not intend that every investor would have to search the public record to find out if every requirement had been met before the town issued the bonds. The bonds' "market-value would be disastrously affected," Strong asserted, "if distant purchasers were under the obligation to inquire before their purchases . . . whether certain contingencies of fact had happened before the bonds were issued,—contingencies the happening of which it would be almost impossible for them in many cases to ascertain with certainty." The Court thus promulgated the doctrine that in cases where a municipality had the lawful power to issue bonds dependent upon certain conditions (such as a popular election), a bondholder had the right to assume that those conditions had been met.[28]

The *Coloma* case was just one of many in 1875 and 1876 in which the Court's majority, over Miller's dissent, upheld the validity of questionable bonds. In *Town of Venice v. Murdock,* for example, the justices considered the validity of municipal bonds that needed the written assent of two-thirds of the town's population before they could be issued. In order to meet this strict requirement, Venice's town officials forged taxpayers' names and placed this fraudulent list in the public record. The Court's majority upheld the bonds' legitimacy. It would be unreasonable to require, Justice Strong argued, that the "holder of bonds should be under obligation to prove . . . that each of the two hundred and fifty-nine names signed to the written assent was a genuine signature." No one, he believed, would invest in bonds that required so much diligence. "No sane person would have a bought a bond with such an obligation," he wrote. The Court reached this conclusion even though New York's highest court had already declared the Venice bonds invalid. In language that echoed Swayne's bombastic opinions in the 1860s, Strong reiterated that the Supreme Court could ignore the decisions of state courts in bond cases, even though such cases almost always involved the interpretation of state laws. We will not, he wrote, "yield our own convictions of . . . right, and blindly follow the lead of others, eminent as we freely concede they are."[29]

Miller dissented in all these decisions but saved his lengthy written dissent for the final bond case of the Court's 1875 term, *Humboldt Township v. Long*. In that dissent, he argued that the majority's decision effectively removed all the barriers to fraud and malfeasance that the state legislatures had erected. What good, he asked, was a law that set strict limits on officials' ability to issue bonds if they could ignore those limitations and issue the bonds anyway? "The simplicity of the device by which this doctrine is upheld as to municipal bonds," Miller felt, "is worthy of the admiration of all who wish to profit from the frauds of municipal officers."[30]

Rather than saddle entire communities with the burden of paying illegally issued bonds, Miller thought these recurring problems could be solved by requiring bondholders to do some preliminary legwork. In *Humboldt*, for example, the township's municipal officers had authority to issue bonds, but only in an amount that did not exceed 1 percent of the value of the town's taxable property. Miller felt that investors could easily have determined if this requirement had been met. "A purchaser," he wrote, "had but to write to the township-clerk or the county-clerk to know precisely the amount of the issue of bonds and the value of the taxable property within the township." Those facts were "all public, all open, all accessible. . . . But in favor of a purchaser of municipal bonds all this was to be disregarded, and a debt contracted without authority, and in violation of express statute, is to be collected out of the property of the helpless man who owns any in that district." The end result was to remove all constraints on unscrupulous officials. "It is . . . clear that, so long as this doctrine is upheld," Miller wrote, "it is not in the power of the legislature to authorize these [cities] to issue bonds under any special circumstances, or with any limitation . . . which may not be disregarded with impunity." For him, these cases should have been decided using a simple moral equation. If one of two innocent persons had to suffer for the unauthorized act of the township or county officers, he asserted, "it is clear that he who could, before parting with his money, have easily ascertained that they were unauthorized, should lose, rather than the property holder, who might not know any thing of the matter, or, if he did, had no power to prevent the wrong."[31]

Shocked by the extremes to which the Court's majority would go to protect bondholders' rights, Miller privately speculated that some of his fellow justices had been bribed by moneyed interests. "Certain members of the Supreme Court are *always* in favour of enforcing bonds, at the expense of all other rights," he told Ballinger, adding that the bondholders "have personal access to certain judges, whose influence on the bench is predominant." The bondholders, Miller said, "understand beyond all men I have ever known the *art* of influencing men. They have unlimited means for they are worth fifty millions of dollars, and they are not illiberal in the use of them." In the end, he lamented, "all that they think worth fighting for they will win."[32]

The capitalists, Miller also observed, were quick to use the law to escape their own debts when necessary. He pointed in particular to abuses surrounding judicially ordered railroad receiverships. In the 1870s, courts first began placing financially unsound railroads under the control of court-appointed supervisors or "receivers," who would manage the failing company's affairs and make sure that creditors were paid. By 1876, over half the nation's railroads had defaulted on their debts and were in receivership. Of the "many thousand miles of railway in my judicial circuit," Miller noted, "hardly a half a dozen have escaped the hands of the receiver." He believed the process was prey to abuse. Interested creditors and stockholders, he alleged, often used their influence to ensure that the Court appointed sympathetic receivers to see that favored creditors and stockholders got paid first, while states and cities that were owed taxes by the railroad or had loaned the corporation money collected nothing. "The rapid absorption of the business of the country of every character by corporations, while productive of much good to the public, is beginning also to develop many evils," Miller asserted in an 1881 corporate receivership case, "not the least of which arises from their failure to pay debts." On the Court, he made it a uniform policy to oppose placing companies in receivership. "He was in principle," Justice Field wrote of Miller, "opposed to putting railroad companies in the hands of receivers."[33]

Miller grew frustrated as he watched the Court bend the law to the will of the bondholders but then twist it in the opposite direction when states tried to collect debts from private businesses. An 1874 case, *Woodson v. Murdock,* was typical of these latter decisions. The case arose when Miller's old Barbourville law partner, Silas Woodson, who had become governor of Missouri, announced that he was putting up for sale the Pacific Railroad, a company whose trains ran between St. Louis and Kansas City. The railroad, Woodson alleged, owed the state $2 million that it refused to pay. Woodson thus felt justified in auctioning the company's assets. During the 1850s, Missouri had loaned $7 million in bonds to the railroad and in return received a first lien or mortgage on the company's assets. At the end of the Civil War, however, the company's tracks lay in ruins, and the railroad subsequently claimed it could not pay its debt in full.

After years of watching railroad bondholders demanding full payment by Missouri's counties and towns, the state's voters were in no mood to forgive the corporations' debts, and they feared that the railroad lobbyists might convince state legislators to do so. As a result, in 1865 Missouri voters approved a special provision in the state's new constitution stipulating that the "General Assembly shall have no power *whatever* to release the lien held by the state upon any railroad." Nevertheless, three years later, state legislators succumbed to the lobbyists' pressure and negotiated a settlement whereby the Pacific Railroad would pay only $5 million of its $7 million debt. To get around the state constitution, proponents of the settlement split legal hairs by arguing that it did not release the lien, but only a portion of the debt. After angry voters tossed out the old governor and elected Woodson, he declared that this compromise with the railroad was unconstitutional and threatened to put the railroad up for sale unless it fully paid its obligations. The railroad's investors sued, and the dispute reached the Supreme Court in 1874.[34]

After countless cases in which the Court had refused to allow towns and states to repudiate or compromise their debts, the justices now sided with a railroad company that wanted to do just that. To do so, Justice Strong ignored the clear intent of Missouri's constitution and accepted the disingenuous argument of its legislature. "Although the legislature had no power to release the lien while the debt remained, . . ." he concluded, "it was not prohibited from . . . commuting the debt."[35]

In his dissent, Miller highlighted the majority's hypocrisy. The language of Missouri's 1865 constitutional convention was clear; it "wholly rejected the idea of leniency to the railroad companies." The purported difference between "lien" and "debt," he continued, was the work of "casuists and linguists" and resulted from the "zeal which springs from a large pecuniary interest." If language as clear as that of Missouri's constitution, Miller charged, was "to be frittered away by construction, then courts themselves become but feeble barriers to . . . legislative corruption, and the interest of the people . . . has but little to hope from the safeguards of written constitutions." Constitutions would fall into disrepute, he predicted, "if they are found to be efficient only for the benefit of the rich and powerful."[36]

Despite his emotional dissents, by the mid-1870s Miller had grown weary of the fight. The uphill battle against a majority that grew more conservative with each passing year and each new appointment had gradually exhausted him. "It is vain to contend with judges who have been at the bar advocates for forty years of railroad companies, and all the forms of associated capital," he said with resignation, "when they are called upon to decide cases where such interests are in contest. . . . All their training, all their feelings are from the start in favor of those who need no such influence." As he told Ballinger in 1875, "I am losing interest in these matters. I will do my duty but will *fight* no more."[37]

The capitalists' influence, Miller knew, went well beyond the Court. The power that they exercised over President Grant also troubled him. Though never one of Grant's most ardent backers, Miller had supported the president throughout his first term and had rejected the conservative alternatives offered by the so-called "Liberal" Republicans. But as the extent of moneyed men's influence over the ex-general became apparent, Miller soured on him. In 1874, Grant alienated many western Republicans when he vetoed the Inflation Bill passed by Congress that year. The bill, a favorite of those who blamed the depression on insufficient currency and the disproportionate power of New York financiers, called for the expansion of the money supply through an increase in national bank notes and greenbacks. Eastern hard-money forces publicly and privately appealed to Grant to veto the bill, which he did.[38]

For Miller, Grant's veto and the pervasive corruption of his administration were symptoms of a tainted presidency. "I am quite disgusted with Grant and his surroundings," he wrote in 1875, calling the president a "weak adorer of moneyed men and moneyed influences." While Miller did not believe Grant himself was dishonest, he thought the president was hopelessly beholden to rich men. "I do not charge or believe that he has ever received a bribe either in money or in property," Miller commented. "But he has habitually bowed himself down and submitted himself to the control and sought the society of men whose only recommendation was their wealth." It was in Grant's "nature to bow the great office he holds in a kind of disgusting worship at the feet of all the coarse rich men he meets without regard to the means which their wealth has been acquired."[39]

Ohio senator John Sherman, head of the Senate Finance Committee and a member of Grant's inner circle, likewise earned Miller's contempt. After western Republicans made political gains by demanding the expansion of the currency through the coining of cheap silver, Sherman and others concocted a bill designed to manipulate these voters. While the Specie Resumption Act of 1876 allowed silver to be coined, the new silver coins only replaced paper currency, not gold coins. The net result—contraction of the money supply—favored bondholders rather than hard-pressed farmers, but it allowed Sherman and his cohort to claim on the stump that they supported the coining of silver. This strategic obfuscation took just enough wind out of the sails of the silverites to prevent a debilitating split in the party on the eve of the presidential election of 1876. Miller found Sherman's machinations offensive, viewing him as a mouthpiece for bondholders and their deflationary desires. "He is a heartless soulless party hack," Miller said of Sherman. "He belongs heart and soul to the money-eyed, bond-holding interest of the country, who no doubt in some shape or other pay him well for his many services to them."[40]

The corruption of the Grant administration hit home for Miller when his Keokuk friend, General William Worth Belknap, a Civil War hero, was implicated in one of the many scandals that plagued Grant's presidency. Before the scandal broke, Belknap and his beautiful wife, Amanda, had been the darlings of Washington society. Newspapers reported what Amanda wore and where she went. People marveled at the Belknaps' gorgeous carriage and the splendid fêtes they hosted. No one asked how Belknap, whose salary as secretary of war was $8,000 a year, could afford to spend $10,000 on a single party. But in 1875 it surfaced that Belknap and his wife had accepted bribes in return for government contracts in the West. Congress promptly impeached Belknap and removed him from office.[41]

To Miller, Belknap's corrupt behavior came as a profound disappointment. He certainly understood the financial pressures his friend faced. No one knew better than Miller the difficulties of maintaining proper appearances while living on a government salary. But unlike Belknap, Miller had done all he could to avoid even the semblance of impropriety. He refused, for example, to let Eliza invest in Washington real estate for fear that he would be accused of speculation. He never accepted the free railroad passes that Stephen J. Field and other justices received from railroad barons; nor did he invest in western mines or elevated railroads, as Field also did. Miller refused to let money dictate his life. On one occasion, he turned down an offer to become a consulting attorney for several New York corporations, a job that would have paid him $100,000 a year. He was thus disheartened when Belknap fell prey to the temptations of the Gilded Age. "I feel a personal chagrin when some man in whom I placed confidence . . . ," Miller said of Belknap, "shows of what poor clay he was made."[42]

With the 1876 election approaching, Miller hoped the Republicans could find a new candidate, someone untainted by scandal and less beholden to the rich than Grant. He wanted a candidate who could restore the party to its role as champion of the common man. Like many of his fellow Iowans, Miller supported the presidential candidacy of the politician he admired "more than any other . . . in public life"—James G. Blaine of Maine. As Speaker of the House from 1869 to 1875, Blaine became one of the most popular and powerful men in Washington. Like Miller, he had lived in Kentucky in the 1830s and 1840s, had joined the Whigs, and had admired Henry Clay. But rather than moving west to seek his fortune, Blaine left Kentucky for Maine, where he carved out a successful career as a "Half-Breed Republican." He broke ranks with the "Stalwarts" who steadfastly supported the corrupt Grant administration, but he also detested the so-called "Liberal" Republicans, who favored making compromises with white southerners. By doing so, Blaine became popular with Iowa Republicans, who also condemned the bribery and scandals in Washington and the mistreatment of blacks in the South. Blaine, moreover, was a bimetallist who favored coining cheap silver and thought that the gold standard only benefited "those already rich." In currency-starved Iowa, bimetallists like Blaine drew fervid support because they offered a solution to the West's financial problems without appearing as radical as greenbackers. At the Republican national conventions in 1876, 1880, and 1884, every one of Iowa's delegates voted for Blaine.[43]

At the 1876 Republican convention, Blaine led the voting through the first six ballots. But when it became clear that his unified support in the West was not enough to secure the presidential nomination, the party turned to Senator John Sherman's pet candidate, Ohio's probusiness governor Rutherford B. Hayes, as its standardbearer. With Blaine defeated, Miller resigned himself to supporting Hayes, despite the fact that on economic issues he saw little difference between Hayes and the Democrats' candidate, Samuel Tilden. Hayes was a fiscal conservative who shared the bondholders' worldview, and Miller dismissed Tilden as an unscrupulous party operative who had "made $5,000,000 by being a Trustee and Director in rotten rail roads." What separated the two candidates, Miller felt, was their position on Reconstruction. Reactionary southern whites uniformly supported Tilden, knowing that if he won he would almost certainly sanction the restoration of total white supremacy in the South. Miller hoped that northern voters recognized this fact and that they would be repulsed by the violent tactics used by Tilden's southern supporters. That July, for example, whites rioted in Hamburg, South Carolina, ransacking the homes and stores of the town's African Americans and killing six black militiamen. The "Hamburg murders" disgusted Miller, and he believed northern voters shared his anger and would express it with their votes. "If your friends will kill negroes," Miller wrote with bitter sarcasm to Ballinger, "I am glad they select the Presidential year for that amusement." White southerners' reactionary behavior, he wrote, was having an "effect in the north, and on the whole I am hopeful, that no such misfortune as Tilden's *providential election* will befall us in the centennial year."[44]

The election of 1876 became one of the most controversial in American history after allegations of electoral fraud by both parties made the final result unclear. Its result hinged on the disputed returns from four states—South Carolina, Florida, Louisiana, and Oregon. In the three southern states, widespread violence against blacks and accusations of fraud tainted the results. Rival Republican and Democratic election boards in each state sent in two different sets of returns. Determining who actually won in those states would be crucial, for if all four states came in for Hayes, he would win by one electoral vote.

With the election undecided and the Constitution providing little guidance as to how to proceed, Congress had to resolve the crisis itself. Since Republicans controlled the Senate and Democrats the House, the debate quickly degenerated into an acrimonious partisan struggle. As passions flared, some southern Democrats resorted to the bellicose sectional language of the 1850s, once again threatening civil war if Tilden were not declared the winner. Such talk made Miller's political blood boil. He chafed at Democrats' assertions that Republicans in Louisiana had been particularly deceitful in their behavior. While Miller acknowledged that Louisiana's Republicans might have engaged in some fraudulent behavior, the Democrats' violent actions against black voters in that state had been far worse. "I think I am unprejudiced enough to admit frankly that the returning board of Louisiana is not what it should be," Miller wrote, "in fact that it is governed if not by corrupt, certainly by partisan influence." "On the other hand," he asked his Democratic ex-brother-in-law, "is it possible that you cannot see and admit that by reason of violence, and the absolute fear of death thus produced, there was no honest vote in that State? And that the laws which governed the returning board were made as the negroes when in power had a right to make them, to protect themselves against this very danger? . . . Suppose I admit the republican party to be more or less corrupt, I am of the opinion that it is purity itself compared to the one which you call your friend." How could it be, Miller wondered, that a decade after Appomattox, even moderate white southerners like Ballinger had failed to learn the lessons of the war? He chided Ballinger for displaying the "same bitterness" and "one-sided spirit" that southerners had shown back in 1857, when they said "if the South could not get their negroes into the Territories" they "could whip us in a fight and would do it."[45]

In January 1877, Congress appointed an electoral commission consisting of ten congressmen and four Supreme Court justices, evenly divided by political affiliation, to resolve the disputed election. From the Court, Miller and Swayne were tapped as the Republicans, and Field and Clifford were appointed as the Democrats. The four justices had the added task of picking a fifteenth, potentially tie-breaking, member of the commission from among their fellow justices. Observers initially assumed that they would choose the fence-straddling David Davis, but Davis left the Court after the Illinois legislature elected him a United States senator. In his place, the justices selected Joseph Bradley, who many considered to be the Court's most open-minded member. Nevertheless, Bradley's selection gave Republicans a bare majority on the commission. Much to the Democrats' disgust, he would remain loyal to his party. As the commission began its work, Bradley often voted with the Democrats on procedural matters, but his critical votes favored Hayes. Miller, for his part, voted with the Republicans throughout the proceedings. Whatever the true results of the disputed election were, the members of commission all voted along strictly partisan lines, and Hayes was declared the winner. Many Democrats complained furiously. But in what became known as the Compromise of 1877, the president-elect and other Republicans secretly placated leading Democrats with assurances that upon assuming office, Hayes would remove all remaining troops from the South and restore "home rule." Reflecting the massive weariness among many northern Republicans over Reconstruction, Hayes had lost enthusiasm for using federal troops to pacify the South. Democrats, in turn, gave halfhearted assurances that blacks' civil rights would still be protected after the troops withdrew.

Miller, who remained guardedly optimistic that the remaining Reconstruction governments in the South could survive, knew nothing of these hidden negotiations.[46]

Although some Democrats roundly criticized Miller for his partisan role on the commission, Republicans cheered him. "I have had a regular ovation wherever I have been this Spring," he wrote from his circuit duties in Minnesota in June 1877. "I have hardly passed a day, except in travel without being invited to a dinner or supper or something of that kind. I do not feel that the abuse heaped upon me by the Democratic press has injured my reputation or injured my usefulness as a judge." The reception accorded to Miller reflected many Republicans' feelings that the electoral commission's decision constituted a great victory, even though the resulting Compromise of 1877 ultimately meant Republican attempts to reshape the South had failed.[47]

When Hayes removed the Union troops from the South, Miller felt betrayed by, and increasingly estranged from, his party. In a letter to Ballinger in October 1877, Miller admitted that during his previous fifteen years on the bench he had often let politics and partisan interests shape his judicial decisions. For the Republican Party, he wrote, he had "rendered fifteen years of faithful irreproachable service." But as his party abandoned their southern allies and became the party of bondholders and corporations, he grew exasperated. "We are quits," Miller wrote. "I shall hereafter feel myself at perfect liberty to oppose or disapprove of any man or any measure as my judgment may dictate." His sense of disillusionment affected his enthusiasm for his judicial duties. "I find myself thus withdrawing active interest, one by one from much that used to absorb me wholly," he wrote, and "I think I have already written to you of my failing interest in the Court. The work there is now merely a matter of duty, often irksome duty. . . . I would gladly accept my salary, or even part of it and retire, before I get too old to seek an interest in something else."[48]

Miller could not afford to leave his position, however; he remained deeply in debt. To retire with his full salary, he would have to stay on the Court until 1886, the year of his seventieth birthday. With most of his Keokuk real estate still unsold, he found it difficult to pay his creditors. Though he was "currently in debt over $20,000," he wrote in 1878, he declared himself "anxious to pay it." Eventually, he resorted to a sad and drastic measure. At the end of the decade, Miller rented his Capitol Hill house and all of its furnishings to a rich congressman from New York for $3,600 a year. While Eliza and their daughter Lida sojourned in Europe, Miller moved back into a hotel. "I may get out of debt and *must and will* live cheap," he vowed. "It will enable me to pay off in two years some debts on which I am paying 10% interest and to relieve the property itself from . . . mortgage now on it." But the decision pained him. "I cannot," he wrote, "but feel that two years of boarding at hotels, abandonment of home and all it implies is a large amount of the few years I can reasonably hope for at my time of life and which I hoped to pass in my own house where I settled down in 1872."[49]

With Eliza in Europe, Miller filled his free time with activities so that he would not dwell on her absence or his financial difficulties. In the evenings he played whist, his favorite card game, with his fellow borders at the Riggs House. "I find . . . the fondness for whist growing on me," Miller wrote, adding that "the hotel has some good players." He also packed his schedule with social activities. "I have been to more formal dinner parties, and more full dress receptions since Christmas day," he told Ballinger, "than I ever have in the same length of time." Given the "absence of my wife," he said, an active social life was "a necessity to prevent moping." But while enjoyable engagements filled his evenings, his continuing struggle on the Court against the vested interests occupied his days.[50]

The Court's justices garnered national attention in 1877 for their decisions in the Granger cases. These cases involved legislation supported by the Grange, an organization of discontented farmers and river-town merchants, mainly from western states, whose members blamed their economic difficulties in the 1870s on railroads, middlemen, and bankers. After Grangers elected majorities in legislatures in Illinois, Iowa, Wisconsin, and Minnesota, those states passed laws that fixed the rates that railroads and grain elevators could charge. In Iowa, for example, the legislature passed an act in 1874 that set maximum rates for the Chicago, Burlington, & Quincy Railroad. Inevitably, the CB&Q and other corporations initiated legal challenges to these statutes. In 1876 and 1877 these cases came before the nation's highest Court, where westerners felt they had a friend in Miller. Miller's longstanding opposition to eastern bondholders resonated among the Grangers, who also criticized the "money power" and Wall Street.[51]

Eight Granger cases eventually reached the Supreme Court, and, of those, the Court chose *Munn v. Illinois* for its lead opinion on the matter. The case involved the owners of grain storage elevators in Chicago, who, farmers alleged, charged exorbitant rates. By 1877, the days when western grain went south on the Mississippi were long gone. Now most grain went by rail to Chicago, where it was stored in giant grain elevators until it could be loaded onto ships bound for eastern markets and Europe via the Great Lakes and the St. Lawrence River. Because these elevators housed all the grain that went through Chicago, their owners had a "vise grip on the flow of commerce." Fourteen elevators owned by nine businesses housed grain from six western states, and the elevators' owners had colluded to fix prices. Charges of monopoly and price gouging followed. When the Grangers took control of the Illinois legislature, they passed statutes that limited the amount the grain elevators could charge.[52]

Conservatives like Justice Field feared the Grangers. He thought they were cut from the same mobocratic cloth as the supporters of the Paris Commune, the revolutionary government that briefly took over the French capital in 1871. And he believed that the Granger laws that regulated private railroads and grain elevators represented a dangerous step towards socialism and communism. Field hoped the Court would use the Fourteenth Amendment's due process clause to strike down those laws, thus building a constitutional firewall between private property and the grasping majority. Surprisingly, in *Munn v. Illinois*, he did not carry the day.[53]

In *Munn*, Miller joined a 7-2 majority that ruled that the Illinois statute was constitutional. States, the majority concluded, had the authority to regulate privately owned businesses like grain elevators that were "affected with a public interest." The majority rejected Field's assertion that the Fourteenth Amendment's due process clause allowed the Court to consider the substance of state legislation and to strike down unjust regulatory and redistributive laws. Instead, the majority deferred to the broad powers of legislatures. "We know that this is a power which may be abused; but that is no argument against its existence," Chief Justice Morrison Waite wrote in his majority opinion. "For protection against abuses by legislatures the people must resort to the polls, not the Courts."[54]

In a dissent that echoed Justice Bradley's opinion in *Slaughter-House*, Field conceded that states had the power to regulate private property in order to protect the health, safety, and morals of the community. But, he adamantly argued, they could not do so solely for economic purposes. "If this be sound law," Field fumed in his dissent, "if there be no protection . . . in the prohibitions of the Constitution against such invasion of private rights, all property and all business in the State are held at the mercy of a majority of the legislature."[55]

Events during the summer of 1877 compounded the anxiety that men of property already felt due to the rise of the Grangers and the Court's decision in *Munn*. In July, a nationwide strike by 80,000 railroad workers brought the United States to a standstill. Hundreds of thousands of other unionists soon joined the work stoppage. When workers sacked and burned railroad company property in Pittsburgh, many observers feared a class revolution was at hand. President Hayes finally restored order by sending the U.S. Army to crush the strike, but the Great Uprising of 1877, as it became known, left businessmen and the middle class badly frightened. As a result, Field's argument that the democratic majority had to be constrained found an increasingly receptive audience. Many propertied men now saw the courts as their best line of defense against the angry masses, and their attorneys embraced Field's substantive view of due process as their most sophisticated weapon. Despite the Supreme Court's decision in *Munn*, these lawyers continued to ask state and federal courts to use the Fourteenth Amendment to thwart what they viewed as redistributive state legislation.[56]

The Supreme Court returned to the issue in 1878 in the case of *Davidson v. New Orleans*. Like the law in *Slaughter-House*, *Davidson* involved an 1871 act of Louisiana's biracial Reconstruction legislature designed to improve sanitary conditions in the Crescent City. The act chartered a private company to drain the swamps in and around New Orleans in order to fight yellow fever. To pay for these efforts, the government assessed fees against the property owners who owned the land. The rationale for asking them to bear these costs was that draining the swamps would dramatically increase the value of their property. Rather than providing the property owners with a windfall at state expense, the legislature required them to help pay for the improvements to their land.[57]

John Davidson, one of the property owners thus taxed, challenged the assessment in state court. Among other claims, Davidson argued that the state's action—forcing him to pay for services he did not request—violated the Fourteenth Amendment by denying him his property without due process of law. Louisiana's state courts rejected this argument, but under a writ of error, he appealed this constitutional question to the United States Supreme Court.

In his majority opinion in *Davidson*, Miller feigned puzzlement about why the dockets of state and federal courts had filled with cases brought by aggrieved property owners who invoked the Fourteenth Amendment's due process clause. The Fifth Amendment's due process clause, he noted, had been around since

1791; in the ensuing decades, few had turned to it for protection. But, for some reason, attorneys had not only latched onto the due process clause of the Fourteenth Amendment, they acted as if it contained substantive powers that the Fifth Amendment's due process clause did not. Miller saw "abundant evidence that there exists some strange misconception of the scope of this provision as found in the Fourteenth Amendment." Because of this misconception, he added, the Court's docket was now "crowded with cases in which we are asked to hold that state courts and state legislatures have deprived their own citizens of life, liberty, or property without due process of law."[58]

Miller's befuddlement about the source of this "strange misconception" was not genuine. He knew, perhaps better than anyone else on the Court besides Field, that railroad, industrial, and financial interests were looking for new legal means to fight regulations then being passed by state legislatures. After his opinion in *Slaughter-House* rendered the Fourteenth Amendment's privileges and immunities clause useless for that purpose, the attorneys for vested interests set their sights on the due process clause. Attorneys, Miller grumbled in *Davidson,* now viewed the due process clause "as a means of bringing . . . this court the abstract opinions of every unsuccessful litigant in a state court."[59]

For Miller, the meaning of due process was clear. In Fifth Amendment cases, it meant that a person's life, liberty, or property could not be taken away without procedural protections. For those accused of a crime, due process meant procedural rights such as the right to a grand jury and a fair trial. In property cases, due process only required that before a person's property could be taken away by the government, that person had to have the right to contest that taking either in court or in front of an administrative body. Miller acknowledged that a law that simply took A's property and gave it to B, without granting A an opportunity for a hearing or legal challenge "in ordinary courts," would violate due process. But in *Davidson,* the plaintiff had the right to challenge the tax assessment; indeed, the law explicitly provided avenues for such challenges. The state notified Davidson of the impending tax, and he "had a full and fair hearing" in both the district court of the state and the state's supreme court. As long as Davis could appeal the assessment, Miller argued, no tax, no matter how oppressive, violated due process.[60]

Although Miller hoped his *Davidson* opinion would discourage the phalanxes of attorneys attempting to expand the meaning of due process, portions of the opinion inadvertently gave those attorneys a glimmer of hope. Miller was reluctant to give a fixed definition of what procedures constituted due process. He instead suggested that the precise meaning of due process be defined by the Court over time, on a case by case basis. "There is wisdom . . . ," Miller concluded, "in ascertaining . . . the intent and application of such an important phrase in the Federal Constitution, by the gradual process of judicial inclusion and exclusion, as the cases presented for decision shall require." Consequently, those who favored substantive due process could take heart in, and hope to exploit, Miller's admission that the definition of due process was still in flux.[61]

The attorneys for propertied men could also find some solace in Justice Bradley's concurring opinion in *Davidson*. Although Bradley did not feel that Louisiana's law unfairly burdened Davidson, he nevertheless argued that the Court had the power to strike down state laws that were unjust but procedurally sound. "It seems to me," he wrote, "that private property may be taken by a State without due process of law in other ways than by mere . . . want of a judicial proceeding." He continued, "I think . . . that in judging what is 'due process of law,' respect must be had to the cause and object of the taking"; if that object was "found too arbitrary, oppressive, and unjust, it may be declared to be not due process of law." Thus, Bradley generally endorsed the "strange misconception" of due process advocated by conservatives. But regardless, *Davidson* was, in the end, a setback for the defenders of untrammeled property rights.[62]

Miller was victorious in *Davidson,* but his losing efforts continued in cases involving bonds and bondholders. Tired of repeatedly arguing the same points, he continued his silent dissents in many bond cases.[63] In others, he simply acquiesced.[64] But in a few cases in the late 1870s, he continued to fight the good fight. In particular, he defended a new strategy developed by states and municipalities to compromise their bonded indebtedness. In these cases, states and cities, rather than trying to renegotiate with bondholders, taxed the interest they paid on their bonds and thereby retained a portion of the money that would otherwise have gone to bondholders. It was a simple but ingenious strategy that infuriated the conservative members of the Court.

Murray v. City of Charleston was typical of this new type of case. During the 1860s, the city of Charleston, South Carolina, had issued a series of bonds that paid 6 percent interest. But when the city ran short of funds in March 1870, it passed "an ordinance to raise supplies for the fiscal year" that included a 2 percent tax on all of the city's interest payments. The bondholders would really only receive a 4 percent dividend from their bonds. As a result, Murray, a bond-holder from Germany, sued the Charleston city council for breach of contract. After the state courts sided with the city, he appealed his case to the United States Supreme Court.[65]

The case had momentous implications both for bondholders and debt-ridden states and cities around the country. If the Court upheld this clever use of a city's taxing power, it would allow states and communities across the country to "renegotiate" their debts without actually consulting the bondholders. In oral arguments, Murray's attorney contended that because the city applied the tax to an existing contract, the tax unconstitutionally impaired that contract. In its defense, Charleston's attorneys argued that the city never renounced its right to tax the bonds and that Murray had bought them "with notice that they were subject to the exercise of that power."[66]

In a 7-2 decision, the Supreme Court sided with Murray and the rights of bondholders. In his majority opinion, Justice Strong acknowledged that the city had broad taxing powers but argued that they were subject to constitutional limitations. "We do not question the existence of a state power to levy taxes," he asserted. "But the power is not without limits, and one of its limitations is found in the clause of the federal Constitution, that no state shall pass a law impairing the obligation of contracts." To Strong, the city's tax was symptomatic of the growing chaos in American life, and it had to be struck down. "The inviolability of contracts, and the duty of performing them, as made," Strong concluded, "are the foundations of all well-ordered societies."[67]

In a concise dissenting opinion, Miller pointed out that Charleston's city charter—written in 1781—gave the city the power to tax. Any contract the city of Charleston made after 1781 was subject to that power unless the city explicitly renounced it. Charleston's power to tax the bonds, in other words, was built into the terms of the contract. "I am of [the] opinion," Miller wrote, "that the power of taxation found in the charter of the City of Charleston, long before the contract was made which is here sued on, entered, like all other laws, into the contract, and became part of it." Thus, he contended, the imposition of the tax could not impair the obligation of Charleston's contract with Murray.[68]

The Court faced the same issues again in *Hartman v. Greenhow* in 1881, when it considered a Virginia law that taxed state bonds by deducting from the interest they paid. Once again, the bondholders were victorious. "If, against the express terms of the contract," Justice Field maintained in his majority opinion, "the state can take a portion of the interest in the shape of a tax on the bond, it may at its pleasure take the whole." It was a "great truth, which all just men appreciate," he moralized, "that there is no wealth or power equal to that which ultimately comes to a state when in all of her engagements she keeps her faith unbroken."[69] Once again relegated to dissent, Miller proffered the same succinct argument he had made in *Murray*, noting that he had long insisted a state could never bargain away its power to tax. In this instance he saw no reason why these bonds "should not be subject to the same taxes as other property taxed by the state."[70]

On a few occasions, Miller scored small victories in bond cases. In 1880, he wrote the majority in a Louisiana case in which the Court declared invalid bonds issued in excess of debt limits set in that state's constitution.[71] But such cases were exceptional. In most, Miller's colleagues characterized efforts by states, counties, and towns to escape their debts as emblematic of dark forces loose in the land. When, for instance, Virginia claimed the state could not be sued by nonresident bondholders because of the Eleventh Amendment, Justice Stanley Matthews called the argument a "doctrine of absolutism, pure, simple, and naked; and of communism, which is its twin; the double progeny of the same evil birth." Justice Field, for his part, urged the Court to use the Constitution as a "barrier against the agrarian and despoiling spirit" that plagued America.[72]

While his fellow justices grew increasingly conservative, Miller, with his critical view of eastern financiers, became a minor folk hero in the West. His regional popularity even led some western Republicans to put his name forward as a presidential candidate. As early as 1872, some of Miller's admirers had suggested that he should replace Grant as the Republicans' standardbearer. Having not yet broken with the president, Miller disavowed such proposals and insisted that he had no desire to undermine Grant or challenge his candidacy. "The friends of Judge Miller," the *New York Times* reported March 29, 1872, "authorize the emphatic contradiction of the report circulating in the West that that gentlemen has permitted the use of his name as a candidate for the Presidency."[73]

During the 1870s, Miller's political popularity continued to increase. Along with his dissents in the bond cases and his concurring votes in the Granger cases, his position on currency issues played well with western Republicans. Like many westerners, Miller was a bimetallist who supported full monetary status for both gold and silver and believed that the demonetization of silver in 1873 had resulted from a conspiracy by British and American bondholders. Creating a dual gold and silver standard, he hoped, would greatly expand the nation's money supply. Not as radical as greenbackers, the bimetallists nevertheless hoped to ease pressures on debt-ridden farmers and towns and provide desperately needed capital to the South and the West. "I belong to a class, a very large one, the dominant one in the Northwest," Miller wrote in 1878, "who believe in a return to specie payments, but who do not believe that either honesty or sound policy require silver to be excluded from the term specie."[74]

Iowa's delegation planned to nominate Miller as a presidential candidate at the 1880 Republican convention if a stalemate occurred between the supporters of the frontrunners—former president Ulysses S. Grant and James G. Blaine, now a senator. Although Miller did not actively support this effort on his behalf, he did not resist it. At the convention, Miller's proponents campaigned among the western delegations with the hope of securing enough support to bring his name to the floor, and for a time they thought they had successfully done so. Then the Wisconsin delegation, which had leaned briefly toward a Miller candidacy, switched its allegiance to James Garfield, thereby destroying Miller's prospects. "If Wisconsin had not made the break for Garfield that it did," J. S. Clarkson, editor of the *Des Moines Register* remembered, "a formidable break of several states would have been for Miller on the next ballot, doubtless resulting in his nomination." In the end, Garfield became the party's nominee. "The Iowa delegation was prepared to offer my name at any time they could honorably abandon Blaine," Miller wrote two days after the convention in 1880, "but that time never came."[75]

When his supporters urged his candidacy in 1884, Miller finally fully embraced the idea. Miller's son-in-law George Corkhill reported that "Miller's heart [was] fixed on it." After surveying the political landscape, Corkhill, editor of the *Washington Chronicle*, concluded that "Miller could be nominated." At the previous two Republican national conventions, western delegates had supported James G. Blaine, but his candidacy had failed each time. Now some westerners concluded that Miller was the candidate who could reclaim the soul of their party from corporate conservatives. Even a few eastern Republican powerbrokers acknowledged that Miller represented the best hope of uniting all of the party's factions. Blaine, who continued to nurse his own presidential ambitions, confessed to Miller that many Republican leaders favored the justice's candidacy "because no man will be so strong with all the wings of the party." Miller took these entreaties seriously. "I find as far as I can trust my own judgment a rather ardent readiness in Iowa and Nebraska among active and influential men to take hold at once," he said of the campaign to draft him as a candidate, "and my hardest task has been to restrain them from present action." Missouri governor Silas Woodson came out in support of a Miller candidacy, and western newspapers described the justice as the "safest man with the required ability who can unite the party."[76]

Unlike his halfhearted candidacies in previous years, Miller believed that this time he stood a credible chance. "*It is serious,*" he told Ballinger. He even ruminated about how assuming the presidency might affect his pocketbook. "If I should become President I lose my retiring pension of $10,000 per annum," he noted. "This is a . . . serious consideration if I survive this to be a very old man as I have but little to leave my family." Corkhill shared these concerns. He feared that if Miller won, resigned from the bench, and lost his pension, "Miller's wife would spend all their salary, & at the end of the term they would be poor & extravagant." Thus, even at the height of the efforts on his behalf, Miller tried to moderate his enthusiasm for the endeavor. "I have . . . an office suitable to my taste," he concluded, "in which I have reached and continue to reach honor which ought to satisfy . . . past ambition. . . . [but] this is not to say to you that I would refuse."[77]

In the end, Miller's and Blaine's supporters reached an agreement in which Miller's western friends would back Blaine on the early convention ballots, but if Blaine's candidacy failed—as it had in the past—Blaine's delegates would actively support Miller. "If he had failed he would have been for me," Miller wrote after the convention, "and I should have been nominated. . . . There were men (leading men) in every delegation from my circuit and from Kentucky and several territories who would have joined the movement." With western Republicans backing him on the early ballots, Blaine secured the nomination, but Miller took mild satisfaction in his brief presidential bid. "Perhaps you would like to know what became of my Presidential Boom," he remarked to Ballinger after the 1884 convention. "Well as I wrote you last spring I never permitted it to rise to the dignity of a boom. It was however the nicest and quietest little scheme."[78]

Miller did win a much smaller election in 1884, when the National Conference of the Unitarian Church chose him to be their president. In the 1880s, the church remained in the forefront of latitudinarian thought, and Miller's coreligionists always impressed him with their erudition and sophistication. Throughout his life, Miller remained a freethinker on legal, political, and theological issues, and the fact that a body of like-minded individuals selected him as their leader pleased him. "It was an honor to be elected," Miller wrote, "and the duties were not burdensome." The annual Unitarian convention was, he believed, "the most cultivated and intelligent body that is gathered together in this Country."[79]

The results of the national political contest in 1884 concerned Miller, as Blaine lost the election to Democrat Grover Cleveland. Miller had supported Blaine's candidacy, although not with the same enthusiasm as in the 1870s. Over the years, Blaine had increasingly embraced the Republicans' corporate emphasis. In the election of 1884 he made raising tariffs the core issue of his campaign. Miller nonetheless preferred Blaine to Cleveland and the Democrats. Because unreconstructed southern whites dominated the Democratic Party, Miller doubted that it was "capable of governing the country well." As he wrote, "It is not to be expected that a party composed of three fourths southern politicians who have learned nothing by misfortune will be impressed with the best feeling for a country of which they constitute so small a part, in numbers, in wealth, in energy or in experience in government." Given the direction his own party had taken on issues of finance and Reconstruction, Miller did not feel that things would have been much different if Blaine had won. "As regards any question of public policy," he concluded, "there is really but little difference so far as the opinions as openly announced between the Democratic and Republican Parties."[80]

The melancholy tone of his political analysis reflected the fact that by the fall of 1884, Miller, now sixty-eight, had abandoned the optimism of his youth. Indeed, few of his early dreams for the nation or for his own personal prosperity had been realized. Even though he held a position of prominence, he had not grown rich, as he had thought he surely would. In the 1880s, Keokuk remained a smallish town, Barbourville had all but disappeared, and Miller continued to struggle to meet his expenses. The Republican Party—the party whose ideology once accurately reflected Miller's own sanguinity—had also changed for the worse. Originally committed to economic mobility for all, its purpose now appeared to be protection of the gains made by a few. And the Supreme Court—the institution into which Miller had poured so much of his life's energies—was now controlled by men who seemed equally committed to this jaded cause.

CHAPTER 10

Danger from Above and Below

I N APRIL 1888, President Grover Cleveland appointed Melville Fuller as chief justice of the United States, filling the seat of Morrison Waite, who had died the month before. When Fuller assumed his duties that fall, seated to his right and left were the two senior members of the bench, Miller and Field, the last of Lincoln's appointees on the Court. Fuller, a congenial Democrat, soon discovered that despite their years, neither Miller nor Field had mellowed with age. "Oh, but there were giants on the Court in those days," Fuller later recalled. The new chief justice found it quite difficult to dictate the Court's agenda, given the indomitable personalities of the elder justices. "I think you will understand," he told a Court employee. "No rising sun for me with these old luminaries blazing away with all their ancient fires."[1]

In the 1880s, the senior justices' "ancient fires" did indeed blaze away. Both born in 1816, Miller and Field had experienced unprecedented social, economic, and political change during their lifetimes. Although the two men had great respect for one another, by the 1880s it was abundantly clear that they viewed their transformed country differently. Justice Field, surrounded by men who prospered in the new economy, saw the postbellum changes in American life as a glorious triumph. Field dined and socialized with railroad men such as Collis Huntington, Cornelius Vanderbilt, and Leland Stanford. Field's brother, Cyrus, who gained lasting fame for organizing the company that laid the first transatlantic telegraph cable, grew rich from railroad investments. In search of his own "moderate fortune," Justice Field himself invested in mines, railroads, and other corporations and saw no conflict of interest in doing so. He believed that if men failed in life it was the result of personal flaws, not market forces. "It is very

strange to see," Field wrote, "how many men fail from some sort of ineffi-
ciency—I know not what to call it except incapacity to succeed." He thus embraced the argument that the individuals later called "robber barons" were
simply successful entrepreneurs whose property needed constitutional protection from the "angry menaces against order" and the "agrarian and nihilistic
element" amongst the laboring masses. By the 1880s, he viewed American politics as a great "contest between civilization on the one hand and anarchy on the
other."[2]

Justice Miller did not share Field's unrestrained enthusiasm for the new economic order. Even though he acknowledged that corporations had some benefits, Miller believed that the concentrated wealth created by national corporate
enterprises had spawned political corruption and material excess. Great wealth,
he warned, had created an explosive situation in the cities where the desperately
poor lived in close proximity to the garish mansions of the wealthy.

By 1888, Miller and Field did agree on one key point. Both men worried
that the growing number of radical voices among the working class threatened
American democracy. After the Haymarket Affair in 1886, in which German
anarchists in Chicago allegedly murdered Chicago policemen, Miller concluded
that the pronounced economic disparity between the idle rich and the working
poor had led many workers to embrace dangerous beliefs. Unlike Field, Miller
blamed capitalists and industrialists for creating the conditions in which socialism, communism, and anarchism flourished.

In June 1888, Miller delivered a poignant commencement address to the
University of Iowa graduating class in which he assessed the state of the nation
and the lessons he had learned about politics and human nature over the course
of his long career. He expressed to the assembled students and parents his concerns about the growing chorus of radical voices in the nation's cities. These
"anarchists, nihilists, socialists, [and] communists," he lamented, believed that
the American system was so corrupt that it could "not be reformed, modified
or gradually changed" but instead had to "be overturned and annihilated."[3]

Although he opposed such extreme solutions, Miller suggested that workers
could not be blamed for looking for solutions to their plight. In America's large
metropolises, he reminded his audience,

the palaces of the rich are surrounded by the hovels of the poor; the glaring
lights of gas and electric lamps illuminating for the wealthy their hours of

hilarity and festivity shine down upon the tenements of the lowly and the poverty stricken, and while the more favored few have all that is best in life in the way of pleasure and enjoyment, another a much larger class of beings a few hundred yards away, or across the street, may be languishing in misery, burdened by poverty, and tortured by disease for which they have not the means to provide the remedy. . . .

Undoubtedly these are not pleasant things for the lover of humanity to witness, and they certainly present the strongest inducement for the introduction of such real and genuine reforms in the fabric of social life as shall tend to ameliorate the hardships of want and to prevent all needless suffering.[4]

Miller empathized with the radical movements' leaders, whom he refused to dismiss as wicked or irrational madmen. "Their leaders are not only learned," he said, "but men of intelligence, speaking and writing many languages, familiar with the world, courageous, and desperate." Often, he continued, these men started out as reasonable reformers. But because alarmist government officials made even sensible union leaders objects of constant harassment and suspicion, many labor organizers learned to hate all elites and to view the entire world through a revolutionary lens. "Whatever they may originally have been in the way of philanthropists," Miller claimed, "they degenerate into haters of prosperity and happiness on the part of those who are more fortunate than themselves." By turning to solutions such as merging all property into "one great common fund," Miller felt radicals looked mistakenly to "some Utopian age founded on the theory that there is no selfishness in human nature, and that the happiness of the whole community is equally dear to every member of it as his own or that of his family."[5]

Jaded by his own experiences, Miller did not share this utopian dream. He had long since lost the idealism of his Barbourville days and now believed that man was "essentially a selfish creature." Men labored to better their own condition and that of their families "rather than that of the world at large," Miller claimed. "Indeed," he told his audience, "there is no doubt that egoism, rather than altruism, is the controlling principle of human nature." The desire for personal gain or profit, "either by the acquisition of property or by the advancement in social position," drove all men, whether they were industrialists, merchants, writers, or artists. If "there were no public to look at, admire, and pay for his works" the artist "would doubtless sit down and smoke his cigar or read his novel in the hours which he now devotes to the finest productions of genius." By depriving individuals of the fruits of their labor, Miller argued, communism and socialism created a "perfect equality, but it is an equality of laziness."[6]

Despite his own misgivings about unbridled capitalism, Miller credited the American economic system with ingeniously harnessing man's selfishness in a manner that created wealth, innovation, and progress, as the U.S. patent system well proved. Noting that the telegraph, the improved steam engine, and the telephone were all American innovations, Miller argued that patents ensured just rewards to the men "whose inventive genius produced these marvelous helps toward the lightening of the burden of human toil." Most inventors, he believed, "never would have spent their nights in vigils, nor their days in toil, if they had known that they would reap no personal benefit."[7]

But Miller also understood the danger of unrestrained greed. The jarring postwar changes in American life, he believed, had destroyed the free-labor society envisioned by antebellum Republicans and replaced it—especially "in our larger cities"—with a dangerous landscape filled with the mansions of the rich and the tenements of the "discontented, the unfortunate, and the poor." The system worked, he believed, when even the poorest citizen had reason to believe that with hard effort they would rise in life. During Reconstruction and the Gilded Age, wealth and power had become concentrated in the hands of the few; consequently, many in the working classes had lost faith that they could succeed. Throughout his career, Miller lamented that bondholders, financiers, and southern reactionaries refused to recognize the folly of denying others the right to rise. As the popularity of anarchism, communism, and socialism in the cities grew, he feared that the selfish elites might reap what they had sowed.[8]

By the end of the 1880s, Miller concluded that the last best hope for American society and time-honored Republican values lay in the fertile fields of Iowa. If a noble free-labor world survived anywhere in America, he maintained, it was there. Though he had hoped once that Keokuk might grow into a great metropolis, Miller now celebrated his state for its rural ways. Iowa, he noted, still had "more good farms than any other state in the Union," and it had "no large city where the disorderly elements seem to gather and become formidable." With the rise of a permanent wage-earning class in the North and tenant farming in the South, Iowa seemed an oasis of virtue and self-sufficiency. It was a "community where almost every man owns, or aspires to own, his plot of ground, and to produce out of that farm a comfortable subsistence for himself and his family." As Miller argued, "Among [Iowa's] population are all the elements of happiness and prosperity, and good government and love of order are developed to as high degree as anywhere in the world." Rather than following selfish capitalists, racist demagogues, or dangerous radicals, the nation needed to turn to Iowa for guidance. It was in Iowa where Americans could look for the "good old-fashioned ideas of honesty, fair-dealing, industry, thrift, and a just regard for the security of the results of individual labor."[9]

In the 1880s, Miller longed for the Republican party of old. Although the party had once served as the reform vehicle of prosperous farmers, small-town professionals, and other members of the antebellum middle class, trans-Mississippi Republicans like Miller watched in dismay in the 1870s as the advocates of corporate industrialism took control of the national organization. But while Miller regularly expressed his distaste for the party's new leadership, he and other old-style western moderates had nowhere else to go. Never radical, they vigorously opposed the socialists and communists. And the Democrats' southern policies continued to make that party anathema to Iowans, who had sacrificed so much during the Civil War. Moderate western Republicans became an anomaly. They opposed their party's new corporate emphasis but could do little about it.

Although Miller often criticized his party's new leadership and policies, some of his judicial opinions eventually aided the very forces he opposed. He lamented the failure of Reconstruction and the Democrats' return to power, for example, but he never acknowledged that some of his decisions had actually helped undermine his party's original southern agenda. Many of his opinions had left substantial authority with the states and had played into the hands of unreconstructed southern whites. His decision in *Slaughter-House* ultimately limited African Americans' ability to use the Fourteenth Amendment to protect many of their civil rights against state action. He also concurred in majority opinions in two cases—the *Civil Rights Cases* and *Cruikshank v. United States*—that severely undermined African Americans' ability to defend their rights against the violent or discriminatory acts of private citizens.[10]

The *Cruikshank* case arose from the Colfax massacre, the "bloodiest single instance of racial carnage in the Reconstruction era." In 1873, after a disputed gubernatorial election in which both Democrats and Republicans claimed victory, armed black residents of Grant Parish, Louisiana, seized the local courthouse to keep it out of the hands of white Democrats. On Easter Sunday, a white militia stormed the courthouse and killed more than one hundred of the African Americans inside, including many who were trying to surrender. After the massacre, the Justice Department indicted ninety-eight of the white attackers but managed to secure only three convictions, all of which were appealed.[11]

When those appeals reached the Supreme Court, Miller and the other justices overturned even those convictions, unanimously concluding that the Fourteenth Amendment applied only to state action and not to the actions of private individuals. They rejected the Justice Department's assertion that the white defendants violated the black victims' Fourteenth Amendment rights of due process and equal protection. "The Fourteenth Amendment," Justice Waite wrote for the majority, "prohibits a state from depriving any person of life, liberty, or property, without due process of law; but this adds nothing to the rights of one citizen against the other." For protection from their fellow citizens, black southerners would have to look to state courts and police. Given that ex-rebels soon regained control of these institutions, African Americans often had no legal recourse for violent crimes committed against them.[12]

In *Cruikshank,* the Court did point out that had the Justice Department's indictments been properly drawn, the perpetrators could have been successfully convicted in federal courts under the Fifteenth Amendment and the Enforcement Act of 1870. The Enforcement Act empowered the federal government to arrest, try, and convict state citizens who interfered with other citizens' voting rights on account of their race. Although the prosecutors in *Cruikshank* had charged the defendants with violating their victims' Fifteenth Amendment rights, the Court found the indictments defective because they did not specifically allege that the defendants attacked their victims because they were black. "We may suspect that race was the cause of the hostility, but it is not so averred," the chief justice concluded. "This is material to a description of the substance of the offence, and cannot be supplied by implication." *Cruikshank* left open the possibility that the federal government could successfully prosecute private citizens who threatened black voting rights if future indictments under the Enforcement Act alleged race as a motive. Nevertheless, by freeing the *Cruikshank* defendants the Court gave the forces of white supremacy an important symbolic victory.[13]

The 1883 *Civil Rights Cases* proved to be even more damaging to black citizens' aspirations for full equality. In that decision, the Supreme Court declared unconstitutional the first section of the Civil Rights Act of 1875, which made it a misdemeanor under federal law for private individuals to deny others access to public accommodations, theaters, and transportation because of their race. In the *Civil Rights Cases,* Miller joined all of the justices except John Harlan in holding that the Thirteenth and Fourteenth Amendments did not prohibit discrimination by private citizens. The justices again declared that for protection against discrimination by private individuals, African Americans would have to depend on their state governments to enforce state laws that prohibited such practices. As Bradley wrote for the majority in the *Civil Rights Cases,* "Innkeepers and public carriers, by the laws of all the States, so far as we are aware, are bound, to the extent of their facilities, to furnish proper accommodations to all unobjectionable persons who in good faith apply for them." But with Reconstruction over and whites fully in control of southern governments, little hope remained that such laws would be enforced. Miller's concurring votes in *Cruikshank* and the *Civil Rights Cases* decisions reflect the limits of his evolving racial views and his unwillingness to abandon the constricted reading of the Fourteenth Amendment that he first presented in *Slaughter-House.*[14]

Yet in an often overlooked opinion written shortly after the *Civil Rights Cases,* Miller revealed that he and other members of the Court had not completely washed their hands of federal efforts to protect African Americans' rights. In *Ex Parte Yarborough,* Miller held that the federal government had broad authority to act when violence perpetrated by private citizens threatened the voting rights of black men. The case originated from an 1883 incident in Banks County, Georgia, involving a white Klansman named Jasper Yarborough. He and several members of his family were members of a Democratic paramilitary group known as the "Pop and Go Club." In 1883, Yarborough and other members of the club made numerous nighttime raids meant to terrorize black voters. In one incident, Yarborough rode with fellow Klansmen to the home of Berry Saunders, an African American who had voted in the federal elections the previous November. In a scene played out thousands of times throughout the South in the late nineteenth century, Yarborough and his disguised associates dragged Saunders from his house and "beat, bruised, wounded, and maltreated" him. What made this case unusual was that Justice Department officials speedily managed to arrest and indict Yarborough and then successfully prosecuted him in federal court. Yarborough was sent to prison in upstate New York for two years of hard labor, but while there he claimed that federal officials had no right to detain him and filed an application for a writ of habeas corpus. After a lower court rejected his contentions, Yarborough appealed to the Supreme Court in January 1884.[15]

In his majority opinion for a unanimous Court, Miller emphatically rejected Yarborough's appeal and endorsed the need for vigorous federal efforts to protect African Americans' voting rights. Federal laws, Miller argued, prohibited Yarborough's acts. Existing statutes authorized federal officials to prosecute anyone who went "in disguise on the highway, or on the premises of another" to hinder a person's "free exercise or enjoyment of his Constitutional rights." Those laws also specifically targeted anyone who conspired to use "force, intimidation, or threat" to prevent another person from voting. While Yarborough did not deny that he had committed these acts, he alleged that the federal laws were unconstitutional because the Fifteenth Amendment, like the Fourteenth Amendment, applied only to state action and did not empower the federal government to prosecute private individuals. Without expressed constitutional authority to prevent private individuals from intimidating other voters, his attorneys argued, the federal government could not act. Miller rejected this contention, concluding that the federal government's power to act could be implied from the Constitution. Yarborough's lawyers' reasoning, he argued, "destroys at one blow, in construing the Constitution of the United States, the doctrine universally applied to all instruments of writing that what is implied is as much a part of the instrument as what is expressed."[16]

To find the implied power by which the federal government could pass laws protecting voting rights, Miller gave a broad interpretation to article 1, section 4 of the Constitution, which provides Congress with the authority to make regulations for the "times, places, and manner of holding elections for senators and representatives." Laws that protected voters from violent intimidation, he reasoned, determined the "manner" of an election. Miller also rejected Yarborough's contention that the Fifteenth Amendment gave no affirmative right to African Americans to vote. He asserted that the language of the Fifteenth Amendment implied that male African Americans had voting rights. The Fifteenth Amendment, he argued, "does, *proprio vigore*, substantially confer on the negro the right to vote, and Congress has the power to protect and enforce that right."[17]

Miller's broad interpretation in *Ex Parte Yarborough* of article 1, section 4, and of the Fifteenth Amendment stood in stark contrast to the conservative construction he gave to the Fourteenth Amendment in *Slaughter-House*. The difference between the two cases stemmed from his concern that the Fourteenth Amendment, broadly interpreted, had the potential to alter dramatically the federal system. If the majority had accepted the dissenters' position in *Slaughter-House*, the Court would have had the ability to strike down valuable state regulatory laws that had nothing to do with race in order to protect rights that had their basis in conservative ideology and natural law. The Supreme Court, Miller feared, would become the perpetual censor of all state legislation. Because he believed that the purpose of the Fourteenth Amendment was to protect African Americans almost exclusively, the amendment's language had to be interpreted strictly or it could lead to all manner of judicial mischief. The Fifteenth Amendment carried no such risks, as its language explicitly limited its effects to matters involving race and voting rights. Even if interpreted broadly, the amendment's impact on federalism would be limited. Thus, in *Yarborough*, Miller was able to give expression and effect to his genuine concern for blacks' voting rights without dramatically altering the Constitution.[18]

In powerful language, Miller described what he saw as the greatest threat to American democracy in the 1880s—the corruption of elections by the wealthy in the North and by reactionary white southerners in the South. "If this government is anything more than a mere aggregation of states," he said, ". . . it must have the power to protect the elections on which its existence depends from violence and corruption. . . . If it has not this power it is left helpless before the two great natural and historical enemies of all republics, open violence and insidious corruption." He continued, "Such has been the history of all republics, and, though ours has been comparatively free from both these evils in the past, no lover of his country can shut his eyes to the fear of future danger from both sources." For Miller, the rise of Klan violence by men like Yarborough, combined with the corrupting influence of capitalists' wealth, endangered America's popular government. "If the recurrence of such acts as these prisoners stand convicted of are too common in one quarter of the country and give omen of danger from lawless violence," Miller expounded, "the free use of money in elections, arising from the vast growth of recent wealth in other quarters, presents equal cause for anxiety."[19]

In his private correspondence, Miller argued that the best hope for saving the democracy lay "in the breaking up of the solid South." He decried the fact that almost all southern whites now voted for the Democratic party and that southern blacks had been increasingly disenfranchised. He hoped decisions like *Yarborough* would convince white southerners to accept black voting rights as a permanent feature of political life in the South, and that white politicians, in turn, would begin to court black votes. Once Democratic politicians appealed to black voters, Miller believed, blacks would quickly be assimilated into the polity and differ little from any other interest group. The politics of race that defined the Democratic party and the South would fall away. "I believe it a great good fortune," he wrote in 1884, "if . . . the next period of general voting in the South would show that every negro voted and half of them voted for the candidates of the democratic party. This I think would presage the speedy dissolution of the democratic party, an event that I think would be the greatest blessing that could come to this country." As things stood in the 1880s, however, the nation was left "at the mercy of the combinations of those who respect no right but brute force, on the one hand, and unprincipled corruptionists on the other."[20]

Considered together, Miller's *Yarborough* opinion and his concurring votes in *Cruikshank* and the *Civil Rights Cases* reflect his belief that if the government protected African Americans' voting rights, black Americans would be able to protect their other civil rights using the ballot rather than the federal courts. Miller put his faith for achieving equality in the political (rather than the legal) process. In retrospect, however, it is clear that he relied too much on the national government's ability or continued willingness to protect black voters and his fellow justices' commitment to African American suffrage.

Miller's hope that federal power would continue to be used to protect blacks' voting rights eventually came to naught. Although the Justice Department continued to prosecute hundreds of voting rights cases in the 1880s, few resulted in convictions. In the 1890s those efforts dwindled, as northerners grew increasingly tired of the "southern question." Despite his forceful conclusions about the need to save the republic from northern corruption and southern violence, Miller's opinion in *Yarborough* was later disregarded. In 1903, thirteen years after his death, the Supreme Court in *James v. Bowman* simply ignored *Yarborough* and held that Congress had no constitutional authority to punish private individuals for violent crimes against black voters. Miller had hoped that with their voting rights protected, blacks might someday be embraced by the leaders of both parties; but by the end of the nineteenth century, few African Americans voted at all.[21]

In the 1880s, Miller also made small but fateful concessions to Justice Field's view of substantive due process—concessions which after Miller's death would also have unintended consequences. In the 1880s, the Supreme Court's docket was filled with cases brought by a new class of skilled, law-school-trained corporate attorneys, who urged the justices to adopt Field's position and the "scientific" doctrines of legal formalism. In the late 1870s, Miller had vigorously resisted those concepts. But after writing the majority opinion in *Davidson v. New Orleans* in 1878, he became uncharacteristically silent in cases involving the Fourteenth Amendment's due process clause.[22] Rather than continuing to fight, as he had in *Davidson*, the "strange misconception" corporate lawyers had about the meaning of due process, Miller instead joined the Court's majority in two opinions that incrementally chipped away at *Munn v. Illinois* and the portions of *Slaughter-House* that called for judicial deference to state legislatures.[23]

In 1887, Miller, without comment, joined the majority in *Mugler v. Kansas*. In that case, the Court rejected the arguments of Peter Mugler, a Kansas brewer, who argued that an 1880 state law prohibiting the sale or manufacture of alcohol denied him of his property without due process of law. The Court upheld the law as a proper use of the state's police powers—its authority to pass laws to protect public health, safety, and morals. But in his majority opinion, Justice Harlan asserted that the Court could, if necessary, strike down redistributive laws that state legislatures disguised as efforts to protect public health, safety, or morals. "The courts are not bound by mere forms, nor are they to be misled by mere pretences," Harlan declared. "They are at liberty—indeed, under a solemn duty—to look at the substance of things. If, therefore, a statute purporting to have been enacted to protect the public health, the public morals, or the public safety, has no real or substantial relation to those objects . . . it is the duty of the Courts to so adjudge and thereby give effect to the Constitution." In the past, Miller had argued that legislatures, not the judiciary, had the sole authority to decide what was or was not a proper use of the police power. Now he concurred in Harlan's opinion that claimed the Court's justices could scrutinize the intent and substance of legislation and strike down laws they believed were illegitimate.[24]

In 1890, Miller weighed in one last time on the issue of due process in *Chicago, Milwaukee and St. Paul Railway Company v. Minnesota*. This case, often referred to as the *Minnesota Milk Rate Case*, arose from an 1887 Minnesota law that gave the power to set railroad freight rates to a newly created state railroad and warehouse commission. The law stipulated that the commission's decisions were final and could not be appealed by the railroads to the courts. When, after a dispute with the commission, attorneys for the Chicago, Milwaukee, & St. Paul Railway tried to take their grievances to Minnesota's state courts, the Minnesota Supreme Court, citing state law, refused to hear the railroad's evidence that the commission had set unreasonable rates. Unlike in *Munn v. Illinois*, the plaintiffs in the Minnesota case did not claim that the state lacked authority to set rates; the railroad's attorneys fully admitted the "right of the legislature to take such proper action as may be necessary to secure to the people reasonable charges for transportation thereon." But, they added, this right did not give the state the power "to arbitrarily and finally fix" rates without giving the railroad the ability to appeal unreasonable rates. By denying their client a right of appeal, the lawyers argued, the state denied the railroad of its property without due process of law.[25]

Despite the railroad attorneys' admission that the state could set rates, their argument challenged the doctrine put forth by the Court in *Munn v. Illinois*. In Munn, the Court ruled that state legislatures had broad powers to regulate private property that served a public purpose. If they abused this power, the remedy was to be found at the polls and not the courts. If the Court sided with the railroad, it would undermine state legislatures' broad authority to regulate such property as they saw fit and would subject regulatory laws to judicial inspection.

In a 6-3 decision, the Court's majority in *Chicago, Milwaukee, & St. Paul Railway* eroded the *Munn* doctrine by holding that the question of reasonableness was a proper subject for judicial review. The majority concluded that if the railroad could not appeal the rates set by the commission, the commission could, at its discretion, set rates that deprived the railroad of any profit whatsoever. Doing so would unconstitutionally deny the railroad its property without due process.[26]

Clearly troubled by the case, Miller joined the majority but offered his own irresolute concurring opinion. "I concur," he wrote, "with some hesitation in the judgment of the Court." He reasserted his conviction that states had broad authority to regulate rates but expressed his discomfort with Minnesota's position that the commission's decision was final and unappealable. He feared such a position might allow railroad commissions to set rates "so unreasonable as to practically destroy the value of the property of persons engaging in the carrying business" or that the commissions might be taken over by corrupt railroad men who could set prices "so exorbitant and extravagant as to be in utter disregard of the rights of the public." In both instances, Miller believed the commissions' rates needed to be appealable. Once the "question of reasonableness becomes a judicial one," he recognized, plaintiffs had to have the right to offer evidence as to the unreasonableness of the rates. He therefore agreed with the majority that the case should be returned to the Minnesota courts and that the railroad's attorneys should be allowed to introduce their evidence, although he cautioned that courts should only overturn a railroad commission's rates in the most extreme circumstances.[27]

The combined effect of the *Minnesota Milk Rate Case* and *Mugler v. Kansas* moved the Court closer towards Field's substantive view of due process. No longer would due process only include procedural protections. Federal courts could look at the substance of regulatory legislation to determine its intent and reasonableness. These were significant concessions to conservatives who opposed government regulations. Miller might have thought he was carving out a moderate position whereby courts would only overturn state legislation in exceptional circumstances, but his concurrences in these cases helped open a Pandora's box. After his death, conservatives on the Court would combine substantive due process with the doctrine of "liberty of contract" in a successful effort to read their laissez-faire ideals into the Constitution. Eventually, these doctrines led to the Court's infamous decision in *Lochner v. New York*.

In that 1905 case, the justices struck down a New York law that set maximum work hours for bakers. Rejecting the state's argument that the law protected the bakers' health, the justices concluded that the statute interfered with the bakers' "liberty" to work sixteen-hour days if they so desired. Given Miller's position in *Slaughter-House*, in which he defended the public health benefits of Louisiana's slaughterhouse law despite the butchers' charges of monopoly and corruption, he almost certainly would have opposed the Court's decision in *Lochner* and subsequent cases in which the Court used the Fourteenth Amendment to strike down state regulations of private businesses. Had he lived to see "liberty of contract" entered into the judicial equation, he probably would have recognized the slippery slope towards laissez-faire jurisprudence down which he and the Court had traveled. By then it might well have been too late, and Miller might have found himself once again relegated to bitter dissents reminiscent of his opinions in the municipal bonds cases.[28]

At the end of his career Miller could look back on some key judicial victories, but on the issues that most mattered to him he had lost the war. Considered by his colleagues to be one of the most formidable intellects on the supreme bench, he ultimately failed to achieve the doctrinal results he desired. In the municipal bond cases, his most eloquent opinions were in dissent. *Slaughter-House,* his most important decision, led to outcomes he did not intend, much less sanction. Despite Miller's ringing language about racial equality under the law, southern whites managed to turn his opinion on its head, using it as a states'-rights precedent that allowed the subjugation of African Americans without federal interference. In the years following Miller's death, the Court sanctioned Jim Crow segregation and the disenfranchisement of black voters. The justices also became notorious for their laissez-faire principles and defense of corporate interests. On all these key issues, Miller's moderate positions were defeated.

Throughout his judicial career, Miller clung to the Republican ideology of the 1850s, an ideology that became impracticable as a result the nation's postwar economic transformations. Abraham Lincoln had embodied that ideology. As a railroad attorney, Lincoln understood the needs of the emerging corporate order. But his economic philosophy also focused on the right of common men, black and white, to rise. Because he did not live to see corporate capitalism in full flower, Lincoln never squarely faced the question of what should happen when some men rose so far, and became so rich and powerful, that they destroyed other men's own right to rise. In the end, Lincoln's two most influential appointments to the Court, Miller and Field, came to represent these two competing strands of the Republican ideology. In his most memorable opinions, Miller sought to defend the rights of common men—westerners burdened by rapacious bondholders and black voters disenfranchised by reactionary southerners. Despite his frequent rhetoric about liberty for all, Field became the champion of laissez-faire, railroad barons, and capitalists. In the 1890s, Field's version of Republicanism proved the more powerful of the two.[29]

Miller fought on until the end of his life, serving as the melancholy legal voice of a lost Republicanism. He remained on the bench despite the fact that in their later years both he and Eliza suffered from a series of physical ailments. Eliza contracted gout and rheumatism and traveled to France in search of treatment.[30] Samuel underwent surgery for kidney stones and endured other minor afflictions and accidents. Throughout his life, however, he retained his mental acuity and remained a fully functioning member of the Court. "The Chief Justice recognizes no claims of old age in me to abatement of service," he wrote in 1887, "for he has given me . . . a full share of opinions to write." Whenever he mentioned retiring, Eliza continued to oppose it. Miller resigned himself to an old age full of work, and indeed concluded that he and Eliza were happier than they "would be in the idleness of wealth."[31]

Miller continued to experience the joys and sorrows of family life. Eliza and his daughter Pattie never reconciled, and their continued bickering at family gatherings pained him, as did the departure of his daughter, Lida, the last of Miller's children to leave home. "Everything augurs well for her happiness," he wrote when Lida married in 1886. "I *must* be satisfied. But I will miss her so. She is the last of the birds of my own nest." Miller also fretted when his hard-drinking son-in-law George Corkhill died of a stomach hemorrhage, leaving his family with debts and doubts. But Samuel and Eliza watched with pleasure as their son Irvine graduated from Cornell and went to work for the best patent law firm in Chicago. Despite their continuing financial difficulties, the couple remained in love to the end. In February 1887, they threw a grand dinner party for "75 or 80 people, mainly intimate friends" to celebrate their thirty years of marriage.[32]

In his final years, Miller grew nostalgic about Barbourville and Keokuk. When he encountered his old friends from those towns, he liked to point out just how successful many of their old acquaintances had become. At one social event, he ran into his old friend Silas Woodson. The two men recalled the Barbourville Debating Society and spoke with reverence about how much the members of that little group, from a largely forgotten town, had achieved. They noted that from the debating society's membership came two judges, a congressman, a Kentucky state legislator, a governor, and a Supreme Court justice. "Under all the circumstances of its locale," Miller observed, "and the limited opportunities for acquiring information and the little assistance any of us have received from personal fortunes or . . . aid from others, I think the result is remarkable." While he had grown increasingly pessimistic about his country's future, Miller remembered the social and economic fluidity of an earlier smaller-scale America with awe.[33]

On October 10, 1890, while walking home from court to his house on Massachusetts Avenue, Miller suffered a stroke that paralyzed his left side. During the next three days physicians treated him at his home as he slipped in and out of consciousness. At times he retained his mental faculties, and the *New York*

Times reported that when doctors advised him not to speak so as not to strain his brain, Miller joked that that was a "compliment for you must think that when I talk I use my brains." But his condition then worsened. He slipped into a coma and died on October 13 at eleven o'clock at night.[34]

The Court held a funeral service for Miller three days later in the Supreme Court room. A wreath of autumnal oak leaves adorned his casket, and a black cloth covered the chair where he had sat, to the right of the Chief Justice Fuller. After the service, Fuller and other mourners boarded a train that carried Miller's body back to Keokuk, where a second service was held at the Unitarian Church that he had helped found.[35]

Though no longer in debt, Miller died poor, with no income to support his wife. His cash assets consisted of the sale of his law books and the balance due on his salary. After his death, an appeal appeared in the *American Law Review* seeking donations for Eliza. Members of the House of Representatives sponsored a bill to pay her one year's salary, but it never emerged from committee. She died in 1900 of heart disease, having outlived her husband by ten years.[36]

On the occasion of Justice Miller's death, the editor of the *Keokuk Gate City* looked back on that city's early years and noted with admiration the great pool of legal talent in antebellum Keokuk. Pointing to Miller, Belknap, Love, and Rankin, the editor tried to explain to his readers why so many eminent lawyers had chosen to settle in Keokuk in the 1850s and 1860s. Thirty years later, Keokuk remained a small, little-known Mississippi River town with fewer than fifteen thousand residents. Why did those lawyers choose such a place? "Just as a great company of strong young men go to any prosperous young territory not for what it is but because of what they hope it and they may become," the editor wrote, "so Keokuk drew to itself the youth and strength of young lawyers who came not to the population that was but to the hundreds of thousands that were expected." After the Panic of 1857, those dreams faded as the expected multitudes failed to arrive.[37]

Today, Keokuk remains a small town. Lined with buildings built in the 1850s, the main street is a poignant place, seemingly frozen in time. Modernity intrudes through the metal smokestacks of a French-owned cornstarch factory that sits beside the river on the site of a former slaughterhouse. Samuel and Eliza are buried in Keokuk's Oakland Cemetery, near the graves of the town's Civil War dead. When one looks up from their gravesite on a winter's day, great plumes of smoke from the cornstarch factory fill the sky. Like Miller, outside capital finally returned to Keokuk, but it was, in the end, too little and too late.

NOTES

Preface

1. William L. Barney, *Passage of the Republic: An Interdisciplinary History of Nineteenth-Century America* (New York, 1987), 293–305; Donald L. Miller, *City of the Century: The Epic of Chicago and the Making of America* (New York, 1996), 55, 305–8; William Cronon, *Nature's Metropolis: Chicago and the Great West* (New York, 1991), 23–54; George Rogers Taylor, ed., *The Turner Thesis Concerning the Role of the Frontier in American History*, 3d ed. (Lexington, Mass., 1972), 3; *World Almanac 1892* (New York, 1892), 274; James M. McPherson, *Battle Cry of Freedom: The Civil War Era* (New York, 1988), 854.

2. Samuel Freeman Miller to William Pitt Ballinger (hereafter W.P.B.), April 28, 1878 ("keen-sighted"), box 2, folder 3, Samuel Freeman Miller Papers, Library of Congress (hereafter SFMP, LC). See also Michael A. Ross, "Cases of Shattered Dreams: Justice Samuel Freeman Miller and the Rise and Fall of a Mississippi River Town," *Annals of Iowa* 57 (summer 1998): 201–39.

3. Darien A. McWhirter, *The Legal 100: A Ranking of the Individuals Who Have Most Influenced the Law* (Secaucus, N.J., 1998), 306. See also Henry Abraham, *Justices, Presidents, and Senators: A History of the U.S. Supreme Court Appointments from Washington to Clinton* (New York, 1999), 370; William D. Pederson and Norman W. Provizer, *Great Justices of the Supreme Court: Ratings and Case Studies* (New York, 1993), 24–7.

4. William Gillette, "Samuel Miller," in *The Justices of the United States Supreme Court, 1789–1969: Their Lives and Major Opinions*, ed. Leon Friedman and Fred Israel (New York, 1969), 1014.

5. Miller to W.P.B., March 21, 1874, box 1, folder 10, and December 5, 1875 ("sow's ear"), box 1, folder 11, both in SFMP, LC; Ballinger diary, November 10, 1865 ("He acts from principle"), Ballinger Family Papers, Center for American History, University of Texas at Austin; Charles Fairman, *Mr. Justice Miller and the Supreme Court, 1862–1890* (Cambridge, Mass., 1939), 320, 424 (Field quote); Charles Noble Gregory, *Samuel Freeman Miller* (Iowa City, 1907), 55 (Chase quote).

6. Fairman, *Mr. Justice Miller*, 299.

7. For a discussion of this literature, see chapter 8.

8. For a discussion of this literature, see chapter 8.

9. Eric Foner, *Free Soil, Free Labor, Free Men: The Ideology of the Republican Party before the Civil*

War (New York, 1970), 13, 33, 316; Gabor Boritt, *Lincoln and the Economics of the American Dream* (Memphis, 1978).

10. Foner, *Free Soil, Free Labor, Free Men*, 13, 16, 17, 21, 33, 40–73, 261–301, 316.

11. For the best discussions of the booster ethos in the trans-Mississippi West, see Timothy Mahoney, *River Towns of the Great West: The Structure of Provincial Urbanization in the American Midwest, 1820–1870* (New York, 1990); Carl Abbott, *Boosters and Businessmen: Popular Economic Thought and Urban Growth in the Antebellum Middle West* (Westport, Conn., 1981), 126, 129, 207; Cronon, *Nature's Metropolis*, 9, 35, 47; Jeffrey S. Adler, *Yankee Merchants and the Making of the Urban West: The Rise and Fall of Antebellum St. Louis* (New York, 1991), 43.

12. David Montgomery has shown how and why Radical Republicans split from labor reformers after the war. But Montgomery's tale is largely an urban one, of major cities where factory owners did battle with wage earners. David Montgomery, *Beyond Equality: Labor and the Radical Republicans, 1862–1872* (New York, 1967).

13. See, for example, David M. Silver, *Lincoln's Supreme Court* (Urbana, Ill., 1956), 57; Laurence Tribe, *God Save This Honorable Court* (New York, 1985), 59–61; Henry J. Abraham, *Justices and Presidents: A Political History of Appointments to the Supreme Court*, 2d ed. (New York, 1985), 115–24.

Chapter 1 "The Athens of the Kentucky Highlands"

1. John Mack Faragher, *Sugar Creek: Life on the Illinois Prairie* (New Haven, Conn., 1986), 99.

2. Tom W. Campbell, *Four Score Forgotten Men: Sketches of the Justices of the United States Supreme Court* (Little Rock, 1950), 212; Eric Hobsbawn, *The Age of Capital, 1848–1875* (1975; reprint, New York, 1996), 197. Descriptions of hardships in Miller's early life are also found in an unpublished biography (author unknown) of him found in the files of the Knickerbocker Publishing Company (1906), State Historical Society of Iowa (hereafter SHSI), Iowa City. Details are also found in *Keokuk Gate City* (hereafter *KGC*), October 14, 1890; T. C. Crawford, interview with Miller, *New York World*, December 11, 1886.

3. Charles Fairman, *Mr. Justice Miller and the Supreme Court, 1862–1890* (Cambridge, Mass., 1939), 5 ("it was fortunate"); Miller to W.P.B., October 24, 1872 ("Owing to my father's habits"), box 1, folder 9, SFMP, LC; James A. Soring, "Judicial Opinions of Mr. Justice Miller" (M.A. thesis, University of Iowa, 1954), 2.

4. John C. Greene, *American Science in the Age of Jefferson* (Ames, Iowa, 1984), 120–3; Robert Peter, *The History of the Medical Department of Transylvania University* (Louisville, Ky., 1905), 159–61.

5. Ibid.

6. Charles Rosenberg, *The Cholera Years* (Chicago, 1962), 4–16; Samuel Freeman Miller, "An Inaugural Dissertation on Cholera Infantum Submitted to the Examination of the Trustees and Medical Professors of Transylvania University for the Degree of Doctor of Medicine" (1838), Transylvania University Archives, Lexington, Ky.

7. Nancy D. Baird, "Asiatic Cholera's First Visit to Kentucky," *Filson Club History Quarterly* 48 (1974): 228–40; John Esten Cooke, "Remarks on Cholera, as It Appeared in Lexington in June 1833," *Transylvania Journal of Medicine and the Associate Sciences* 6 (July 1833): 17; Rosenberg, *Cholera Years*, 4–16.

8. Peter, *History of the Medical Department of Transylvania University,* 67–76; Frederick Eberson, "A Great Purging—Cholera or Calomel?" *Filson Club Historical Quarterly* 50 (April 1976): 32; Hardin Weathorford, *A Treatise on Cholera, Symptoms, Mode of Prevention, and Cure on a New and Successful Plane* (Louisville, Ky., 1833).

9. Miller, "Inaugural Dissertation," 16, 21.

10. Rosenberg, *Cholera Years,* 1–5; Weathorford, *A Treatise on Cholera,* 8.

11. Lunsford P. Yandell, *A Lecture on the Duties of Physicians Delivered before the Medical Class of Transylvania University,* February 4, 1837, Yandell Family Papers, record group 188, Rare Books and Manuscripts, Kornhauser Health Sciences Library, University of Louisville, Louisville, Ky., 20.

12. Ibid.

13. Crawford, interview with Miller, *New York World,* December 11, 1886.

14. In 1850, Barbourville still only had 184 residents and 21 dwelling houses. *1850 Knox County Census* (Louisville, Ky., 1850), Filson Club Historical Society (hereafter FCHS).

15. "Samuel Freeman Miller," *The Green Bag* 9 (1897): 310; K. S. Sol Warren, *A History of Knox County* (Barbourville, Ky., 1976), 2.

16. Robert L. Kincaid, *The Wilderness Road* (Harrogate, Tenn., 1955), 210. See also Harriet Simpson Arnow, *Flowering of the Cumberland* (New York, 1963), 373; James McCague, *The Cumberland* (New York, 1973), 191.

17. Samuel Freeman Miller, autobiographical sketch, June 7, 1882, microfilm, reel 2, book 5, p. 11, Caleb Forbes Davis Collection (hereafter CFDC), SHSI, Iowa City.

18. Elmer Decker, "History of Knox County and Eastern Kentucky," 34, 95, FCHS; John Anthony Moretta, *William Pitt Ballinger: Texas Lawyer, Southern Statesman, 1825–1888* (Austin, 2000), 15; Fairman, *Mr. Justice Miller,* 16.

19. Decker, "History of Knox County," 185–6; Irving Richman, *Ioway to Iowa: The Genesis of a Corn and Bible Commonwealth* (Iowa City, 1931), 353.

20. *1850 Knox County Census.* See also Sherman Oxendine, "Foreword," in Michael C. Mills, *Barbourville, Kentucky* (Barbourville, Ky., 1977), 6.

21. Decker, "History of Knox County," 185–6.

22. William Lynwood Montell, *Upper Cumberland Country* (Jackson, Miss., 1993), 7–8; McCague, *The Cumberland,* 189–93.

23. Oxendine, "Foreword," in Mills, *Barbourville, Kentucky,* 6; Kincaid, *Wilderness Road,* 215–6; Decker, "History of Knox County," 104, 106, 108.

24. Decker, "History of Knox County," 101, 178. See also Timothy Mahoney, *River Towns in the Great West: The Structure of Provincial Urbanization in the American Midwest, 1820–1870* (New York, 1990), 38; Oxendine, "Foreword," in Mills, *Barbourville, Kentucky,* 6; Lewis Collins, *History of Kentucky,* 2 vols. (1874; reprint, Frankfort, Ky., 1966) 2:455–6; McCague, *The Cumberland,* 190–1.

25. Decker, "History of Knox County," 109.

26. An edited version of these minutes was published by Charles Fairman in the *Mississippi Valley Historical Review* 17 (June 1930–March 1931), 595–601.

27. Miller argued in the negative to the following questions: "Has wealth more influence than talent?" and "Will wealth enable a man to pass through the world with greater honor to himself than education?" Ibid., 597–601.

28. Ibid., 598. Another question included "Apart from Revelation and Human Tradition have we any evidence of the existence of Deity?" Miller, a freethinker on religious issues who later became

president of the National Unitarian Conference, voted no. Later, during his judicial career, he again argued against capital punishment. See, for example, *United States v. Gleason,* 1 Woolworth 128 (1867).

29. William W. Freehling, *The Road to Disunion: Secessionists at Bay, 1776–1854* (New York, 1990), 308–36.

30. Fairman, "Minutes of the Barbourville Debating Society," 595–601.

31. *Lexington Herald,* August 3, 1913; Fairman, *Mr. Justice Miller,* 15.

32. Crawford, interview with Miller, *New York World,* December 11, 1886.

33. Richard D. Sears, *The Day of Small Things: Abolitionism in the Midst of Slavery* (New York, 1986), 30–1; William Henry Townsend, *The Lion of White Hall* (Dunwoody, Ga., 1967); Roberta Baughman Carl'ee, *The Last Gladiator: Cassius M. Clay* (Berea, Ky., 1979); H. Edward Richardson, *Cassius Marcellus Clay: Firebrand of Freedom* (Lexington, Ky., 1976); Horace Greeley, ed., *The Writings of Cassius Marcellus Clay (Including Speeches and Addresses)* (New York, 1848); Jeffrey Brooke Allen, "The Debate over Slavery and Race in Antebellum Kentucky: 1792–1850" (Ph.D. dissertation, Northwestern University, 1973); Mac Swinford, "Mr. Justice Samuel Freeman Miller," *Filson Club History Quarterly* 34 (1960): 37.

34. David L. Smiley, *Lion of White Hall: The Life of Cassius M. Clay* (Madison, Wis., 1962), 22, 26, 29–30.

35. Ibid., 29–30.

36. Ibid., 46–50. Clay's views on the detrimental effects of slavery on free laborers and the economy were shared by free-soilers in other sections of the country. See Eric Foner, *Free Labor, Free Soil, Free Men: The Ideology of the Republican Party before the Civil War* (New York, 1970).

37. Smiley, *Lion of White Hall,* 46, 47, 53.

38. Ibid., 83, 108.

39. By 1850, slaves equaled the number of whites in several tobacco counties in the bluegrass region. In the mountains along the eastern border, however, slaves were only 2 or 3 percent of the population. Asa Earl Martin, *The Anti-Slavery Movement in Kentucky prior to 1850* (Louisville, Ky., 1918), 7.

40. Smiley, *Lion of White Hall,* 56–7 (quotes); Sears, *Day of Small Things,* 28.

41. Decker, "History of Knox County," 167.

42. Miller to W.P.B., March 19, 1854 ("An abolitionist has been"), box 1, folder 1, SFMP, LC; Fairman, *Mr. Justice Miller,* 17 ("nearly all the blood relations"); Campbell, *Four Score Forgotten Men,* 213. See also Richard L. Aynes, "Constricting the Law of Freedom: Justice Miller, the Fourteenth Amendment, and the *Slaughter-House Cases,*" *Chicago-Kent Law Review* 70 (1994): 627, 658.

43. Miller, *Inaugural Dissertation,* 9, 15.

44. Ibid., 14–6; Rosenberg, *Cholera Years,* 42, 59. See also Charles Rosenberg, "The Cause of Cholera: Aspects of Etiological Thought in Nineteenth-Century America," in *Sickness and Health in America,* ed. Judith W. Leavitt and Ronald L. Numbers (Madison, Wis., 1978), 257–72.

45. Miller, *Inaugural Dissertation,* 16; Weathorford, *Treatise On Cholera,* 11; Rosenberg, *Cholera Years,* 3.

46. Quote taken from Tom W. Campbell, *Four Score Forgotten Men,* 212.

47. Rosenberg, *Cholera Years,* 65.

48. Miller to Charles Lanman, April 16, 1869 ("After some three or four years"), Manuscript Department, FCHS; Truman S. Stevens, "Miller and Henderson," *Iowa Magazine,* 18 October 1923, p. 671, SHSI, Des Moines.

49. Quotes taken from Miller's letter to Lanman, April 16, 1869. The fact that his friends cautioned him against changing careers was recalled by Miller in an interview with T. C. Crawford of the *New York World,* December 11, 1886.

50. Decker, "History of Knox County," 63; Miller, autobiographical sketch, 11.

51. Mahoney, *River Towns,* 51, 52, 84; Michael A. Ross, "Cases of Shattered Dreams: Justice Samuel Freeman Miller and the Rise and Fall of a Mississippi River Town," *Annals of Iowa* 57 (summer 1998): 201–39; Robert P. Swierenga, *Pioneers and Profits: Land Speculation on the Iowa Frontier* (Ames, Iowa, 1968), 21; Allan Bogue, *From Prairie to Corn Belt: Farming on the Illinois and Iowa Prairies in the Nineteenth Century* (Chicago, 1963); Faye Erma Harris, "'A Frontier Community': The Economic, Social, and Political Development of Keokuk, Iowa, from 1820 to 1866" (Ph.D. dissertation, University of Iowa, 1965), 85, 185.

52. Mahoney, *River Towns,* 145–8; Ross, "Cases of Shattered Dreams," 204–5; *History of Lee County, Iowa* (Chicago, 1879), 624–5.

53. Harris, "A Frontier Community," 94; Richman, *Ioway to Iowa,* 275.

54. *History of Lee County;* Harris, "A Frontier Community," 98; Ross, "Cases of Shattered Dreams," 205; William Worth Belknap to Clara Belknap, May 3, 1853, William Worth Belknap Papers, Special Collections and Manuscripts, Princeton University Library, Princeton, N.J.

55. *Keokuk Register,* September 2, 1847, September 6, 1849.

56. Michael A. Ross, "Hill-Country Doctor: The Early Life and Career of Supreme Court Justice Samuel F. Miller in Kentucky, 1816–1849," *Filson Club History Quarterly* 71 (1997): 457.

57. Miller to Lanman, April 16, 1869; biography of Miller (author unknown) from the files of the Knickerbocker Publishing Company (1906), SHSI, Iowa City; Smiley, *Lion of White Hall,* 132.

58. Fairman, *Mr. Justice Miller,* 16 ("stand openly in favor"); Miller to Lanman, April 16, 1869 ("When the proposition").

59. Sears, *Day of Small Things,* 33.

60. *Louisville Examiner,* August 11, 1849, quoted in Fairman, *Mr. Justice Miller,* 17; Martin, *Anti-Slavery Movement in Kentucky,* 134; Sears, *Day of Small Things,* 31, 33.

61. Miller to Lanman, April 16, 1869; Mills, *Barbourville, Kentucky,* 6; Constitution of Kentucky, 1850, Art. 10, Secs. 1, 2, 3, quoted in Martin, *Anti-Slavery Movement in Kentucky,* 134–5.

62. Miller to Lanman, April 16, 1869 ("The new constitution"); Miller, autobiograpical sketch, 15 ("would never be"); Ross, "Hill-Country Doctor," 459–60.

63. Kincaid, *Wilderness Road,* 211–2.

64. Decker, "History of Knox County," 169, 109, 206; *KGC,* July 16, 1856.

65. Miller, autobiographical sketch, 15.

Chapter 2 Keokuk Rising

1. Samuel Freeman Miller, autobiographical sketch, microfilm, reel 2, book 5, p. 11, CFDC, SHSI, Iowa City. Reeves's reputation as a gambler is described in a letter by James L. Estes to Charles Mason, December 15, 1853, Charles Mason Papers, SHSI, Des Moines.

2. A good description of the history of the Half-Breed Tract can be found in *Coy v. Mason,* the Supreme Court decision that attempted permanently to settle this difficult issue. *Coy v. Mason,* 58

U.S. 580 (1855). An example of a Half-Breed Tract–related mob action is described in James L. Estes to Charles Mason, September 6, 1853, Charles Mason Papers, SHSI, Des Moines.

3. Quote is from the *Christian Times*, July 22, 1862, reprinted in *KGC*, August 12, 1862; Douglas Atterberg, *Samuel Freeman Miller: A Home in Keokuk, A Place in History* (Keokuk, 1990), 10. The *Iowa Reports* contain a number of examples of Half-Breed Tract litigation in which the firm of Reeves & Miller was involved. See: *Rowan v. Lamb*, 4 Iowa 468 (1854); *Marshall v. McLean*, 3 Iowa 363 (1852); *Tiffany v. Glover*, 3 Iowa 387 (1852); *Walker v. Stannis*, 3 Iowa 440 (1852); *Wright v. Meek*, 3 Iowa 472 (1852).

4. Henry Strong, "Samuel Miller," *Annals of Iowa* 3 (1894): 255.

5. Samuel Miller, "Address of Mr. Justice Miller," *Albany Law Journal* 20 (1879): 25–9.

6. Charles Fairman, "Keokuk Debating Society," *Mississippi Valley Historical Review* 17 (June 1930–March 1931): 595–601; Conrad Wright, ed., *A Stream of Light: A Short History of American Unitarianism* (Boston, 1975), 23.

7. Wright, ed., *Stream of Light*, 38 ("probably the most convinced"); Charles Noble Gregory, *Samuel Freeman Miller* (Iowa City, 1907), 59.

8. Miller, autobiographical sketch, 11–2; Charles Fairman, *Mr. Justice Miller and the Supreme Court, 1862–1890* (Cambridge, Mass., 1939), 19; Gregory, *Samuel Freeman Miller*, 62, 63.

9. In terms of the number of cases argued by Keokuk attorneys before the Iowa Supreme Court, Miller's closest competitor was the firm of Edwards & Turner, which handled seven cases. The fifteen cases Miller argued before the Iowa Supreme Court in 1855 were: *Claggett v. Gray*, 1 Iowa 19 (1855); *Hinds v. Hinds*, 1 Iowa 36 (1855); *Farner v. Turner*, 1 Iowa 53 (1855); *Cox v. Burns & Rentgen*, 1 I.R. 64 (1855); *Houston v. Walcott & Co.*, 1 Iowa 86 (1855); *Stowers v. Milledge*, 1 Iowa 150 (1855); *Hyde v. Woolfolk and Bacon*, 1 Iowa 159 (1855); *Young v. Wolcott*, 1 Iowa 174 (1855); *Mathews v. Gilliss*, 1 Iowa 242 (1855); *Harkins v. Edwards & Turner*, 1 Iowa 296 (1855); *Pipe v. Bateman*, 1 Iowa 369 (1855); *Oswald & Company v. Broderick & Co.*, 1 Iowa 380 (1855); *Death v. Bank of Pittsburgh*, 1 Iowa 382 (1855); *Wickersham v. Reeves & Miller*, 1 Iowa 413 (1855); *Harkins v. Edwards & Turner*, 1 Iowa 426 (1855).

10. William Pitt Ballinger diary, April 18, 1857, Ballinger Papers, Center for American History, University of Texas at Austin ("rather handsome"); Randolph Keim, *Society in Washington: Its Noted Men, Accomplished Women, Established Customs, and Notable Events* (Washington, D.C., 1887), 122–4 ("resemblance").

11. Ballinger diary, April 9, 1857.

12. Ibid., April 18, 1857.

13. Ibid., July 10, 11, and 17, 1860.

14. Miller to W.P.B., December 28, 1866, box 1, folder 3, SFMP, LC; Ballinger diary, August 25, 1865 ("Miller is entirely").

15. Reporter from the Davenport Gazette, quoted in the *Keokuk Register*, July 20, 1848; *History of Lee County, Iowa* (Chicago, 1879), 624; *Keokuk Daily Post*, December 16, 1855; R. M. Reynolds to C. Throop, May 27, 1856, SHSI, Iowa City.

16. *KGC*, March 11, 1856; William Rees, *Description of the City of Keokuk* (Keokuk, 1855), 20, 22.

17. William Worth Belknap to Clara Belknap, March 17, 1853, Belknap Papers, Princeton University; *Keokuk Dispatch*, November 8, 1854.

18. Orion Clemens, *City of Keokuk in 1856: A View of the City . . .* (Keokuk, 1856), 19; Rees, *Description of the City of Keokuk*, 2 (quote).

19. Interregional partnerships between frontier wholesalers and New York merchants were crucial to the growth of emerging western cities. See William Cronon, *Nature's Metropolis: Chicago and the Great West* (New York, 1991), 62; Lewis Atherton, *The Frontier Merchant in Mid-America* (Columbia, Mo., 1971); James E. Vance Jr., *The Merchant's World: The Geography of Wholesaling* (Englewood Cliffs, N.J., 1970). For the growth of Keokuk's wholesale trade and its position in the larger regional context, see: Timothy Mahoney, *River Towns of the Great West: The Structure of Provincial Urbanization in the American Midwest, 1820–1870* (New York, 1990), 211–3, 272; "Inaugural Address of Mayor Curtis," May 9, 1856, reprinted in Clemens, *City of Keokuk,* 4; *KGC,* May 4, 1861.

20. Samuel Clemens lived in Keokuk during the boom years of 1854–56. Andrew Hoffman, *Inventing Mark Twain: The Lives of Samuel Langhorne Clemens* (New York, 1997), 42–5; Fairman, *Mr. Justice Miller,* 21–2.

21. Clemens, *City of Keokuk in 1856,* 8; *History of Lee County, Iowa,* 623.

22. Douglas Atterberg of the Lee County Historical Society has searched the land records of Lee County and prepared a comprehensive map of Miller's property holdings. The map is in the society's collection. For a summary, see Atterberg, *Samuel Freeman Miller,* 26, 27.

23. *Coy v. Mason,* 58 U.S. 580 (1855); Rees, *Description of the City of Keokuk,* 22; M. L. Townsend, "Liberal Religion in Iowa," unpublished manuscript (1930), SHSI, Iowa City.

24. Morton Rosenberg, *Iowa on the Eve of the Civil War: A Decade of Frontier Politics* (Norman, Okla., 1972), 81, 232, 233.

25. Atchison quote reprinted in James McPherson, *Battle Cry of Freedom: The Civil War Era* (New York, 1988), 122. See also William E. Parrish, *David Rice Atchison of Missouri: Border Politician* (Columbia, Mo., 1961), 121–32.

26. McPherson, *Battle Cry of Freedom,* 58, 122 ("hell of a storm"), 123.

27. David M. Potter, *The Impending Crisis, 1848–1861* (New York, 1976), 145–76; McPherson, *Battle Cry of Freedom,* 123, 125.

28. Miller to W.P.B., March 19, 1854, box 1, folder 1, SFMP, LC.

29. Ibid.

30. Robert W. Johannsen, *Stephen A. Douglas* (New York, 1973); Robert Johanssen, *The Frontier, the Union, and Stephen A. Douglas* (Urbana, Ill., 1989); Harry V. Jaffa, *Crisis of the House Divided: An Interpretation of the Lincoln-Douglas Debates* (Garden City, N.Y., 1959), 104–80; *KGC,* June 17, 1856.

31. Atchison quote in James A. Rawley, *Race and Politics: "Bleeding Kansas" and the Coming of the Civil War* (Philadelphia, 1969), 21–57; Seward quote in McPherson, *Battle Cry of Freedom,* 145; Parrish, *David Rice Atchison,* 164.

32. Rawley, *Race and Politics,* 88; Atchison quote in McPherson, *Battle Cry of Freedom,* 145–7.

33. *Keokuk Dispatch,* July 26, 1854: *KGC,* May 12, 1855.

34. *KGC,* May 26, 1856 ("Kansas War Commenced!"), May 28, 1856 ("blood boil," "Lawrence destroyed!").

35. McPherson, *Battle Cry of Freedom,* 149, 150; David Donald, *Charles Sumner and the Coming of the Civil War* (New York, 1960), 285 ("hirelings" and "harlot" quotes), 289–97 ("libel on South Carolina").

36. *KGC,* May 31, 1856. In addition to the sensational national events, Iowa's Republican Party benefited from a new wave of immigration into the state from the Middle Atlantic states, New England, and Ohio. Robert Cook, *Baptism of Fire: The Republican Party in Iowa* (Ames, Iowa, 1994), 50; Rosenberg, *Iowa on the Eve of the Civil War,* 234.

37. Cook, *Baptism of Fire*, 17; *KGC*, May 31, 1856 ("national and patriotic"), June 17, 1856.

38. *KGC*, July 17, 1856.

39. Ibid.

40. Ibid.

41. Ibid.

42. Rosenberg, *Iowa on the Eve of the Civil War*, 166; Fairman, *Mr. Justice Miller*, 32.

43. Each town hoped, at the very least, to secure the role of secondary entrepôt north of St. Louis. Mahoney, *River Towns*, 273; Burlington Hawkeye, July 28, 1857, reprinted in *KGC*. For a useful discussion of the rivalry between Keokuk and Burlington, see George A. Boeck, "A Decade of Transportation Fever in Burlington, Iowa, 1845–1855," *Iowa Journal of History* 56 (April 1958) 2: 130–1.

44. Mahoney, *River Towns*, 191.

45. Cronon, *Nature's Metropolis*, 74; *KGC*, January 6, 1860, March 12, 1860. "If we receive one weekly while the river is closed," William Belknap said of Keokuk's winter mail deliveries in 1852, "we consider ourselves doing very well indeed." William W. Belknap to Clara Belknap, January 18, 1852, Special Collections and Manuscripts, Princeton University.

46. *KGC*, February 19, 1858 ("a very considerable"); "Inaugural Address of Mayor Curtis," May 9, 1856, reprinted in Clemens, *City of Keokuk in 1856*, 12.

47. *Des Moines Valley (Keokuk) Whig*, January 29, 1852 (quote), June 24, 1852; Fairman, *Mr. Justice Miller*, 26.

48. "Inaugural Address of Mayor Taylor," reprinted in O. Clemens, *Keokuk Directory and Business Mirror for the Year 1857* (Keokuk, 1857), 145–6.

49. Charles Fairman, *Reconstruction and Reunion, 1864–88*, part 1, in *Oliver Wendell Holmes Devise History of the Supreme Court of the United States* (New York, 1971), 934.

50. Dissenting opinion of Judge John Kinney in *Dubuque County v. Dubuque and Pacific Railroad*, 4 Greene 1 (1853).

51. *Dubuque County v. Dubuque and Pacific Railroad*, 4 Greene 1 (1853). See also: James W. Ely Jr., *Railroads and American Law* (Lawrence, Kans., 2001), 19–26; Michael A. Ross, "Cases of Shattered Dreams: Justice Samuel Freeman Miller and the Rise and Fall of a Mississippi River Town," *Annals of Iowa* 57 (1998): 201–39.

52. *Inaugural Address of D. W. Kilbourne, Esq.* (Keokuk, 1955); Ross, "Cases of Shattered Dreams," 215.

53. *KGC*, June 11, 1862 (description of Miller on board).

54. Richard C. Overton, *Burlington West: A Colonization History of the Burlington Railroad* (Cambridge, Mass., 1941), 164–85; Arthur M . Johnson and Barry E. Supple, *Boston Capitalists and Western Railroads: A Study in the Nineteenth-Century Railroad Investment Process* (Cambridge, Mass., 1967), 156–80, 223, 224; *KGC*, September 5, 1859, January 13, 1860.

55. *St. Louis Democrat*, May 22, 1860.

56. Jeffrey Adler, *Yankee Merchants and the Making of the Urban West: The Rise and Fall of Antebellum St. Louis* (New York, 1991), 3, 11, 123–36, 139, 141, 144, 155; Wyatt Belcher, *The Economic Rivalry between Chicago and St.Louis* (New York, 1947), 15; Carl Abbott, *Boosters and Businessmen: Popular Economic Thought and Urban Growth in the Antebellum Middle West* (Westport, Conn., 1981), 97, 98; Cronon, *Nature's Metropolis*, 60, 62.

57. "Inaugural Address of Mayor Curtis," in Clemens, *Keokuk Directory and Business Mirror for the Year 1857*, 12; *KGC*, January 13, 1860.

58. Mahoney, *River Towns,* 241. Not until much later did commentators in Keokuk finally come to grips with this grim reality. "Railroads are great equalizers," observed the *Gate City* in 1863, "by which we mean to say that much of the trade which in former years found its way to the banks of the Mississippi is now concentrated at the more important places on the railroad in the interior." *KGC,* May 26, 1863.

59. The *Chicago Democratic Press,* quoted in Marquis W. Childs, *Mighty Mississippi: Biography of a River* (New Haven, Conn., 1982), 95, 96.

60. Benedict K. Zobrist, "Steamboat Men versus Railroad Men: The First Bridging of the Mississippi River," *Missouri Historical Review* 59 (1965): 159–72; John C. Parish, "The First Mississippi Bridge," *Palimpsest* 3 (1922): 145; Childs, *Mighty Mississippi,* 99, 102.

61. Childs, *Mighty Mississippi,* 98.

62. Ibid., 100.

63. Zobrist, "Steamboat Men versus Railroad Men," 166–8; Parish, "The First Mississippi Bridge," 137; "Lincoln and the Bridge Case," *Palimpsest* 3 (1922): 142–54 (quotes); Childs, *Mighty Mississippi,* 100.

64. The best discussion of the relative importance of steamboats and railroads to the nineteenth-century economy can be found in George Rogers Taylor, *The Transportation Revolution, 1815–1860* (New York, 1951). The best description of the case Miller made for steamboats can be found in the decision of the United States Supreme Court on this issue: *The Mississippi & Missouri Railroad Company v. Ward,* 67 U.S. (2 Black) 485 (1862).

65. *Mississippi & Missouri Railroad Company v. Ward,* 67 U.S. 485, 486 (1862); *KGC,* March 22, 1860, February 6, 1863; Parish, "The First Mississippi Bridge," 139.

66. *Mississippi & Missouri Railroad Company v. Ward,* 67 U.S., at 496 (1862); *KGC,* March 22, 1860, February 6, 1863.

Chapter 3 The Panic of 1857

1. George W. Van Vleck, *The Panic of 1857* (New York, 1943), 53–8; Albert Fishlow, *American Railroads and the Transformation of the American Economy* (Cambridge, Mass., 1965), 114–5; James L. Huston, *The Panic of 1857 and the Coming of the Civil War* (Baton Rouge, La., 1987), 5, 13–4, 22, 29, 32, 34; Timothy Mahoney, *River Towns of the Great West: The Structure of Provincial Urbanization in the American Midwest, 1820–1870* (New York, 1990), 203; Carl Abbott, *Boosters and Businessmen: Popular Economic Thought and Urban Growth in the Antebellum Middle West* (Westport, Conn., 1981), 17. For an intriguing hypothesis that events in Bleeding Kansas helped cause the panic, see Charles Calomiris and Larry Schweikart, "The Panic of 1857: Origins, Transmission, and Containment," *Journal of Economic History* 51 (1991): 807–34. For representative reactions in Keokuk to the onset of the crisis, see *KGC,* May 30, June 10, September 3, October 9 and 17, 1857.

2. *KGC,* October 27, 1857 ("To raise money"); Mahoney, *River Towns,* 235; Huston, *Panic of 1857,* 18. For the extent of crisis in Keokuk, see *KGC,* October 6, 1857 ("We think we have"), November 14, 1857, October 30, 1857, March 4, 1858; R. M. Reynolds to C. Throop, September 9, 1857, R. M. Reynolds Collection, SHSI, Iowa City.

3. *KGC,* February 9, December 20, 1859.

4. On February 15, 1859, for example, Rankin, Miller, and their new partner, Enster, ran twenty-

seven legal notices in the *Keokuk Gate City*. Rankin's reputation as a first-rate collections attorney is described in his profile in the Caleb Forbes Davis Collection, microfilm, reel 2, book 5, p. 259, SHSI, Iowa City. "Hard, selfish times" quote taken from *KGC*, November 17, 1857. For an example of Miller's role as trustee, see *KGC*, July 20, 1860.

5. Samuel Miller, letter to the editor, ibid., September 17, 1858.

6. Ibid., September 8 ("quit suing") and September 17, 1858 (Miller quote).

7. Abbott, *Boosters and Businessmen*, 17; *KGC*, July 10, July 12, 1858; Mildred Throne, "'Book Farming' in Iowa, 1840–1870," *Iowa Journal of History* 49 (April 1951): 121.

8. *KGC*, June 18, 1858 ("silent and gloomy"), December 29, 1858, November 23, 1859 ("Alas, for Second Street"), October 26, 1859, February 12, 1864; *Davenport Gazette*, May 17, 1859 ("monument of the folly").

9. C. H. Pierson quote, *Chicago Tribune*, June 16, 1858, reprinted in *KGC*, June 21, 1858.

10. *KGC*, April 20, 1863, November 5, 1858, November 29, 1859, December 9 ("shrill and piercing") and December 17 ("kicking, squirming, agonizing"), 1862.

11. Ibid., November 5, 1858, October 24, 1859 ("perfidious traffic"), August 4, 1860, June 12 and 21, 1862, December 9 and 17, 1862.

12. Ibid., June 21, 1858.

13. Article reprinted in ibid., October 8, 1858.

14. Ibid., October 26, 1858, October 8, 1858; *Davenport Gazette*, May 17, 1859. For discussions of the relationship between eastern capital and the success and failure of western communities, see: Jeffrey Adler, *Yankee Merchants and the Making of the Urban West: The Rise and Fall of Antebellum St. Louis* (New York, 1991), 9, 43; John D. Haeger, "Capital Mobilization and the Urban Center," *Mid-America* 60 (April–July 1978): 88; John D. Haeger, "Eastern Money and the Urban Frontier," *Journal of the Illinois Historical Society* 64 (autumn 1971): 267–84; John D. Haeger, "The Abandoned Townsite on the Midwestern Frontier," *Journal of the Early Republic* 3 (summer 1983): 165–83.

15. *KGC*, April 15, 1859, June 7, 1858, June 2, 1859, March 8, 1860 ("condition of decadence"), November 8, 1859, November 12, 1859, October 2, 1860, December 6, 1860, November 18, 1859, October 31, 1860 ("The wharf is full"), September 19, 1859, March 21, 1861; *History of Keokuk: 1820 to 1906* (Keokuk, 1906), 8, 42.

16. *KGC*, July 7, 1859, September 22, 1860, June 29, 1858.

17. "Inaugural Address of H. W. Sample," reprinted in *KGC*, April 16, 1858. See also Mahoney, *River Towns of the Great West*, 240.

18. Ibid.; "Statement of City Council," printed in *KGC*, July 8, 1858; "Inaugural Address of Mayor Leighton," reprinted in *KGC*, April 14, 1859 ("settled on some honorable basis"); *KGC*, January 29, 1859 ("We can't pay now"), April 14, 1859, February 15, 1859.

19. *Clapp v. County of Cedar*, 5 Iowa 15 (1857). See also Michael A. Ross, "Cases of Shattered Dreams: Justice Samuel Freeman Miller and the Rise and Fall of a Mississippi River Town," *Annals of Iowa* 57 (summer 1998): 229.

20. *KGC*, September 17, 1858.

21. Love's quotes in *Robert Moir v. Jefferson County* reprinted in *KGC*, April 14, 1860.

22. In determining against the county, Love relied on *State Bank of Ohio v. Knoop*, 57 U.S. (16 Howard) 376 (1853). The case of *Robert Moir v. Jefferson County* is described in detail in *KGC*, April 14, 1860. "Report of the Anti-Railroad Tax Meeting" of April 16, 1860, reprinted in *KGC*, April 19, 1860; "Report of Anti-Railroad Tax Mass Meeting" of October 6, 1860, reprinted in *KGC*, October 13, 1860.

23. *KGC*, May 6, 1858 ("paying off debts"), August 5, 1859 ("hoarded up"); James McPherson, *Battle Cry of Freedom: The Civil War Era* (New York, 1988), 191.

24. Even some prominent Keokuk Democrats—David Kilbourne and Hugh Reid—tried to get in on the act, attempting to organize a competing state bank branch in town. But because only one branch could be awarded per city, Miller's Republican group was awarded control. Miller defended this decision by saying that Kilbourne and Reid did not have the confidence of Keokuk's merchant community. *KGC*, July 7, October 1 and 14, 1858; Robert Cook, *Baptism of Fire: The Republican Party in Iowa* (Ames, Iowa, 1994), 22, 98; Morton Rosenberg, *Iowa on the Eve of the Civil War: A Decade of Frontier Politics* (Norman, Okla., 1972), 137.

25. *KGC*, May 31, 1858, September 29, 1860.

26. For a more thorough discussion of the *Dred Scott* decision see: McPherson, *Battle Cry of Freedom*, 170–8; Don E. Fehrenbacher, *The Dred Scott Case: Its Significance in American Law and Politics* (New York, 1978).

27. In that case, the Supreme Court held that slaves from Kentucky taken temporarily to Ohio remained slaves under Kentucky law. *Strader v. Graham*, 51 U.S. 82 (1851).

28. *Dred Scott v. Sandford*, 60 U.S. 393, 405, 412, 417 (1857).

29. Ibid., at 432–52.

30. *New York Tribune*, March 7, 1857; *KGC*, March 10, 1857 ("The decision"), March 18, 1857 ("by every patriot"); McPherson, *Battle Cry of Freedom*, 183.

31. *New York Evening Post*, March 7, 1857; Paul Finkelman, *Dred Scott v. Sandford: A Brief History* (Boston, 1997), 46; McPherson, *Battle Cry of Freedom*, 173; Fehrenbacher, *Dred Scott Case*, 200.

32. Remarks of Miller's friend H. E. Davis, a member of the Supreme Court bar, on December 6, 1890, at the memorial services for Justice Miller held by the Supreme Court, *Proceedings of the Bench and Bar of the Supreme Court of the United States in Memoriam Samuel F. Miller* (Washington, D.C., 1891), addenda, 17.

33. McPherson, *Battle Cry of Freedom*, 164.

34. Ibid., 166, 168.

35. See the *Keokuk Gate City* throughout the fall of 1857 for dozens of articles on the *Dred Scott* decision. The debates in Congress over the Lecompton constitution appear throughout late March and early April 1858. See, for example, *KGC*, April 1, 2, 3, 4, 1858. For some of the many accounts of the Lincoln-Douglas debates, see *KGC*, July 27, 28, 29, 1858, August 9, 1858.

36. Ibid., July 17, 1856; Paul M. Angle, ed., *Created Equal? The Complete Lincoln-Douglas Debates of 1858* (Chicago, 1958), 323, 326.

37. Cook, *Baptism of Fire*, 66, 67, 76, 93; *KGC*, June 4, 1857.

38. Gabor Boritt, *Lincoln and the Economics of the American Dream* (Memphis, 1978), 8, 9, 19 (quote), 47, 58; David Donald, *Lincoln* (New York, 1995), 110.

39. Francis Wayland, *Elements of Political Economy* (New York, 1835), quote in Donald, *Lincoln*, 110.

40. Donald, *Lincoln*, 178 ("to prevent"); Boritt, *Lincoln and the Economics of the American Dream*, 71 ("respectable scoundrels").

41. David S. Sparks, "Iowa Republicans and the Railroads, 1856–1860," *Iowa Journal of History* 53 (1955): 274, 276, 275, 283; Earl S. Beard, "Local Aid to Railroads in Iowa," *Iowa Journal of History* 50 (1952): 15–6.

42. *KGC*, May 24, 1860 (quote); Beard, "Local Aid to Railroads in Iowa," 15–6; Eric Foner, *Free*

Soil, Free Labor, Free Men: The Ideology of the Republican Party before the Civil War (New York, 1970); John Lauritz Lutz, *Bonds of Enterprise: John Murray Forbes and Western Development in America's Railway Age* (Cambridge, Mass., 1984), 79, 81, 90. See also Alan Jones, "Republicanism, Railroads, and Nineteenth-Century Midwestern Constitutionalism," in *Liberty, Property, and Government: Constitutional Interpretation before the New Deal,* ed. Ellen Paul and Howard Dickman (Albany, N.Y., 1989), 239–65. For the view that the shift of Republican party leaders on the issue of railroad bonds was less ideological and more cynical, see Cook, *Baptism of Fire,* 115.

43. *KGC,* June 1, 1859.

44. Rosenberg, *Iowa on the Eve of the Civil War,* 193, 198, 199; *KGC,* August 12, September 27 and 28, October 1, 1859, May 28, 1860 (Miller appointed to State Executive Committee).

45. McPherson, *Battle Cry of Freedom,* 205, 206; Rosenberg, *Iowa on the Eve of the Civil War,* 207; Cook, *Baptism of Fire,* 120, 121.

46. *KGC,* October 20, 1859. Howells and Kirkwood quoted in McPherson, *Battle Cry of Freedom,* 210, 212. See also: *KGC,* December 2, 1860; Stephen B. Oates, *To Purge This Land with Blood: A Biography of John Brown* (New York, 1970), 354–6; Cook, *Baptism of Fire,* 120, 121.

47. *KGC,* May 24, 1860; Cook, *Baptism of Fire,* 124–6.

48. *KGC,* May 14 and 26, 1860.

49. Ibid., July 14, 1860, August 17, 23, 28, 30, 1860; Ballinger diary, July 14, 1860, Ballinger Collection, Center for the Study of American History, University of Texas at Austin.

50. *KGC,* September 11, October 11 and 30, 1860; Charles Fairman, *Mr. Justice Miller and the Supreme Court, 1862–1890* (Cambridge, Mass., 1939), 34.

51. McPherson, *Battle Cry of Freedom,* 216, 221 (platform quote).

52. Rosenberg, *Iowa on the Eve of the Civil War,* 225.

53. In Keokuk, the southern candidate, John Breckinridge, received only six votes. *KGC,* November 7, 1860; Fairman, *Mr. Justice Miller,* 35; McPherson, *Battle Cry of Freedom,* 232; Rosenberg, *Iowa on the Eve of the Civil War,* 225.

54. Miller to W.P.B., November 11, 1860, box 1, folder 1, SFMP, LC.

55. Ibid.

56. Abraham Lincoln, *Collected Works of Abraham Lincoln,* ed. Roy P. Basler. 9 vols. (New Brunswick, N.J., 1952–55), 4: 95; McPherson, *Battle Cry of Freedom,* 230.

57. *New York Weekly Tribune,* November 3, 1860; *New York Tribune,* November 9, 1860. See also Adam-Max Tuchinsky, "Horace Greeley's Lost Book: *The New-York Tribune* and the Origins of Social Democratic Liberalism in America" (Ph.D. dissertation, University of North Carolina at Chapel Hill, 2001), 469–70.

58. McPherson, *Battle Cry of Freedom,* 252.

59. Miller to W.P.B., November 11, 1860, box 1, folder 1, SFMP, LC.

60. McPherson, *Battle Cry of Freedom,* 253.

61. Congress would also be forbidden from abolishing slavery on federal property such as forts and naval bases within slave states. In addition, it could not abolish slavery in the District of Columbia without the consent of its inhabitants and unless slavery had first been abolished by both Virginia and Maryland. McPherson, *Battle Cry of Freedom,* 253 (quote); Patsy S. Ledbetter, "John J. Crittenden and the Compromise Debacle," *Filson Club History Quarterly* 51 (1977): 125–42.

62. Lincoln to Lyman Trumbull, December 10, 1860, quoted in McPherson, *Battle Cry of Freedom,* 253–4. See also David E. Woodard, "Abraham Lincoln, Duff Green, and the Mysterious Trumbull Letter," *Civil War History* 42 (1996): 211–9.

63. *KGC,* January 24, 25 (Love quote), 28 ("no compromise"), 1861.

64. Ibid., January 28, 1861.

65. Ibid., February 20, 1861.

66. Douglas quote in McPherson, *Battle Cry of Freedom,* 274; *KGC,* April 25, 1861 (Belknap quote); Cook, *Baptism of Fire,* 136.

67. *KGC,* April 19, 1861 (speech), April 20, 1861 ("war spirit").

68. Ibid., May 4, 1861; Cyrus Bussey to Samuel Kirkwood, August 6, 1861, Samuel Kirkwood Papers, SHSI, Des Moines; Fairman, *Mr. Justice Miller,* 37.

69. *KGC,* May 25, 1861.

70. Ibid., February 4, April 24, July 26, August 10, December 10, 1861, January 20, 1862.

71. Ibid., July 1, 1861, June 22, 1861 (quote).

72. Ibid., May 30, 1861 (soldiers exercising), June 1, 1861 ("prostrated"), July 13, 1862, December 8, 1862 ("blockade").

73. Ibid., May 31, 1861, May 29, 1861 ("smashed everything"), June 3, 1861, July 13, 1861, March 29, 1862 ("making themselves").

74. Ibid., July 28, 1862, March 29, 1862, August 5, 1862.

75. Because the bondholder lived in Ohio, the case went to Love's federal district court because of diversity of citizenship. Miller to W.P.B., November 11, 1860, box 1, folder 1, SFMP, LC.

Chapter 4 Lincoln Appoints a Justice

1. *Dred Scott v. Sandford,* 60 U.S. 393 (1857); Paul Finkelman, *Dred Scott v. Sandford: A Brief History with Documents* (Boston, 1997), 29; Abraham Lincoln, *Collected Works of Abraham Lincoln,* ed. Roy P. Basler. 9 vols. (New Brunswick, N.J., 1953–55), 2:401, James McPherson, *Battle Cry of Freedom: The Civil War Era* (New York, 1988), 176–7.

2. "Brooding proslavery fanatic" in Don E. Fehrenbacher, *The Dred Scott Case: Its Significance in American Law and Politics* (New York, 1978), 234. See also McPherson, *Battle Cry of Freedom,* 174; David Silver, *Lincoln's Supreme Court* (Urbana, Ill., 1956), 3, 9, 10.

3. *Ex parte Merryman,* 17 Fed. Cas. 144. (C.C.D.Md. 1861) (No. 9,487).

4. McPherson, *Battle Cry of Freedom,* 287; David Donald, *Lincoln* (New York, 1995), 297–300; Mark E. Neely, *The Fate of Liberty: Abraham Lincoln and Civil Liberties* (New York, 1991), 4; J. G. Randall, *Constitutional Problems under Lincoln* (rev. ed.; Urbana, Ill., 1951).

5. Neely, *Fate of Liberty,* xii; Donald, *Lincoln,* 299; Silver, *Lincoln's Supreme Court,* 28; Milton Cantor, "The Writ of Habeas Corpus: Early American Origins and Development," in *Freedom and Reform: Essays in Honor of Henry Steele Commager,* ed. Harold Hyman and Leonard Levy (New York, 1967), 74; Lincoln's message to Congress, July 4, 1861, *Collected Works,* ed. Basler, 4:421–41 (Lincoln quote).

6. Under the organization of the federal court system at the time, the Supreme Court judge from each of the nine circuits served also as the presiding judge of the circuit court. Silver, *Lincoln's Supreme Court,* 28; Randall, *Constitutional Problems under Lincoln,* 120–1 ("no longer living under"); Donald, *Lincoln,* 299; Fehrenbacher, *Dred Scott Case,* 575.

7. Neely, *Fate of Liberty,* 14, 15, 24.

8. Ibid., 25, 145; Silver, *Lincoln's Supreme Court,* 104, 105.

9. *New York Tribune,* December 13, 1861; *Chicago Tribune,* March 4, 1861; Fehrenbacher, *Dred Scott,* 576–7; Silver, *Lincoln's Supreme Court,* 39, 40.

10. The nine circuits in 1860 were organized as follows: 1st Circuit (Rhode Island, Massachusetts, New Hampshire, and Maine), 2d Circuit (New York, Vermont, and Connecticut), 3d Circuit (Pennsylvania and New Jersey), 4th Circuit (Maryland, Delaware, and Virginia), 5th Circuit (Alabama and Louisiana), 6th Circuit (North Carolina, South Carolina, Georgia), 7th Circuit (Ohio, Indiana, Illinois, Michigan), 8th Circuit (Kentucky, Tennessee, Missouri), 9th Circuit (Mississippi, Arkansas). It was in his capacity as circuit court judge that Taney issued his decision in *Ex Parte Merryman.* Silver, *Lincoln's Supreme Court,* 42, 43; Fehrenbacher, *Dred Scott,* 576–7.

11. *Chicago Tribune,* June 5, 1862; *KGC,* July 29, 1862 (Wilson quote).

12. Lincoln's first annual message to Congress, December 3, 1861, *Collected Works,* ed. Basler, 5:35–53.

13. The bill was entitled "An Act to Amend the Judicial System of the United States." Silver, *Lincoln's Supreme Court,* 50, 51; Michael A. Ross, "Justice for Iowa: Samuel Freeman Miller's Appointment to the United States Supreme Court during the Civil War," *Annals of Iowa* 60 (spring 2001): 111–38.

14. *Congressional Globe,* 37th Cong., 2d sess., 187–8, 469.

15. Noah H. Swayne to Benjamin F. Wade, January 10, 1861 ("must appoint Browning"), Wade Manuscript Collection, LC; Silver, *Lincoln's Supreme Court,* 51, 60.

16. Maurice Baxter, *Orville Browning: Lincoln's Friend and Critic* (Bloomington, Ind., 1957), 57, 68, 111, 224.

17. Silver, *Lincoln's Supreme Court,* 51; Richard L. Aynes, "Constricting the Law of Freedom: Justice Miller, the Fourteenth Amendment, and the *Slaughter-House Cases,*" *Chicago-Kent Law Review* 70 (1994): 674, 675; Jonathan Lurie, "Noah Haynes Swayne," in *The Oxford Companion to the Supreme Court,* ed. Kermit Hall (New York, 1992), 850.

18. *Mad River & Lake Erie R.R. v. Barber,* 5 Ohio State Reports 541 (1856).

19. Silver, *Lincoln's Supreme Court,* 59; W. B. Ogden to A. Lincoln, May 25, 1861, quoted in Carl B. Swisher, *The Taney Period, 1836–64,* in *Oliver Wendell Holmes Devise History of the Supreme Court of the United States* (New York, 1974), 816.

20. Ernest Bates, *The Story of the Supreme Court* (Indianapolis, Ind., 1936), 168 (quote); Silver, *Lincoln's Supreme Court,* 59.

21. Senate Misc. Document. No. 73, 37th Cong., 2d sess., p. 1.

22. Robert Cook, *Baptism of Fire: The Republican Party in Iowa, 1838–1878* (Ames, Iowa, 1994), 103, 123, 107, 109; Fred B. Lewellen, "Political Ideas of James W. Grimes," *Iowa Journal of History and Politics* 42 (October 1944): 339–404; Silver, *Lincoln's Supreme Court,* 55.

23. Speech of Iowa congressman James F. Wilson, June 4, 1862, *Congressional Globe,* 37th Cong., 2d sess., p. 2562; Swisher, *Taney Period,* 826; Charles Fairman, *Mr. Justice Miller and the Supreme Court, 1862–1890* (Cambridge, Mass., 1939), 47; Silver, *Lincoln's Supreme Court,* 55.

24. Speech of Iowa congressman James F. Wilson, June 4, 1862.

25. *Congressional Globe,* 37th Cong., 2d sess., pp. 3276–8.

26. Ibid.

27. Heather Cox Richardson, *The Greatest Nation of the Earth: Republican Economic Policies during the Civil War* (Cambridge, Mass., 1997), 2, 12, 13, 15, 80.

28. *Chicago Tribune,* June 5, 1862, 2.

29. Silver, *Lincoln's Supreme Court,* 55 (quote).

30. Edward Johnstone to Abraham Lincoln, December 20, 1861 ("The citizens"), microfilm, reel 30, doc. 13503, Lincoln Papers, LC; D. F. Miller to Abraham Lincoln, December 10, 1861 ("I hope your excellency"), microfilm, reel 30, doc. 13327, Lincoln Papers, LC.

31. Joseph C. Knappe (former U.S. attorney in Iowa) to Abraham Lincoln, January 4, 1862, microfilm, reel 31, doc. 13822; C. C. Norse (Iowa attorney general) to Abraham Lincoln, December 14, 1861 ("conscientious Republican"), microfilm, reel 30, doc. 13423; Caleb Baldwin (Iowa Supreme Court judge) to Abraham Lincoln, December 16, 1861, microfilm, reel 30, doc. 13424; George C. Wright (Iowa Supreme Court judge) to Abraham Lincoln, December 16, 1861, microfilm, reel 30, doc. 13454; Francis Springer (Iowa attorney) to Abraham Lincoln, December 11, 1861, microfilm, reel 30, doc. 13368; J. M. Love (Iowa federal district court judge), January 1, 1862, microfilm, reel 31, doc. 13746; Daniel F. Miller (former Iowa congressman) to Abraham Lincoln, December 10, 1861, microfilm, reel 30, doc. 13327; Edward Johnstone to Lincoln, December 20, 1861 ("unwavering"). All in Lincoln Papers, LC.

32. J. M. Love to Abraham Lincoln, January 1, 1862.

33. Michael A. Ross, "Cases of Shattered Dreams: Justice Samuel Freeman Miller and the Rise and Fall of a Mississippi River Town," *Annals of Iowa* 57 (summer 1998): 221, 231.

34. Samuel F. Miller, "Address of Mr. Justice Miller," *Albany Law Journal* 20 (1879): 25–29; Eric Foner, *Reconstruction: America's Unfinished Revolution, 1863–1877* (New York, 1988), 31; Frank L. Klement, "Economic Aspects of Middle Western Copperheadism," *Historian* 14 (autumn 1951): 27–44; Frank L. Klement, "Middle Western Copperheadism and the Genesis of the Granger Movement," *Mississippi Valley Historical Review* 38 (March 1952): 679–94.

35. John A. Kasson to Charles Aldrich, November 10, 1893, quoted in Henry Strong, "Justice Samuel Freeman Miller," *Annals of Iowa* 3 (January 1894): 241, 252.

36. Silver, *Lincoln's Supreme Court,* 66. Governor Kirkwood's avid support of Miller might also have been spurred by a desire to remove a political rival. In 1861 Miller made an abbreviated attempt to challenge Kirkwood for the governorship. For a discussion of the brief and muted rivalry between the two men, see Miller's letter to Samuel Kirkwood, August 3, 1861, Samuel Kirkwood Papers, SHSI, Des Moines. For a discussion of Iowans' efforts on Miller's behalf, see Cook, *Baptism of Fire,* 59, 68, 93, 111, 114, 121; Morton M. Rosenberg, *Iowa on the Eve of the Civil War: A Decade of Frontier Politics* (Norman, Okla., 1972), 191; *KGC,* August 3, 5, 1861; Fairman, *Mr. Justice Miller,* 36, 37, 48.

37. Henry J. Abraham, *Justices and Presidents: A Political History of Appointments to the Supreme Court,* 2d ed. (New York, 1985), 109; Fairman, *Mr. Justice Miller,* 50; Silver, *Lincoln's Supreme Court,* 65.

38. James Lee McDonough, *Shiloh—In Hell before Night* (Knoxville, Tenn., 1977); Robert G. Tanner, *Stonewall in the Valley: Thomas J. "Stonewall" Jackson's Shenandoah Valley Campaign, Spring 1862* (Garden City, N.Y., 1976); McPherson, *Battle Cry of Freedom,* 358 (Lincoln quote), 413–4, 457–9.

39. Abraham, *Justices and Presidents,* 109; Henry Strong, "Samuel Freeman Miller," *Annals of Iowa* 1 (January 1894): 252 (Lincoln quote).

40. Mark E. Neely, *The Last Best Hope of Earth: Abraham Lincoln and the Promise of America* (Cambridge, Mass., 1993), 10 ("Lincoln fought"), 11; Gabor Boritt, *Lincoln and the Economics of the American Dream* (Memphis, Tenn., 1978), 1, 14, 93, 101, 105, 119 ("all is cold"); Donald, *Lincoln,* 110.

41. Lincoln quote in Boritt, *Lincoln and the Economics of the American Dream,* 177; Donald, *Lincoln,* 234.

42. Richardson, *Greatest Nation on Earth*, 15, 21; Eric Foner, *Free Soil, Free Labor, Free Men: The Ideology of the Republican Party before the Civil War* (New York, 1970), 16, 17.

43. Lincoln, *Collected Works*, ed. Basler, 7:259–60; Boritt, *Lincoln and the Economics of the American Dream*, 96, 98; Foner, *Free Soil, Free Labor, Free Men*, 20, 177.

44. Because Miller was in Washington when Lincoln announced his appointment, the process moved quickly from there. Swisher, *The Taney Period*, 828; Abraham, *Justices and Presidents*, 109.

45. Report from Washington in *KGC*, July 26, 1862; Charles Noble Gregory, *Samuel Freeman Miller* (Iowa City, 1907), 12–3 (Miller quote).

46. *KGC*, July 18, 1862 ("He is the model"); Silver, *Lincoln's Supreme Court*, 69 ("little systematic approach"); *Daily State Register*, July 22, 1862 ("The appointment"). See also: *Daily State Register*, July 19, 1862; *Burlington Hawkeye*, July 18, 1862; Fairman, *Mr. Justice Miller*, 22–4.

47. *New York Tribune*, July 18, 1862; *Chicago Tribune*, July 18, 1862; *New York Times*, July 17, 1862; *Baltimore Sun*, July 17, 1862; *Washington Daily Globe*, July 17, 1862; *New York World*, July 17, 1862.

48. *Christian Times*, July 22, 1862, reprinted in *KGC*, August 12, 1862.

49. *KGC*, July 26, 1862.

50. Ibid., August 8, 1862.

51. Antietam was the single bloodiest day in American military history. Almost five thousand Union and Confederate soldiers died in the fighting. Stephen Sears, *Landscape Turned Red: The Battle of Antietam* (New Haven, Conn., 1983); McPherson, *Battle Cry of Freedom*, 494, 496, 505, 557 (Emancipation Proclamation quote); *Congressional Globe*, 34th Cong., 2d sess., January 14, 1862, 327–32 (Julian quote).

52. The best analysis of Miller's views as to the causes of the war can be found in his lengthy discussion of the matter in the *Slaughter-House Cases*, 83 U.S. 36, 68 (1873).

53. Robert Dykstra, *Bright Radical Star: Black Freedom and White Supremacy on the Hawkeye Frontier* (Cambridge, Mass., 1993), 197–8; *Atlantic Monthly* quote in McPherson, *Battle Cry of Freedom*, 686; Dudley T. Cornish, *The Sable Arm: Negro Troops in the Union Army* (New York, 1966), 285–7; Joseph T. Glatthaar, *Forged in Battle: The Civil War Alliance of Black Soldiers and White Officers* (New York, 1990), 182–5; Mary F. Berry, *Military Necessity and Civil Rights Policy: Black Citizenship and the Constitution, 1861–1868* (Port Washington, N.Y., 1977); *Slaughter-House Cases*, 83 U.S., at 41–57, 68 (Miller quote).

54. Wendell Phillips quote in Silver, *Lincoln's Supreme Court*, 137–8; *New York Times*, January 3, 1863, 4.

55. Stephen R. Wise, *Lifeline of the Confederacy: Blockade Running during the Civil War* (Columbia, S.C., 1988), 46–73; Frank L. Owsley, *King Cotton Diplomacy: Foreign Relations of the Confederate States of America*, 2d rev. ed. (Chicago, 1959), 229, 250–90; Silver, *Lincoln's Supreme Court*, 106; Robert Carse, *Blockade: The Civil War at Sea* (New York, 1954); Neely, *Fate of Liberty*, 145.

56. Silver, *Lincoln's Supreme Court*, 105–6; Phillip Shaw Paludan, *A People's Contest: The Union and the Civil War, 1861–1865* (New York, 1988), 34; Harold M. Hyman and William Wiecek, *Equal Justice under Law: Constitutional Development, 1835–1875* (New York, 1982), 264–5; Randall, *Constitutional Problems under Lincoln*, 67–72.

57. Silver, *Lincoln's Supreme Court*, 71–81, 108 ("lifeblood"); George Leyh, "David Davis," in *The Oxford Companion to the Supreme Court of the United States*, ed. Kermit L. Hall (New York, 1992) 218–9; Willard L. King, *Lincoln's Manager David Davis* (Cambridge, Mass., 1960), 102–3, 124, 157, 166, 195, 310.

58. The proposal to add a tenth circuit had been left out of the act of 1862 because, it was argued,

the population of the Far West did not yet warrant adding a tenth justice. Silver, *Lincoln's Supreme Court,* 50, 85–7; *New York World,* January 5, 1864; *Congressional Globe,* 37th Cong., 3d sess., 1300; *New York Times,* March 4, 1863. For a contrary view, see Stanley Kutler, *Judicial Power and Reconstruction Politics* (Chicago, 1968), 18–9.

59. *Prize Cases,* 67 U.S. 635, 665–82 (1863); Robert C. Grier to Nathan Clifford, July 24, 1861, quoted in Silver, *Lincoln's Supreme Court,* 16, 22 (quote).

60. *Prize Cases,* 67 U.S., at 666–7.

61. Ibid., at 666.

62. Fairman, *Mr. Justice Miller,* 81.

63. *Prize Cases,* at 690, 696.

64. Act of Congress of July 13, 1861, secs. 5, 6; *Prize Cases,* at 695.

65. Paul Finkelman, "The Prize Cases," in *The Oxford Companion to the Supreme Court of the United States,* ed. Hall, 681 (quote); Paludan, *A People's Contest,* 34; Randall, *Constitutional Problems under Lincoln,* 72; Stewart L. Bernath, *Squall across the Atlantic: American Civil War Prize Cases and Diplomacy* (Berkeley, 1970).

66. *The Cornelius,* 70 U.S. 214 (1865); Willie Lee Rose, *Rehearsal for Reconstruction: The Port Royal Experiment* (Indianapolis, Ind., 1964); Neely, *Fate of Liberty,* 145.

67. *The Cornelius,* at 223–4.

68. Ibid.

69. Paul Kens, *Justice Stephen Field: Shaping Liberty from the Gold Rush to the Gilded Age* (Lawrence, Kans., 1997), 96 (quote).

70. Ibid., 88–9, 95–7; Carl Brent Swisher, *Stephen J. Field: Craftsman of the Law* (Washington, D.C., 1930), 116–7; Abraham, *Justices and Presidents,* 111–2; Jan S. Stevens, "Stephen J. Field: A Gold Rush Lawyer Shapes the Nation," *Journal of the West* 29 (1990): 40–53.

71. *The State of Iowa ex rel. v. The County of Wapello,* 13 Iowa R. 388, 423, 424 (1862).

72. Ibid.

73. *Gelpcke v. Dubuque,* 68 U.S. (1 Wall.) 175 (1864).

74. *Leffingwell v. Warren,* 67 U.S. (2 Black) 599 (1862).

75. If the Court somehow distinguished *Leffingwell* from the case at hand, the bondholders could hope for a result similar to that in the Court's 1859 decision, *Knox County v. Aspinwall.* In *Knox County,* the Court held that in order to protect innocent investors, municipal bonds that appeared valid on their face had to be honored, even if they had been issued improperly. Thus, Dubuque's bonds, although unconstitutionally issued, would have to be honored. *Knox County v. Aspinwall,* 62 U.S. (21 Howard) 539 (1859).

76. *Gelpcke v. Dubuque,* 68 U.S., at 205 (1864).

77. Ibid., at 206, 209, 214, 220.

78. *Meyer v. City of Muscatine,* 68 U.S. 384–93 (1864).

79. Ibid., at 386–92.

80. Ibid., at 395–6.

81. Ibid., at 398.

82. *Philadelphia Press,* October 14, 1864; Charles Sumner to Abraham Lincoln, October 12, 1864, quoted in Kutler, *Judicial Power and Reconstruction Politics,* 21; Fairman, *Mr. Justice Miller,* 52.

83. Abraham, *Justices and Presidents,* 112–4; Miller to W.P.B., October 15, 1876; Harold M. Hyman, *The Reconstruction Justice of Salmon P. Chase* (Lawrence, Kans., 1997), 70–1; George S.

Boutwell, *Reminiscences of Sixty Years in Public Service*, 2 vols. (New York, 1902), 2:29; Donald, *Lincoln*, 552–3.

84. In 1833, in *Barron v. Baltimore*, the Supreme Court ruled that the Constitution's Bill of Rights applied only to the federal government. Citizens had to look to their state constitutions for protection of their civil and political rights. *Barron v. Baltimore*, 32 U.S. 243 (1833); Hyman and Wiecek, *Equal Justice under Law*, 276, 277, 300; Earl Maltz, *Civil Rights, the Constitution, and Congress, 1863–1869* (Lawrence, Kans., 1990).

85. Hyman and Wiecek, *Equal Justice under Law*, 316; Donald G. Nieman, *To Set the Law in Motion: The Freedman's Bureau and the Legal Rights of Blacks, 1865–1868* (Millwood, N.Y., 1979), introduction; William S. McFeely, *Yankee Stepfather: General O. O. Howard and the Freedmen* (New York, 1968).

86. Foner, *Reconstruction*, 74 (quote); McPherson, *Battle Cry of Freedom*, 852.

87. Foner, *Reconstruction*, 20–2; Foner, *Free Soil, Free Labor, Free Men*, 11–72.

Chapter 5 The Consequences Attendant upon Treason

1. Eric Foner, *Reconstruction: America's Unfinished Revolution, 1863–1877* (New York, 1988), 176.

2. Dan T. Carter, *When the War Was Over: The Failure of Self-Reconstruction in the South, 1865–1867* (Baton Rouge, La., 1986), 24 (Johnson quote); Foner, *Reconstruction*, 176–8; Michael Les Benedict, *A Compromise of Principle: Congressional Republicans and Reconstruction, 1863–1869* (New York, 1974), 100, 101; W. R. Brock, *An American Crisis: Congress and Reconstruction, 1865–1867* (New York, 1963), 31.

3. Foner, *Reconstruction*, 177, 178 (Sumner quote).

4. Miller to W.P.B., August 31, 1865, box 1, folder 2, SFMP, LC.

5. Wade quote in Benedict, *Compromise of Principle*, 101.

6. Miller to W.P.B., August 31, 1865.

7. Ibid.

8. Ibid.

9. Ibid.; Brock, *An American Crisis*, 101 (Stevens quote).

10. Miller to W.P.B., August 31, 1865.

11. Carter, *When the War Was Over*, 25; Foner, *Reconstruction*, 183.

12. Foner, *Reconstruction*, 187, 216; Benedict, *Compromise of Principle*, 103, 107.

13. Foner, *Reconstruction*, 190; Carter, *When the War Was Over*, 28.

14. Although in the first months of the war, Lincoln had also acted while Congress was out of session, he acknowledged that his actions were tentative and reversible. Lincoln also called Congress into special session to ratify or reject his decisions. Harold Hyman and William Wiecek, *Equal Justice under Law: Constitutional Development, 1835–1875* (New York, 1982), 304, 309.

15. Foner, *Reconstruction*, 189.

16. Miller to W.P.B., August 31, 1865.

17. Carter, *When the War Was Over*, 68–70 (quote, 70); Foner, *Reconstruction*, 196.

18. Brock, *An American Crisis*, 16.

19. Carter, *When the War Was Over*, 229, 230; Foner, *Reconstruction*, 196.

20. Carter, *When the War Was Over*, 63, 64 (quotes); Benedict, *Compromise of Principle*, 121.

21. Hyman and Wiecek, *Equal Justice under Law*, 305.

22. Christopher Waldrep, "Substituting Law for the Lash: Emancipation and Legal Formalism in a Mississippi County Court," *Journal of American History* 82 (March 1996): 1425; William C. Harris, *Presidential Reconstruction in Mississippi* (Baton Rouge, La., 1967), 99–100, 112–5, 130–1; Brock, *An American Crisis*, 36, 37; Hyman and Wiecek, *Equal Justice under Law*, 319, 320; Carter, *When the War Was Over*, 148–50, 177, 217–27 (quotes); Foner, *Reconstruction*, 199–200.

23. Hyman and Wiecek, *Equal Justice under Law*, 317, 322–5.

24. Chicago editor Charles Dana to Isaac Sherman, September 17, 1865, quoted in Foner, *Reconstruction*, 225.

25. John Hope Franklin, *Reconstruction: After the Civil War* (Chicago, 1961), 53; Kenneth M. Stampp, *The Era of Reconstruction, 1865–1877* (New York, 1965), 72–3; Carter, *When the War Was Over*, 2 ("entire South").

26. Miller to W.P.B., January 11, 1866, box 1, folder 2, SFMP, LC.

27. Foner, *Reconstruction*, 221–2, 226 (Howard quote), 241.

28. Charles A. Jellison, *Fessenden of Maine* (Syracuse, N.Y., 1962), 198–201; Brock, *An American Crisis*, 96 ("calamity").

29. Miller to W.P.B., February 6, 1866, box 1, folder 2, SFMP, LC.

30. Miller to W.P.B., January 11, 1866; Benedict, *Compromise of Principle*, 129–30; Brock, *An American Crisis*, 45, 96; Foner, *Reconstruction*, 226, 227, 231, 241; Carter, *When the War Was Over*, 232.

31. Miller to W.P.B., January 11, 1866; Hyman and Wiecek, *Equal Justice under Law*, 311.

32. Miller to W.P.B., January 11, 1866.

33. Ibid.; Foner, 228–30 ("will escape for years"), 241 (Fessenden quote); Benedict, *Compromise of Principle*, 57, 112.

34. Miller to W.P.B., January 11, 1866.

35. Ibid.

36. Foner, *Reconstruction*, 226, 238; Mark M. Krug, *Lyman Trumbull: Conservative Radical* (New York, 1965), 231–2.

37. *Statutes at Large* 14 (1866): 173.

38. Ibid., 27.

39. *Congressional Globe*, 39th Cong., 1st sess., 319, 474, 1266.

40. Foner, *Reconstruction*, 243; Carter, *When the War Was Over*, 234; Benedict, *Compromise of Principle*, 148; Hyman and Wiecek, *Equal Justice under Law*, 406–7.

41. Lyman Trumbull to Dr. William Jayne, January 11, 1866, quoted in Foner, *Reconstruction*, 245; Benedict, *Compromise of Principle*, 148; Carter, *When the War Was Over*, 236; Donald Nieman, "Andrew Johnson, the Freedmen's Bureau, and the Problem of Equal Rights, 1865–1866," *Journal of Southern History* 44 (August 1978): 399–420.

42. Johnson quote in Benedict, *Compromise of Principle*, 164.

43. Johnson quote in Foner, *Reconstruction*, 248, 250 (quote).

44. Hyman and Wiecek, *Equal Justice under Law*, 418; Benedict, *Compromise of Principle*, 155–6.

45. *Ex Parte Milligan*, 71 U.S. 2, 6, 7 (1866).

46. Allan Nevins, "The Case of the Copperhead Conspirator," in *Quarrels That Have Shaped the Constitution*, ed. John A. Garraty (New York, 1964), 103, 111–3.

47. Charles Fairman, *Mr. Justice Miller and the Supreme Court, 1862–1890* (Cambridge, Mass., 1939), 93; David Silver, *Lincoln's Supreme Court* (Urbanna, Ill., 1956), 228; *Ex Parte Milligan*, at 4–9.

48. *Ex Parte Milligan,* at 4–9.

49. Ibid., at 16, 17, 20.

50. Ibid., at 21.

51. Field quote in Daun van Ee, *David Dudley Field and the Reconstruction of the Law* (New York, 1986), 207.

52. *Ex Parte Milligan,* at 22, 29, 30, 31, 32, 60–2.

53. Ibid., at 85–7.

54. Ibid.; Nevins, "The Case of the Copperhead Conspirator," 101, 118; Silver, *Lincoln's Supreme Court,* 232.

55. *Ex Parte Milligan,* at 109.

56. Ibid., at 121, 124, 125.

57. Ibid., at 126, 127.

58. Ibid.

59. Nevins, "The Case of the Copperhead Conspirator," 118.

60. *Ex Parte Milligan,* at 132.

61. Ibid., at 133, 136, 137, 139, 140, 142.

62. *Indianapolis Daily Herald,* April 5, 1866.

63. *Cummings v. the State of Missouri,* 71 U.S. 277 (1866); *Ex Parte Garland,* 71 U.S. 333 (1866).

64. Harold M. Hyman, *To Try Men's Souls: Loyalty Tests in American History* (Berkeley, 1959), 139–98.

65. *Cummings v. the State of Missouri,* at 279.

66. James M. McPherson, *Battle Cry of Freedom: The Civil War Era* (New York, 1988), 784–6 (quote); Jay Monaghan, *Civil War on the Western Border, 1854–1865* (Boston, 1955), 274–89; Richard S. Brownlee, *Gray Ghosts of the Confederacy: Guerrilla Warfare in the West, 1861–1865* (Baton Rouge, La., 1958), 110–57; Michael Fellman, *Inside War: The Guerrilla Conflict in Missouri during the American Civil War* (New York, 1989), 42, 46, 60–1, 233, 236.

67. *Cummings v. Missouri,* at 282; Hyman and Wiecek, *Equal Justice under Law,* 350; Louis S. Gerteis, *Civil War St. Louis* (Lawrence, Kans., 2001), 316–20.

68. *Cummings v. Missouri,* at 282–92; Hyman and Wiecek, *Equal Justice under Law,* 373.

69. *Cummings v. State of Missouri,* 71 U.S. 282–9 (1866); *Dodge v. Woolsey,* 59 U.S. 331 (1856).

70. *Cummings v. State of Missouri,* at 295, 305, 306.

71. Ibid.

72. Ibid., at 306, 307.

73. Ibid., at 295, 305, 306.

74. *Ex Parte Garland,* 71 U.S. 333 (1866); Hyman, *To Try Men's Souls,* 164.

75. *Ex Parte Garland,* at 336, 337, 374.

76. Ibid.; Miller to W.P.B., February 6, 1867, box 1, folder 4, SFMP, LC.

77. Miller to W.P.B., July 31, 1866; Fairman, *Mr. Justice Miller,* 130–2; Hyman, *To Try Men's Souls,* 260.

78. Hyman and Wiecek, *Equal Justice under Law,* 380; Miller to W.P.B., July 31, 1866.

79. Miller to Salmon P. Chase, June 5, 1866, quoted in Carl Brent Swisher, *Stephen J. Field: Craftsman of the Law* (Washington, D.C., 1930), 142.

80. Stephen J. Field to Salmon P. Chase, June 30, 1866, quoted in ibid., 143.

Chapter 6 Men Incapable of Forgiving or Learning

1. Kevin R. Hardwick, "'Your Old Father Abe Lincoln Is Dead and Damned': Black Soldiers and the Memphis Riot of 1866," *Journal of Social History* 27 (fall 1993): 109–29; *Cleveland Leader*, June 4, 1866 (quote); Eric Foner, *Reconstruction: America's Unfinished Revolution, 1863–1877* (New York, 1988), 261, 262.

2. Miller to W.P.B., August 29, 1869, folder 6, box 1, SFMP, LC; Michael A. Ross, "Justice Miller's Reconstruction: The *Slaughter-House Cases*, Health Codes, and Civil Rights in New Orleans, 1861–1863," *Journal of Southern History* 64 (November 1998): 649, 661; James G. Hollandsworth, *An Absolute Massacre: The New Orleans Race Riot of July 30, 1866* (Baton Rouge, La., 2001); Joe Gray Taylor, *Louisiana Reconstructed, 1863–1877* (Baton Rouge, La., 1974), 106–10; Ted Tunnell, *Crucible of Reconstruction: War, Radicalism, and Race in Louisiana, 1862–1877* (Baton Rouge, La., 1984), 104–7; Foner, *Reconstruction*, 262–3.

3. After the convention, Johnson compounded his problems by campaigning for candidates around the country. Many observers thought his behavior during this tour was undignified and unpresidential. At several stops, he shouted back at hecklers and generally behaved in a rough manner. Foner, *Reconstruction*, 263–6.

4. Ibid., 253.

5. Michael Les Benedict, "Preserving the Constitution: The Conservative Basis of Radical Reconstruction," *Journal of American History* 61 (1974): 65–90; Foner, *Reconstruction*, 254–9. For a discussion of some of the extensive literature on the intent of the framers of the Fourteenth Amendment, see chapter 8, note 49. For the best one-volume discussion, see William E. Nelson, *The Fourteenth Amendment: From Political Principle to Judicial Doctrine* (Cambridge, Mass., 1988).

6. Michael Les Benedict, "Constitutional History and Constitutional Theory: Reflections on Ackerman, Reconstruction, and the Transformation of the American Constitution," *Yale Law Journal* 108 (1998): 2011, 2024–6.

7. Miller to David Davis, October 12, 1866, quoted in Charles Fairman, *Reconstruction and Reunion, 1864–88, Part 1* (New York, 1971), 180; Foner, *Reconstruction*, 267–8; Michael Les Benedict, *A Compromise of Principle: Congressional Republicans and Reconstruction, 1863–1869* (New York, 1974), 212.

8. Benedict, *Compromise of Principle*, 212; Foner, *Reconstruction*, 268.

9. Foner, *Reconstruction*, 271–2 (quotes).

10. *New York World*, December 8, 1866; *Washington Chronicle*, December 8, 1866; *New York Herald*, December 10 and 20, 1866.

11. *New York Times*, January 3, 1867; *Indianapolis Journal*, January 2, 1867; John Jay to Salmon Chase, January 5, 1867, quoted in Charles Warren, *The Supreme Court in United States History* (Boston, 1937), 428; *Cleveland Herald*, January 7, 1867.

12. *Independent*, January 10, 1867; *New York Herald*, January 8, 1867.

13. *Harper's Weekly*, January 19, 1867; *Richmond Enquirer*, December 28, 1866.

14. Warren, *Supreme Court*, 442; *Detroit Tribune*, January 2, 1867, quoted in Warren, *Supreme Court*, 444; *Congressional Globe*, 39th Cong., 2d sess., January 3, 1867.

15. *Harper's Weekly*, January 19 and March 2, 1867; *Congressional Globe*, 39th Cong., 2d sess., 500–3 (Bingham quote); *KGC*, January 8, 1867.

16. *Cummings v. the State of Missouri*, 71 U.S. 277, 318, 319, 322 (1866).

17. Ibid., at 325–8.

18. *Ex Parte Garland*, 71 U.S. 333, 376–7 (1866).

19. Ibid., at 377, 380–1.

20. Ibid., at 382.

21. Ibid., at 384, 385.

22. Ibid., at 390, 392.

23. Ibid., at 393.

24. Ibid., at 397.

25. Ibid., at 392.

26. *Washington Chronicle*, February 16, 1867; *Harper's Weekly*, March 2, 1867.

27. Numerous bills were introduced in Congress to reorganize the Court and to keep former rebels from serving as attorneys before that tribunal. See, for example, *Congressional Globe*, 39th Cong., 2d sess., January 22, 1867, 646–73. *New York Herald*, January 23, 1867; *Boston Daily Advertiser*, January 23, 1867.

28. *New York Times*, February 13, 1867, quoted in Benedict, *Compromise of Principle*, 246.

29. Miller to John Rankin, February 4, 1867, box 1, folder 4, SFMP, LC.

30. Miller to W.P.B., February 6, 1867, box 1, folder 4, SFMP, LC.

31. Ibid.

32. Ibid.

33. Ibid.

34. Foner, *Reconstruction*, 277–8.

35. Ibid., 273, 276; Miller to W.P.B., August 29, 1869 ("absorb us all"), SFMP, LC; Michael A. Ross, "Hill-Country Doctor: The Early Life and Career of Samuel F. Miller in Kentucky, 1816–1849," *Filson Club History Quarterly* 71 (October 1997): 430–62.

36. Miller to W.P.B., April 24, 1867, box 1, folder 4, SFMP, LC.

37. Harold Hyman and William Wiecek, *Equal Justice under Law: Constitutional Development, 1835–1875* (New York, 1982), 382.

38. Warren, *Supreme Court*, 458; *Independent*, April 17, 1867.

39. *Mississippi v. Johnson*, 71 U.S. 475, 498, 500 (1867).

40. *Georgia v. Stanton*, 73 U.S. 50 (1867); Warren, *Supreme Court*, 462–4; *Nation*, May 23, 1867.

41. William L. Barney, *Battleground for the Union* (Englewood Ciffs, N.J., 1990), 250.

42. *Boston Daily Advertiser*, September 2, 1867, quoted in Benedict, *Compromise of Principle*, 255; Barney, *Battleground for the Union*, 255.

43. Benedict, *Compromise of Principle*, 272–5, 284, 288; Barney, *Battleground for the Union*, 255; Foner, *Reconstruction*, 314–5; Miller to W.P.B., December 22, 1867 ("Many thinking men"), box 1, folder 4, SFMP, LC.

44. *Ex Parte McCardle*, 74 U.S. 506, 508 (1869).

45. Ibid.; Warren, *Supreme Court*, 465. The Court agreed to hear McCardle's appeal in *Ex Parte McCardle*, 73 U.S. 318, 320 (1868).

46. Warren, *Supreme Court*, 466; *Congressional Globe*, 40th Cong., 2d sess., 478 et seq.; *Independent*, January 23, 1868 ("The Reconstruction acts"); *Indianapolis Journal*, January 25, 1868 ("lift judicial decisions"); *Chicago Republican*, January 15, 24, 25, 27, 31, 1868; *Springfield Republican*, January, 13, 18, 25, February 1, 1868.

47. Benedict, *Compromise of Principle*, 288–94.

48. Miller to W.P.B., January 19, 1868.

49. Benedict, *Compromise of Principle,* 295–309; Miller to W.P.B., December 22, 1867, box 1, folder 4, SFMP, LC; Michael Les Benedict, *The Impeachment and Trial of Andrew Johnson* (New York, 1973), 26–34; Foner, *Reconstruction,* 314–5, 334–7.

50. Miller to W.P.B., March 1, 1868, box 1, folder 5, SFMP, LC.

51. Benedict, *Compromise of Principle,* 298–9 ("wilted"); Foner, *Reconstruction,* 335–7.

52. Henry D. Ashley, "Matthew Hale Carpenter as a Lawyer," *Green Bag* 6 (1894): 441, 443.

53. *Independent,* March 19, 1868; *Springfield Republican,* March 27, 1868; Warren, *Supreme Court,* 475–8.

54. *Boston Post,* March 19, 1868, quoted in Warren, *Supreme Court,* 480.

55. *Springfield Republican,* March 28, 1868.

56. *Indianapolis Journal,* March 18, 1868.

57. *Ex Parte McCardle,* 74 U.S., at 506, 510–2.

58. Benedict, *Compromise of Principle,* 315.

59. *Texas v. White,* 74 U.S. 700, at 703–7, 734.

60. Ibid., at 708, 709, 711.

61. Warren, *Supreme Court,* 488.

62. Ibid., 490.

63. *Texas v. White,* 74 U.S., at 718, 725–6.

64. Ibid., at 730.

65. Ibid., at 732–6.

66. Ibid., at 737–41.

67. Ibid., at 741.

68. Ibid., at 740; Michael B. Dougan, "Robert Cooper Grier" in *The Oxford Companion to the Supreme Court of the United States,* ed. Kermit Hall (New York, 1992), 349.

69. *Texas v. White,* 74 U.S., at 741.

70. *Congressional Globe,* 41st Cong., 2d sess., 167 et seq., speech of Trumbull, December 16, 1869.

71. Barney, *Battleground for the Union,* 257; Robert M. Goldman, *Reconstruction and Black Suffrage: Losing the Vote in Reese and Cruikshank* (Lawrence, Kans., 2001), 15.

72. Benedict, *Compromise of Principle,* 328–32; Barney, *Battleground for the Union,* 24; Miller to W.P.B., December 22, 1867, box 1, folder 4, SFMP, LC; Goldman, *Reconstruction and Black Suffrage,* 14.

73. Foner, *Reconstruction,* 343; Miller to W.P.B., August 1869, box 1, folder 6, SFMP, LC.

74. Miller to W.P.B., July 30, 1869, box 1, folder 6, SFMP, LC..

75. Robert R. Dykstra, *Bright Radical Star: Black Freedom and White Supremacy on the Hawkeye Frontier* (Cambridge, Mass., 1993), 170, 177, 208–9, 227, 262, 266, 270.

Chapter 7 A New Class That Produces Nothing

1. Miller to W.P.B., March 1, 1868, box 1, folder 5, SFMP, LC.

2. William Pitt Ballinger diary, July 1867, Ballinger Collection, Center for American History, University of Texas at Austin.

3. Miller to W.P.B., July 2, 1866, July 18, 1867, box 1, folder 4, SFMP, LC.

4. *KGC,* July 2, 1868; Miller to W.P.B., December 8, 1866 ("strong possibility"), Miller box 1, folder 2, and November 13, 1868 ("canal in progress"), box 1, folder 5, SFMP, LC.

5. Charles Noble Gregory, *Samuel Freeman Miller* (Iowa City, 1907), 70–1.

6. Keokuk Constitution, quoted in *KGC,* September 24, 1868; Democratic speaker and editor quoted in Robert Dykstra, *Bright Radical Star: Black Freedom and White Supremacy on the Hawkeye Frontier* (Cambridge, Mass., 1993), 225.

7. Miller to W.P.B., August 27, 1868 ("hottest summer"), box 1, folder 5, SFMP, LC; *KGC,* July 8, 1868, August 15, 1868.

8. *KGC,* August 20, 1868.

9. *Riggs v. Johnson County,* 73 U.S. 166, 197 (1868); *Weber v. Lee County,* 73 U.S. 210, 213 (1868).

10. *Riggs v. Johnson County,* at 200 ("evil consequences"), 201 ("no matter how"), 205 ("judicial subtleties").

11. *Butz v. City of Muscatine,* 75 U.S. 575, 576, 587 (1869).

12. Ibid., at 576.

13. Ibid., at 576.

14. Ibid., at 577, 580–1.

15. Miller to W.P.B., June 17, 1869, box 1, folder 6, SFMP, LC.

16. Miller to W.P.B., December 25, 1880, box 2, folder 5, SFMP, LC.

17. *Leffingwell v. Warren,* 67 U.S. 599 (1862); *Butz v. Muscatine,* at 585–7.

18. *Butz v. Muscatine,* at 587. Some of his more notable dissents include: *Olcott v. The Supervisors,* 83 U.S. (16 Wallace) 678 (1873); *Pine Grove Township v. Talcott,* 86 U.S. (19 Wallace) 666 (1874); *Riggs v. Johnson County,* 73 U.S. (6 Wallace)166 (1868); *Butz v. Muscatine,* 75 U.S. (8 Wallace) 575 (1869); *Marsh v. Fulton County,* 77 U.S. (10 Wallace) 676 (1871); *Mercer County v. Hackett,* 68 U.S. (1 Wallace) 83 (1864); *Meyer v. Muscatine,* 68 U.S. (1 Wallace) 384 (1864); *Rogers v. Burlington,* 70 U.S. (3 Wallace) 654 (1866); *Lynde v. Winnebago,* 83 U.S. (16 Wallace) 6 (1873); *Humboldt Township v. Long,* 92 U.S. 642 (1876); *Nugent v. The Supervisors,* 86 U.S. (19 Wallace) 241 (1874); *United States v. County of Clark,* 96 U.S. 211 (1878). On a few occasions Miller was able to carry the day in a municipal bond case. See *Nashville v. Ray,* 86 U.S. (19 Wallace) 468 (1874); *Buchanan v. Litchfield,* 102 U.S. 278 (1880); *Litchfield v. Ballou,* 114 U.S. 190 (1885).

19. Charles Fairman, "Justice Miller and the Mortgaged Generation," *Iowa Law Review* 23 (1938): 351, 356 ("an exemplar"); Howard J. Graham, *Everyman's Constitution: Historical Essays on the Fourteenth Amendment, the "Conspiracy Theory," and American Constitutionalism* (Madison, Wis., 1968), 296; Kevin Christopher Newsom, "Setting Incorporationism Straight: A Reinterpretation of the *Slaughter-House Cases,*" *Yale Law Journal* 109 (2000): 693; *Loan Association v. Topeka,* 87 U.S. 655, 663 ("limitations") (1875). For the opposite view see Richard Aynes, "Charles Fairman, Felix Frankfurter, and the Fourteenth Amendment," *Chicago-Kent Law Review* 70 (1995): 1197, 1212–3 n. 102.

20. Quote taken from the dissent by Justice Clifford in *Loan Association v. Topeka,* 87 U.S., at 655, 669 (1875).

21. Miller to W.P.B., June 17, 1869, box 1, folder 5, and January 13, 1878, box 2, folder 3, SFMP, LC.

22. Miller to W.P.B., April 28, 1878, box 2, folder 3, SFMP, LC.

23. Ibid.

24. Richard Franklin Bensel, *Yankee Leviathan: The Origins of Central State Authority in America*

(New York, 1990), 252–3; Richard Sylla, "Federal Policy, Banking Market Structure, and Capital Mobilization in the United States, 1863–1913," *Journal of Economic History* 29 (December 1969): 657–86; William L. Barney, *Battleground for the Union: The Era of the Civil War and Reconstruction, 1848–1877* (Englewood Cliffs, N.J., 1990), 258.

25. *KGC,* July 1, August 15, and October 10, 1868.

26. Miller to W.P.B., August 27, 1868, box 1, folder 5, SFMP, LC.

27. Miller to W.P.B., November 13, 1868, box 1, folder 5, SFMP, LC.

28. Barney, *Battleground for the Union,* 259. See also Thomas S. Mach, "George Hunt Pendleton, the Ohio Idea, and Political Continuity in Reconstruction America," *Ohio History* 108 (summer–autumn 1988): 125–44.

29. Miller to W.P.B., April 28, 1878, box 2, folder 3, SFMP, LC; Barney, *Battleground for the Union,* 251.

30. *Hepburn v. Griswold,* 75 U.S. 603 (1870); *Legal Tender Cases,* 79 U.S. 457 (1871); Barney, *Battleground for the Union,* 164–5.

31. *Hepburn v. Griswold,* 75 U.S., at 605.

32. Ibid., at 604–6.

33. Gerald T. Dunne, "Legal Tender Cases," in *The Oxford Companion to the Supreme Court of the United States,* ed. Kermit Hall (New York, 1992), 498.

34. *Hepburn v. Griswold,* at 609–11.

35. Ibid., at 614, 623.

36. Ibid., at 606–26.

37. Ibid., at 633.

38. Ibid., at 632–3.

39. Ibid., at 634–5.

40. Ibid., at 634–8.

41. Ibid., at 637–8.

42. Ibid., at 638–9.

43. *Washington Chronicle,* February 12, 1870; *Boston Advertiser,* April 19, 1870.

44. Irwin Unger, *The Greenback Era: A Social and Political History of American Finance, 1865–1879* (Princeton, N.J., 1964), 174–5; Charles Fairman, "Mr. Justice Bradley's Appointment to the Supreme Court and the Legal Tender Cases," *Harvard Law Review* 14 (May 1941): 1131; Bensel, *Yankee Leviathan,* 293; Michael B. Dougan, "William Strong," in *The Oxford Companion to the Supreme Court,* ed. Kermit Hall, 845–6.

45. *American Law Review* 5 (1870) 158, 366; Henry J. Abraham, *Justices and Presidents: A Political History of Appointments to the Supreme Court,* 2d ed. (New York, 1985), 117–9.

46. *Boston Daily Advertiser,* April 12, 1870; Miller to W.P.B., April 21, 1870, box 1, folder 7, SFMP, LC. See also G. Edward White, "Reconstructing the Constitutional Jurisprudence of Salmon P. Chase," *Northern Kentucky Law Review* 21 (fall 1993): 41–116.

47. *Legal Tender Cases,* 79 U.S. 457, 529, 553 (1871).

48. Ibid., at 564.

49. Ibid., at 580, 669, 674.

50. Barney, *Battleground for the Union,* 251, 256.

51. Miller to W.P.B., May 1, 1871, box 1, folder 8, and January 13, 1877, box 2, folder 1, SFMP, LC; *Railroad Company v. County of Otoe,* 83 U.S. 667 (1873); *Olcott v. The Supervisors,* 83 U.S. 678 (1873).

52. Miller to W.P.B., December 8, 1870, box 1, folder 7; June 23, 1872 ("As I should never probably"), box 1, folder 7; October 13, 1875 ("I have been peculiarly"), box 1, folder 11. All in SFMP, LC.

53. Miller to W.P.B., October 24, 1872, box 1, folder 9, SFMP, LC.

Chapter 8 The *Slaughter-House Cases*

1. *New Orleans Daily Picayune*, June 27, 1869; Louisiana Legislature, Act No. 118, March 8, 1869, appears in *Slaughter-House Cases*, 83 U.S. 36 (1873), at 38–43. See also Michael A. Ross, "Justice Miller's Reconstruction: The *Slaughter-House Cases*, Health Codes, and Civil Rights in New Orleans, 1861–1873," *Journal of Southern History* 64 (November 1998): 649–76.

2. John Duffy, "Pestilence in New Orleans" in *The Past as Prelude: New Orleans, 1718–1968*, ed. Hodding Carter (New Orleans, 1968), 107; Paul Kens, *Justice Stephen Field: Shaping Liberty from the Gold Rush to the Gilded Age* (Lawrence, Kans., 1997), 118; Joe Gray Taylor, *Louisiana Reconstructed, 1863–1877* (Baton Rouge, La., 1974), 6; Ronald M. Labbé, "New Light on the Slaughterhouse Monopoly Act of 1869," in *Louisiana's Legal Heritage*, ed. Edward F. Haas (Pensacola, Fla., 1983), 149–50; Oliver Evans, *New Orleans* (New York, 1959), 51 (Audubon quote).

3. *The State of Louisiana, ex rel. S. Belden, Attorney General v. Wm. Fagan, et al.*, 22 La. Ann. 545, 551 (quote) (1870).

4. Testimony of Dr. E. S. Lewis before the Louisiana House of Representatives Special Committee on the Removal of the Slaughterhouses in 1867, quoted in Kens, *Justice Stephen Field*, 118.

5. *State v. Fagan*, 22 La. Ann., at 553; Labbé, "New Light on the Slaughterhouse Monopoly Act of 1869," 150.

6. *State v. Fagan*, at 551; Labbé, "New Light on the Slaughterhouse Monopoly Act of 1869," 150; William Novak, *The People's Welfare: Law and Regulation in Nineteenth-Century America* (Chapel Hill, 1996), 230.

7. Herbert Hovenkamp, *Enterprise and American Law, 1836–1937* (Cambridge, Mass., 1991), 119; Labbé, "New Light on the Slaughterhouse Monopoly Act of 1869," 149–50; Evans, *New Orleans*, 55–56; Duffy, "Pestilence in New Orleans"; Mitchell Franklin, "The Foundations and Meaning of the Slaughterhouse Cases: General Butler, Yellow Fever, and the Slaughter-House Monopoly," *Tulane Law Review* 18 (December 1943): 222–3.

8. John Duffy, *A History of Public Health in New York City, 1866–1966* (New York, 1974), 8, 9, 24, 25, 33, 36, 39, 48.

9. Labbé, "New Light on the Slaughterhouse Monopoly Act of 1869," 145–6, 150–7; *New Orleans Republican*, June 23, 1869; Hovenkamp, *Enterprise and American Law*, 123; Franklin, "Foundations and Meaning of the Slaughterhouse Cases," 34, 225; Dr. R. Delrieu, *Les Abattoirs publics de la Nouvelle-Orléans* (New Orleans, 1869), 17–18; *New Orleans Bee*, July 4, 1869.

10. Labbé, "New Light on the Slaughterouse Monopoly Act of 1869," 158 (quote); Kens, *Justice Stephen Field*, 119.

11. *New Orleans Daily Picayune*, June 6, 1869; *New Orleans Bee*, May 3 and June 21, 1870, February 28, June 2, October 19, 1871, and March 21, 1872. See also: Leo Pfeffer, *This Honorable Court: A History of the United States Supreme Court* (Boston, 1965), 198; Bernard Schwartz, *A History of the Supreme Court* (New York, 1993), 159; Richard C. Cortner, *The Supreme Court and the Second Bill of Rights: The Fourteenth Amendment and the Nationalization of Civil Liberties* (Madison, Wis., 1981),

6; Robert J. Kaczorowski, *The Politics of Judicial Interpretation: The Federal Courts, Department of Justice and Civil Rights* (New York, 1985), 144; Ella Lonn, *Reconstruction in Louisiana* (New York, 1918), 28.

12. "The New Orleans press," historian Herbert Hovenkamp points out, "most of which represented the interests of the Old South, was responsible for the allegations of bribery and corruption, and historians have taken most of their facts at face value from these editorials." Hovenkamp, *Enterprise and American Law, 1836–1937*, 123. See also: Ross, "Justice Miller's Reconstruction," 657 n. 26; James Keith Hogue, "Five New Orleans Street Battles and the Rise and Fall of Radical Reconstruction" (Ph.D. dissertation, Princeton University, 1998), 121–4.

13. The *New Orleans Republican* noted, for example, that in the past the "franchises of the state were granted in the most lavish fashion to gentlemen belonging to the superior race." *New Orleans Republican*, March 12, 1870. The prevalence of corruption in antebellum Louisiana is widely acknowledged. Evans, *New Orleans*, 59; Taylor, *Louisiana Reconstructed*, 49, 82, 201, 251, 258; Kens, *Justice Stephen Field*, 119.

14. Hovenkamp, *Enterprise and American Law*, 119–20 (quote); Evans, *New Orleans*, 62.

15. Labbé, "New Light on the Slaughterhouse Monopoly Act of 1869," 151; Duffy, "Pestilence in New Orleans," 112; Evans, *New Orleans*, 62; Franklin, "Foundations and Meaning of the Slaughterhouse Cases," 221–6.

16. Ted Tunnell, *Crucible of Reconstruction: War, Radicalism, and Race in Louisiana* (Baton Rouge, 1984), 152 (quote); Lonn, *Reconstruction in Louisiana*, 32.

17. Lonn, *Reconstruction in Louisiana*, 32 (quote); Taylor, *Louisiana Reconstructed*, 189–96; Franklin, "Foundations and Meaning of the Slaughterhouse Cases," 58–9; Tunnell, *Crucible of Reconstruction*, 175; Mark W. Summers, *Railroads, Reconstruction, and the Gospel of Prosperity: Aid under the Radical Republicans, 1865–1877* (Princeton, N.J., 1984), 13–5.

18. Lonn, *Reconstruction in Louisiana*, 17–18; Taylor, *Louisiana Reconstructed*, 178, 314–6, 318, 319, 340, 343–5; John Blassingame, *Black New Orleans* (Chicago, 1973), 49–50.

19. Lonn, *Reconstruction in Louisiana*, 17; Labbé, "New Light on the Slaughterhouse Monopoly Act of 1869," 154; *New Orleans Bee*, March 21, 1872.

20. Miller to W.P.B., August 29, 1869, box 1, folder 6, SFMP, LC; Tunnell, *Crucible of Reconstruction*, 104–7; Taylor, *Louisiana Reconstructed*, 106–10; Eric Foner, *Reconstruction: America's Unfinished Revolution, 1863–1877* (New York, 1988), 262–3.

21. Tunnell, *Crucible of Reconstruction*, 107 (quote); Taylor, *Louisiana Reconstructed*, 146–7.

22. *New Orleans Bee*, January 24, 1869; Roger Fischer, "The Post–Civil War Segregation Struggle," in *The Past as Prelude: New Orleans, 1718–1968*, ed. Hodding Carter, 293–4.

23. *New Orleans Commercial Bulletin*, November 17, 1869.

24. *New Orleans Bee*, January 1, 1869, December 23, 1869, January 22, 1870, February 19, 1869, July 14, 1869.

25. Blassingame, *Black New Orleans*, 183; Taylor, *Louisiana Reconstructed*, 211; *New Orleans Daily Picayune*, September 22, 1868; *New Orleans Bee*, February 7, 1869.

26. *New Orleans Bee*, March 20, 1869; April 28, 1870; Tunnell, *Crucible of Reconstruction*, 153, 159.

27. *New Orleans Bee*, March 23, 1869, June 13, 1869 (first two quotations), June 22, 1869 (third quotation), February 28, 1871, October 19, 1871 (last two quotations).

28. *New Orleans Republican*, March 22, 1870.

29. Franklin, "Foundations and Meaning of the Slaughterhouse Cases," Part 2, 225; *New Orleans Bee*, June 22, 1869, June 13, 1869, July 7, 1869 (three quotations from *Bee* in order cited).

30. Robert J. Saunders, *John Archibald Campbell: Southern Moderate, 1811–1889* (Tuscaloosa, Ala., 1997), 186, 187, 226; Franklin, "Foundations and Meaning of the Slaughterhouse Cases," 18.

31. John A. Campbell to his daughter, April 9, 1871, box 11, folder 10, Campbell Family Papers, Southern Historical Collection, University of North Carolina at Chapel Hill.

32. John A. Campbell to Nathan Clifford, June 25, 1871, Clifford Papers, Maine Historical Society (Portland, Maine); Ross, "Justice Miller's Reconstruction," 665–6.

33. *Slaughter-House Cases,* 83 U.S. 36 (1873) at 45, 48, 60.

34. Ibid., at 51, 53.

35. Miller to W.P.B., March 18 and October 15, 1877, box 2, folder 2, SFMP, LC.

36. *Slaughter-House Cases,* 83 U.S., at 78–9.

37. Akhil Reed Amar, "The Bill of Rights and the Fourteenth Amendment," *Yale Law Journal* 101 (1992): 1259.

38. For critics of Miller's position on the privileges or immunities clause, see: Michael K. Curtis, "Resurrecting the Privileges and Immunities Clause and Revising the *Slaughter-House Cases* without Exhuming *Lochner:* Individual Rights and the Fourteenth Amendment," *Boston College Law Review* 38 (December 1996): 1–106; Michael K. Curtis, *No State Shall Abridge: The Fourteenth Amendment and the Bill of Rights* (Durham, N.C., 1990), 91; Pamela Brandwein, *Reconstructing Reconstruction: The Supreme Court and the Production of Historical Truth* (Durham, N.C., 1999); Akhil Reed Amar, *The Bill of Rights: Creation and Reconstruction* (New Haven, Conn., 1998); Richard L. Aynes, "On Misreading John Bingham and the Fourteenth Amendment," *Yale Law Journal* 103 (October 1993): 57–104; Schwartz, *A History of the Supreme Court,* 159; Laurence Tribe, *American Constitutional Law* (Mineola, N.Y., 1978), 415–26, 567–9; George P. Fletcher, *Our Secret Constitution: How Lincoln Redefined American Democracy* (New York, 2001), 130. For the view that the Fourteenth Amendment did not incorporate the Bill of Rights, see: Charles Fairman, "Does the Fourteenth Amendment Incorporate the Bill of Rights?" *Stanford Law Review* 2 (1949): 5–139; Felix Frankfurter's concurring opinion in *Adamson v. California,* 332 U.S. 46, 59–68 (1947); Raoul Berger, *Government by Judiciary: The Transformation of the Fourteenth Amendment* (Cambridge, Mass., 1977), chap. 8; George C. Thomas III, "When Constitutional Worlds Collide: Resurrecting the Framers' Bill of Rights and Criminal Procedure," *Michigan Law Review* 100 (October 2001): 145–233.

39. Richard L. Aynes, "Constricting the Law of Freedom: Justice Miller, the Fourteenth Amendment, and the *Slaughter-House Cases,*" *Chicago-Kent Law Review* 70 (1994): 627–88; Julius J. Marke, "The Banded Butchers and the Supreme Court: Herein of the Slaughterhouse Cases," *New York University Law Center Bulletin* 12 (spring 1964): 8, 10; Pfeffer, *This Honorable Court,* 199–200; Russell W. Galloway, *Justice for All? The Rich and Poor in Supreme Court History, 1790–1990* (Durham, N.C., 1991).

40. Xi Wang, *The Trial of Democracy: Black Suffrage and Northern Republicans, 1860–1910* (Athens, Ga., 1997), 121–4; Robert G. McCloskey, *The American Supreme Court,* 2d ed., revised and expanded by Sanford Levinson (Chicago, 1994), 81; Broadus Mitchell and Louise Mitchell, *A Biography of the Constitution of the United States: Its Origin, Formation, Adoption, Interpretation* (New York, 1964), 289–90; Aynes, "On Misreading John Bingham," 57–104; Michael W. McConnell, "The Forgotten Constitutional Moment," *Constitutional Commentary* 11 (1994): 115, 133; Loren Miller, *The Petitioners: The Story of the Supreme Court of the United States and the Negro* (New York, 1966), 105; Curtis, *No State Shall Abridge,* 177–8; Lou Falkner Williams, *The Great South Carolina Ku Klux Klan Trials, 1871–1872* (Athens, Ga., 1996), 132–4.

41. Amar, *The Bill of Rights,* 213 (quote); Fletcher, *Our Secret Constitution,* 130; Robert J. Kaczo-rowski, "The Chase Court and Fundamental Rights: A Watershed in American Constitutionalism," *Northern Kentucky Law Review* 21 (fall 1993): 151–202; Kaczorowski, *The Politics of Judicial Interpre-tation,* 143, 159; Loren P. Beth, "The Slaughter-House Cases—Revisited," *Louisiana Law Review* 23 (1963): 487, 494, 501; Peter Irons, *A People's History of the Supreme Court* (New York, 1999), 196–201.

42. *Slaughter-House Cases,* 83 U.S., at 64, 71 (quote).

43. Michael A. Ross, "Hill-Country Doctor: The Early Life and Career of Supreme Court Jus-tice Samuel Freeman Miller in Kentucky, 1816–1849," *Filson Club History Quarterly* 71 (October 1997): 430–5, 445–51; Wendy E. Parmet, "From Slaughter-House to Lochner: The Rise and Fall of the Constitutionalization of Public Health," *American Journal of Legal History* 40 (October 1996): 476–505.

44. *KGC,* November 5, 1858, October 24, 1859, August 4, 1860, June 12, 1862, June 21, 1862, Decem-ber 9 ("porkopolis") and 17, 1862.

45. Miller to W.P.B., April 9, 1871, box 1, folder 1, SFMP, LC.

46. *Slaughter-House Cases,* 83 U.S., at 36, 64 (1873).

47. Ibid., at 36, 45.

48. Ross, "Hill-Country Doctor," 430–62; Miller to WPB, July 30, 1869, box 1, folder 6, SFMP, LC.

49. *Slaughter-House Cases,* 83 U.S., at 96, 101.

50. Ibid., at 97.

51. Stephen J. Field to Matthew Deady, April 20, 1868 ("colored brethren"), Matthew Deady Papers, Oregon Historical Society, Portland; *Slaughter-House Cases,* 83 U.S. at 88, 89, 93, 96, 101, 104, 105, 110; Charles W. McCurdy, "Justice Field and the Jurisprudence of Government-Business Relations: Some Parameters of Laissez-Faire Constitutionalism, 1863–1897," *Journal of American History* 61 (March 1975): 1000; Kens, *Justice Stephen Field,* 118–28; Carl B. Swisher, *Stephen J. Field: Craftsman of the Law* (Washington, D.C., 1930), 376–83, 418–20, 429; Howard Jay Graham, *Every-man's Constitution: Historical Essays on the Fourteenth Amendment, the "Conspiracy Theory," and American Constitutionalism* (Madison, Wis., 1968), 132.

52. *Slaughter-House Cases,* 83 U.S., at 111–24, 122; John A. Scott, "Justice Bradley's Evolving Con-cept of the Fourteenth Amendment from the *Slaughter-House Cases* to the *Civil Rights Cases,*" *Rutg-ers Law Review* 25 (summer 1971): 552–69.

53. *Slaughter-House Cases,* 83 U.S. at 81.

54. Ibid., at 126, 128.

55. Ibid., at 78, 81, 82.

56. Beth, "The Slaughter-House Cases—Revisited," 487, 490 (quote); Kaczorowski, *Politics of Judicial Interpretation,* 143, 159. Some scholars and commentators have countered this argument by claiming that Miller actually intended to incorporate the Bill of Rights using the privileges or im-munities clause (or that he at least left open the possibility that many of those rights could be incor-porated). These arguments are intriguing but inconclusive due to the fact that Miller never in any of his subsequent opinions, public speeches, or extant private correspondence said that that was what he intended in *Slaughter-House.* See: Kevin Christopher Newsom, "Setting Incorporationism Straight: A Reinterpretation of the *Slaughter-House* Cases," *Yale Law Journal* 109 (2000): 643–744; Robert C. Palmer, "The Parameters of Constitutional Reconstruction: *Slaughter-House, Cruikshank,* and the Fourteenth Amendment," *University of Illinois Law Review* 3 (1984): 739–70; Bryan Wilden-thal, "The Lost Compromise: Reassessing the Early Understanding in Court and Congress on

Incorporation of the Bill of Rights in the Fourteenth Amendment," *Ohio State Law Journal* 61 (2000): 1051–74.

57. Michael Les Benedict, "Preserving Federalism: Reconstruction and the Waite Court," *Supreme Court Review* (1978): 39–62; G. Edward White, "Reconstructing the Constitutional Jurisprudence of Salmon P. Chase," *Northern Kentucky Law Review* 21 (fall 1993): 41–116; Loren Beth, *The Development of the American Constitution* (New York, 1971), 191–9; Swisher, *Stephen J. Field*, 420; Cortner, *The Supreme Court and the Second Bill of Rights*, 9, 10; Parmet, "From Slaughter-House to Lochner," 474–505.

58. J. Taylor, *Louisiana Reconstructed*, 503; Franklin, "Foundation and Meaning of the Slaughterhouse Cases," 58, 59; Tunnell, *Crucible of Reconstruction*, 210. For a good general history of the last years of Reconstruction, see Michael Les Benedict, *The Fruits of Victory: Alternatives in Restoring the Union, 1865–1877*, 2d ed. (New York, 1986), 53–63.

59. *Slaughter-House Cases*, 83 U.S., at 81.

60. See the remarks of Senators Morton and Howe in the *Congressional Record*, 43d Cong., 1st sess., 4147, 4148, 4149 (Senator Howe's remarks are on p. 4149); *Congressional Record*, 43d Cong., 1st sess., Appendix, 360–1 (first and fourth quotations from Senator Morton are on p. 361; second and third quotations on p. 360) (May 21–2, 1874).

61. *Slaughter-House Cases*, 83 U.S., at 68, 70.

62. Miller to W.P.B., January 11, 1866, box 1, folder 2, SFMP, LC.

63. Miller to W.P.B., August 29, 1869, box 1, folder 6, SFMP, LC.

64. Miller to W.P.B., June 29, 1879, box 2, folder 4, SFMP, LC.

Chapter 9 Shattered Dreams

1. *Washington Republic*, July 18, 1880 ("well-contented"), 341; Charles Fairman, *Mr. Justice Miller and the Supreme Court, 1862–1890* (Cambridge, Mass., 1939), 5 ("fortunate he was born poor"), 428; Profile of Stephen J. Field from a news clipping in a scrapbook of Justice Harlan, John Marshall Harlan Papers, Special Collections, University of Louisville, Louisville, Ky.

2. Ballinger diary, October 8, 1871, August 25, 1883, Ballinger Family Papers, Center for American History, University of Texas at Austin.

3. Miller to W.P.B., February 6, 1867, box 1, folder 4, SFMP, LC.

4. Kathryn Allamong Jacob, *Capital Elites: High Society in Washington, D.C., after the Civil War* (Washington, D.C., 1995), 218; Madeline Dahlgren, *Etiquette of Social Life in Washington* (Lancaster, Pa., 1873), 121.

5. Randolph Keim, *Society in Washington: Its Noted Men, Accomplished Women, Established Customs, and Notable Events* (Harrisburg, Pa., 1887), 122–4 ("Mrs. Miller"); Jacob, *Capital Elites*, 69. William Pitt Ballinger listed a number of the Millers' dinner guests in his diary. Ballinger diary, December 8 and 14, 1877.

6. E. N. Chapin, *American Court Gossip; or, Life at the National Capitol* (Marshalltown, Iowa, 1887), 249.

7. Keim, *Society in Washington*, 120–1; Ballinger diary, April 4, 1886.

8. Miller to W.P.B., November 6, 1870, box 1, folder 7, SFMP, LC; Ballinger diary, October 14, 1871.

9. Miller to W.P.B., July 27, 1873, box 1, folder 9, SFMP, LC; Joseph P. Bradley to his wife, May 16, 1873, Joseph P. Bradley Papers, New Jersey Historical Society, Newark.

10. Miller to W.P.B., October 18, 1870, box 1, folder 7, and July 27, 1873, box 1, folder 9, SFMP, LC.

11. *Des Moines Daily Republican,* May 13, 1873; *KGC,* May 13, 1873.

12. Miller to W.P.B., January 18, 1874, reprinted in Fairman, *Mr. Justice Miller,* 265; *Washington National Republican,* November 10, 1873 (quote); Ben Perley Poore, *Perley's Reminiscences of Sixty Years in the National Metropolis,* vol. 2 (Philadelphia, 1886), 299.

13. Miller to W.P.B., Dec 10, 1873, box 1, folder 10, SFMP, LC; Jacob, *Capital Elites,* 104–6; James Whyte, *The Uncivil War: Washington during Reconstruction, 1865–1878* (New York, 1958), 192; Fairman, *Mr. Justice Miller,* 257–9.

14. *Washington Chronicle,* January 11, 1874; Miller to W.P.B., January 18, 1874, box 1, folder 10, SFMP, LC; Fairman, *Mr. Justice Miller,* 264.

15. Stephen Field to Matthew Deady, March 16, 1874, Matthew Deady Papers, Oregon Historical Society, Portland; Miller to W.P.B., March 21, 1874 ("mediocre"), box 1, folder 10, and December 5, 1875, box 1, folder 11, SFMP, LC.

16. Miller to W.P.B., March 7, 1875, box 1, folder 11, SFMP, LC.

17. Charles Hurd, *Washington Cavalcade* (New York, 1948), 108; Poore, *Perley's Reminiscences,* 94, 261–3, 269; Carl Abbott, *Political Terrain: Washington, D.C., from Tidewater Town to Global Metropolis* (Chapel Hill, N.C., 1999), 71–3; Jacob, *Capital Elites,* 169.

18. Fairman, *Mr. Justice Miller,* 427 (Miller quote); Keim, *Society in Washington,* 217 ("The seat of government").

19. Ballinger diary, October 10, 1871; Poore, *Perley's Reminiscences,* 269; Jacob, *Capital Elites,* 25.

20. Irwin Unger, *The Greenback Era: A Social and Political History of American Finance, 1865–1879* (Princeton, N.J., 1964), 213–5; William L. Barney, *Battleground for the Union: The Era of the Civil War and Reconstruction, 1848–1877* (Englewood Cliffs, N.J., 1990), 303–6; Eric Foner, *Reconstruction: America's Unfinished Revolution, 1863–1877* (New York, 1988), 512–3.

21. Miller to W.P.B., April 28, 1878, box 2, folder 3, SFMP, LC. See also: Gretchen Ritter, *Goldbugs and Greenbacks: The Antimonopoly Tradition and the Politics of Finance in America* (New York, 1997), 37; Barney, *Battleground for the Union,* 304, 312–3.

22. *The Mayor v. Ray,* 86 U.S. 468 (1874).

23. Ibid., at 476, 478.

24. Miller to W.P.B., December 13, 1874, quoted in Fairman, *Mr. Justice Miller,* 231.

25. *The Mayor v. Ray,* at 478.

26. *Humboldt Township v. Long,* 92 U.S. 642 (1876); *Town of Coloma v. Eaves,* 92 U.S. 484 (1876); *Town of Venice v. Murdock,* 92 U.S. 494 (1876); *Town of Genoa v. Woodruff et al.,* 92 U.S. 502 (1876); *County of Moultrie v. Rockingham Ten-Cent Savings-Bank,* 92 U.S. 631 (1876); *Marcy v. Township of Oswego,* 92 U.S. 637 (1876).

27. *Town of Coloma v. Eaves,* 92 U.S., at 485.

28. Ibid., at 485, 487, 488.

29. *Town of Venice v. Murdock,* at 92 U.S., at 497, 498, 501, 502.

30. *Humboldt Township v. Long,* 92 U.S., at 648.

31. Ibid., at 642, 647, 649, 650–1.

32. Miller to W.P.B., August 27, 1868, box 1, folder 5, SFMP, LC.

33. *Barton v. Barbour,* 104 U.S. 126, 137 (1881); *Sawyer v. Hoag,* 84 U.S. 610 (1873); Stephen J. Field to Matthew Deady, May 22, 1888 ("He was in principle"), Deady Papers, Oregon Historical Society, Portland. See also Foner, *Reconstruction,* 512; Fairman, *Mr. Justice Miller,* 237–49.

34. *Woodson v. Murdock et al.,* 89 U.S. 351 (1874).

35. Ibid., at 371.

36. Ibid., at 376, 380, 381.

37. Miller to W.P.B., December 5, 1875, box 1, folder 11, SFMP, LC.

38. Ritter, *Goldbugs and Greenbacks,* 29–37; Unger, *The Greenback Era,* 235–44.

39. Miller to W.P.B., March 29, 1875, box 1, folder 11, SFMP, LC.

40. Miller to W.P.B., October 28, 1877, box 2, folder 2, SFMP, LC; Ritter, *Greenbacks and Goldbugs,* 41; Barney, *Battleground for the Union,* 324.

41. Whyte, *The Uncivil War,* 191–2; Jacob, *Capital Elites,* 108.

42. Miller to W.P.B., March 29, 1875 (quote), box 1, folder 11, SFMP, LC ; Fairman, *Mr. Justice Miller,* 427; Barney, *Battleground for the Union,* 328. For evidence of Justice Field accepting railroad passes from Coliss Huntington, see his letters to Judge Matthew Deady, May 19, 1876, and May 14, 1881, Deady Papers, Oregon Historical Society, Portland. Field's investments in mines and the New York Elevated Railway—run by his brother Cyrus—are well documented in his letters to his brother. See, for example, Stephen J. Field to Cyrus Field, June 25, 1861, Field Papers, New York Public Library, Special Collections. See also George W. Barge, *The Free Pass Bribery System: Showing How the Railroads, through the Free Pass Bribery System, Procure the Government away from the People* (Lincoln, Neb., 1905), xi, 41.

43. Miller to W.P.B., July 26, 1876 ("more than any other"), box 2, folder 1, SFMP, LC; Poore, *Perley's Reminiscences,* 212; Norman Tutorow, *James Gillespie Blaine and the Presidency: A Documentary Study and Source Book* (New York, 1989), 1–8, 45–51, 107, 186, 202, 278; Gail Hamilton, *Biography of James G. Blaine* (Norwich, Conn., 1899), 432; Edward Stanwood, *James Gillespie Blaine* (New York, 1905), 206–7; John H. Landis, *Life and Speeches of James Gillespie Blaine* (Lancaster, Pa., 1884), 77, 78 ("already rich"), 90; George Alfred Townsend, *Events at the National Capital and the Campaign of 1876* (Hartford, Conn., 1876), 407–8, 416.

44. Townsend, *Events at the National Capital,* 407–8, 416; Miller to W.P.B., July 26, 1876 ("rotten railroads"), box 2, folder 1, SFMP, LC; Foner, *Reconstruction,* 571.

45. Miller to W.P.B., December 25, 1877, quoted in Fairman, *Mr. Justice Miller,* 285.

46. C. Vann Woodward, *Reunion and Reaction: The Compromise of 1877 and the End of Reconstruction* (New York, 1951), 8–10, 182, 188–96, 239; Charles Fairman, *Five Justices and the Electoral Commission of 1877,* in *Oliver Wendell Holmes Devise History of the Supreme Court of the United States,* supp. to vol. 7 (New York, 1988); Michael Les Benedict, "Southern Democrats in the Crisis of 1876–1877: A Reconsideration of *Reunion and Reaction,*" *Journal of Southern History* 46 (November 1980): 497, 512–6; Sean Dennis Cashman, *America in the Gilded Age: From the Death of Lincoln to the Rise of Theodore Roosevelt* (New York, 1984), 232.

47. Miller to W.P.B., June 22, 1877, box 2, folder 2, SFMP, LC.

48. Miller to W.P.B., October 28, 1877, box 2, folder 1, and June 10, 1880, box 2, folder 5, SFMP, LC; Ballinger diary, April 4, 1886.

49. Miller quote in Fairman, *Mr. Justice Miller,* 427; Miller to W.P.B., May 14, 1879, box 2, folder 4; June 29, 1879, box 2, folder 4; October 31, 1879, box 2, folder 4, SFMP, LC.

50. Miller to W.P.B., February 17, 1880, box 2, folder 5, SFMP, LC.

51. *Chicago, Burlington, & Quincy Railroad v. Iowa*, 94 U.S. 155 (1877); *Munn v. Illinois*, 94 U.S. 113 (1877); *Chicago, Burlington, & Quincy R.R. Co. v. Cutts*, 94 U.S. 155 (1877); *Peik v. Chicago & Northwestern Ry. Co.*, 94 U.S. 164 (1877); *Chicago, Milwaukee & St. Paul R.R. Co. v. Ackley*, 94 U.S. 179 (1877); *Winona & St. Peter Co. v. Blake*, 94 U.S. 180 (1877); *Stone v. Wisconsin*, 94 U.S. 181 (1877). See also: Ritter, *Greenbacks and Goldbugs*, 51; Barney, *Battleground for the Union*, 310–1; George H. Miller, *Railroads and the Granger Laws* (Madison, Wis., 1971), 187–93; Edwin W. Sigmund, "The Granger Cases: 1877 or 1876?" *American Historical Review* 58 (April 1953): 571–4.

52. *Munn v. Illinois*, 94 U.S. 113 (1877); *Chicago Burlington & Quincy Railroad v. Cutts*, 94 U.S. 155 (1877); *Peik v. Chicago & Northwestern Railway*, 94 U.S. 164 (1877); *Chicago, Milwaukee & St. Paul Railroad Company v. Ackley*, 94 U.S. 179 (1877); *Winona & St. Peter Railroad Company v. Blake*, 94 U.S. 180 (1877); *Stone v. Wisconsin*, 94 U.S. 181 (1877). See also Paul Kens, *Justice Stephen Field: Shaping Liberty from the Gold Rush to the Gilded Age* (Lawrence, Kans., 1997), 155.

53. Howard Jay Graham, "Justice Field and the Fourteenth Amendment," *Yale Law Journal* 52 (1943): 852; Charles Warren, *The Supreme Court in United States History*, vol. 2, (Boston, 1937), 577–8; Kens, *Justice Stephen Field*, 164–7, 257.

54. *Munn v. Illinois*, 94 U.S., at 134.

55. Ibid., at 140.

56. William L. Barney, *The Passage of the Republic: An Interdisciplinary History of Nineteenth-Century America* (New York, 1987), 386.

57. *Davidson v. New Orleans*, 96 U.S. 97 (1878).

58. Ibid., at 103, 104.

59. Ibid., at 104.

60. Ibid., at 102, 104, 105.

61. Ibid.

62. Ibid., at 107.

63. See, for example, *County of Morgan v. Illinois*, 103 U.S. 498 (1880).

64. In 1877, for example, Miller dissented in a case where the Court ruled that a state legislature could pass a law that retroactively cured a defect in a bond's issuance. But three years later, Miller, having recognized that the die was cast, failed to dissent in a similar case. See Miller's dissent in *County of Warren v. Marcy*, 97 U.S. 96 (1877); *Thomas v. Perrine*, 103 U.S. 806 (1880). For examples of other cases where Miller acquiesced in the majority decision in a bond case, see *County of Jasper v. Ballou*, 103 U.S. 745 (1880); *County of Clay v. Society for Savings*, 104 U.S. 579 (1881).

65. *Murray v. Charleston*, 96 U.S. 432, 433, 435, 444 (1878).

66. Ibid., at 438.

67. Ibid., at 432, 444, 449.

68. Ibid., at 449.

69. *Hartman v. Greenhow*, 102 U.S. 672 (1881).

70. Ibid., at 686. For examples of cases where Miller argued that the state has no power to bargain away its taking power, see: *Washington v. Rouse*, 8 Wallace 439 (1869); *Pacific Railroad Company v. Maguire*, 20 Wallace 36 (1874).

71. *Williams v. Louisiana*, 103 U.S. 637 (1880). See also: *Durkee v. Board of Liquidation*, 103 U.S. 646 (1880); *Railroad Company v. Falconer*, 103 U.S. 821 (1880); *Smith v. McCullough*, 104 U.S. 25 (1881).

72. *Poindexter v. Greenhow*, 114 U.S. 270 (1885). Miller dissented in *Poindexter* and argued that the Eleventh Amendment overrode the contract clause; *Louisiana v. Jumel*, 107 U.S. 711, 733 (Field quote) (1883).

73. *New York Times*, March 28, 1872; Fairman, *Mr. Justice Miller*, 299.

74. Miller to W.P.B., April 28, 1878, box 2, folder 4, SFMP, LC. For discussions of westerners' stands on silver, see Ritter, *Greenbacks and Goldbugs*, 51, 66–70, 168; Unger, *The Greenback Era*, 230–2; Elmer Ellis, "The Silver Republicans in the Election of 1896," *Mississippi Valley Historical Review* 18 (1932): 519–34.

75. Quote by J. S. Clarkson, editor of the *Des Moines Register*, found in Edward Stiles, *Recollections and Sketches of Notable Lawyers and Public Men of Early Iowa* (Des Moines, 1916), 178; Miller to W.P.B., June 10, 1880 ("prepared to offer my name"), box 2, folder 5, and May 9, 1883, box 2, folder 8, SFMP, LC.

76. Miller to W.P.B., May 27, 1883, box 2, folder 8, SFMP, LC; Ballinger diary, August 25, 1883 (Corkhill quote).

77. Ibid.

78. Miller to W.P.B., June 15, 1884, box 2, folder 9, SFMP, LC.

79. Miller to W.P.B., October 8, 1886, box 2, folder 11, SFMP, LC; Fairman, *Mr. Justice Miller*, 14 n. 22.

80. Miller to W.P.B., November 23, 1884, box 2, folder 9, and January 18, 1885, box 2, folder 9, SFMP, LC. For an analysis of the campaign and Blaine's positions, see Cashman, *America in the Gilded Age*, 260–1.

Chapter 10 Danger from Above and Below

1. James W. Ely, *The Chief Justiceship of Melville W. Fuller, 1888–1910* (Columbia, S.C., 1995), 25 ("No rising sun for me"), 27, 31; Willard L. King, *Melville Weston Fuller: Chief Justice of the United States, 1888–1910* (New York, 1950), 125 ("Oh, but there were"), 127; John V. Orth, "Melville Weston Fuller" in *The Oxford Companion to the Supreme Court*, ed. Kermit Hall (New York, 1992), 320–1.

2. The Field Papers in the New York Public Library contain letters that discuss the justice's machinations with Huntington, his various investments, and payments to him from his wealthy brother. See, for example, Stephen J. Field to Cyrus Field, May 29, 1879, June 25, 1881 ("moderate fortune"), June 29, 1883, Field Papers, New York Public Library Special Collections. For the report of Field socializing with Huntington and Vanderbilt, see *New York Saturday Journal*, April 13, 1880. Other quotes found in: Field to Matthew Deady, July 25, 1884 ("incapacity to succeed"), April 8, 1885 ("nihilistic element" and "contest"), Matthew Deady Papers, Oregon Historical Society, Portland. See also Paul Kens, *Justice Stephen Field: Shaping Liberty from the Gold Rush to the Gilded Age* (Lawrence, Kans., 1997), 226, 266–75.

3. Samuel Freeman Miller, "The Conflict in the Country between Socialism and Organized Society," reprinted in the appendix of Charles Noble Gregory, *Samuel Freeman Miller* (Iowa City, Iowa, 1907), 158–70.

4. Ibid., 165–7.

5. Ibid., 158, 162, 168.

6. Ibid., 158 ("selfish creature"), 159 ("Indeed there is no doubt"), 160 ("either by acquisition of property"), 161 ("there were no public"), 162 ("perfect equality of laziness").

7. Ibid., 163–4.

8. Ibid., 167.

9. Ibid., 169–70. See also Miller to W.P.B., October 15, 1885, box 2, folder 10, and May 30, 1885, box 2, folder 10, SFMP, LC.

10. *United States v. Cruikshank,* 92 U.S. 542, 553–6 (1875); *The Civil Rights Cases,* 109 U.S. 3 (1883).

11. For a more detailed description of the tragic events in Grant Parish, see Robert M. Goldman, *Reconstruction and Black Suffrage: Losing the Vote in Reese and Cruikshank* (Lawrence, Kans., 2001), 44–59; Joel M. Sipress, "From the Barrel of a Gun: The Politics of Murder in Grant Parish," *Louisiana History* 42 (2001): 303–21.

12. *United States v. Cruikshank,* 92 U.S, at 554.

13. Ibid., at 542, 553–6. The Court issued a similarly narrow decision in *United States v. Reese,* in which the justices declared some portions of the Enforcement Acts to be unconstitutional while at the same time explicitly confirming the federal government's authority to protect black voters from discrimination with properly drawn legislation. See *United States v. Reese et al.,* 92 U.S. 214 (1876); Goldman, *Reconstruction and Black Suffrage,* 60–107.

14. *The Civil Rights Cases,* 109 U.S. 3 (1883).

15. *Ex Parte Yarborough,* 110 U.S. 651–6 (1883); Goldman, *Reconstruction and Black Suffrage,* 113.

16. *Ex Parte Yarborough,* 110 U.S., at 651–6, 658.

17. Ibid., at 651–6, 658.

18. For other examples of the Court continuing to uphold federal authority under the Enforcement Acts, see *Ex Parte Clarke,* 100 U.S. 399; *Ex Parte Siebold,* 100 U.S. 371 (1879).

19. *Ex Parte Yarborough,* 110 U.S., at 657, 666–7.

20. Miller to W.P.B., November 23, 1884, box 2, folder 9, SFMP, LC.

21. *James v. Bowman,* 190 U.S. 127 (1903); Goldman, *Reconstruction and Black Suffrage,* 123, 134.

22. For discussions of the growth of law schools, corporate law firms, and the class of corporate attorneys generally, see: Lawrence M. Friedman, *A History of American Law* (New York, 1973), 525, 535, 549, 552–5; Wayne K. Hobson, *The American Legal Profession and the Organizational Society, 1890–1930* (New York, 1896), 76, 90–1, 104, 108, 112, 114, 141–2, 165; Gerard W. Gawalt, "The Impact of Industrialization on the Legal Profession of Massachusetts, 1870–1890," in *The New High Priests: Lawyers in Post–Civil War America,* ed. Gerard W. Gawalt (Westport, Conn., 1984), 97–124; Kermit L. Hall, "Introduction," in The Legal Profession: Major Historical Interpretations, ed. Kermit L. Hall (New York, 1987), xiii–xiv.

23. *Davidson v. New Orleans,* 96 U.S. 97, 103, 104 (1878).

24. *Mugler v. Kansas,* 123 U.S. 623, 661 (1887). In 1886, Miller also joined the majority in *Santa Clara v. Southern Pacific Railroad Company,* 118 U.S. 394, 396 (1886), in which the Court ruled that corporations were "persons" within the meaning of the Fourteenth Amendment.

25. *Chicago, Milwaukee and St. Paul Railway Company v. Minnesota,* 134 U.S. 418, 445 (1890).

26. Ibid., at 452–9.

27. Ibid., at 458–61.

28. *Lochner v. New York,* 198 U.S. 45 (1905). The doctrine of "liberty of contract" was introduced seven years after Miller's death in *Allgeyer v. Louisiana,* 165 U.S. 578 (1897).

29. For a study of Lincoln's economic ideology, see Gabor Boritt, *Lincoln and the Economics of the American Dream* (Memphis, Tenn., 1978). For a discussion of Field's use of Jacksonian rhetoric to defend laissez-faire jurisprudence, see Kens, *Justice Stephen Field,* 266–74.

30. Miller to W.P.B., November 13, 1868, box 1, folder 5, October 31, 1869, box 1, folder 6, SFMP, LC.

31. Miller to W.P.B., February 13, 1887, box 2, folder 11 ("The Chief Justice"), September 5, 1880 ("idleness of wealth"), box 2, folder 5, SFMP, LC.

32. Miller to W.P.B., May 16, 1886, box 2, folder 11 (Lida); July 18, 1886, February 13, 1887 ("75 or 80 people"), September 22, 1878, box 2, folder 3 (Cornell), SFMP, LC.

33. Miller to W.P.B., May 30, 1885, box 2, folder 10, SFMP, LC.

34. David N. Atkinson, *Leaving the Bench: Supreme Court Justices at the End* (Lawrence, Kans., 1999), 65 (quote).

35. Gregory, *Samuel Freeman Miller,* 58.

36. Ibid., 62–3; Charles Fairman, *Mr. Justice Miller and the Supreme Court, 1862–1890* (Cambridge, Mass., 1939), 431.

37. *KGC,* October 18, 1890.

SELECTED BIBLIOGRAPHY

Manuscripts

BANCROFT LIBRARY, UNIVERSITY OF CALIFORNIA AT BERKELEY
Stephen J. Field Collection

THE CENTER FOR AMERICAN HISTORY, UNIVERSITY OF TEXAS AT AUSTIN
Ballinger Family Papers

FILSON CLUB HISTORICAL SOCIETY, LOUISVILLE, KY.
Charles Lanman Papers
Marshall Family Papers

KORNHAUSER HEALTH SCIENCES LIBRARY, UNIVERSITY OF LOUISVILLE,
LOUISVILLE, KY.
Yandell Family Papers

LIBRARY OF CONGRESS, MANUSCRIPT DIVISION, WASHINGTON, D.C.
Salmon P. Chase Papers
Melville Weston Fuller Papers
Abraham Lincoln Papers
Samuel Freeman Miller Papers
Franklin Pierce Manuscripts
Benjamin Wade Manuscripts
Morrison R. Waite Papers

MAINE HISTORICAL SOCIETY, PORTLAND
Nathan Clifford Papers

NEW JERSEY HISTORICAL SOCIETY, NEWARK
Joseph P. Bradley Papers

NEW YORK HISTORICAL SOCIETY, NEW YORK CITY
Thomas J. Durant Papers

NEW YORK PUBLIC LIBRARY, SPECIAL COLLECTIONS
Cyrus W. Field Papers

OREGON HISTORICAL SOCIETY, PORTLAND
Matthew Deady Papers

SOUTHERN HISTORICAL COLLECTION, UNIVERSITY OF NORTH CAROLINA
AT CHAPEL HILL
Campbell Family Papers
John Rogers Clarke Papers
Henry Clay Warmoth Papers

SPECIAL COLLECTIONS AND MANUSCRIPTS, PRINCETON UNIVERSITY,
PRINCETON, N.J.
William Worth Belknap Papers

SPECIAL COLLECTIONS AND MANUSCRIPTS, YALE UNIVERSITY, NEW
HAVEN, CONN.
Field Family Papers

STATE HISTORICAL SOCIETY OF IOWA, DES MOINES
Samuel Kirkwood Papers

STATE HISTORICAL SOCIETY OF IOWA, IOWA CITY
Caleb Forbes Davis Collection
R. M. Reynolds Collection

STATE HISTORICAL SOCIETY OF MISSOURI, COLUMBIA
Silas Woodson Papers

TRANSYLVANIA UNIVERSITY ARCHIVES, LEXINGTON, KY.
Samuel Miller Dissertation

UNIVERSITY OF LOUISVILLE SCHOOL OF LAW, LAW LIBRARY
John Marshall Harlan Papers

Newspapers and Magazines

Baltimore Sun
Boston Daily Advertiser
Burlington (Iowa) Hawkeye
Chicago Tribune
(Des Moines) Daily State Register
Davenport (Iowa) Gazette

Harper's Weekly
Indianapolis Daily Herald
(Burlington) Iowa State Gazette
Keokuk (Iowa) Dispatch
Keokuk (Iowa) Gate City
Lexington (Ky.) Herald
New Orleans Bee
New Orleans Commercial Bulletin
New Orleans Daily Picayune
New Orleans Republican
New York Times
New York Tribune
New York World
Philadelphia Press
Richmond (Va.) Enquirer
St. Louis Democrat
St. Louis Republican
Washington Daily Globe

Published Primary Sources

Angle, Paul, ed. *Created Equal? The Complete Lincoln-Douglas Debates of 1858*. Chicago, 1958.

Boutwell, George. *Reminiscences of Sixty Years in Public Service*. New York, 1902.

Chapin, E. N. *American Court Gossip, or Life at the National Capitol*. Marshalltown, Iowa, 1887.

Clemens, Orion. *City of Keokuk in 1856: A View of the City. . . .* Keokuk, Iowa, 1856.

———. *Keokuk Directory and Business Mirror for the Year 1857*. Keokuk, Iowa, 1857.

Cooke, John Esten. "Remarks on Cholera, As It Appeared in Lexington in June 1833." *Transylvania Journal of Medicine and the Associate Sciences*. 6 (July 1833): 7.

Dahlgran, Madeline. *Etiquette of Social Life in Washington*. Lancaster, Pa., 1873.

Delrieu, Dr. R. *Les Abattoirs Publics de la Nouvelle-Orléans*. New Orleans, 1869.

Field, Henry M. *The Life of David Dudley Field*. New York, 1898.

Keim, Randolph. *Society in Washington: Its Noted Men, Accomplished Women, Established Customs, and Notable Events*. Washington, D.C., 1887.

Landis, John. *Life and Speeches of James Gillespie Blaine*. Lancaster, Pa., 1884.

Lincoln, Abraham. *Collected Works of Abraham Lincoln*. 9 vols. Edited by Roy P. Basler. New Brunswick, N.J., 1959.

Poore, Benjamin Perley. *Perley's Reminiscences of Sixty Years in the National Metropolis*. Philadelphia, 1886.

Townsend, George Alfred. *Events at the National Capital and Campaign of 1876*. Hartford, Conn., 1876.

Weathorford, Hardin. *A Treatise on Cholera, Symptoms, Mode of Prevention, and Cure on a New and Successful Plane.* Louisville, Ky., 1833.

Secondary Sources

BOOKS AND ESSAYS IN BOOKS

Abraham, Henry. *Justices and Presidents: A Political History of Appointments to the Supreme Court.* 2d ed. New York, 1985.
————. *Justices, Presidents, and Senators: A History of the U.S. Supreme Court Appointments from Washington to Clinton.* New York, 1999.
Ackerman, Bruce. *We the People: Transformations.* Cambridge, Mass., 1998.
Adler, Jeffrey. *Yankee Merchants and the Making of the Urban West: The Rise and Fall of Antebellum St. Louis.* New York, 1991.
Abbott, Carl. *Boosters and Businessmen: Popular Economic Thought and Urban Growth in the Antebellum Middle West.* Westport, Conn., 1981.
————. *Political Terrain: Washington, D.C., from Tidewater Town to Global Metropolis.* Chapel Hill, 1999.
Amar, Akhil Reed. *The Bill of Rights: Creation and Reconstruction.* New Haven, Conn., 1998.
Aynes, Richard. "Unintended Consequences of the Fourteenth Amendment." In *Unintended Consequences of Constitutional Amendment.* Edited by David D. Kyvig. Athens, Ga., 2000.
Barney, William L. *Battleground for the Union: The Era of the Civil War and Reconstruction, 1848–1877.* Englewood Cliffs, N.J., 1990.
————. *Passage of the Republic: An Interdisciplinary History of Nineteenth-Century America.* New York, 1987.
————. *Road to Secession: A New Perspective on the Old South.* New York, 1972.
Belcher, Wyatt. *The Economic Rivalry between Chicago and St. Louis.* New York, 1947.
Benedict, Michael Les. *A Compromise of Principle: Congressional Republicans and Reconstruction, 1863–1869.* New York, 1974.
————. *The Fruits of Victory: Alternatives in Restoring the Union, 1865–1877.* 2d ed. New York, 1986.
————. *The Impeachment and Trial of Andrew Johnson.* New York, 1973.
Bensel, Richard Franklin. *Yankee Leviathan: The Origins of Central State Authority in America.* New York, 1990.
Berger, Raoul. *Government by Judiciary: The Transformation of the Fourteenth Amendment.* Cambridge, Mass., 1977.
Bernath, Stewart. *Squall across the Atlantic: American Civil War Prize Cases and Diplomacy.* Berkeley, Calif., 1970.
Beth, Loren P. *The Development of the American Constitution.* New York, 1971.
Bogue, Allan. *From Prairie to Corn Belt: Farming on the Illinois and Iowa Prairies in the Nineteenth Century.* Chicago, 1963.

Boritt, Gabor. *Lincoln and the Economics of the American Dream.* Memphis, 1978.

Brandwein, Pamela. *Reconstructing Reconstruction: The Supreme Court and the Production of Historical Truth.* Durham, N.C., 1999.

Brock, W. R. *An American Crisis: Congress and Reconstruction, 1865–1867.* New York, 1963.

Carter, Dan T. *When the War Was Over: The Failure of Self-Reconstruction in the South, 1865–1867.* Baton Rouge, La., 1986.

Chase, Anthony. *Law and History: The Evolution of the American Legal System.* New York, 1997.

Coclanis, Peter A. *Shadow of a Dream: Economic Life and Death in the South Carolina Lowcountry, 1670–1920.* New York, 1989.

Cook, Robert. *Baptism of Fire: The Republican Party in Iowa.* Ames, Iowa, 1994.

Cornish, Dudley. *The Sable Arm: Negro Troops in the Union Army.* New York, 1966.

Cronon, William. *Nature's Metropolis: Chicago and the Great West.* New York, 1991.

Curtis, Michael Kent. *No State Shall Abridge: The Fourteenth Amendment and the Bill of Rights.* Durham, N.C., 1990.

Donald, David. *Charles Sumner and the Coming of the Civil War.* New York, 1960.

———. *Lincoln.* New York, 1995.

Duffy, John. *A History of Public Health in New York City, 1866–1966.* New York, 1974.

Dykstra, Robert. *Bright Radical Star: Black Freedom and White Supremacy on the Hawkeye Frontier.* Cambridge, Mass., 1993.

Ely, James, Jr. *The Chief Justiceship of Melville W. Fuller, 1888–1910.* Columbia, S.C., 1995.

———. *Guardian of Every Other Right: A Constitutional History of Property Rights.* New York, 1992.

———. *Railroads and American Law.* Lawrence, Kans., 2001.

Fairman, Charles. *Five Justices and the Electoral Commission of 1877.* In *Oliver Wendell Holmes Devise History of the Supreme Court of the United States.* Supplement to vol. 7. New York, 1988.

———. *Mr. Justice Miller and the Supreme Court, 1862–1890.* Cambridge, Mass., 1939.

———. *Reconstruction and Reunion, 1864–88.* In *Oliver Wendell Holmes Devise History of the Supreme Court of the United States.* Vols. 6 and 7. New York, 1971.

Faragher, John Mack. *Sugar Creek: Life on the Illinois Prairie.* New Haven, Conn., 1986.

Fehrenbacher, Don E. *The Dred Scott Case: Its Significance in American Law and Politics.* New York, 1978.

Finkelman, Paul. *Dred Scott v. Sandford: A Brief History with Documents.* Boston, 1997.

———. *An Imperfect Union: Slavery, Federalism, and Comity.* Chapel Hill, N.C., 1981.

Fishlow, Albert. *American Railroads and the Transformation of the American Economy.* Cambridge, Mass., 1965.

Fletcher, George P. *Our Secret Constitution: How Lincoln Redefined American Democracy.* New York, 2001.

Foner, Eric. *Free Soil, Free Labor, Free Men: The Ideology of the Republican Party before the Civil War.* New York, 1970.

———. *Politics and Ideology in the Age of the Civil War.* New York, 1980.

———. *Reconstruction: America's Unfinished Revolution, 1863–1877.* New York, 1988.

Franklin, John Hope. *Reconstruction: After the Civil War.* Chicago, 1961.

Freehling, William. *The Road to Disunion: Secessionists at Bay, 1776–1854.* New York, 1990.

Friedman, Lawrence M. *A History of American Law.* New York, 1973.

Friedman, Leon, and Fred Israel, eds. *The Justices of the United States Supreme Court, 1789–1969: Their Lives and Major Opinions.* New York, 1969.

Gillman, Howard. *The Constitution Besieged: The Rise and Demise of Lochner Era Police Powers Jurisprudence.* Durham, N.C., 1993.

Glatthaar, Joseph T. *Forged in Battle: The Civil War Alliance of Black Soldiers and White Officers.* New York, 1990.

Goldman, Robert M. *A Free Ballot and a Fair Count: The Department of Justice and the Enforcement of Voting Rights in the South, 1877–1893.* New York, 2001.

———. *Reconstruction and Black Suffrage: Losing the Vote in Reese and Cruikshank.* Lawrence, Kans., 2001.

Graham, Howard. *Everyman's Constitution: Historical Essays on the Fourteenth Amendment, the "Conspiracy Theory," and American Constitutionalism.* Madison, Wis., 1968.

Gregory, Charles Noble. *Samuel Freeman Miller.* Iowa City, Iowa, 1907.

Hale, Grace Elizabeth. *Making Whiteness: The Culture of Segregation in the South, 1890–1940.* New York, 1998.

Hall, Kermit L., ed. *The Legal Profession: Major Historical Interpretations.* New York, 1987.

———. *The Oxford Companion to the Supreme Court of the United States.* New York, 1992.

Harris, William. *Presidential Reconstruction in Mississippi.* Baton Rouge, La., 1967.

Hobsbawm, Eric. *The Age of Capital, 1848–1875.* New York, 1975.

Holt, Michael F. *The Political Crisis of the 1850s.* New York, 1978.

Hovenkamp, Herbert. *Enterprise and American Law, 1836–1937.* Cambridge, Mass., 1991.

Huebner, Timothy. *The Southern Judicial Tradition: State Judges and Sectional Distinctiveness, 1790–1890.* Athens, Ga., 1999.

Huston, James L. *The Panic of 1857 and the Coming of the Civil War.* Baton Rouge, La., 1987.

Hyman, Harold. *A More Perfect Union: The Impact of the Civil War and Reconstruction on the Constitution.* New York, 1973.

———. *The Reconstruction Justice of Salmon P. Chase.* Lawrence, Kans., 1997.

———. *To Try Men's Souls: Loyalty Tests in American History.* Berkeley, Calif., 1959.

Hyman, Harold, and William Wiecek. *Equal Justice under Law: Constitutional Development, 1835–1875.* New York, 1982.

Irons, Peter. *A People's History of the Supreme Court.* New York, 1999.

Jacob, Kathryn Allamong. *Capital Elites: High Society in Washington, D.C., after the Civil War.* Washington, D.C., 1995.

Jaffa, Harry A. *Crisis of the House Divided: An Interpretation of the Lincoln-Douglas Debates.* Garden City, N.Y., 1959.

Johannsen, Robert. *The Frontier, the Union, and Stephen A. Douglas.* Urbana, Ill., 1989.

———. *Stephen A. Douglas.* New York, 1973.

Kaczorowski, Robert. *The Politics of Judicial Interpretation: The Federal Courts, Department of Justice, and Civil Rights.* New York, 1985.

Karst, Kenneth L. *Belonging to America: Equal Citizenship and the Constitution.* New Haven, Conn., 1989.

Keller, Morton. *Affairs of State: Public Life in Late Nineteenth-Century America.* Cambridge, Mass., 1977.

Kens, Paul. *Judicial Power and Reform Politics: The Anatomy of Lochner v. New York.* Lawrence, Kans., 1990.

———. *Justice Stephen Field: Shaping Liberty from the Gold Rush to the Gilded Age.* Lawrence, Kans., 1997.

King, Willard. *Lincoln's Manager David Davis.* Cambridge, Mass., 1960.

Kutler, Stanley. *Judicial Power and Reconstruction Politics.* Chicago, 1968.

Lofgren, Charles. *The Plessy Case: A Legal-Historical Interpretation.* New York, 1987.

Lonn, Ella. *Reconstruction in Louisiana.* New York, 1918.

Lutz, John Lauritz. *Bonds of Enterprise: John Murray Forbes and Western Development in America's Railway Age.* Cambridge, Mass., 1984.

Mahoney, Timothy. *Provincial Lives: Middle-Class Experience in the Antebellum Midwest.* New York, 1999.

———. *River Towns in the Great West: The Structure of Provincial Urbanization in the American Midwest, 1820–1870.* New York, 1990.

Maltz, Earl. *Civil Rights, the Constitution, and Congress, 1863–1869.* Lawrence, Kans., 1990.

McCague, James. *The Cumberland.* New York, 1973.

McCloskey, Robert Green. *American Conservatism in the Age of Enterprise, 1865–1910.* New York, 1951.

McDonough, James Lee. *Shiloh—In Hell before Night.* Knoxville, 1977.

McPherson, James M. *Battle Cry of Freedom: The Civil War Era.* New York, 1988.

———, ed. *"We Cannot Escape History": Lincoln and the Last Best Hope of Earth.* Urbana, Ill., 1995.

Miller, George. *Railroads and the Granger Laws.* Madison, Wis., 1971.

Mills, Michael C. *Barbourville, Kentucky.* Barbourville, Ky., 1977.

Mitchell, Broadus, and Louise Pearson Mitchell. *A Biography of the Constitution of the United States: Its Origin, Formation, Adoption, Interpretation.* New York, 1964.

Montgomery, David. *Beyond Equality: Labor and the Radical Republicans, 1862–1872.* New York, 1967.

Moretta, John Anthony. *William Pitt Ballinger: Texas Lawyer, Southern Statesman, 1825–1888.* Austin, Tex., 2000.

Neely, Mark E. *The Fate of Liberty: Abraham Lincoln and Civil Liberties.* New York, 1991.

————. *The Last Best Hope of Earth: Abraham Lincoln and the Promise of America.* Cambridge, Mass., 1993.

Nelson, William E. *The Fourteenth Amendment: From Political Principle to Judicial Doctrine.* Cambridge, Mass., 1988.

Nieman, Donald. *To Set the Law in Motion: The Freedmen's Bureau and the Legal Rights of Blacks, 1865–1868.* Millwood, N.Y., 1979.

Oates, Stephen B. *To Purge This Land with Blood: A Biography of John Brown.* New York, 1970.

Paludan, Phillip Shaw. *A People's Contest: The Union and the Civil War, 1861–1865.* New York, 1988.

Peter, Robert. *The History of the Medical Department of Transylvania University.* Louisville, Ky., 1905.

Potter, David M. *The Impending Crisis, 1848–1861.* New York, 1976.

Przybyszewski, Linda. *The Republic According to John Marshall Harlan.* Chapel Hill, N.C., 1999.

Randall, J. G. *Constitutional Problems under Lincoln.* Urbana, Ill., 1951.

Rawley, James. *Race and Politics: "Bleeding Kansas" and the Coming of the Civil War.* Philadelphia, 1969.

Richardson, H. Edward. *Cassius Marcellus Clay: Firebrand of Freedom.* Lexington, Ky., 1976.

Richardson, Heather Cox. *The Death of Reconstruction: Race, Labor, and Politics in the Post–Civil War North, 1865–1901.* Cambridge, Mass., 2001.

————. *The Greatest Nation of the Earth: Republican Economic Policies during the Civil War.* Cambridge, Mass., 1997.

Ritter, Gretchen. *Goldbugs and Greenbacks: The Antimonopoly Traditions and the Politics of Finance in America.* New York, 1997.

Rose, Willie Lee. *Rehearsal for Reconstruction: The Port Royal Experiment.* Indianapolis, Ind., 1964.

Rosenberg, Charles. *The Cholera Years.* Chicago, 1962.

Rosenberg, Morton. *Iowa on the Eve of the Civil War: A Decade of Frontier Politics.* Norman, Okla., 1972.

Saunders, Robert. *John Archibald Campbell: Southern Moderate, 1811–1889.* Tuscaloosa, Ala., 1997.

Schwartz, Bernard. *A History of the Supreme Court.* New York, 1993.

Sears, Richard D. *The Day of Small Things: Abolitionism in the Midst of Slavery.* New York, 1986.

Sears, Stephen. *Landscape Turned Red: The Battle of Antietam.* New Haven, Conn., 1983.

Semonche, John. *Charting the Future: The Supreme Court Responds to a Changing Society, 1890–1920.* Westport, Conn., 1978.

————. *Keeping the Faith: A Cultural History of the U.S. Supreme Court.* New York, 1998.

Silver, David. *Lincoln's Supreme Court.* Urbana, Ill., 1956.

Stampp, Kenneth. *The Era of Reconstruction, 1865–1877.* New York, 1965.

Starr, John W. *Lincoln and the Railroads*. New York, 1927.

Summers, Mark W. *Railroads, Reconstruction, and the Gospel of Prosperity: Aid under the Radical Republicans, 1865–1877*. Princeton, N.J., 1984.

Swierenga, Robert P. *Pioneers and Profits: Land Speculation on the Iowa Frontier*. Ames, Iowa, 1968.

Swisher, Carl B. *Stephen J. Field: Craftsman of the Law*. Washington, D.C., 1930.

———. *The Taney Period, 1836–64*. In *Oliver Wendell Holmes Devise History of the Supreme Court of the United States*. Vol. 5. New York, 1974.

Tanner, Robert G. *Stonewall in the Valley: Thomas J. "Stonewall" Jackson's Shenandoah Valley Campaign, Spring 1862*. Garden City, N.Y., 1976.

Taylor, George Rogers. *The Transportation Revolution, 1815–1860*. New York, 1951.

Taylor, Joe Gray. *Louisiana Reconstructed, 1863–1877*. Baton Rouge, La., 1974.

Tribe, Laurence. *God Save This Honorable Court*. New York, 1985.

Tunnell, Ted. *Crucible of Reconstruction: War, Radicalism, and Race in Louisiana, 1862–1877*. Baton Rouge, La., 1984.

Tushnet, Mark. *The American Law of Slavery, 1810–1860: Considerations of Humanity and Interest*. Princeton, N.J., 1981.

Tutorow, Norman. *James Gillespie Blaine and the Presidency: A Documentary Study and Source Book*. New York, 1989.

Unger, Irwin. *The Greenback Era: A Social and Political History of American Finance, 1865–1879*. Princeton, N.J., 1964.

Van Ee, Daun. *David Dudley Field and the Reconstruction of the Law*. New York, 1986.

Van Vleck, George. *The Panic of 1857*. New York, 1943.

Wang, Xi. *The Trial of Democracy: Black Suffrage and Northern Republicans, 1810–1910*. Athens, Ga., 1997.

Warren, Charles. *The Supreme Court in United States History*. Boston, 1937.

Warren, K. S. Sol. *A History of Knox County*. Barbourville, Ky., 1976.

White, G. Edward. *The American Judicial Tradition: Profiles of Leading American Judges*. New York, 1976.

Whyte, James. *The Uncivil War: Washington during Reconstruction, 1865–1878*. New York, 1958.

Williams, Lou Falkner. *The Great South Carolina Ku Klux Klan Trials, 1871–1872*. Athens, Ga., 1996.

Wise, Stephen. *Lifeline of the Confederacy: Blockade Running during the Civil War*. Columbia, S.C., 1988.

Woodward, C. Vann. *Reunion and Reaction: The Compromise of 1877 and the End of Reconstruction*. New York, 1951.

ARTICLES

Amar, Akhil Reed. "The Bill of Rights and the Fourteenth Amendment." *Yale Law Journal* 101 (1992): 1259–84.

Aynes, Richard. "*Bradwell v. Illinois:* Chief Justice Chase's Dissent and the 'Sphere of Women's Work.'" *Louisiana Law Review* 59 (winter 1999): 521.

————. "Constricting the Law of Freedom: Justice Miller, the Fourteenth Amendment, and the *Slaughter-House Cases*." *Chicago-Kent Law Review* 70 (1994): 627–88.

————. "On Misreading John Bingham and the Fourteenth Amendment." *Yale Law Journal* 103 (October 1993): 57–104.

Baird, Nancy D. "Asiatic Cholera's First Visit to Kentucky." *Filson Club History Quarterly* 48 (1974): 228–40.

Benedict, Michael Les. "Constitutional History and Constitutional Theory: Reflections on Ackerman, Reconstruction, and the Transformation of the American Constitution." *Yale Law Journal* 108 (1998): 2011–38.

————. "Laissez-Faire and Liberty: A Reevaluation of the Meaning and Origin of Laissez-Faire Constitutionalism." *Law and History Review* 3 (fall 1985): 243–331.

————. "Preserving Federalism: Reconstruction and the Waite Court." *Supreme Court Review* (1978): 39–62.

————. "Preserving the Constitution: The Conservative Basis of Radical Reconstruction." *Journal of American History* 61 (1974): 65–90.

————. "Southern Democrats in the Crisis of 1876–1877: A Reconsideration of *Reunion and Reaction*." *Journal of Southern History* 46 (November 1980): 497–524.

Beth, Loren P. "The Slaughter-House Cases—Revisted." *Louisiana Law Review* 23 (1963): 487–505.

Braukman, Stacy L., and Michael A. Ross. "Married Women's Property and Male Coercion: United States' Courts and the Role of the Privy Examination, 1864–1887." *Journal of Women's History* 12 (2000): 57–80.

Conant, Michael. "Antimonopoly Tradition under the Ninth and Fourteenth Amendments: *Slaughter-House Cases* Reexamined." *Emory Law Journal* 31 (1982): 785–832.

Curtis, Michael Kent. "Resurrecting the Privileges and Immunities Clause and Revising the *Slaughter-House Cases* without Exhuming *Lochner:* Individual Rights and the Fourteenth Amendment." *Boston College Law Review* 38 (December 1996): 1–106.

Eberson, Frederick. "A Great Purging—Cholera or Calomel?" *Filson Club History Quarterly* 50 (April 1976): 28–55.

Ely, James, Jr. "The Railroad Question Revisited: *Chicago, Milwaukee & St. Paul Railway v. Minnesota* and the Constitutional Limits on State Regulations." *Great Plains Quarterly* 12 (spring 1992): 121–34.

Foner, Eric. "The Strange Career of the Reconstruction Amendments." *Yale Law Journal* 108 (1999): 2003–9.

Hardwick, Kevin. "'Your Old Father Abe Lincoln Is Dead and Damned': Black Soldiers and the Memphis Riot of 1866." *Journal of Social History* 27 (fall 1993): 109–29.

Kens, Paul. "Liberty and the Public Ingredient of Private Property." *Review of Politics* (winter 1993): 85–116.

Klement, Frank. "Middle Western Copperheadism and the Genesis of the Granger Movement." *Mississippi Valley Historical Review* 38 (March 1952): 679–94.

Lurie, Jonathan. "One Hundred and Twenty-Five Years after *Slaughter-House:* Where's the Beef?" *Journal of Supreme Court History* 24 (1999): 269–81.

Mahoney, Timothy. "Urban History in a Regional Context: River Towns and the Upper Mississippi, 1840–1860." *Journal of American History* 72 (September 1985): 318–9.

McCurdy, Charles W. "Justice Field and the Jurisprudence of Government-Business Relations: Some Parameters of Laissez-Faire Constitutionalism, 1863–1897." *Journal of American History* 61 (March 1975): 970–1005.

———. "The Roots of 'Liberty of Contract' Reconsidered: Major Premises in the Law of Employment, 1867–1937." *Yearbook of the Supreme Court Historical Society* (1984): 20–33.

———. "Stephen J. Field and Public Land Law Development in California, 1850–1866: A Case Study of Judicial Resource Allocation in Nineteenth-Century America." *Law and Society* 10 (winter 1976): 235–66.

Newsom, Kevin Christopher. "Setting Incorporationism Straight: A Reinterpretation of the *Slaughter-House* Cases." *Yale Law Journal* 109 (2000): 643–744.

Nieman, Donald. "Andrew Johnson, the Freedmen's Bureau, and the Problem of Equal Rights, 1865–1866." *Journal of Southern History* 44 (August 1978): 399–420.

Orth, John V. "Taking From A and Giving to B: Substantive Due Process and the Case of the Shifting Paradigm." *Constitutional Commentary* 14 (1997): 337–43.

Palmer, Robert C. "The Parameters of Constitutional Reconstruction: *Slaughter-House, Cruikshank,* and the Fourteenth Amendment." *University of Illinois Law Review* 3 (1984): 739–70.

Powell, Lawrence N. "Reinventing Tradition: Liberty Place, Historical Memory, and Silk-Stocking Vigilantism in New Orleans Politics." *Slavery and Abolition* 20 (1999): 127–49.

Ross, Michael A. "Cases of Shattered Dreams: Justice Samuel Freeman Miller and the Rise and Fall of a Mississippi River Town." *Annals of Iowa* 57 (summer 1998): 201–39.

———. "Hill-Country Doctor: The Early Life and Career of Supreme Court Justice Samuel F. Miller in Kentucky, 1816–1849." *Filson Club History Quarterly* 71 (October 1997): 430–62.

———. "Justice for Iowa: Samuel Freeman Miller's Appointment to the United States Supreme Court during the Civil War." *Annals of Iowa* 60 (spring 2001): 111–38.

———. "Justice Miller's Reconstruction: The *Slaughter-House Cases,* Health Codes, and Civil Rights in New Orleans, 1861–1863." *Journal of Southern History* 64 (November 1998): 649–76.

Scott, John A. "Justice Bradley's Evolving Concept of the Fourteenth Amendment from the *Slaughter-House Cases* to the *Civil Rights Cases.*" *Rutgers Law Review* 25 (summer 1971): 552–69.

Sipress, Joel M. "From the Barrel of a Gun: The Politics of Murder in Grant Parish." *Louisiana History* 42 (2001): 303–21.

Stevens, Jan S. "Stephen J. Field: A Gold Rush Lawyer Shapes the Nation." *Journal of the West* 29 (1990): 40–53.

Tregle, Joseph G. "Thomas Durant, Utopian Socialism, and the Failure of Presidential Reconstruction in Louisiana." *Journal of Southern History* 45 (November 1979): 485–512.

Waldrep, Christopher. "Substituting Law for the Lash: Emancipation and Legal Formalism in a Mississippi County Court." *Journal of American History* 82 (March 1996): 1425–51.

White, G. Edward. "Reconstructing the Constitutional Jurisprudence of Salmon P. Chase." *Northern Kentucky Law Review* 21 (fall 1993): 41–116.

Wildenthal, Bryan, "The Lost Compromise: Reassessing the Early Understanding in Court and Congress on Incorporation of the Bill of Rights in the Fourteenth Amendment." *Ohio State Law Journal* 61 (2000): 1051–174.

Zobrist, Benedict. "Steamboat Men versus Railroad Men: The First Bridging of the Mississippi River." *Missouri Historical Review* 59 (1965): 159–72.

THESES AND DISSERTATIONS

Allen, Jeffrey Brooke. "The Debate over Slavery and Race in Antebellum Kentucky, 1792–1850." Ph.D. diss., Northwestern University, 1973.

Harris, Faye Erma. "'A Frontier Community': The Economic, Social, and Political Development of Keokuk, Iowa, from 1820 to 1866." Ph.D. diss., University of Iowa, 1965.

Hogue, James Keith. "Bayonet Rule: Five Street Battles in New Orleans and the Rise and Fall of Radical Reconstruction." Ph.D. diss., Princeton University, 1998.

Sipress, Joel M. "The Triumph of Reaction: Political Struggles in a New South Community, 1865–1878." Ph.D. diss., University of North Carolina at Chapel Hill, 1993.

Soring, James A. "Judicial Opinions of Mr. Justice Miller." Master's thesis, University of Iowa, 1954.

Tuchinsky, Adam-Max. "Horace Greeley's Lost Book: The *New-York Tribune* and the Origins of Social Democratic Liberalism in America." Ph.D. diss., University of North Carolina at Chapel Hill, 2001.

INDEX

Abolitionism, 8, 10–1, 15–6, 20, 29, 31, 55–6, 66, 165. *See also* Slavery

African Americans: and *Slaughter-House Cases*, xiii–xiv, 189, 196–7, 200–2, 207–10, 245, 249; Clay on character of, 10; lynching of, 10; Lincoln on rights for, 52–3, 94, 95; Miller on rights of, 52, 116, 164–5, 202, 207–10; rights for, 52–3, 94–5, 114, 115–6, 118–21, 136, 146, 163–5, 195–6, 202, 207–10; voting rights for, 53, 95, 106, 110, 115–6, 119, 120, 136, 147–8, 151, 163–5, 169, 195, 246–50, 291*n*13; as soldiers in Civil War, 82, 95, 114, 165, 209; and Freedmen's Bureau, 94–5, 114, 119–21, 127, 128, 140; and Thirteenth Amendment, 94, 113; Johnson and rights for, 106, 110, 118, 120–1; and Black Codes, 113–5, 117, 120, 136, 195, 208–10; southern attitudes toward freedmen, 113–4, 115, 135–6, 164; farming by freedmen, 114; violence against, 135–6, 146–7, 163, 227, 245–6, 247, 249; citizenship for, 136; and Fourteenth Amendment, 136–8, 146–8, 158, 199–210, 245, 246, 247; and Fifteenth Amendment, 163–4, 202; in Louisiana legislature, 196; segregation of, 196–7, 254; and *Cruikshank v. United States*, 245–6, 247, 250; and *Civil Rights Cases*, 246–7; discrimination against, 247; and *Ex Parte Yarborough*, 247–9, 250. *See also* Race; Slavery

Agriculture. *See* Farming

Alabama, 59, 115, 153

Allgeyer v. Louisiana, 291*n*28

American Party (Know-Nothings), 27–8, 30

American System, 9, 77

Amnesty for ex-Confederates. *See* Pardons and amnesty for ex-Confederates

Anarchism, 242–4

Anderson, "Bloody Bill," 129

Andersonville prison camp, 110

Antietam, battle of, 81, 272*n*51

Arkansas, 131, 153

Ashley, James, 145

Atchison, David Rice, 26, 28, 29

Atlantic Monthly, 82

Atterberg, Douglas, 263*n*22

Attorneys. *See* Lawyers

Audubon, John James, 190

Bakers' working hours, 253

Ballinger, Franklin, 5

Ballinger, James, 5, 12, 17, 22

Ballinger, Lucy. *See* Miller, Lucy Ballinger

Ballinger, William Pitt: as lawyer, 5; move

ing, 67, 68, 83–8; battle of Shiloh during, 76; Seven Days' battle during, 76; in Shenandoah Valley, 76; in West, 76; battle of Antietam during, 81, 272n51; and Emancipation Proclamation, 81–3, 94; African American soldiers in, 82, 95, 114, 165, 209; Grier on, 85; Nelson on, 86; end of, 95; Andersonville prison camp during, 110; and Confederate war debt, 113, 136; in Indiana, 121–6; and *Milligan* case, 121–8, 133; New York draft riots during, 163; federal government's debt from, 177; and greenbacks, 177–8, 181; Union occupation of New Orleans during, 193

Claggett v. Gray, 262n9

Clapp v. County of Cedar, 46

Clark, William, 19

Clarke, Ex Parte, 291n18

Clarkson, J. S., 237

Clay, Cassius M., 8–11, 14–6, 77, 203, 260n36

Clay, Henry, 9, 15, 77, 226

Clemens, Samuel, 24

Cleveland, Grover, 239, 241

Clifford, Nathan: as Democrat, 66, 215; and *Prize Cases*, 86; and test-oath cases, 141; and *McCardle* case, 153, 155, 156; and bond cases, 170, 219; and *Legal Tender Cases*, 178, 179; and *Slaughter-House Cases*, 200; and presidential election of 1876, 228–9

Colfax massacre, 124, 245–6

Coloma case, 219–20

Communism, 242–4, 245

Compromise of 1850, 158

Compromise of 1877, 208, 228–9

Confederacy: and secession of southern states, 59, 105; foreign countries' recognition of, 68, 87; Lincoln's view of, 68, 84, 85–6, 159, 160; status of, as sovereign state, 68, 84, 85–7; and Emancipation Proclamation, 81; pardons and amnesty

for ex-Confederates, 106–10, 112, 132, 142, 143, 147; treason trials and death sentences for leaders of, 106–10; war debts of, 113, 136. *See also* Civil War; Secession and secessionists

Congress, U.S.: antislavery sentiment in, 8; Gag Rules in, 8; and Missouri Compromise, 25–7, 31, 32, 50; and Kansas-Nebraska Act, 26–7, 29–30; caning of Sumner in, 29–30; and slavery in territories, 50; and Lecompton constitution for Kansas, 52; and Crittenden compromise, 59–60, 268n61; powers of, in Constitution, 67, 179; and suspension of habeas corpus, 67, 122–4, 126; and Lincoln's extraconstitutional actions during Civil War, 68, 122, 274n14; and reorganization of federal judicial circuits, 69–74, 79; representation in, 69, 136; and Miller's appointment to U.S. Supreme Court, 79; and Union blockade during Civil War, 83, 86–7; Supreme Court bills in, 84–5, 144, 153, 278n27; and African American freedom, 94–5; and emancipation of slaves, 94; and Freedmen's Bureau, 94–5, 119–21; and Legal Tender Act (1862), 94, 177, 179; and Reconstruction during Johnson presidency, 110–1, 116–21, 138; southern delegations to, at beginning of Reconstruction, 112–3, 116–7, 121; refusal of, to seat ex-Confederates in, 116–7, 121; and ironclad loyalty test oath, 117, 132, 133, 141; and Civil Rights Act (1866), 119–21; and Fourteenth Amendment, 136–8, 158, 201; and Habeas Corpus Act (1867), 148, 156, 157; and Military Reconstruction Act, 148–51, 160–1; and Tenure of Office Act, 151, 154; and jurisdiction of Supreme Court, 156–7, 162–3; and *McCardle* case, 156; and return to peacetime Constitution in 1868, 158; war powers of, 178–80, 185; and bankruptcy laws, 182; and Ku Klux Klan Act, 208; and Civil Rights Act (1875), 209; and Inflation Bill (1874), 224; and Specie Resumption Act (1876), 225; and presidential election of 1876, 227–8; and financial support for Eliza Miller, 256. *See also* specific bills and laws

Conkling, Roscoe, 214

Constitution, U.S.: Miller on, 62, 145–6, 154, 174, 182–3; and habeas corpus, 66–7; powers of Congress in, 67, 179; three-fifths clause in, 136; separation of powers in, 146, 149, 154; Congress and appellate jurisdiction of Supreme Court, 156–7; guarantee clause of, 160; strict construction of, 164; necessary and proper clause of, 179–80; contracts clause of, 180, 235, 289*n*72. *See also* Bill of Rights; Due process; and specific amendments

Constitutional Union Party, 57

Consumption, 21

Contracts clause, 180, 235, 289*n*72

Cooke, Jay, 217

Cooke, John Esten, 3

Copperheads, 75, 121–2, 129

Corkhill, George, 215, 237, 238, 255

Cornelius case, 87–8

Corwin, Edgar, 118

County of Jasper v. Ballou, 289*n*64

County of Morgan v. Illinois, 289*n*63

County of Moultrie v. Rockingham Ten-Cent Savings-Bank, 287*n*26

County of Warren v. Marcy, 289*n*64

Court system. *See* Federal court system; Supreme Court, U.S.

Cox v. Burns & Rentgen, 262*n*9

Coy v. Mason, 25, 261–2*n*2

Crittenden, John J., 59–60

Cruikshank v. United States, 245–6, 247, 250

Cummings, John, 129–30, 141–3

Cummings v. the State of Missouri, 128–34, 138–44, 149

Currency issues. *See* Monetary policy

Curtis, Samuel, 24, 33, 36

Cushing, Caleb, 215

Daniel, Peter, 65

Davidson, John, 232

Davidson v. New Orleans, 232–4, 251

Davis, David: as Lincoln appointee to U.S. Supreme Court, 84; as Lincoln's campaign manager in 1860 presidential election, 84; and *Milligan* case, 122–3, 125–6, 127, 139–40; and Fourteenth Amendment, 138; and *McCardle* case, 153, 155, 156; and bond cases, 170; and *Legal Tender Cases*, 178; and *Slaughter-House Cases*, 200; resignation of, from Supreme Court, 228

Davis, H. E., 267*n*32

Davis, Jefferson, 32, 107, 146

Death penalty. *See* Capital punishment

Death v. Bank of Pittsburgh, 262*n*9

Debating Society of Barbourville, 7–8, 12, 20, 78, 255, 259–60*nn*27–8

Debt: and railroad bonds, 34–5, 45–8, 53–5, 64, 70–1, 73, 79, 89–93, 168–77, 186–7, 222–3, 269*n*75, 273*n*75; of Keokuk, Iowa, 45–8, 168–9, 176–7; repudiation of, 53–4, 56, 79, 180, 185–6, 217, 222–3; Confederate war debt, 113, 136; federal government's war debt, 177; and *Legal Tender Cases*, 177–86; and bankruptcy laws, 182; and Panic of 1873, 217–8

Declaration of Independence, 62, 147, 204

Democratic Party: and Kentucky Constitutional Convention of 1849, 15–6; on banks, 27, 48–9, 267*n*24; and Kansas-Nebraska Act, 27, 29, 30; and slavery question, 27, 31–2; free-soil Democrats, 30; in Iowa, 31, 32, 48–9, 75, 169; secession threatened by southern Democrats,

Howard, Jacob, 72–3, 115, 201
Howe, Timothy O., 209
Howells, William Dean, 56
Humboldt Township v. Long, 221, 280*n*18, 287*n*26
Hunt, Ward, 200
Huntington, Collis P., 89, 241, 288*n*42
Hurd, John, 38
Hurd v. Railroad Bridge Company, 38
Hyde v. Woolfolk and Bacon, 262*n*9

Illinois, 219–20, 230–1. *See also* Chicago
Immigration and immigrants, 7, 199
Impeachment and trial of Johnson, 145–6, 151–5
Indiana, 121–6, 139–40
Industrialism, xii, xiv–xvii, 8–9, 77–8. *See also* Capitalists
Inflation Bill (1874), 224
Internal improvements, 7, 27, 31, 35, 53, 77, 203. *See also* Railroads
Interracial marriage, 121
Inventions, 88, 241, 244
Iowa: Republican Party in, xiv–xv, 28, 30–2, 48, 52–5, 75, 165, 169, 263*n*36; economic growth of Keokuk in, 13–4, 22–5, 77; farming in, 13, 23, 41, 43, 244–5; lawyers in, 14, 19–20, 24, 262*n*9; Unitarians in, 20, 21; Miller as Republican candidate for state senate in, 30–2; Democratic Party in, 31, 32, 48–9, 75, 169; economic rivalry between Burlington and Keokuk, 32–6; railroads in, 33–40, 45–6, 54–5, 265*n*58; and Panic of 1857, 41–9; state bank for, 48–9; black suffrage in, 53, 169; constitutional convention of 1857 in, 53; rights for African Americans in, 53; and Civil War, 61–4, 72, 81, 82; and reorganization of judicial circuits, 70–4; and Miller's appointment to U.S. Supreme Court, 74–81; and railroad bonds, 89–92, 167–77, 269*n*75; support

for Miller's nomination as Supreme Court chief justice, 214; and Blaine's presidential campaigns, 226; railroad and grain elevator rates in, 230; and Miller's presidential candidacy, 237, 238; and free-labor ideology, 244–5; Miller's praise of, 244–5. *See also* Keokuk, Iowa
Iowa Supreme Court, 21, 35, 46–7, 55, 89–91, 169–72, 262*n*9

Jackson, Andrew, 51, 54, 85
Jackson, Stonewall, 76
James, Frank and Jesse, 129
James v. Bowman, 250
Jay, John, 139
Jay Cooke and Company, 217
Johnson, Andrew: family background of, 105; on planter class, 105–6, 109–10; Reconstruction policy of, 105–6, 109–11, 113, 115, 116, 118, 120–1, 128, 136, 137, 195; secession opposed by, 105; and African Americans' rights, 106, 110, 118, 120–1, 151; and pardons and amnesty for ex-Confederates, 109, 110, 112, 132, 142, 143; and federal patronage appointees, 136; and National Union movement, 136; and Fourteenth Amendment, 137, 138; and military trials of civilians in South, 140; Miller's criticism of, 146; and Military Reconstruction Act, 148, 149–51; and Tenure of Office Act, 151, 153–5; firing of Stanton by, 153, 154, 155; and elections of 1866, 277*n*3; impeachment and trial of, *following p. 96*, 145–6, 151–5
Johnson, Reverdy, 124, 130, 132–4, 150
Judicial Reorganization Act (1862), 74, 79, 272–3*n*58
Judicial system. *See* Federal court system; and Supreme Court headings
Julian, George, 81
Justice Department, U.S., 246, 250

pointees of, xvi, 65–6, 70, 71–2, 74–81, 84, 88, 93–4, 95, 254, 272*n*44; as lawyer, 38, 56, 254; on African Americans' rights, 52–3, 94, 95; debates between Douglas and, 52–3; and debt repudiation, 53–4, 56, 79; and capitalists, 54, 56, 79, 254; and presidential election of 1860, 56–8, 84, 88; and secession of southern states, 58–60; and Civil War, 61, 62, 66–8, 76, 81–3, 122, 123, 163, 274*n*14; and *Dred Scott* decision, 65; and suspension of habeas corpus during Civil War, 66–8, 122; extraconstitutional actions of, during Civil War, 67–8, 85, 122, 124, 274*n*14; and Union blockade during Civil War, 67, 68, 83–8; wartime powers of, 67–8, 85, 123, 124; on Confederacy as not sovereign state, 68, 84, 85–6, 159, 160; and reorganization of federal judicial circuits, 69, 74; compared with Miller, 77–9; on industrialization, 77–8; in Whig Party, 77; in Republican Party, 78; and Emancipation Proclamation, 81–3; assassination of, 95; portrait of, *following p. 96*; Stanton as appointee of, 155

Litchfield v. Ballou, 280*n*18

Loan Association v. Topeka, 174, 183

Lochner v. New York, 253

Longstreet, James, 164

Louisiana: secession of, 59; Black Codes in, 114, 195; test-oath statute in, 128; New Orleans race riot (1866) in, 135–6, 147, 151, 195; health and sanitary regulations in, 189–200, 202–3, 232–34, 253; slaughtering industry in, 189–93, 197–200, 202–3; yellow fever and cholera in, 191, 193, 210, 232; corruption in, 192, 195, 283*n*12; Reconstruction government in, 193–200, 203, 205, 208, 210; Union occupation of New Orleans during Civil War, 193; economy of, after Civil War, 194–5; internal improvements in, 194;

school desegregation in, 195, 196–7; state constitution of 1868, 195–7, 207; African Americans in state legislature, 196; and *Slaughter-House Cases,* 199–210, 253; and presidential election of 1876, 227; *Davidson v. New Orleans,* 232–4; bond case from, 236; Colfax massacre in, 245–6

Louisiana v. Jumel, 289*n*72

Love, James M., 39, 40, 47–8, 60, 64, 75, 256, 266*n*22, 269*n*75

Lowe, Ralph P., 32, 89

Loyalty oaths. *See* Test oaths

Lynchings, 10

Lynde v. Winnebago, 280*n*18

Mad River & Lake Erie Railroad, 71

Marcy v. Township of Oswego, 287*n*26

Marsh v. Fulton County, 280*n*18

Marshall, John, 179

Marshall v. McLean, 262*n*3

Martial law, 122, 125–7

Maryland, 66–7, 128, 130

Mathews v. Gilliss, 262*n*9

Matthews, Stanley, 236

Mayor of Nashville v. Ray, 218–9, 220, 280*n*18

McCallister, George, 5

McCardle, William, 152, 156

McCardle, Ex Parte, 152–3, 155–7, 158, 278*n*45

McCulloch v. Maryland, 179

McDonald, David, 122–3

McLean, John, 65–6, 69, 71

Medical education/medical profession, 2–5, 8, 11–2, 202–3

Memphis race riot (1866), 135, 147

Mercer County v. Hackett, 280*n*18

Merryman, John, 66–7

Merryman, Ex Parte, 66–7, 68, 87

Meyer v. City of Muscatine, 91–3

Meyer v. Muscatine, 280*n*18

Military Reconstruction Act, 148–53, 155–7, 160, 160–3
Military trials of civilians, 122, 125–7, 139–40, 152
Miller, Alida (Lida), 22, 229–30, 255
Miller, Daniel F., 75, 80, 176
Miller, Eliza Winter Reeves: Ballinger's view of, 21–2, 213; children of, 21–2, 167, 187, 211–2, 229–30, 255; marriage of, to Samuel Miller, 21; wealth and property of, 24; during Civil War, 62; social life of, in Keokuk, Iowa, 80–1; in Keokuk, Iowa, after Samuel Miller's appointment to Supreme Court, 167, 187; move to Washington, D.C. by, 187, 211; conflicts between daughter Pattie and, 211–2, 255; social life and social status of, in Washington, D.C., 211–3, 216; interest of, in Washington real estate, 225; trip to Europe by, 229–30; health problems of, 254; opposition of, to Miller's retirement from Supreme Court, 255; thirtieth wedding anniversary of, 255; death of, 256; financial situation at husband's death, 256
Miller, Frederick, 2
Miller, Irvine, 22, 255
Miller, Jane, 21
Miller, Lucy Ballinger, 5, 12, 17, 21
Miller, Olivia (Olly), 21
Miller, Patricia (Pattie), 21, 211–2, 255
Miller, Patsy, 2, 187
Miller, Samuel Freeman: changes during lifetime of, xi–xii, 187–8; significance and legacy of, xi–xvii, 253–4; personality of, xii–xiii; as populist hero, xiii, xiv; birth of, 1; education of, 1, 2–5; physical appearance of, 1; youth of, 1–2; medical education and medical career of, 2–5, 8, 11–2, 202–3; mother of, 2, 187; in Barbourville, Ky., 5–9, 11–3, 16–7, 20, 34, 77; marriage of, to Lucy Ballinger, 5; as

slaveholder, 5, 11; and debating society in Barbourville, 7–8, 12, 20, 78, 255, 259–60nn27–8; children of, 12, 17, 21–2, 167, 187, 211–2, 229–30, 255; law practice of, in Barbourville, Ky., 12–3; in Whig Party, 14–5, 31, 77, 80; in Keokuk, Iowa, 17, 19–22, 77; law practice of, in Keokuk, Iowa, 19–21, 38–40, 42–3, 47–8, 62–3, 64, 75, 79, 262n9, 265–6n4; legal style and philosophy of, 20, 80, 174, 183, 213–4; and religious issues, 20, 238–9, 259–60n28; and death of wife Lucy, 21; marriage of, to Eliza Winter Reeves, 21–2, 24, 62, 80–1, 167, 211–3, 216, 225, 229–30, 255; finances and property of, 24–5, 42, 80, 167–8, 176, 187, 211, 216, 229–30, 238, 239, 256, 263n22; as Republican Party member and leader, 28, 30–2, 52, 55, 75, 78, 229; as Republican candidate for Iowa senate, 30–2; and Lincoln's 1860 presidential campaign, 56–8; and Civil War, 61–2, 77, 81–2; compared with Lincoln, 77–9; portraits of, *following p. 96;* and impeachment of Johnson, 145–6, 154–5; friendships of, while on U.S. Supreme Court, 167; and summers in Keokuk while on U.S. Supreme Court, 167–9, 176; in Washington, D.C., without family after Supreme Court appointment, 167, 187, 229–30; and family's move to Washington, 187, 211–2; leisure and social life of, in Washington, 211–3, 230; social status of, in Washington, 212–3, 216–7; and corruption of Grant administration, 224–6; and presidential election of 1876, 226–9; as presidential candidate, 236–8; health problems of, 254; final illness and death of, 255–6; thirtieth wedding anniversary of, 255; gubernatorial ambitions of, 271n36
—views of: capitalists, xii, xiv, xvi, 78–9, 174–7, 217, 221–4, 242–4, 249; optimistic

delegations during, 112–3, 116–7, 121; southern state elections during, 112–3; and Black Codes, 113–5, 117, 120, 136, 195, 208–10; and Confederate war debt, 113, 136; southern legislatures during, 113–4, 138, 196–7; southern courts during, 114; refusal of Congress to seat ex-Confederates during, 116–7; and Democratic Party, 117, 118; and conservative Republicans, 118, 136; and Civil Rights Act (1866), 119–21, 137; U.S. Supreme Court cases on, 121–34, 138–45; and test-oath cases, 128–34, 138, 140–4, 149; and Fourteenth Amendment, 136–8, 146–8, 158, 199–210; Military Reconstruction Act, 148–53, 155–7, 160–3; new state constitutions in 1868, 157–8, 195–7, 207; resumption of normal relations between southern states and Union, 157–8; in Louisiana, 193–200, 203, 205, 210; end of, 208, 228–9

Reeves, Eliza Winter. *See* Miller, Eliza Winter Reeves

Reeves, Lewis, 19, 21, 168

Reid, Hugh, 267*n*24

Republican Party: and capitalists, xii, xv–xvii, 239, 245, 254; free-labor ideology of, xiv–xv, xvi, 49, 73, 95–6, 244, 254; in Iowa, xiv–xv, 28, 30–2, 48, 52–5, 75, 165, 169, 263*n*36; and Whigs' demise, 27; antislavery position of, 28, 31–2, 50–2, 56, 80; Miller's membership in and leadership of, 28, 30–2, 52, 55, 75, 78, 229; and Kansas violence over slavery, 29; Miller as candidate for Iowa senate from, 30–2; and Union, 32; and Panic of 1857, 48; and Lincoln-Douglas debates, 52–3; and presidential election of 1860, 56–8, 84, 88; and secession of southern states, 58–60; and Civil War, 61, 81; and *Dred Scott* decision, 65, 68; regional tensions in, 73–4; western Republicans, 73–4,

235–6, 245; and Miller's appointment to U.S. Supreme Court, 75, 80; and Emancipation Proclamation, 81–2; and additional justice for Supreme Court, 84–5; Radical Republicans during Reconstruction, 106, 107, 108, 110, 115, 117–8, 121, 139, 140, 145, 147–50, 153–4, 159, 209; and Reconstruction, 106–8, 110, 115–21, 139, 140, 145, 147–50, 153–4, 159; and treason trials and death sentences for ex-Confederates, 107; moderate Republicans and Reconstruction, 110, 115–21, 137, 147–50, 153; and black suffrage, 115, 163–5; conservative Republicans and Reconstruction, 118, 136; and Fourteenth Amendment, 136–8; and National Union movement, 136; in 1867 elections, 151–2; and presidential election of 1868, 152, 163; and impeachment and trial of Johnson, 154–5; and *McCardle* case, 156–7; and *Texas v. White*, 159–60; and *Legal Tender Cases*, 183; and *Slaughter-House Cases*, 208–9; "Liberal" Republicans, 224, 226; "Half-Breed" Republicans, 226; and presidential election of 1876, 226–9; "Stalwart" Republicans, 226; and Miller's presidential candidacy, 236–8; and presidential election of 1880, 237; and presidential election of 1884, 237–9

Restless (ship), 87–8

Riggs v. Johnson County, 170, 280*n*18

Robert Moir v. Jefferson County, 47

Rock Island bridge, 37–40, 75, 79, *following p. 96*

Roe v. Wade, 189

Rogers v. Burlington, 280*n*18

Roosevelt, Franklin D., xiii

Rowan v. Lamb, 262*n*3

Sample, Hugh W., 46, 64, 176

Sanitation regulations. *See* Health and sanitation regulations

Santa Clara v. Southern Pacific Railroad Company, 291n24
Saunders, Berry, 247
School desegregation, 195, 196–7
Scott, Dred, 50–1
Scott, Winfield, 66
Secession and secessionists, 32, 57–61, 66–7, 105, 111–2, 129, 134, 147, 160
Segregation, 196–7, 254. See also Race
Senate, U.S. See Congress, U.S.
Separation of powers, 146, 149, 154
Seven Days' battle, 76
Seward, William H., 28, 113
Seymour, Horatio, 163
Sharkey, William, 149, 150, 157
Shenandoah Valley, battles of, 76
Sheridan, Philip H., 135, 151, 195
Sherman, John, 69–70, 115, 224–5, 226
Sherman, William Tecumseh, 212
Shiloh, battle of, 76
Sickles, Daniel, 151
Siebold, Ex Parte, 291n18
Silver, 225, 226, 237
Sixth Amendment, 123, 125
Slaughter-House Cases, xiii–xiv, 199–210, 233, 245, 247, 249, 253, 254, 285n56
Slaughtering industry, 13–4, 23, 43–4, 168, 189–93, 197–200, 202–3
Slavery: in Barbourville, Ky., 5, 10; in Kentucky, 5, 8–10, 14–6, 260n39; Miller as slaveholder, 5, 11; Cassius Clay on, 8–10; Miller's antislavery position, 8, 10–1, 15, 16, 26–7, 31–2, 52, 77, 78, 80, 81–2; emancipation of slaves, 9–10, 15–6, 81–3, 94, 109; lynching of slaves, 10; Miller's freeing of his slaves, 11; Unitarians' opposition to, 20; in Kansas, 25–30, 51–2; and Kansas-Nebraska Act, 25–30; and Missouri Compromise, 25–7, 31, 32, 50, 59; in territories, 25–30, 32, 50–1, 65, 78; Democratic Party on, 27, 31–2; Republican Party's antislavery position, 28, 31–2, 50–2,

56, 80; and Dred Scott decision, 50–1, 52, 65–6, 68, 82, following p. 96, 133, 136, 139, 140, 189, 198, 207, 215; and Brown's raid on Harpers Ferry, Va., 55–6, 121; and Crittenden compromise, 59–60, 268n61; and Emancipation Proclamation, 81–3, 94, 109; Chase's antislavery position, 94. See also Abolitionism; African Americans; Race
Smith, Adam, 204
Smith, Gerritt, 31
Smith v. McCullough, 289n71
Socialism, 242–4, 245
Sons of Liberty, 121, 122, 125
South Carolina, 59, 61, 112, 115, 227, 234–5
Specie Resumption Act (1876), 225
Speed, James, 123, 126
St. Louis, 13, 22, 24, 34, 36, 37, 38
"Stalwart" Republicans, 226
Stanberry, Henry, 149, 150
Stanford, Leland, 89, 241
Stanton, Edwin M., 150, 151, 153, 154, 155
State Bank of Ohio v. Knoop, 266n22
States' rights: and Slaughter-House Cases, xiv, 254; and nullification doctrine, 32; and secession, 32; after Civil War, 111; and Johnson, 120–1; and test-oath case, 130–1; and Military Reconstruction Act, 160
Steamboats, 6, 13, 14, 33, 34, 37–40, 63, 72, 74, 93
Steam engine, 244
Stephens, Alexander, 113
Stevens, Thaddeus, 108, 110, 117–8, 140, 145, 209
Stone v. Wisconsin, 289nn51–2
Stowers v. Milledge, 262n9
Strader v. Graham, 50, 267n27
Strike of railroad workers (1877), 232
Strong, William, 183–6, 200, 219–21, 235
Substantive due process, 205, 251, 253
Suffrage. See Voting rights

Sumner, Charles, 29–30, 94, 106, 110, 117–8, 209
Supreme Court, California, 88–9
Supreme Court, Iowa, 21, 35, 46–7, 55, 89–91, 169–72, 262n9
Supreme Court, Missouri, 129
Supreme Court, U.S.: Miller's criticism of justices of, xiii, 51, 93–4, 172–3, 200, 215; Miller's relationships with staff of, xiii; *Slaughter-House Cases,* xiii–xiv, 189, 199–210, 231, 233, 245, 247, 249, 253, 254, 285n56; Lincoln's appointees to, xvi, 65–6, 70, 71–2, 74–81, 84, 88, 93–4, 95, 254, 272n44; railroad cases, 39–40, 251–3; slavery cases, 50–1, 65, 68, 82, 133, 139, 140, 189, 207, 215, 267n27; Jackson's appointee to, 51; permission for Miller to argue cases before, 64; *Merryman* opinion, 66–7, 68, 87; federal judicial circuits supervised by justices of, 68–9, 269n6; reorganization of judicial circuits under, 69–74, 79; support for capitalists in, 71–2, 173, 174–5, 221–4, 239, 241–2, 254; Miller's appointment to, 74–81, 272n44; blockade cases, 83–8; *Prize Cases,* 83–7; proposed bills on, in Congress, 84–5, 144, 153, 278n27; tenth justice for, 84–5; bond cases, 89–93, 169–74, 186–7, 217–24, 234–6, 254, 273n75, 280n18, 289nn63–4; portrait of, in 1888, *following p. 96;* Reconstruction cases, 121–34, 138–45; *Milligan* case, 123–8, 130, 133, 138–40, 149, 151; test-oath cases, 128–34, 138, 140–4, 149; reorganization of, called for, 140, 145; Military Reconstruction Act cases, 148–53, 155–7, 160–3; Congress and jurisdiction of, 156–7, 162–3; *Texas v. White,* 158–63; appointment of southerner to, 164; and strict construction of Constitution, 164; judicial restraint versus expansive reading of Constitution, 174; *Legal Tender Cases,* 177–86; Grant's appointees

to, 183, 184; and Fourteenth Amendment, 199–210, 231–3, 245, 246, 247, 249, 251, 291n24; Miller's workstyle on, 211, 254–5; wives of justices of, 212–3; aspirations of Miller for becoming chief justice of, 213–4; Miller's reservations about chief justice position of, 214; and Miller's avoidance of impropriety, 225–6; and presidential election of 1876, 228–9; Granger cases, 230–2, 289nn51–2; *Davidson v. New Orleans,* 232–4, 251; Cleveland's appointee to, 241; *Cruikshank v. United States,* 245–6, 247, 250; *Civil Rights Cases,* 246–7; Enforcement Act cases, 246, 291n13, 291n18; *Ex Parte Yarbrough,* 247–9, 250; and Fifteenth Amendment, 248–9; and corporate lawyers, 251; and laissez-faire principles, 253, 254; and Miller's funeral, 256. *See also* specific Supreme Court justices and cases
Swayne, Noah: as Lincoln appointee to Supreme Court, xvi, 71–2; antislavery position of, 71; and railroad cases, 71; support for capitalists by, 71–2, 173; wealth of, 80; and *Prize Cases,* 85; and bond cases, 90–2, 172–3, 219; and *Milligan* case, 126–7, 139; and Republican Reconstruction, 144, 145; and *McCardle* case, 153; and *Texas v. White,* 161–2; Miller's criticisms of, 172–3, 203; and greenbacks, 177–8; and *Legal Tender Cases,* 178–81, 184; and *Slaughter-House Cases,* 206, 210; and presidential election of 1876, 228–9

Taney, Roger: proslavery position of, xvi; and *Dred Scott* decision, 50–1, 65, 66, 82, 136, 207; and Bank of the United States, 51; Miller's criticism of, 51; and *Ex Parte Merryman,* 66, 67, 68; illness of, 71; and Miller's oath of office as Supreme Court

Wilderness Road, 4, 6

Williams, George, 213, 214–5

Williams v. Louisiana, 289*n*71

Wilson, James F., 69, 72, 74, 76, 80, 132

Winona & St. Peter Co. v. Blake, 289*nn*51–2

Wirz, Henry, 110

Wisconsin, 230, 237

Women's suffrage, 116, 163

Woodson, Silas, 12–7, 222–3, 238, 255

Woodson v. Murdock, 222–4

Woodward, William, 46

Working class, 232, 242–4

Wright, George, 47

Wright v. Meek, 262*n*3

Yandell, Lunsford P., 4

Yarborough, Jasper, 247–8, 249

Yarborough, Ex Parte, 247–9, 250

Yellow fever, 191, 193, 210, 232

Young v. Wolcott, 262*n*9

www.ingramcontent.com/pod-product-compliance
Lightning Source LLC
Chambersburg PA
CBHW050332270326
41926CB00016B/3428